SINGAPORE

SINGAPORE

A Modern History

Michael D. Barr

BLOOMSBURY ACADEMIC
LONDON • NEW YORK • OXFORD • NEW DELHI • SYDNEY

BLOOMSBURY ACADEMIC
Bloomsbury Publishing Plc
50 Bedford Square, London, WC1B 3DP, UK
1385 Broadway, New York, NY 10018, USA

BLOOMSBURY, BLOOMSBURY ACADEMIC and the Diana
logo are trademarks of Bloomsbury Publishing Plc

First published in Great Britain by I. B. Tauris & Co. Ltd in 2018
This edition published in Great Britain by Bloomsbury Academic in 2020

Cover design by: Graham Robert Ward
Cover images: Front: Ludham, Norfolk, medieval rood screen painting, St. Edmund,
Anglo-Saxon King of East Anglia, Saint with arrow, 15th century art
(picture credit: Neil Holmes/Getty Images). Back: St Edmund by Dame Elisabeth Frink
(picture credit: East Anglian Picture Service/Alamy Stock Photo).

A catalogue record for this book is available from the British Library.

A catalog record for this book is available from the Library of Congress.

ISBN: PB: 978-1-3501-8566-1
ePDF: 978-1-7867-3527-0
eBook: 978-1-7867-2527-1

Typeset by Jones Ltd, London

To find out more about our authors and books visit
www.bloomsbury.com and sign up for our newsletters.

Michael Barr is Associate Professor in International Relations, Flinders University, Australia. This is his fifth authored book, following *Lee Kuan Yew: The Beliefs Behind the Man* (2000, 2009), *Cultural Politics and Asian Values: The Tepid War* (2002, 2004), *Constructing Singapore: Elitism, Ethnicity and the Nation-Building Project* (written with Z. Skrbiš, 2008), and *The Ruling Elite of Singapore: Networks of Power and Influence* (2014). He also co-edited *Paths Not Taken: Political Pluralism in Post-War Singapore* with C.A. Trocki (2008) and *The Limits of Authoritarian Governance in Singapore's Developmental State* with L.Z. Rahim (2019). He was Editor-in-Chief of *Asian Studies Review* from 2012 to 2017.

Contents

List of Maps

Maps 3.1, 3.2, 3.4–3.8, 4.1–4.3 and 5.1 were created by Michael Barr using base cartography sourced from d-maps.com

List of Figures

Foreword

CARL A. TROCKI

The Australian scholar, Michael Barr, has written extensively on contemporary Singapore politics and its political economy. Over the past two decades he has published works on the thought of Lee Kuan Yew, on the political economy of Singapore Inc., on Asian values and on the social impact of Singapore's educational system, among other things. In all of this he has pioneered looking behind the curtains of mythology and self-congratulation that have become hallmarks of the 'story' of Singapore's success, as told by its elite class. With this book, Barr makes an important contribution to the literature on Singapore's history and sets a new standard for scholarly treatment of the state.

While I have never thought of him as an outspoken critic of the regime, his work has provided considerable evidence that the self-portrait of Mr Lee and his government is not always what they would wish us to believe. At the same time he has not been slow to recognise the legitimate and considerable accomplishments of the city-state. In some cases he argues that these might be more impressive than those for which People's Action Party (PAP) claims credit. The current work offers a number of examples of this view.

Although much of his recent work has been in contemporary political study, this book revisits his original discipline, which is history. Speaking as a historian myself, I find this cross-over of history and contemporary politics both gratifying and extraordinary. Rarely do students of politics do more than provide a cursory and stereotypical view of the historical developments that have shaped their subjects. I hasten to add that Barr himself is not usually guilty of this blind spot but, even allowing for that, he has approached Singapore's past in a unique manner. Although six of the eight substantive chapters deal mainly with the years before 1965, the entire book is truly grounded in the issues and problems of the twenty-first century. Rather than a standard chronological approach, Barr has opted for what I see as a thematic approach, or perhaps a problem-based approach.

The main 'problem' as Barr sees it, is 'The Singapore Story'. This is the title of Lee Kuan Yew's historical autobiography – himself and Singapore – as if the two could not be separated. In this sense, Barr's book is frankly in the category of 'revisionist' history. It is important to understand that 'history' in Singapore has a rather interesting history. At first, when Singapore became independent under the rule of Lee and his PAP, the government felt there was little need for history. In their eyes, as of 1965, the world was made anew. The British colonial past was little more than a period in which many Chinese had come to settle on the island. Singapore had been born out of a series of crises beginning with the Japanese Occupation, the communist 'threat' and the experience as part of Malaysia. In any case, the past was now irrelevant. These three 'crises' had been overcome by the wise leadership of the PAP and Lee Kuan Yew and there was no need to probe further. In Singapore's schools and in the public discourse of the 1960s and 1970s, there was virtually no history beyond this.

By the 1980s, the government's view on the uselessness of history had changed. A new generation had arisen which had not known the strife of the past and it was deemed necessary to inform them about the history of those who had built this new Singapore. Thus we see the origins of the Singapore Story. This was a tale of great men, such as Thomas Stamford Raffles who had founded this dynamic port city where only a sleepy Malay fishing village had formerly existed in 1819. It had been populated by rags-to-riches Chinese immigrants supplying tin, rubber and pepper to Britain and the world. Mary Turnbull had written the history of British Singapore. Then came a series of crises: the Japanese Occupation, the communist threat and the unhappy experience with Malaysia. Singapore faced a grim economic future and was surrounded by danger on all sides. Luckily, Singapore had been steered through these recent difficulties by the leadership of Lee Kuan Yew. Today, Singapore lives with this 'mythology', as Loh Kah Seng has described it.

Barr begins his attempt to redress this somewhat lopsided version of the past by looking at three 'problems' that force us to readjust our thinking about Singapore. These include Singapore's 'place', secondly its 'size' and thirdly, whether it is a city or a nation. In discussing place, Barr begins with a circumstance of which few would be aware. He offers us a map showing Singapore as a major node of the global undersea cable network. These cables carry about 95% of the world's electronic communications. His map shows that Singapore is on a level with London, New York, San Francisco and Tokyo in terms of importance. Perhaps this centrality could be explained by the fact that gutta-percha, the substance that was initially used to coat those marine cables, was a product of the Johor rainforests and was 'discovered' in Singapore and exported to the world from Singapore. It is also important to remember that the network was created in the nineteenth century, and except for the fibre-optic cables that now make up the bulk of the network, it remains an example of nineteenth-century technology. But, there is more to Singapore's position than this.

In terms of global shipping, it is likewise important as a major node between the Indian and Pacific oceans at the entrance to the Straits of Malacca. This centrality is nothing new, but has been the case since the mid-nineteenth century. Today, Singapore is also a global node of airline traffic, a financial centre, a petroleum centre and, of course, a shopping centre. Moreover, recent archaeological evidence has shown that Singapore had been the site of a prominent entrepôt on the Indian Ocean–South China Sea trade routes perhaps as early as the twelfth century. On the other hand, this centrality was not inevitable.

In 1819, Raffles' choice of Singapore as a British port was actually quite arbitrary. Barr argues that Raffles chose the site largely because it was *available* at the time. In fact, he and William Farquhar had originally hoped to found a settlement at nearby Riau, on Bentan Island, but the Dutch had managed to pre-empt their scheme. They then turned to Karimun, but finally settled on Singapore because the Malay prince, the Temenggong Abdul Rahman, had set up a residence there. The Temenggong, who possessed the island by hereditary right, offered a slight cover of legitimacy to Raffles' claim. For the Temenggong, Raffles offered the chance to make Singapore an important node of Asian commerce. Also, in this story, it is important to acknowledge the role of Farquhar who had the on-the-ground knowledge to lead Raffles to Singapore Island.

Singapore, despite its excellent harbour, was not necessarily destined to be the great port of the Straits. Although Singapore had flourished in the fourteenth century and again in the sixteenth, in other times, other sites had been equally significant, including Malacca, Riau, Johor, Palembang, Aceh and Kedah. Barr's argument clearly undercuts a number of key myths of Singapore's history. The first is the wisdom and foresight attributed to Raffles and the importance of the 1819 date. As I have suggested earlier in my own work, the whole period between 1795 and 1824, when the Napoleonic Wars shook the world, was transitional. In the eighteenth century both Holland and France were considerable counter-weights to British power. Britain's position in Asia (and Singapore's especially) was not secured until well after Waterloo. Barr places the narrative of Raffles' 'foundation' of Singapore squarely as a minor consequence of this shift in hegemonic power rather than as part of a grand design. Finally, as Barr makes clear, for most of the nineteenth century, Singapore remained an 'Asian' port, or an Indian Ocean port. It was one more reincarnation in the succession of multicultural entrepôts that have made up what John Miksic has styled the 'silk road of the sea' for nearly two millennia. The East India Company gained nothing from the possession, even though its merchants prospered.

On the other hand, Barr also makes clear that while Lee Kuan Yew and the PAP did much to overhaul and renovate Singapore's economy after 1965, it was not really a case of 'Third World to First' as the myth boasts. The British and European contribution to Singapore's economic situation became crucial in the late nineteenth century and maintained its importance through the early twentieth century. Such factors as the development of steam travel, the railroad, the modernisation of Singapore's port facilities, its shipbuilding industry, its place in the oil industry, the trans-oceanic cable network and even Singapore's early industrialisation and its public housing programme were all elements that were already in place before 1959.

Although Singapore was in a rather insecure position in 1965 when it left Malaysia, the crisis was never so great as pretended. The possible loss of the Malaysian hinterland and a possible threat from Indonesia were matters for concern. But perhaps the anticipated reactions from Britain and Australia to Singapore's independence were seen by Singapore's leaders as more significant threats.

The real contributions of Lee Kuan Yew and the PAP were, however, considerable. They included the decision to containerise the port in 1969 and the creation of an alliance with American and Japanese capital to power Singapore's industrialisation. The policy pushed by Goh Keng Swee to finance Singapore's housing and urban development with the Central Provident Fund was a key element in Singapore's success. So too was the creation of the financial and management structures which included a carefully balanced partnership between business and government that has developed into 'Singapore Inc.'. Likewise, one might consider the creation of a 'leadership class' and a system for self-renewal and perpetuation of the family-based political economy as one of Lee Kuan Yew's unique contributions. Barr notes that experts on state capitalism '[regard] Singapore Inc. as being the most efficient form of state capitalism in the world'. Barr's focus on Singapore's 'place' in the global economic network and the ability of Lee and his associates to parley that situation in the late twentieth century are really the key elements in the city-state's success.

The creation of social stability as well as the quiescence of the labour force has also been an important accomplishment of Singapore's ruling elite. Barr warns, however, that the long-term success of this system now that its architects have passed on is an open question. So too, is the fact that much of this quiescence was achieved by sidelining local capital and most of Singapore's small and medium-sized enterprises (SMEs). These were not only economic entities, but also had considerable cultural and social power that Lee Kuan Yew saw as a threat to his own prominence.

In terms of size, Barr correctly reflects again on the history of Singapore as an important centre of the Malay world. Singapore has always been more than merely an island full of Chinese. The pre-nineteenth-century entrepôts that flourished in and around Singapore were always Malay centres. Singapore was always part of the islands to the south and the west and the peninsula to the north. Johor, Riau-Lingga and eastern Sumatra had been a joint maritime zone since the earliest times. It remained so in the nineteenth century as I have shown in my discussion of the pepper and gambier agriculture and the revenue farming systems of the era, despite the European attempts to divide the area into British and Dutch spheres. This local coherence has been resurrected since the 1980s with the development of Singapore–Johor–Riau (SIJORI) growth triangle.

Yet in the years between World War II and 1980, the geographic consciousness of official Singapore was really quite blinded to this reality. Particularly, in the 1960s and 1970s, one felt particularly isolated in Singapore. The sense of being on an island, surrounded by 'enemies', was pervasive. Of course, this was not true of the tens of thousands of Singaporeans and Malaysians who commuted daily across the Causeway. To the government, this often seemed like an unwelcome anomaly. Thanks to official foot-dragging on both sides, this border crossing remains one of the more tedious commutes I know of.

Even though it was long the case that newspapers were confiscated when one crossed the Causeway, the governments and peoples of Malaysia, Singapore and Indonesia always retained many links. Inhabitants of Riau and Johor constantly watched Singapore television and listened to Singapore radio. People moved constantly across these borders, and now money, technology and expertise likewise flow along their 'natural' and historic patterns. This ambiguity of Singapore's sense of its size is part of the uncertainty surrounding the issues of Singapore's identity as a city-state or a nation-state.

Much of Singapore's continued success will probably depend on the development of Singapore's society and culture. This is where the question of Singapore's identity comes in, and we can see the relevance of Barr's query about whether Singapore is a city or a nation. As a city, Singapore aspires to be 'world class', a global city – one that is open and welcomes all with talent, one that is cosmopolitan, affluent, competitive and dynamic – but it also presents itself as a nation-state. It must protect its borders, serve the needs of its citizens and promote the 'national interest'. There are many contradictions in attempting to pursue these two paths. One cannot be a neo-liberal and a nationalist at the same time forever. At some point, the 'heartlanders' will find it compelling to reject the cosmopolitan agenda. Can its self-perpetuating elite continue to rule in its arbitrary and sometimes arrogant fashion and still pretend that they rule by democratic consensus? Can a city-state be a nation-state?

Related to this is the question of Singapore's idea of multiculturalism. Can the nation-state continue to coexist with the CMIO (Chinese, Malays, Indians and 'Others') consciousness that pervades the entire system? Particularly when ethnic Chinese constitute such an important element of the population? Barr has shown that the system from education to military service has been quietly rigged to promote Chinese over the other races. Part of the reluctance to acknowledge Singapore's history as well as its place in Southeast Asia stems from the consciousness that such awareness would require an acknowledgement of the important role of the Malay peoples in Singapore.

This attention to place, size and city- or nation-state identifies many of the important, but often unacknowledged, issues that lie beneath the surface of Singapore. Barr gives us what we may justly see as a much more balanced picture of Singapore's past than we have from the Singapore Story. He has done a thorough survey of much of the recent scholarship on Singapore and its history and has produced a readable and engaging work that analyses and unpacks the current mythologies. He also shows us that Singapore's actual history has some of the real depth that the mythologies ignore. He likewise provides us with some of the tools that make it possible to understand key issues that Singapore will face in the future. In structuring his study around these three issues, he completely deflates the Singapore Story, and in the process reveals its fundamental emptiness.

Prologue

At the outset of writing a history of Singapore, it is humbling to realise that I am able to present the basic outline in four paragraphs:

1. Singapore is a largish island (currently just over 700 square kilometres) at the mouth of Malaysia's Johor River. It was formerly part of the Johor-Riau Sultanate and home to traders and pirates who maximised the benefits to be gained from its strategic location across the Straits of Malacca. In 1819 it became a British trading port-cum-colony and a free port welcoming all traders and taxing none, thanks to the initiative of the colony's founder, Sir Stamford Raffles. Chinese flocked in as labourers and entrepreneurs, along with natives from the region (mostly from places that today are parts of Malaysia and Indonesia).
2. As part of the British Straits Settlements (comprising Singapore, Malacca and Penang) Singapore was administered from Calcutta from 1826 until 1867, and then directly by the Colonial Office in London until the Japanese Occupation in 1942. After the war the Colonial Office disestablished the Straits Settlements and Singapore became a Crown Colony while Malacca and Penang were integrated more fully into British Malaya. The British granted the new Federation of Malaya independence in 1957 but retained Singapore as a colony until it joined with Malaya and Britain's North Borneo colonies (Sarawak and Sabah) in 1963 to form the new Federation of Malaysia.
3. The integration of Singapore into Malaysia ended in bitter recrimination after less than two years, and the Republic of Singapore was born in 1965 despite no one wanting its creation – not the British, nor the government in Kuala Lumpur and not even the ruling elite in Singapore itself.
4. Having had independence thrust upon it, the Singapore Government set about making it a success by integrating the new country into the global capitalist order. Over the half-century since independence its government has milked to the full the advantages provided by the island's British heritage and connections

> (capitalism, a strong administration, the inheritance of tangible assets, the use of English) while dispensing with inconvenient legacies such as civil liberties and full democracy. The young republic has emerged as a well-ordered and professionally run bastion of state capitalism.

At less than 400 words, this thumbnail sketch even outperforms Wikipedia for brevity. For any reader who knows Singapore as little more than that place with the nice airport, it might even be a useful point of orientation. But it is hardly an adequate description; nor is it free of value judgements. Just to take two points: the description of Singapore as an island at the mouth of the Johor River, and the choice of the pre-colonial Johor-Riau Sultanate as a starting point. The absence of any mention of Singapore's second 'founding father', Lee Kuan Yew, and its post-independence ruling party, the People's Action Party (PAP), will also raise some eyebrows, as will the failure to mention the country's two primary foundation myths – the operation of meritocracy and multiculturalism (which in Singapore is known as 'multiracialism').

◆ ◆ ◆ ◆ ◆

I have kept this little exercise in subjective brevity separate from the main text because it really is an affront to the notion of writing a national history to presume to condense it thus, and yet I have retained it as a Prologue precisely because it hints at some of the enigmas and challenges of writing a national history.

Benedict Anderson[1] assures us that any national history is a constructed entity, with a starting point, stories of change, shifting emphases and even potential futures that are selected by national myth-makers: variously aristocrats and royalty, religious and political leaders, scholars and journalists, novelists and poets, and sometimes even educational bureaucrats. These disparate people may collude with each other in making such selections, but they are just as likely to be operating in competition with each other or feeding off each other or their long-dead ancestors without any sense of collusion. The narrative they weave between them is in some form a truly 'national' story in the sense that it is representative of a dominant national self-image. In another sense it is just the self-representation of the winners in the society and so national histories change as the locus of power shifts within the society, or as the fortunes of the nation itself wax and wane. Furthermore there can be competing national narratives, each playing to a different domestic constituency.

That such traps lie in wait even for the author of a 400-word national history of a very small and young country like Singapore emphasises the contingent nature of the picture presented in the pages of this book.

Singapore's national history is a battleground between rival visions of the country. Unlike the case with larger, older countries, the practical parameters of this battleground are highly restrictive, but the very smallness, closeness and newness of the field makes it a highly volatile one. Members of the current national elite consider (and want) the national narrative to be more or less settled as it now stands because it concludes with the presumption of their continued rule and the country's continued prosperity. They might have their way but I do not see my role as helping this along. If I have a mission, it is to pull the national narrative apart and see how it can be put together differently. With this goal in mind, I have written a revisionist national history that devotes a great deal of attention to an interrogation of the narratives and myths that comprise the national history – and the very role of national history in national identity and national politics. I even question whether the 'national' perspective is the most appropriate way to study Singapore's history and include a chapter that interrogates the presumptive 'idea' of Singapore.

Yet for all my questioning of the national perspective, I open the book writing about Singapore's 'national' achievements and close with thoughts about its 'national future'. It really is difficult to escape this perspective when writing about a city-state in the early twenty-first century. Perhaps my underlying nation-based perspective is a reflection of my personal methodological bias, which I admit gravitates towards elite politics, but I think it also says something about the hegemonic place of the 'nation-state' in our understandings of the location of power in the modern international system – where both imperial states like China and city-states like Singapore have to be fitted neatly into an international system of 'nation-states'. In this book I have certainly made a major effort to break free of the rigidity of the national prism. I leave it to readers to judge how fully I have succeeded.

Acknowledgements

This book has been in gestation since 2012 while I was still working on *The Ruling Elite of Singapore*, and has been a serious work in progress since 2014. In that time I have accumulated numerous debts of gratitude that have contributed to the finished product.

Institutionally, I need to begin by thanking Flinders University for its support in providing me with a semester's sabbatical in 2015, and financial assistance to buy archival photos and some editorial assistance. The National University of Singapore Department of History and the National University of Singapore Library were both generous to my needs – and my special thanks goes to Mr Tim Yap Fuan at the Library, who was as helpful as he could be, as always. I am especially grateful to the National Archives of Singapore and the National Archives of Australia for permission to use archival photos. Thanks also goes to the Asia Research Centre at Murdoch University, the Malaysia and Singapore Society of Australia, the International Convention of Asia Scholars, and Universiti Malaysia Terengganu, each of which provided me with venues at which I could try out sections of my book on unsuspecting audiences. I would also like to thank the team at I.B.Tauris – especially Joanna Godfrey, who commissioned this book, and Sophie Campbell, who saw it through to production. I would also like to make a special mention of Chris Reed of BBR, who has proved himself to be an exceptionally diligent copy-editor – and who saved me from many a slip! I am exceptionally impressed with IBT for going the extra step of taking my amateurish maps and getting Chris to turn them into professional, publishable graphics.

In terms of scholarly and collegial support, I owe huge debts of gratitude that I can never hope to repay to a collection of very senior figures in the field of Singapore history. First there is Peter Borschberg, who I knew only slightly before I began this project, but who I now count as a good friend and colleague. Peter was so generous with his time, advice and friendship – and eventually advance samples of his own publications – that it is humbling. He had a fundamental impact on the shape and scope of the book, over and above the feedback he gave me on the chapters that he read for me. Carl Trocki was already a friend and colleague of long standing when he agreed to read the first full draft of the manuscript. His detailed, extensive (and brutally honest!) feedback was just what I needed to save me from many errors and lift the quality of the book. I have never met or had any dealings directly with John Miksic, but I thought I should mention him for his decades of work on the *longue durée* framework that was so important to my project.

Moving beyond historians, I need to thank Garry Rodan who has engaged with me and mentored me (I suspect rather patiently) as I have worked to appreciate more fully the political economy dimensions of his analysis of Singapore politics. Being trained as a historian, I find it both refreshing and challenging to learn from those who come from outside my home discipline, and yet with whom I have so much in common. I need to thank my former students, Anantha Raman Govindasamy, who gave me a tour of Kampung Baru Nilai, and Rizwana Abdul Azeez, who, among other things, gave me access to her research on the Iskandar development in 'North Singapore'. Thanks also to Stephen Dobbs who wrote such a beautifully crafted social history of the Singapore River that I not only used his work as part of my framework for the first half of Chapter 8, but I asked if I could borrow some of his photos – and he gifted them with such unaffected generosity that I was quite overwhelmed by the show of goodwill. Stephen was one of several social historians of Singapore who influenced me, both through their scholarship and through more personal and direct interactions. James Warren, Loh Kah Seng and Ernest Koh come readily to mind. Scholars such as Kevin Tan, Lily Rahim, Terence Lee, Jason Lim, Wang Gungwu, Geoff Wade, Kenneth Paul Tan, Thum Ping Tjin, Hong Lysa, Tim Huxley, Tim Harper, Fr James Minchin, Huang Jianli and Brian Farrell all deserve my thanks for their input to my work – though perhaps not all of them would be aware of it until reading this acknowledgement. I cannot repay my debts, but at least I can express my gratitude.

In terms of scholarly input, I also need to give a special thanks to the two anonymous reviewers of my manuscript. They worked me very hard indeed after I had received their feedback, and I thank them for it most sincerely. I doubt that I fully met all of their expectations or fully dealt with all their criticisms, but rest assured I took them all to heart and I hope they find that the book is considerably improved from the version that they read.

A special mention goes to my Masters and now-PhD student, Abdul Rahman Yaacob, specifically for finding a good photo of Goh Keng Swee for me when I had left it almost too late, but more generally for giving me the pleasure of teaching such an enthusiastic and innovative student of Singapore history. Thanks also to Rosa Evaquarta, for doing the index.

My final vote of gratitude is the most fundamental of all – and it goes to my wife, Shamira, who has carried me through the downs and helped me celebrate the ups as I worked through this project while carrying a full teaching load at Flinders University. As if that wasn't enough, she has also made more than her share of direct contributions to my understanding of Singapore society over the years. Many thanks and all my love go out to Shamira, as always.

MDB, Adelaide, July 2018

List of Abbreviations

ABL	Anti-British League
ASEAN	Association of Southeast Asian Nations
BMA	British Military Administration
CEO	chief executive officer
CPF	Central Provident Fund
CPM	Communist Party of Malaya (a variation of MCP, Malayan Communist Party)
DBS	Development Bank of Singapore (now known as DBS Bank)
EDB	Economic Development Board
EIC	[English] East India Company
FDI	foreign direct investment
GDP	gross domestic product
GIC	Government of Singapore Investment Corporation
GLC	government-linked company
KMM	Young Malay Union (Kaum Melayu Muda) (Malay)
KMT	Chinese Nationalist Party (Kuomintang) (Mandarin)
MCA	Malayan/Malaysian Chinese Association
MCP	Malayan Communist Party (sometimes called the CPM, Communist Party of Malaya)
MIC	Malayan/Malaysian Indian Congress
MP	Member of Parliament
MPAJA	Malayan People's Anti-Japanese Army
MRT	Mass Rapid Transit (train system)
NIDL	New International Division of Labour
OFDI	outward foreign direct investment
PAP	People's Action Party

PP	Progressive Party
SAF	Singapore Armed Forces
SIJORI	Singapore–Johor–Riau [growth triangle]
SME	small and medium-sized enterprise
UMNO	United Malays National Organisation
VOC	Dutch East India Company

Glossary of Asian-Language Terms

baba	Straits-born Chinese, descended from early immigrants, a distinct cultural group; can be used either to specify males, or to refer to both males and females (Malay)
Bahasa Melayu	Malay language (Malay)
Barisan Sosialis	Socialist Front (Malay)
Bendahara	de facto prime minister and law giver (Malay)
guanxi	Chinese mutual-obligation networks (Mandarin)
Indonesia Raya	Greater Indonesia (Malay)
kampung/kampong	village/town (Malay)
kangchu	'lord of the river' or 'lord of the port' (Hokkien)
kerajaan	Malay polity (Malay)
Konfrontasi	Confrontation (Malay/Indonesian)
kongsi	Chinese business partnership-cum-secret society (Hokkien)
Laksamana	admiral (Malay)
Malai	Japanese-occupied Malaya (Japanese)
negeri	geographical place ruled by a sultan (Malay)
nyonya	the specifically female form of *baba* (Malay)
orang laut	sea people/nomads (Malay)
peranakan	Straits-born, usually Chinese but sometimes Indian; sometimes used interchangeably with *baba* (Malay)
raja	king/sultan (Malaya)
Syonan-To	Japanese-occupied Singapore (Japanese)
Temenggong	mayor/police chief/chief justice (Malay)
towkay	rich and powerful businessman (Hokkien)

Timeline

PREMODERN SINGAPORE

Before the Seventeenth Century

1025	Indian (Chola) attacks begin the decline of the Srivajaya Empire, which had been based at Palembang on the north-east coast of Sumatra
1126	Song dynasty opens up China and encourages maritime trade to the south; new period of prosperity in Southeast Asia
1290	Beginning of Singapore's first period of prosperity
1325	Temasik (Singapore) sends a tributary mission to China
1340s	Singapore attacked by Siamese forces
1349	Wang Dayuan writes of Dragon Tooth's Gate/Old Singapore Strait (between Sentosa and Singapore Island) as the gateway between oceans
1390	Sang Nila Utama flees Javanese attacks on Palembang and invades Singapore; changes its name from Temasik to Singapura and settles there with his followers
1396	Sang Nila Utama leaves Singapore for Malacca with most of his followers; founds Malacca Sultanate; end of Singapore's first period of prosperity
1436	Ming dynasty bans Chinese participation in maritime trade
1511	Portuguese sack Malacca; Sultanate returns to Riau/Johor area and continues as the Johor Sultanate; beginning of Singapore's second period of prosperity
1570s	Portuguese consider building a fortress on or near Singapore
1580s	New Singapore Strait (south of Sentosa) starts being used for maritime passage and the Old Singapore Strait starts falling out of use
1594	Jacques de Coutre reports a significant settlement on Singapore

The Seventeenth Century

1600	Formation of the Honourable [English] East India Company (EIC)
1602	Formation of Dutch East India Company (VOC)
1603	Dutch establish first settlement in Java; Dutch and Portuguese fight a naval battle off Singapore
1606	Dutch Admiral Cornelius Matelieff de Jonge reports the presence of a harbour master at Singapore; negotiates treaty of alliance with Sultan of Johor
1630s	Dutch identify five strategic points of control around Johor, Singapore and Malacca
1641	Dutch capture Malacca from Portuguese; Sultan Iskander Thani of Aceh dies, ending a century of Acehnese attacks on Johor
1669	EIC establishes a factory in Kedah (which survives only four or five years)
1699	Murder of Sultan Mahmud Syah of Johor; effectively the end of the Johor Sultanate; gradual depopulation of Singapore and Johor; the end of Singapore's second period of prosperity

The Eighteenth Century

1703	Sultan Abdul Jalil offers Singapore to the British (but they decline)
1718	Raja Kecil of Siak (Sumatra) captures Johor, claiming to be the heir of Sultan Mahmud Syah
1724	Raja Kecil defeated and returns to build his kingdom in Siak; the final end of Johor Sultanate
1720s	Bugis begin filling the vacuum left by fall of Johor Sultanate; establish themselves in Riau as a Riau Sultanate; begin opening the waters and harbours of Riau to the British
1756	Riau engages in open warfare with the Dutch
1782	Governor General of (British) India begins seeking a base in the Straits of Malacca in response to a military setback by French forces in the Bay of Bengal
1784	Riau attacks the Dutch in Malacca; the Dutch repel the attack and take Riau, signing a treaty with Sultan Mahmud
1784	Dutch cede free navigation of the Far East seas to Britain
1786	British accept sovereignty of Penang from Sultan of Kedah; establish a colony

1787 Sultan Mahmud attacks the Dutch on Riau with the help of mercenaries; the Dutch retaliate successfully but Riau is razed and destroyed as a regional centre, leaving settlement of Chinese gambier and pepper farmers to work the island

1795 Sultan Mahmud returns to Riau under a new treaty with the Dutch

1799 The end of the VOC; the Dutch state takes over its colonies

1801–1867

1811 Temenggong Abdul Rahman begins settling thousands of his followers on Singapore; establishes a large settlement at Kampong Glam and begins enticing Chinese gambier and pepper farmers from Riau; British invade and occupy Dutch Java as part of the politics of the Napoleonic Wars; Sir Stamford Raffles installed as Lieutenant Governor of Java

1812 Death of Sultan Mahmud; succeeded by his younger son, Sultan Abdul Rahman, overlooking his elder son, Hussain/Hussein Mahummud Shah; Temenggong Abdul Rahman aligns himself with Hussein

1814 The British return Java to the Dutch at the end of the Napoleonic Wars

1817 Raffles appointed Lieutenant Governor of Bencoolen, on the south-west coast of Sumatra

1818 The Dutch arrive in Riau, and sign a treaty with Sultan Abdul Rahman, thus recognising his claim to the throne and re-establishing their sovereignty over Riau; Temenggong Abdul Rahman relocates to Singapore, making it his main base; the Governor General of India dispatches Raffles to Penang with the mission of establishing a base at the southern end of the Straits of Malacca

1819 Raffles and Colonel William Farquhar arrive in Singapore; Raffles and Temenggong Abdul Rahman sign an interim treaty to establish an EIC factory; a week later the Temenggong, 'Sultan' Hussain and Raffles sign a Treaty of Friendship and Alliance. These treaties confirm the Temenggong as the 'Ruler of Singapore' and Hussain as 'Sultan of Johore'; together they are confirmed as comprising 'the Government of Singapore-Johore', and the EIC is recognised as a tenant with rights in the river district. Raffles returns to Bencoolen with authority over the Singapore settlement; Farquhar appointed Resident of Singapore.

1822 A colonial town planning committee plans the segregation of Singapore town on racial lines

1823	Sultan Hussain, Temenggong Abdul Rahman and Raffles sign a new treaty, giving Britain sovereignty over all of Singapore except for the Sultan's and Temenggong's personal compounds; Sir John Crawfurd replaces Farquhar as Resident of Singapore; Raffles retires; Singapore becomes an Indian Presidency, administered from Calcutta
1824	Signing of the Treaty of London, which legitimises the British claim to Singapore and the Temenggong's claim to Johor, but gives his southern island holdings to the Dutch; Malacca is given to the British – Singapore's third period of prosperity has now unambiguously begun; publication of Singapore's first local newspaper, the English-language *Singapore Chronicle*
1825	Death of Temenggong Abdul Rahman; succeeded by his 15-year-old son, Daing Ibrahim
1826	Singapore, Penang and Malacca are formed into a single Indian Presidency called the Straits Settlements owned by the EIC and administered from Calcutta
1829	Beginnings of Singapore's shipping industry
1830s	Seat of government of the Straits Settlements begins shifting from Penang to Singapore
1830	Straits Settlements downgraded from a Presidency to a Residency
1833	Renewal of EIC Charter; the EIC loses its monopoly of the China trade
1834	Singapore Free School, which subsequently became Singapore Institution (forerunner of the Raffles Institution) opens as Singapore's first school, teaching in English and initially in Malay, Mandarin and Tamil
1835	Sultan Hussain dies in poverty and without any successor; Governor Samuel Bonham begins building up Daing Ibrahim's stature and importance as a means of controlling piracy
1837	Building of Singapore Free School completed
1840s	Secret society violence in Singapore on the rise; Singapore's inland roads programme begins
1841	Daing Ibrahim officially installed as Temenggong, having notionally held the title since 1825
1842	End of the First Opium War with the signing of the Treaty of Nanjing
1843	Discovery of gutta-percha in Johor
1844	Temenggong Daing Ibrahim begins developing Johor through gambier and pepper farms

1845 Beginning of the age of steam ships

1850s Singapore emerges as a major coaling station; Christian missionary societies begin opening schools in Singapore

1851 Opening of the Horsburgh Lighthouse on Pedra Branca

1852 Opening of New Harbour (Keppel Harbour)

1853 Americans force 'free trade' on Japan

1855 British force 'free trade' on Siam

1856 Judiciary shifts from Penang to Singapore, finally ending the last vestige of Penang's role as the seat of government and administration

1857 Indian Mutiny

1858 EIC is dissolved; the Colonial Office assumes control of the Straits Settlements, though it still administers them through Calcutta; the seat of Johor's government and administration is transferred from Singapore to Johor Baru

1860 End of the Second Opium War

1862 Death of Temenggong Daing Ibrahim; succeeded as Temenggong by his son, Abu Bakar

1864 Beginning of development of New Harbour (Keppel Harbour) by Tanjong Pagar Dock Company

MODERN SINGAPORE BEFORE INDEPENDENCE, 1867–1965

1867 Colonial Office in London takes direct control of the Straits Settlements; creation of a Straits Civil Service; a nominated, advisory Legislative Council formed

1868 Tanjong Pagar Dock Company opens Singapore's first dry dock

1869 Opening of Suez Canal

1871 Opening of the first submarine cable between Singapore and London

1876 Publication of first Malay newspaper, *Jawi Peranakan*

1870s Tin and rubber replace gambier and pepper as Malaya's main exports; British hold over central-western Malay peninsula tightens, with Abu Bakar's assistance

1876	Redevelopment and expansion of Singapore's sewage and water system begins
1879	First telephone line begins operation in Singapore
1881	Publication of first Chinese newspaper in Singapore, *Lat Pau*
1885	Maharajah Abu Bakar given title 'Sultan' of Johor by the British; the beginning of Chinese schools in Singapore
1886	Invention of the motor car and petrol engine; electrification of the docks in New Harbour
1887	Invention of the pneumatic tyre
1888	The 'Veranda Riots' in Chinatown
1890	Secret societies outlawed
1892	M. Samuel and Co. (Shell) builds a kerosene bunker on Pulau Bukum
1895	Federated Malay States formed from Selangor, Perak, Negeri Sembilan and Pahang; death of Sultan Abu Bakar of Johor and succession by his son, Sultan Ibrahim
1896	First rubber plantation on Singapore; Singapore's first motor car drives through the city
1897	Shell begins bunkering oil on Pulau Bukum; Sir Henry Ridley perfects rubber planting and tapping techniques in Singapore Botanical Gardens
1899	Malaya is producing half the world's rubber
1902	Government commits to providing English-medium schools on a small scale
1903	Government takes control of Raffles Institution; foundation of Cold Storage company
1904	Last tiger shot in the wild in Singapore
1905	Colonial government takes over the Tanjong Pagar Dock Company and its four dry docks; the peak of Malaya's tin production
1906	Electrification of the town centre completed
1907	Shell merges with Royal Dutch Company to become Royal Dutch Shell and bases its bunkering at Pulau Bukum
1910	End of the revenue farms; de-privatisation of opium industry
1911	Nationalist revolution in China; foundation of the Republic of China by the Kuomintang (Chinese Nationalist Party, KMT)

1912	Foundation of the Singapore Harbour Board; foundation of the KMT in Malaya
1913	Sultan of Johor accepts a British 'Adviser' for the first time
1914–19	World War I
1915	First aeroplane lands in Singapore at Farrer Park; first wireless radio station; Indian soldiers mutiny
1920s	Expansion of Singapore's public buildings programme; flowering of Malayan nationalism
1921	Britain decides to build a naval base in Singapore; foundation of the Chinese Communist Party (CCP)
1923	Causeway between Singapore and Johor Baru is opened; KMT–CCP common front formed in China
1925	KMT declared illegal in Malaya
1927	KMT–CCP split in China
1928	Admiralty builds Singapore's first floating dock
1929	Beginning of the Great Depression
1930s	Age of mechanised vehicles begins in Singapore
1930	Foundation of the (illegal) Malayan Communist Party (MCP)
1931	Mobil begins bunkering oil at Pulau Sebarok
1937	Japan invades China
1938	Singapore Naval Base completed in Sembawang; Admiralty builds Singapore's first graving dock; foundation of pro-Japanese Young Malay Union (Kaum Melayu Muda, KMM)
1942	Japanese attack on Pearl Harbor; Japanese invasion of Malaya and Singapore; beginning of Japanese Occupation of Malaya as Malai and Singapore as Syonan-To; launch of the Malayan People's Anti-Japanese Army (MPAJA) resistance who worked with British commandos
1943	Subhas Chandra Bose arrives in Singapore as head of the Indian National Army
1945	Japan surrenders; end of Japanese Occupation; return of British; establishment of British Military Administration; demobilisation of the MPAJA
1946	Britain breaks up the Straits Settlements and separates Singapore from the rest of the peninsula which is planned as the Malayan Union; foundation of the United Malays National Organisation (UMNO) on the peninsula

1947	Foundation of the Progressive Party
1948	Declaration of the 'Malayan Emergency'; MCP declared illegal; a partially elected Legislative Council instituted in Singapore
1949	CCP victory in China
1950	Dismantling of the MCP's Singapore Town Committee; 'Maria Hertogh Riots'
1950–3	Korean War
1954	Foundation of the People's Action Party (PAP); 'National Service Riot'
1955	Introduction of limited self-government with an elected Legislative Assembly; foundation of the Labour Front; David Marshall appointed Chief Minister, heading a coalition led by the Labour Front; 'Hock Lee Riot'; creation of the Central Provident Fund
1956	'Middle School Riots'; abortive negotiations in London over self-government; opening of Nanyang University; Lim Yew Hock appointed Chief Minister heading an ever-changing coalition; Lim Yew Hock begins programme of detentions
1957	Successful negotiations in London for self-government; foundation of Workers' Party by David Marshall; PAP wins inaugural City Council elections; foundation of the Federation of Malaya
1958	Nanyang University opens; Lee Kuan Yew enters a united front with the MCP
1959	Singapore granted almost complete self-government; PAP wins Legislative Assembly elections; Lee Kuan Yew appointed Prime Minister
1960	Foundation of the Housing and Development Board; announcement of plans for Jurong Industrial Estate
1961	Bukit Ho Swee fire; two PAP by-election losses; Tunku Abdul Rahman, Prime Minister of Malaya, declares support for merger between Singapore and Malaya; splits in PAP; foundation of Barisan Sosialis (Socialist Front) and the United People's Party; foundation of the Economic Development Board (EDB); formation of National Trades Union Congress (NTUC)
1962	Mobil approaches EDB about expansion; plebiscite on 'Merger' with Malaya; the beginning of Indonesian Konfrontasi
1963	Operation Coldstore; PAP wins general election, Barisan forms opposition; formation of Malaysia, including Singapore, Sarawak and Sabah; beginning of Konfrontasi

1964 'Singapore Race Riots'

1965 Lee Kuan Yew, Goh Keng Swee and E.W. Barker negotiate Singapore's exit from Malaysia

INDEPENDENT SINGAPORE, 1965–

1965 Foundation of the Republic of Singapore with Lee Kuan Yew as Prime Minister, heading a PAP government; the last Singapore Legislative Assembly becomes the first Singapore Parliament; first American troops deployed in Vietnam

1966 Mobil opens Singapore's first oil refinery at Jurong; in Indonesia Sukarno falls, Suharto rises; end of Indonesia's Konfrontasi

1967 UK devalues the pound stirling

1968 PAP wins every seat in parliament; foundation of the Development Bank of Singapore (DBS); decision taken to turn Singapore into a financial centre; UK announces early closure of naval base; foundation of Sembawang Shipyards Pty Ltd, forerunner of Sembcorp; Lee Kuan Yew begins his sabbatical at the Kennedy School of Government, Harvard University

1969 'Malaysian Race Riots'; Nixon announces the Guam Doctrine, partially withdrawing from Asia; Lee Hsien Loong passes matriculation in Catholic High School; decision taken to containerise the Port of Singapore

1970s Traditional Chinese schools wither and are all but extinguished

1970 First junior college, National Junior College, opens; Lee Hsien Loong passes matriculation at National Junior College

1971 Nixon defaults on US commitment to the gold standard; Singapore Armed Forces Overseas Scholarship announced, with Lee Hsien Loong a first-round winner

1972 Port of Singapore is containerised

1974 Formation of Sheng-li Holdings (later Singapore Technologies and ST Engineering) and Temasek Holdings; scholarship scheme for serving Singapore Armed Forces (SAF) officers instituted, with Lee Hsien Loong in first round of winners

1975 End of Vietnam War

1978 Singapore's 'Second Industrial Revolution'; Deng Xiaoping visits Singapore; Lee Hsien Loong enrols in US Army Command and General Staff College at Fort Leavenworth

1979	Lee Hsien Loong enrols in Kennedy School of Government, Harvard University; Government reintroduces Chinese schools as Special Assistance Plan schools
1980s	China begins opening up
1981	J.B. Jeyaretnam wins the seat of Anson for the Workers' Party, breaking PAP's monopoly; creation of Government of Singapore Investment Corporation (GIC)
1984	Central Provident Fund (CPF) contribution rate reaches 50% of income; Goh Keng Swee retires from parliament; Lee Hsien Loong enters parliament; Non-Constituency MPs introduced
1985	1980s recession begins
1987	Operation Spectrum: detention of alleged Marxist conspirators
1988	Group Representation Constituencies introduced
1989	Launch of Singapore–Johor–Riau growth triangle; MCP officially surrenders
1990	Release of the last of the 1987 detainees, Vincent Cheng; some easing of restrictions on the last of the 1963 detainees, Chia Thye Poh; Goh Chok Tong becomes Prime Minister; Lee Hsien Loong becomes Deputy Prime Minister; Lee Kuan Yew becomes Senior Minister; Nominated MPs introduced
1991	Elected Presidency introduced
1993	Singapore begins 'Growing a Second Wing'
1994	Temasek Holdings absorbs Singapore Engineering
1998	Chia Thye Poh released from all detention-related restrictions
2004	Lee Hsien Loong becomes Prime Minister; Lee Kuan Yew becomes Minister Mentor; Goh Chok Tong becomes Senior Minister
2005	Lee Hsien Loong begins programme to boost immigration
2006	Formation of Iskandar Development Region and South Johor Economic Region
2007	US Navy Region Centre opens in Singapore
2008	Singapore River sealed from the sea to make it a freshwater reservoir; Singapore Public Service Commission announces incentives for scholars to study in China

2011	PAP vote in general election down to 60%; PAP loses six seats to Workers' Party in general election; Tony Tan narrowly elected President; worst electoral outcomes for PAP since independence
2012	Breakdowns on Mass Rapid Transit (MRT) emerge as a recurring problem affecting all lines
2013	Workers' Party wins Tampines East from PAP in by-election
2015	Death of Lee Kuan Yew; Fiftieth Anniversary of Singapore's independence; PAP wins 70% of the vote in general election, regains Tampines East but fails to win back any of the losses from 2011
2016	Lee Hsien Loong aligns with USA over South China Sea; sale of Neptune Orient Lines; China impounds nine of Singapore's armoured vehicles in Hong Kong
2017	Lee Hsien Loong not invited to Xi Jinping's Belt and Road Forum; Lee Hsien Loong visits Beijing and signs up to the Belt and Road initiative

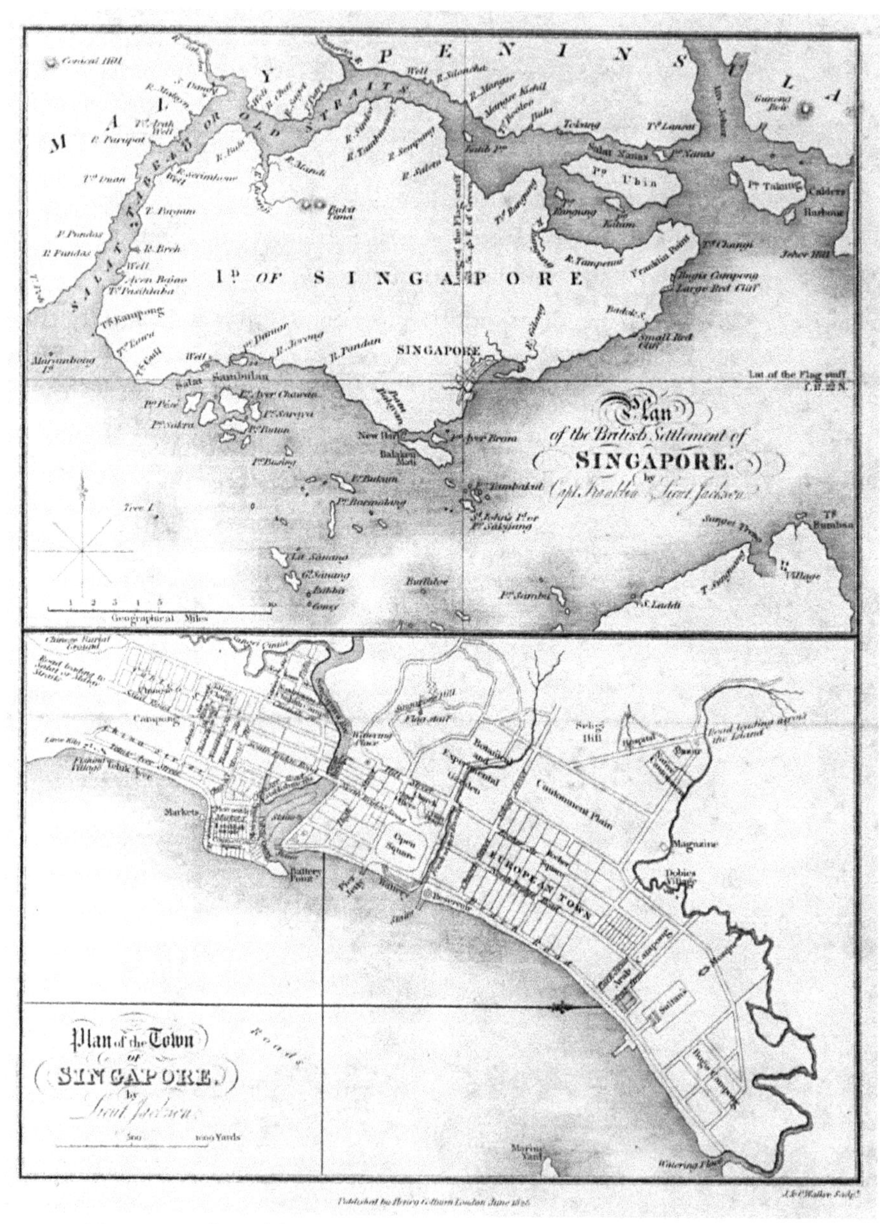

Map 1.1 *Plan of the Town of Singapore* by Lieutenant Jackson, 1828

1

Let's Talk About 1819: Reorienting the National Narrative

> Not one stick or stone of present-day Singapore was standing on the morning of Friday, the 29th day of January, 1819. Towards noon of that day two men, the Temenggong Abdul Rahman and Sir Stamford Raffles, with whom the story of the modern city begins, met for the first time in the shade of a cluster of coconut palms on the southern shore of the island.
>
> The opening words of H.F. Pearson's *Singapore: A Popular History* (1961)[1]

Singapore has many honours and awards to its name. It routinely tops the World Bank listings for 'ease of doing business'. As a city it won a 2010 United Nations Habitat Award and as a country it has been recognised as having one of the best health systems in the world. It brims with such confidence in its own international standing that it even gives awards to other countries and other cities – such as its Global City Prize, awarded by the Urban Redevelopment Authority. By any measure it is a remarkable place, especially considering its size. As a country Singapore is tiny (less than 6 million people living on an island at the mouth of the Johor River) and even as a city it is smaller than Sydney, Bangkok, Jakarta and almost any major metropolis you could mention. It is, enigmatically, the largest city-state in the world, beating its nearest rivals, Monaco and the Vatican City, hands down.

In 2018 it was also confirmed for the fifth year in a row as the most expensive place in the world in which to live. This latter point is one of the few honours that is not a matter for boasting by the government and yet being in the league of expensive cities should not be unexpected, since it has been working to a deliberate and substantially successful agenda for many years to become a 'global city' like London and New York, one of the characteristics of which is a high cost of living. Yet even on this score, neither the aspiration nor the costly outcome should be taken as being free of nuance. Singapore's government likes to think that it is different from other global cities in at least one positive respect: that it actively redistributes enough social goods (notably housing, health and education) to ensure that ordinary citizens who are not direct beneficiaries of the wealth generated by the city are at least indirect beneficiaries. Leaving aside the government's severely limited notions of redistribution and disputes over its success in achieving this goal, it is significant to note that such a neo-Fabian objective is rarely taken on by a city (the experience of London in the 1970s notwithstanding). If this role is undertaken by any level of government it is usually the central, federal or state/ regional government, not the municipality.

The government's social conscience therefore underlines the plain oddity of the extraordinary amount of attention paid to Singapore as a subject of scholarly and public policy study: it is a city-state in an age of nation-states. City-states have enjoyed several historical periods of pre-eminence and in their days have dominated their worlds, but those days are long gone. They disappeared even before the withering of the age of empires roughly a century ago. It is undeniable that the average size of nation-states is getting smaller by the decade (think of the impact of recent additions such as Timor Leste, Macedonia and Kosovo), but this has not translated into a renaissance for city-states. Not a single enduring city-state emerged from the break-up of the Soviet, German, Hapsburg, Japanese, Portuguese or Ottoman empires. The French and British empires gave us just one city-state each (Monaco and Singapore, though Dubai, Abu Dhabi and Hong Kong have survived as quasi-city-states operating with varying degrees of comfort within larger entities). Unprecedented levels of connectivity in both transport and communications and the new importance of service and information as tradable commodities mean that this is a good time for an economy to be based on a great city, and yet every one of the great cities of the modern world remains stubbornly embedded in a nation-state. The twentieth century was very much the century of nationalism, not 'civic-ism'.

The sobering truth is that it takes a decidedly unusual set of circumstances to create an environment in which the international community will recognise a city as a sovereign state. Such a peculiar set of circumstances accidentally and reluctantly flowed together in 1965 for the Federation of Malaysia to give birth to the Republic of Singapore. With rather more deliberation they flowed together for Mussolini's Italy and the old Papal States to give birth to the Vatican City in 1929. But the same fortune has failed to smile upon other likely candidates for city-based sovereignty. There is little doubt, for instance, that both Hong Kong and Jerusalem would have been better off as independent statelets with carefully crafted relations with their immediate neighbours, but it was not to be.

A study of Singapore is therefore a study in difference. It may not be *sui generis*, but it is certainly a rare bird. This particular difference is part of the reason it is so interesting and we can say with a reasonable level of confidence that it is one of the critical factors that explains why it is successful on so many fronts. There is an orthodoxy in Singapore that its small size makes it vulnerable and it has to struggle to prosper – a minnow swimming with the sharks and whales. There can be little doubt that being small creates a distinctive set of vulnerabilities with which a larger entity need not concern itself, and yet short of a direct existential threat there is little reason to think that a city-state like Singapore is more vulnerable to a myriad of formidable challenges than larger countries. Indeed there is much reason to regard the city-state as being an enviable model of an economy/polity. Writing in *Foreign Affairs* on sovereign risk and regime durability, Nassim Nicholas Taleb and Gregory F. Treverton make this point thus:

> City-states both old and new – from Venice to Dubai to Geneva to Singapore – owe their success to their smallness. Those who compare political systems by looking at their character without taking into account their size are thus making an analytical error.[2]

Smallness, they argue, brings with it many strengths, though in itself it is no guarantee of success. Largeness likewise brings with it a baggage-load of its own problems, especially if it is coupled with inflexibility – or a 'lack of political variability', to use Taleb and Treverton's terminology.[3]

LOOKING PAST RAFFLES AND LEE KUAN YEW

I have opened this history of Singapore with this somewhat tangential discourse on the bifurcated nature of Singapore (city and country) as a modest beginning of an antidote to the standard mythology of Singapore, which is premised on the city-state's vulnerability – primarily due to its size. In this narrative, the future and security of tiny Singapore is guaranteed only by the cleverness and benevolence of the country's political leaders. The mythology to which I refer finds its zenith in the official, state-constructed narrative of Singapore, which is known as 'The Singapore Story'[4] and has provided the template for teaching history throughout the island's schools and junior colleges since the introduction of the National Education programme in 1997.[5] The Singapore Story also utterly dominates the historical narrative in universities, newspapers and other media. It has even been reproduced on the Discovery Channel.[6] Ernest Koh was, if anything, understating the case when he wrote in 2010 that the Singapore Story submerges 'all forms of remembrance in Singapore, especially among the English-literate majority of the population'.[7] Kwa Chong Guan, Derek Heng and Tan Tai Yong extend this criticism, calling it a 'misuse' of history, but offer some understanding of this misuse by pointing out that this weakness is shared with 'other national histories'.[8] At its heart the Singapore Story is, to return to the critique offered by Koh, 'a triumphal narrative of deliverance from political, economic, and social despair ... through the ruling regime's scientific approaches to solving the problems faced by a developing and industrialising society'.[9] T.N. Harper goes further, describing it as a 'biblical narrative of deliverance'.[10] The enemies from which Singapore was 'delivered' are very clearly delineated in this narrative: the chaos of communal discord (most notably Malay 'ultras' and Chinese 'chauvinists'); the pull of extra-national loyalties by ethnic homelands (China; India; Malaysia; Indonesia); communism and leftist subversives, students and unionists; overbearing regional neighbours (Malaysia and Indonesia); and poverty. More recent additions to this litany include Western decadence and liberalism, and religious 'extremists' (most notably Catholics and Muslims). The Singapore Story was the product of a state-directed campaign that was launched in the late 1990s, but it built directly on an earlier national(ist) narrative adopted in the 1980s. The earlier iteration underlined explicitly one major feature that is implicit and taken as a given in its successor: that the story of Singapore's triumphal march to success is essentially a British-colonial and a Chinese-immigrant story. The explicit premise of the national narrative is that before Raffles arrived in 1819 there was, basically, nothing on the island and nothing in the region that need be considered when accounting for Singapore's success; and without the leadership of Lee Kuan Yew and the followership of industrious, clever and frugal Chinese citizens, Singapore would still be in the Third World.

NATIONAL(IST) HISTORIES

The mythology of Singapore as a British–Chinese–Lee Kuan Yew success story lies in the perspective generated by the undisputed 'mother' of Singaporean history, Mary Turnbull, who denied Singapore's pre-British past when she opened her seminal *A History of Singapore* with the memorable words:

> Modern Singapore dates from 30 January 1819, when the local chieftain, the Temenggong of Johor, signed a preliminary treaty with Sir Stamford Raffles, agent of the East India Company, permitting the British to set up a trading post.[11]

Turnbull's contribution to the Singapore national narrative is her lasting achievement, alongside her exhaustive attention to archival material. She stands apart from her contemporaries partly because no other historian matched the way she meticulously and painstakingly mined the colonial archives and then used this material to weave a narrative that was straightforward, readable and informative. Without the archival foundation, it is doubtful that her work would have been so durable that in the second decade of the twenty-first century her books still comprise basic texts for historians researching the colonial period. But this is not the core of her distinctiveness; that is primarily attributable to the fact that she single-handedly, deliberately and successfully created the narrative of Singapore (including colonial Singapore) as a consciously national history. In her national history, Singapore's story was separate from the history of both Malaya and from Singapore's

Figure 1.1
Secondary One History textbook, 1984–99

pre-colonial past – which until her work triumphed, had been a common and mainstream perspective among historians. Furthermore, she did so as a ten-year project beginning in the 1960s when there was no obvious market for such a national history. At that time the government was actively discouraging the teaching of history, regarding it as irrelevant – and even detrimental – to the task of building a successful Singapore.

Turnbull's *A History of Singapore* was published in 1977. As luck would have it, just a few years after publication – in 1980 – the attitude at the top of government began to change: ministers began ruminating in public about the importance of history as a nation-building tool. Turnbull's work was promptly embraced by the Ministry of Education and so she provided the template for the teaching of Singapore history in Singaporean schools, junior colleges and the local university. The Turnbull approach was on graphic display in the first generation of History textbooks. Consider the cover of the Secondary One textbook shown in Figure 1.1. It features a statue of Raffles superimposed over a 1959 photo of Lee Kuan Yew and his Cabinet colleagues marching in front of City Hall after being sworn in.[12]

Allowing for some relatively minor changes of inflection, this situation has lasted to today. Turnbull's history served the nation-building agenda so well precisely because it created a new myth in which the whole of Singapore's colonial history was presented as the backdrop for its triumphal march to success, delivered by Prime Minister Lee Kuan Yew and his People's Action Party (PAP) government. This history was uncompromisingly anchored fore and aft by Sir Stamford Raffles and Lee Kuan Yew and it provided the new nation with, as Karl Hack has eloquently expressed it, a 'genealogy'. Less simply, but more profoundly, Hack described Turnbull's *A History of Singapore* as 'a teleological exercise in endowing a modern "nation-state" with a coherent past that should explain the present'.[13] That it was such an important book for its time was due to its intrinsic strengths: the quality of the research and the groundbreaking analysis. That it has lasted so well beyond its time is due more to its facility to a ruling elite seeking a foundation myth that reinforces its own place in history and politics.

REVISIONIST HISTORY

The Turnbull story, followed by the hegemony of the Singapore Story, planted two pivotal dates in Singapore's national narrative: 1819 as the foundation of 'modern Singapore', and 1965 as the foundation of independent Singapore. The triumph of each of these narratives in turn was absolute in institutional terms and yet they never went completely unchallenged, either by historians or by scholars from other disciplines. Sadly, however, during the 1980s and most of the 1990s none of these critiques came from Singaporeans themselves. This task was left to 'foreign talent' because in those decades it would have been a career-killing exercise for a local scholar to have questioned the orthodoxy. Even today, 'revisionist history' is a politically charged term wielded by the Establishment as an accusation. In the 2010s, revisionists (labelled by one Establishment scholar as 'Alternates')[14] engage in provocative exercises such as seeking evidence before accepting official narratives, especially on matters concerning the 'riots', strikes and rounds of detention that have become part of Singapore's foundational mythology. One of the more contentious exercises a revisionist can engage in is to question the way the official narrative about the 1960s and 1970s carelessly accuses people of being communist or 'pro-communist' – the latter being a label that seems to be applied to almost anyone of whom the government disapproved.[15] In the 1970s and 1980s it was worse: you were a revisionist if you merely suggested that Singapore had a history before 1819.

One of the more innovative revisionists of the 1980s was Philippe Regnier, a French scholar whose history opened with a very substantial introduction in which he explored the lines of continuity between Singapore's pre-colonial past as a regional meeting point and its colonial and subsequent role as a trading city, rather than as a colony or as a nation.[16] Carl Trocki was busy throughout the entire period from the 1970s onwards, producing social histories focused on the Singapore-Johor region that deliberately cast aside and challenged the significance of the colonial (and by implication, the national) borders as the boundary of delineation in local history.[17] James Warren's bottom-up social histories of the 1980s and 1990s mounted less direct challenges to the national narrative, but were nevertheless notable for their complete disregard for the colonial boundaries, treating Singapore essentially as a city that was part of an East Asian political economy.[18]

Perhaps it should not be surprising, however, that the greatest advances in decentring Singapore's history from its colonial past and its national present have been made by scholars who are not actually historians of Singapore: John Miksic, an American archaeologist of Southeast Asia for whom Singapore is just one site of interest among many; and Peter Borschberg, an Austrian historian who focuses on Southeast Asia in the period from the fifteenth to the seventeenth century. Miksic's work on pre-fifteenth-century Singapore was a game-changer in Singapore historiography. The archaeological digs that he ran at Fort Canning from 1984 onwards and which he wrote up for the National Museum confirmed the importance of Singapore as an outpost of the Java-based Majapahit Empire before becoming part of the Malacca Sultanate, which in turn became the Johor-Riau Sultanate.[19] This history was already known, but tended to be sidelined in most accounts. It continued to be mostly ignored even after Miksic's scholarship started appearing in print because the new material was emerging at exactly the same time that the Turnbull version of the national history was being newly promoted as the country's official history.

Yet for all its strengths, the work of Miksic and his collaborators has had an unintended consequence: it intensified the focus on Singapore the island, generating a parochial compulsion in official, popular and academic discourse to tie 'Singaporean' historical perspectives rigidly to the current national boundaries of the city-state. This was a danger that Wang Gungwu explicitly warned the Ministry of Education about as long ago as 1982, when he wrote that 'it is a mistake to see Singapore's history in terms of the physical island'.[20] The mindset against which Prof. Wang was warning, and which subsequently became entrenched in Singapore historiography, is that if it happened across the water, in Johor or Riau, it is someone else's history, not 'ours'. Let us admit that a parochial and present-ist focus is to some extent intrinsic to any national history. Such engagement is arguably the legitimate purpose of a national history and I certainly have no illusions that I have been able to escape the island boundary either: not in this book and certainly not in my earlier works, in which the acceptance of Singapore-as-nation (or Singapore-as-colony) was accepted without demure. This is where Peter Borschberg's contributions are critical, since he is a transnational historian and so is completely free of the national-history genre's limitations. His contributions are also critical for another reason: he can read Spanish, Portuguese and Dutch archives, which has opened up new vistas of transnational and trans-colonial historiography.[21] Borschberg's scholarship is so firmly fixed on the pre-British past and so focused on the minutiae of discrete historical episodes from the fifteenth to the seventeenth century that it is easily possible to bypass its implications for current national history and Singapore's founding mythology,[22] yet it provides a perspective that should be front and centre of any effort to place Singapore in history: that Singapore is, in the final analysis, 'an island in the mouth of the Johor River'.[23]

Separately to these efforts, the 1980s, 1990s and early 2000s saw selected facets of the national narrative being challenged with increasing frequency and intensity as time went on, even if none were actually written as national histories. At the latter end of the time spectrum, the 2000s and 2010s also saw direct challenges by both scholars and former victims of repression to some of the core political elements of the Singapore Story, notably the official accounts of two sets of detentions: the 1963 sweep of over 100 alleged communists in 'Operation Coldstore' and the 1987 sweep of 22 alleged Marxist conspirators in 'Operation Spectrum'.

In retrospect it is clear that during the 1990s and the first decade of the 2000s, Singapore historiography had begun shifting in a major way – seemingly as a direct reaction to the Singapore Story's oppressive dominance of the public space. Karl Hack reports that by the mid-2000s both the National University of Singapore and Nanyang Technological University had begun – or at least provided the option of – including a study of Singapore's pre-colonial past as part of the history curriculum for trainee teachers and others.[24] Local scholars were even joining with international colleagues to challenge the construction of an official national history in books dedicated explicitly to that purpose. Such is the extent of the shifting grounds in the national debates that an approved Secondary One History textbook published in 2014 explicitly considers pre-colonial history back to 1300. Yet such is the power of the institutional ballast held by the Singapore Story that the same textbook claims to trace the making of the Singapore nation-state back to 1300. And Raffles is still on the cover[25] (Figure 1.2).

Thus, a formidable armada of revisionist scholarship has been arrayed against the national history and the Singapore Story, and yet The Singapore Story remains dominant in pedagogy, publishing and global consciousness. There is a long struggle being played out for the high ground in Singapore historiography – with an Establishment that dispenses research funding and jobs on one side, and an array of independent scholars and critics on the other. This is a history war, but it is not just about history. It is ultimately about politics and power, a point that was explicitly recognised in May 2014 by National University of Singapore History Professor Tan Tai Yong when he warned History teachers about succumbing to the lure of 'revisionist history'.[26] In these debates, the Establishment holds all the institutional advantages, but it is concerned that this

Figure 1.2
Secondary One History textbook, 2014–

advantage is withering as scholarship – particularly local scholarship – is emboldened, thus making contrarian interpretations of history increasingly mainstream.

It is in this context that I approach my task, which operates at several levels. First I tell what I hope is an interesting and informative story about Singapore for those readers who know it mostly through its nice airport or a casual knowledge of its reputation. Second, it sets out to overturn the established national narrative, with the intention of creating the intellectual room necessary for consideration of fresh approaches to both Singaporean historiography and national identity. This brings me to the third point. This is a history book, written for students of history and serious general readers who are interested in considering new ways of looking at Singapore's place on the expansive landscape of colonial, pre-colonial and contemporary history. Lastly – and somewhat in tension with the previous point – this book is an alternative national history. Like the Singapore Story it seeks to impose the order of a linear narrative onto the disparate events of the past, specifically to provide an understanding of the contemporary, living nation, but unlike the Singapore Story it places present-day Singapore in the context of history, rather than vice versa. One of its more provocative elements is its challenge to the place of 1819 in the national narrative, denying its role as the decisive point of discontinuity with what had gone before and shifting the foundation of 'modern Singapore' to a point much later in the nineteenth century.

My contribution in this volume is not, for the most part, directly confrontational. There are particular passages that challenge the veracity of accepted 'facts', but my primary challenge to the established narrative is made by taking accepted facts and telling a substantially different story. I present a narrative in which modern Singapore is not a simple story of brilliant leadership, whether the leader be named Raffles or Lee. Starting from a point much earlier than either independence in 1965 or the planting of a British flag in 1819, I focus on a bigger picture in which the island and its immediate neighbours to the north and south have for centuries hosted social and commercial networks that have given the region importance beyond that suggested by its relatively minor place in global history. Singapore itself has routinely been either central or important to these regional networks because of its location, but it has never been separated from them in the past nor, I suggest, in the present. I argue that this is the most basic truth of Singapore's story.

When considering the various flows of peoples, commerce, shipping and communications, both over the centuries and today, it is a problematic exercise to separate the achievements of Singapore from a broader web of regional relationships, and so for the most part I have not tried to do so. Until Singapore became a sovereign political entity with clearly defined geographical boundaries in 1965, the island had always been part of a greater whole, and that is how I have treated it. Any attempt to imprison history in the 719 square kilometres that make up present-day Singapore is bound to stunt and distort it, and whatever other weaknesses this book may have, I am confident that I have avoided that particular trap. Even when late-colonial and post-colonial Singapore started notching achievements that distinguished the island from its neighbours, there were remarkably few that could be fairly described without considering Singapore's place in regional networks; in other words, its achievements amounted to Singapore being given or taking a head start over its neighbours in ventures that concerned the region as a whole, and then running furiously to keep ahead of the pack. Think of shipping, ship servicing, air traffic and oil. Each is an entry in independent Singapore's list of success stories, but they all had their origins well before independence and are anchored in the strategic geography of the island and the region. The common factors in all of these achievements and many others included not just courageous and prudent investment-cum-leadership (though that factor was certainly pivotal) but also geography and historical inheritance. The region per se was pivotal, and the island of Singapore was a rather useful base from which to work the region. The Singapore that we know succeeded because it successfully captured the region's intrinsic and historical advantages for its own profit, while pursuing the regional partnerships that were necessary to make the achievements possible. This is the underplayed – though never quite denied – key factor in Singapore's success. This book places this line of analysis in prime position and so sets out to identify and study those advantages over the *longue durée.*

This is not the first national history to consider the region's pre-colonial past, but it is the first to override 1819 by drawing firm lines of continuity that straddle it. Other accounts tend to treat Singapore's pre-colonial past as mere background at best: interesting, but ultimately disconnected from what came after. In such accounts, 1819 continues to loom large as the pivotal point at which everything changed. The current volume sets out to reduce the significance of 1819 to the point where it is a punctuation mark, rather than a headline. Hence the book is broken into thematic chapters that for the most part show scant regard for 1819. Chapter 2 considers different configurations of the idea of Singapore, starting in the present and working backwards. Chapter 3 looks at the role of geography in Singapore's history, placing British settlement in the context of history, rather than vice versa. Chapters 4, 5 and 6 study governance since *c.*1390 to the present, with periodisation markers at 1867 and 1965 (but not 1819). Chapter 7 presents an economic history in which 1819 is recognised as a critical turning point, but not the beginning of everything. Chapter 8 considers Singapore society and its development as a city, starting with the establishment of Kampong Glam and the beginnings of gambier and pepper farming in about 1811.

Thanks to its thematic approach, the advent of independence in 1965 appears in several chapters in this book and on each appearance it marks a change of pace and focus. This is neither accidental nor incidental. Independence heightened the agency of Singaporeans in determining their own destiny in a fundamental way. Indeed it was only with the advent of sovereignty that it started to make sense to speak of 'Singaporeans' at all. The year 1965 must therefore remain a headline, not a punctuation mark, in any Singapore story. Without shunning the regional and global connectivity that is a major theme of this book, this change in status demands a change in focus each time this book breaches it. Even beyond the imperatives of a linear national history, the decisiveness of the shift is further exaggerated because the metanarrative of the post-1965 story is dominated utterly by a small leadership group that has successfully perpetuated itself over half a century and continues to rule. As a national history, this book must accept the pathway laid out by this metanarrative, even as it interrogates and questions the official versions of that story and seeks to maintain a regional and trans-regional perspective.

2

The Idea of Singapore

Singapore runs probably one of the most rational governments in the world. Some say it operates almost like a business. …

Singapore is an ongoing experiment in plurality and multiculturalism in an era of globalisation. …

Venice and the cities of the Hanseatic League prefigured the future in their time. Singapore, Hong Kong, Shanghai, and now Bangalore: these free cities provide glimpses of what the future in Asia and to some extent the world will look like.

George Yeo, then Minister for Trade and Industry, 17 May 2001[1]

There is an idea of Singapore that lives in the minds of the country's ruling elite somewhere beyond the prosaic realities of the small city-state that sits at the end of the southern tip of the Malay Peninsula. The idea is both an aspirational ideal and a Platonic ideal-type: an essence of government-cum-society to which other societies and Singapore itself should aspire. The idea presumes that Singapore enjoys perfection (or something close to it) in the country's meritocratic, talent-driven system of government, which itself is seen as an extension and perfection of the Singaporean social order as a whole. This idea is the most basic of the Singapore elite's regime-legitimating mythologies and it provides the foundation for a further series of closely related legitimating mythologies for a government and society whose democratic and egalitarian credentials are weak. It is a natural and logical consequence of such a starting point that it has created expectations of world-class outcomes among Singaporeans. Indeed this logic is made explicit in both the avidness with which government and other Singaporean agencies seek and highlight international awards and tributes, and also in the rationale by which members of Cabinet and senior civil servants are rewarded with world-class salaries that dwarf those of their counterparts overseas.

Until recently this idea of Singapore has been internalised by most of the population to the point where it can be regarded as a new foundational myth for the country: an existential mythology that has been retrofitted onto the history and national identity of Singapore. Freed of hyperbole, a prosaic version of this idea can be seen in the 2012 White Paper on ministerial salaries:

Singapore has succeeded over the years as a small nation in a competitive and uncertain world. A key reason for this has been Government policies that have built up our capabilities

> and attracted investments, and developed a cohesive society. The Government has also taken a long term perspective, envisioning Singapore's future and dealing with challenges and opportunities in advance. It has made careful strategic choices so that we have lived within our means and invested in our future, avoiding national debts that will burden future generations. The result has been a safe home, shared prosperity and a better life for all Singaporeans. ... Being a small country with a small citizen population and an open economy, our talent pool is naturally limited, and our margin for error is slim.[2]

The extract is more modest than might have been expected from a reading of my opening paragraph, but bear in mind that it was written as a defensive document issued in the wake of a series of major policy and administrative failures[3] and a major backlash against the government. It was a period when expressions of humility and hints of self-doubt on the part of the ruling elite had become politically expedient. The crucial elements driven underground by the imposed modesty of 2012 are the self-proclaimed brilliance of the members of the national elite, the national obsession with collecting international accolades, and a didactic drive to share the wisdom and experience of the Singapore elite with the world. Also missing from this passage is the mythology of Singapore as a meritocracy (or a 'macho-meritocracy' according to one overenthusiastic acolyte).[4] Add to that a multiracial society that gives equal opportunity to all, but where Chinese always seem to dominate, and we have a fair description of the idea of Singapore in its full glory.

THREE DECADES OF A NEW IDEA

This idea of Singapore is not in any sense a natural phenomenon. Nor is it a permanent fixture, having been built on a series of much more modest ideas of Singapore. The ruling elite began constructing and cultivating the current idea at the beginning of the 1980s. Its public seminal moment can be traced to a speech delivered in 1982 by Goh Chok Tong, speaking as Minister for Health eight years before he became Prime Minister. Goh declared that Singapore's health system was already among the 'best in the world' but tempered his satisfaction by expressing a need to pursue infinite improvement: 'We should not rest on our laurels, looking down from Mount Everest. In organisational efficiency, in the pursuit of quality and excellence, there can be no highest peak.'[5]

This speech marked the beginning of a spiralling round of self-congratulatory hyperbole from government politicians that was very different from the official rhetoric of the preceding decades. Throughout the 1960s and 1970s the rhetoric of government had been bound up in the quest for survival and development. It was dominated by imagery of struggle and striving, crafted and led by the founding father of independent Singapore, Prime Minister Lee Kuan Yew. By the early 1980s there was a sense that this quest had been substantially achieved and much of the rhetoric of 'struggle' was replaced by the rhetoric of 'success'. In fact, the Singapore government was struggling with the problems of success:

society was changing, and expectations were rising along with the standards of living and education. It was a nice problem to have, and the government could have taken the opportunity to steer the rhetoric in the direction of ordinary political management. Under the explicit inspiration and direction of Prime Minister Lee, however, the government chose instead to identify a new national quest, which was flagged for the first time in Goh Chok Tong's 'no highest peak' speech of 1982. This new vision employed the rhetoric of Singapore as the epitome of rational, technocratic success: the ideal, self-correcting, self-perpetuating machine of modern governance. It was not merely a 'success', which is an idea that was already and justifiably well established in the national mythology. Nor were its leaders merely 'talented' (which was also well entrenched in government rhetoric). No, there emerged a sense in which Singapore was a light on the hill for more ordinary governments.

Beginning in 1982, the rhetoric of the uniqueness of Singaporean governance was maintained for nearly a decade by the spectacle of Cabinet ministers, journalists and even academics displaying stage-managed public angst over the succession from the 'Old Guard' of government leaders (Lee Kuan Yew's 'classes of 1959 and 1963') to what had been dubbed the 'Second Generation' of 'young' leaders (Goh Chok Tong, Ong Teng Cheong, Tony Tan and several others). The professional care and managerial approach taken with the selection, training and appointment of the succession team became part of the logic of Singapore's exceptionalism. There was even a five-year transition period from 1985 to the end of 1990 during which Lee Kuan Yew stayed on as Prime Minister and his successor, Goh Chok Tong, became First Deputy Prime Minister. 'My colleagues have decided that I should play centre forward. They have asked me to play the role of striker in the new team. The prime minister … will play the role of goalkeeper,' Deputy Prime Minister Goh told the press at the beginning of the long transition.[6] Leaving aside scepticism as to whether such a micromanaged and drawn-out handover is really best professional practice, we can identify in these events and the surrounding rhetoric the guided evolution of the idea of Singapore.

Nearly 20 years later, over April and May 2001, Minister for Trade and Industry (and later Foreign Minister) George Yeo captured the core of this idea of successful Singapore in a series of claims made in an interview and a separate speech. By that time the claims were so commonplace that they passed without remark: 'Singapore runs probably one of the most rational governments in the world.'[7] He described Singapore as 'an ongoing experiment' and observed that

> Singapore plays a role in the region and the world out of proportion to its size. We are entering a creative phase of our history. While we do not offer ourselves as a model to anyone, many cities in Asia view us as an interesting experiment in social and economic management.[8]

A few years later (2004), in the first year of his premiership, Prime Minister Lee Hsien Loong defined his mission in government in terms of perpetual achievement and improvement:

> We can never afford to be satisfied with the status quo, even if we are still okay, even if our policies are still working. People say, 'If it ain't broke, don't fix it.' I say, if it ain't broke, better maintain it, lubricate it, replace it, upgrade it, try something better and make it work better than before. …
>
> And this is true not just of the government but also of Singapore, also of society.[9]

Note that the claim made in this passage is not that of perfection per se, but of perpetual improvement based on rational analysis and trial and error – an ideal that Lee explicitly applies as much to society as he does to government.

More than three decades after it was seeded in Goh's speech, the mythology of rational and perpetual improvement is very obviously starting to wear thin in the popular imagination, and yet it seems to be stronger than ever in the imaginings of the ruling elite itself. By 2015, Prime Minister Lee had toned down the government's triumphalist rhetoric on health from 'probably the best in the world' to 'it works reasonably well for us',[10] yet at the same time he is also convinced that it is, at the very least, 'exceptional' and 'special' to the point where it left others agog at its achievements. At the 2015 May Day Rally, held a month after his father died, Lee Hsien Loong told the nation:

> The most difficult part of [our] job is to keep Singapore exceptional, special. Brother [Minister Without Portfolio Lim] Swee Say showed you workers making exceptional contributions, ordinary people doing exceptional things. We as a country have to be ordinary people doing exceptional things. We as a country have to be ordinary people creating an exceptional nation because we are a small country in this part of the world and to survive you have to be exceptional. …
>
> Most dramatically you ask yourself, why did so many foreign leaders come for Mr Lee [Kuan Yew]'s funeral service? … Would they have done that if Mr Lee had been an ordinary leader? But because we are exceptional, because we had an extraordinary leader, people have regard for us. …
>
> It's very, very important you don't lose that magic and to stay exceptional, we need a successful economy, we need hardworking and skilful workers, we need outstanding leadership. …
>
> This place could not have been built and cannot be kept going without exceptional leadership.[11]

This extensive monologue on Singapore's exceptionalism built on themes developed and refined by his father over his long public life, and to which he had given witness only four years earlier, in 2011: 'If we don't have a government and a people who differentiate themselves from the rest of the neighbourhood in a positive way and can defend Singapore and its rights, it will cease to exist.'[12] Significantly, both Lees linked the uniqueness of the country directly to the exceptional quality and character of the country's leadership.

It is not unique for an elite to link the nation with an idea or a vision that takes on something of an existential quality. John L. O'Sullivan arguably performed this service for the United States of America when, in a magazine article published in 1845, he called for the fulfilment of America's 'manifest destiny to overspread the continent allotted by Providence for the free development of our yearly multiplying millions'.[13] Although he cannot claim such longevity for his idea, Sukarno performed a comparable service when he dedicated his new Republic of Indonesia to the New Emerging Forces. Abraham Lincoln, Charles de Gaulle, Mustafa Kemal Atatürk, Vladimir Lenin, Mao Zedong, Ho Chi Minh, Ayatollah Khomeini and Elizabeth I are also members of this club of visionaries. Yet giant ideas do not necessarily translate into trans-generational visions and they are rarely the key to understanding a country's history.

The mythology embedded in national ideas is necessarily the construction of a victor (however transient the victory might prove to be), and is often laden with retrospective reconstructions: something akin to what Eric Hobsbawm and Terence Ranger have called 'the invention of tradition'.[14] Developing an understanding of a new national history routinely necessitates the exercise of deliberate effort to break free from the hegemonic ideas that have constructed the idea of nation. After all, the very notion of a 'national' history implies the construction of a narrative to back-fill a political-cum-cultural outcome that happens to be extant at the time of writing. This is especially true when 'nation' is being used as shorthand for 'nation-state'. Nations and nation-states come and go and their boundaries shift like rivers in soft soil, but national histories usually treat contemporary national boundaries as if they are permanent lines of inclusion and exclusion. Thus a national history of Malaysia has to include Sarawak and Sabah, but not Singapore or Brunei, either of which might easily have been part of Malaysia today if history had worked out differently. Ideas of national identity and constructions of national history smooth over such arbitrariness at the expense of non-hegemonic understandings of the nation.

NATION OR CITY?

Such cautionary tales about national histories tend not to apply with such force to the histories of cities, but this certainly does not mean that the histories of cities are free of myth-making. Just think of the myth-making and imagery that surrounds Rome, Paris, London, New York and Moscow, and the spiritual significance attributed to Jerusalem, Mecca and Ayodhya. Cities thus play central roles, not only in their own histories, but also on more expansive historical and political landscapes. Furthermore, they can be wilfully constructed and reconstructed to serve national projects and symbolise national self-images.

This digressive focus on cities is important because Singapore is, of course, a city as well as a country. There are aspects to the idea of Singapore that centre specifically on its identity as a city. C.M. Turnbull described the Singapore of the 1920s as 'the Chicago of the East, the haven of gunmen and street gangs'.[15] In 1962, Malayan Prime Minister Tunku Abdul Rahman described colonial Singapore as 'the New York of Malaysia', by which he was both recognising its role as a regional hub and discouraging any notion that it might be the Washington (i.e. political centre) of Malaysia when it joined the Federation soon after.[16] Ten years later, in 1972, S. Rajaratnam – Foreign Minister of the now-independent republic – declared Singapore to be a 'Global City' and a 'World City', which he presented as a step up from its role as 'the Change Alley of Asia' (referring to the narrow mercantilist entrepôt role that had been the lifeblood of the city during its colonial period).[17] After this little outing, the language of Singapore as a city took a back seat to the idea of Singapore as a nation, but by the 1990s the idea of Singapore as a city had moved to the front and centre of government thinking. A series of government reports and initiatives throughout that decade referred to Singapore as a 'global city', a 'people's city', a 'business city' and a 'transit city', among other descriptors.[18] In 2000 the 'city' imagery was stepped up with an official report on Singapore as a 'Renaissance city'.[19]

Indeed, consideration of Singapore as a global city is now a routine entrée into histories of Singapore[20] – and rightly so since Singapore was a city at least a hundred years before it was a nation. British Singapore was, in fact, a late member of the network of indigenous and colonial 'port cities' that are mapped and analysed in detail by Anthony Reid in volume two of his *Southeast Asia in the Age of Commerce, 1450–1680*. These cities were the direct inheritors of the pre-colonial port cities described by O.W. Wolters in his *History, Culture, and Region in Southeast Asian Perspectives*.[21] Singapore's historical roles as a port and as a city serving an Asian clientele – and variously the British Empire and the capitalist West more generally[22] – distinguish it from being 'merely' a nation.

Cities can and should be studied in their own right, but Singapore's place since independence in 1965 as a city-state singles it out in multiple ways. Cities are essentially parochial. New York is a vitally important city in its own right, but discussions of its politics and its mayors generally remain municipal unless they take on national importance for some particular reason – such as providing a presidential candidate, affecting a national election, showcasing racial or policing issues that might have national implications, or being singled out for a particularly spectacular terrorist attack. Despite having seen plenty of downtimes, London remains one of the world's most important cities and it has been the subject of more histories and 'biographies' than most, but its significance today is viewed primarily through the twin prisms of its role in international markets and its relationship with England and the rest of the United Kingdom. Cities are studied in their own right by some specialist fields of scholarship and for their relationship with other cities by scholars such as Saskia Sassen, but for the most part they are discussed for their roles in and relationships with larger entities, most commonly the nation-state in which they are situated. Going just up the road from Singapore we find that Ross King's *Kuala Lumpur and Putrajaya: Negotiating Urban Space in Malaysia* is essentially about how Prime Minister Mahathir was crafting these two cities into an emblem and mirror of his vision of the nation.[23] Going across the water from Singapore we find in Jakarta a much bigger city than Singapore, but one that receives much less scholarly and global attention. Part of the reason for this is undoubtedly the exceptional level of interest that Singapore generates because of its achievements. A more basic reason, however, is that Jakarta is 'just' a city (albeit the capital of the fourth-largest country and the third-largest democracy in the world) whereas Singapore is a country in its own right.

In a real sense, all important cities must be outward looking, whether to other cities or to a host nation, in order to be important in the first place. The complete absence of examples of large cities that operate in a state of political or economic autarky establishes this point for practical purposes. In the case of Singapore, its expansiveness is what defines it in the early decades of the twenty-first century – as it did throughout the nineteenth and twentieth centuries – but its concomitant 'national' perspective gives it a fused identity. When Daniel A. Bell and Avner de-Shalit set out to characterise the 'identity' of nine major cities for their book, *The Spirit of Cities: Why the Identity of a City Matters in a Global Age*, they characterised Singapore as the 'City of Nation Building'.[24] Thus they highlighted an element of tension that sits at the heart of contemporary Singapore's identity: once it was 'just' a city; now it is a city-state that takes its place among nation-states.

BIG SINGAPORE

The state's nation-building project is not the focus of this book, but I do want to draw attention to the debilitating smallness of either a rigidly nation-focused or city-focused perspective when considering Singapore. Nations might usually be bigger than the cities they host, but not in the case of Singapore. Taking either a rigidly national or civic perspective when studying Singapore ironically leads to an indecently small 'big picture'. And such a surrender is not necessary. Thanks to George Yeo's intervention in 2001, we already have the beginnings of a rival 'idea of Singapore'. In the speech and interview of April and May 2001 that was cited earlier, he introduced the idea of a 'big Singapore' that effectively sidestepped the nation-building project and spoke of Singapore primarily as a city and a place; as a node in history and the region and the world. This, he argued, is a big vision of Singapore.[25] Yeo all but denied Singapore's nation status, highlighted Singapore's city status, and emphasised its current and historical connectivity with the world and the region.[26] Even Singapore's colonial past was presented as a connectivity to be grasped as Yeo urged Singaporeans to 'think not only in terms of our island geography, but also against the backdrop of our Asian and Anglo-Saxon history and connections'.[27]

This speech was remarkable for the clever way in which Yeo – a Cabinet minister at the time – packaged a set of messages that challenged how the government thought of its own role, and yet still maintained a comfortable resonance with the accepted orthodoxy. We have already seen that the notion of Singapore as a global city was not new to government thinking. Yet when Yeo posed a binary opposition of 'Big Singapore vs Small Singapore' he was trying to lift the Singapore government and not just ordinary Singaporeans out of obsessive introspection. Yeo bridged the tension between the outward-looking vision of Singapore as a global city and the established inward-looking 'national' vision of Singapore as a highly ethnicised (racialised) community and turned them both into something that looked outwards and seemed to complement each other. In doing so he took the 'national' vision to a new level, removing many of the ambiguities about ethnicity and citizenship that had been papered over for two decades. His picture of a 'big Singapore' effectively called for the cultivation of a 'long-distance nationalism' – an overt identification with an ancestral 'homeland' that may or may not have ever been a personal home. Such ideas would have been regarded as close to sedition in the 1970s when the government was jealously building and establishing its credentials as a nation, and Yeo's speech might therefore be taken as an indication of Singapore's new-found comfort as a nation. If this were the case, however, it was an indication laced with irony, since he was describing the comfortable attributes of a cosmopolitan, global city; attributes that sit most uncomfortably with nation.

Yeo's call for a 'big Singapore' was also limited in another major respect, which has been highlighted by Huang Jianli: Yeo focused particularly on Chinese identity, and his call for a 'big Singapore' has a distinct Sinocentric tinge.[28] There are three distinct reasons for claiming such a Sinocentrism in Yeo's 'big Singapore' speech. First, and most basic, was that at the time of the speech ethnic Chinese had comprised 75% of the population for several decades, with Malays, Indians and 'Others' comprising the remainder, so encouragement of ethnic identification was itself sufficient to empower the Chinese as a group and to emphasise the minority status of the non-Chinese. Beyond this implied logic of demography, the ostensible purpose of Yeo's speech was to lay claim to a Singapore connection with the Chinese Nationalist Revolution (on the basis that Sun Yat-Sen stopped over several times and used Singapore as a base for a few months in 1908). Finally, the speech was loaded with rich and value-laden talk of the virtues and foibles of Chinese culture in particular, and the way that local (Singaporean Chinese) culture differed from that found in China.

The Anglo connection in Yeo's speech sits oddly here, but it needs to be remembered that in the final analysis he was a member of the government and as such he was interested in pursuing any forms of connectivity that would help the Singapore economy. Also remember that Yeo, like Lee Kuan Yew and Lee Hsien Loong and many other members of Cabinet, the civil service and the Singapore Armed Forces (SAF) Officer Corps, is a graduate of a British university. (The United Kingdom remains the favourite destination for Singapore overseas scholars, so the connection would not seem odd to anyone in the elite.) We are also reminded of a major theme of Chapter 1: Singapore's orthodox national narrative is bounded by Raffles and Lee Kuan Yew. Thus, Yeo's 'big Singapore' ultimately remains an heir of the dominant national narrative established between the 1960s and the 1980s: a narrative that might be characterised as 'small Singapore', and to which we now turn our attention.

BEFORE SINGAPORE GREW 'BIG' ...

In the two decades or so after Singapore left Malaysia, the idea of Singapore was really very modest and, it should be said, 'small' and defensive. It looked to the world, but only in the spirit of looking out from the trenches: a mercantilist state, seeking markets for its goods and capital for its industry.[29] It was Singapore, the nation forged in adversity; Singapore, the beachhead of modernity and capitalism in Southeast Asia; Singapore, the Chinese island in a Malay-Muslim sea; Singapore, the survivor.[30] Gazing wistfully to ancestral homelands was condemned as Singaporean leaders invented their nation. The central idea linking all these features was Singapore the vulnerable success – a land of wonderful achievements, but forever on the edge of disaster. The objective was to survive, prosper and stake a secure place in a hostile region and in a volatile global economy. A decades-long elite-led nation-building campaign became the utensil into which these ideas were poured, and in which they fermented, but the core ideas were more basic and visceral: success and survival.

Vulnerability – Domestic

I have already considered the idea of 'success' in Singapore's identity when giving background to the idea of 'big' Singapore, but I have not yet touched on its symbiotic twin, vulnerability. In independent Singapore's metanarrative, vulnerability comes in two varieties: domestic and imported. Domestically the idea was one of near-comprehensive vulnerability to social (communal/racial/religious) disharmony, communist insurrection, industrial friction, political insecurity and economic failure. The solution to these myriad threats was complex and multifaceted in its detail but essentially simple at its core: trust the government, give it a free hand and allow it to exercise quasi-dictatorial powers to keep the peace and get the job done. By the mid-1980s this formula was starting to wear thin with the electorate, but in the 1970s it was widely accepted. Even many of the social groups that were being brought to heel – and at this time this included the Chinese clans, schools, associations and small businesses – were mostly quiescent, offering only muted and limited opposition. They saw this programme as being relatively even-handed between groups, and they thought that the alternative was worse – a dystopian future epitomised by a series of violent riots and other purported threats to social order in Singapore and Malaysia stretching back to 1950.

The riots of the past were, in fact, used by the government as a series of morality plays that used the imagery of the past to threaten the population with a foreboding future. The 'Maria Hertogh Riots' of 1950 were the earliest in the series. Directed against the colonial authorities (which are presented as inept rather than evil), they have been woven into the regime's standard litany of cautionary tales of the dangers posed by religion and communal identity. The issue at stake was a custody battle between the Dutch Catholic natural mother and the Malay-Muslim adoptive mother of a little girl called Maria Hertogh who had been baptised Catholic but raised Muslim. It was a heart-rending private story about a family torn apart by the war, but it became public property, initially because some Malay supporters of the adoptive mother rioted, and subsequently because Lee Kuan Yew was a junior barrister defending some of the rioters from a murder charge – and he wrote it into the Singapore Story, using it to warn about the dangers of communalism (language- and race-based identity politics) and religious passion.

The next iconic 'riot' was just a few years later. In 1954, about 900 Chinese schoolboys and schoolgirls assembled at Government House to offer moral support to eight of their number who were presenting a petition to the Governor. The petition asked for a guarantee that the boys' call-up for National Service would be automatically postponed until after graduation. All was peaceful until the Riot Squad charged the students with batons, injuring 30 and arresting 44. This episode entered national mythology as a 'student riot' rather than as a warning about the brutality of the colonial police. The Singapore Story presents it as one of its central morality plays about the dangers of both communalism and communism. Significantly, even the Chinese press at the time drew a direct connection between these riots and the Maria Hertogh riots, despite being substantially in sympathy with the students and being appalled at the brutality of the Riot Squad.[31] Their musings on the vulnerability of Singapore to such incidents suggest that the government's later construction of a metanarrative based on riots and domestic vulnerability was building on a natural reaction and did not need to be fully constructed and imposed from above.

The next riot in the litany came a year later and is known as the 'Hock Lee Riot'. It is presented explicitly as a lesson in the dangers of communism and implicitly as a lesson in the dangers posed by Chinese communalism. Just weeks after Singapore was granted self-government in April 1955, a strike and picket at the Hock Lee Bus Company, in reaction to the mass sacking of the entire unionised workforce, was transformed into a mass action by the efforts of Lim Chin Siong. Lim was a charismatic young radical leftist with (at the very least) close ties to the Malayan Communist Party (MCP). He held sway over a number of other unions and – critically – thousands of firebrand Chinese-educated school students. The mass action degenerated into a riot that led directly to several deaths which, in the official discourse, are blamed exclusively on communists – without any regard for the employer's provocation, the workers' grievances or the fluidity of events on the day. Communists were unquestionably involved, yet it is now clear that the violence was an outcome of their lack of tight control, rather than their deliberate efforts.[32] This episode entered the lexicon of stories about the domestic dangers Singapore faced. There was then a nine-year hiatus in the calendar of riots until fighting broke out between Chinese and Malays in July and August 1964, each time degenerating into riots that left dozens dead. At this stage Singapore was a state of Malaysia and the Singapore government had given control of the police to the central government in Kuala Lumpur. In his memoirs, Lee Kuan Yew provided a convincing case that elements within the central government in Kuala Lumpur had been stirring up local Malays and orchestrating the trouble, but this episode is nevertheless written into the national narrative as a lesson about the generic dangers of ethnic and religious communalism. The year 1969 saw a new round of race riots between Malays and Chinese in Kuala Lumpur, accompanied by some minor disturbances in Singapore. The details of this episode are not central to the official narrative because they happened in Malaysia, but what is significant is how seamlessly they have been given a role in the Singapore narrative of domestic insecurity.

Separately to the litany of riots, a security sweep called 'Operation Coldstore' assumed a foundational place in the Singapore Story as evidence of its vulnerability to subversion. Operation Coldstore was a massive preventative security action in February 1963 that detained 133 people: nine fully identified MCP 'underground' operatives who had no role in public life; over 100 left-wing activists and leaders who had varying degrees of association with the MCP and the colony's broader left-wing networks; and three members of the opposition United People's Party. The latter three were known to have no communist connections or sympathies at all, but were targeted because they were political opponents of Lee Kuan Yew.[33] It is doubtful whether many of those detained were communists, especially since C.C. Chin tells us that a major security sweep had been widely anticipated by the MCP and most of its operatives had fled the colony in advance.[34] The Singapore Story makes great play of this episode and insists that Operation Coldstore was targeted at an organised communist threat.[35] Defenders of the official narrative routinely claim that Operation Coldstore destroyed the communist threat – for example, Kumar Ramakrishna said it was 'decisive in destroying the subversive threat posed by the Communist Party of Malaya'[36] – and yet the national narrative continues, seemingly unthinkingly, as if communism were alive and well in Singapore. In fact there is no reason to doubt that Operation Coldstore not only finally and fully destroyed communism as a force in Singapore but that it gutted the entire left-wing movement. The MCP, in particular, was left with no personnel, no leaders and no structure.[37] According to the official narrative, communism was defeated in 1963, but the same narrative managed to keep the threat alive in the national imagination for the next quarter-century. Its final desperate outing was in 1987 when it was used against a group of Catholics and alternative theatre activists,[38] thus demonstrating the looseness with which the label was applied and the political utility to which it was put.

Singapore separated from Malaysia under acrimonious circumstances on 9 August 1965, and the dominant idea of Singapore over the following decade and more was comprehensively captured by local scholar Chan Heng Chee in the titles of her books from the period. Her first book, *The Politics of Survival*, caught the essence of the idea of Singapore in the late 1960s. The challenges to Singapore's 'survival' were primarily external in origin. They were indisputably real and will be covered in the next section, but there was also a strong domestic dimension that was less obviously valid: insecurity deriving from domestic unrest. This led seamlessly to the logic of Chan Heng Chee's remaining books from the period: *Politics in an Administrative State: Where Has the Politics Gone?* and *The Dynamics of One Party Dominance*.[39] In short, the government projected an apocalyptic picture of threats from enemies within society that it used to justify the destruction of its political and social rivals. The only solution on the table was to restrict personal and political freedoms and trust the government blindly. The early victims were the opposition Barisan Sosialis (Socialist Front) MPs and dozens of other party activists who were on the left of politics but had not been targeted in Operation Coldstore, despite the breadth of that sweep.[40] This pattern of harassment was not new in itself: since February 1963, Barisan leaders had been systematically defamed, vilified, arrested, fined and driven off the island on the flimsiest of grounds and with the maximum of rhetorical flourish that sometimes drew a direct connection to the 'bloody riots' of earlier years.[41] The post-independence burst of persecution seemed like the final stage of this long play, but with a new twist: the government took to itself new permanent powers that treated almost any activity with political implications (other than supporting the government or being/supporting a candidate standing for parliament) as sedition, a breach of the peace or vandalism.[42] Sacrifices of freedoms and political rights seemed to most Singaporeans in the 1960s and 1970s to be a reasonable price to pay for the positive side of the struggle for survival: economic and industrial development, jobs, peace on the streets and a highly successful programme of housing development. Yet if the non-English newspapers of the late 1960s are indicative of public opinion, it is clear that everyone was nevertheless hoping for a return to a democratic 'normal'.[43] *Nanyang Siang Pau* wrote in an editorial, 'It will be an irony in history if we still cannot talk about liberation of thought and speech after attaining political freedom.'[44] These were prescient words, since *Nanyang Siang Pau* was closed down soon afterwards as part of a crackdown on the press. The threat motif on this occasion took two distinct forms: fear of Chinese 'chauvinism' in the case of several Chinese newspapers that were challenging the government's language and education policies, and fear of allegedly suspicious motivations of their domestic and overseas financial backers in the case of two English-language start-ups.[45]

In 1987 the government invested in a new round of detentions to smash a supposed 'Marxist Conspiracy' to overthrow the state. As I indicated above, this security sweep marked the last serious outing for the government's theme of vulnerability from within. Not that it actually disappeared thereafter. It continued to exercise a role in politics and society, but the disconnection between the seriousness of the government's charges against the alleged 'Marxist Conspirators' and the public's obvious scepticism over the dangers posed by 22 young 'do-gooders' showed that the currency of this narrative had been exhausted as a pivotal source of political legitimacy. The government used the episode to elicit compliance from a series of social actors who had been becoming uncomfortably independent-minded since the beginning of the 1980s – Christian churches, international media, English-educated civil society[46] – but it recognised that fear of domestic unrest was a diminishing asset and began nuancing its programmes accordingly.

Vulnerability – Imported

The second element in the discourse of vulnerability was fear of international challenges. This imagery had very specific, if rather eclectic targets: Malaysia, China, America and 'Western liberalism'. During Konfrontasi, Sukarno's Indonesia had also been a major and indisputably valid source of fear. As a target, Indonesia effectively evaporated in the mid-1960s with Singapore's exit from Malaysia and the rise of Suharto, but was retained in defence thinking and public rhetoric as an extension of fear of Malaysia.

It was natural that Malaysia would loom large in public rhetoric. During Singapore's brief membership of Malaysia (1963–5), Malay nationalists in the government had made too many intemperate and inflammatory speeches about Lee, his government, Singapore and Singaporeans to be easily overlooked. Singapore was demographically and politically dominated by Chinese and the government in Kuala Lumpur was run by Malays, thus feeding naturally from and into the standard suite of racial pressures and tensions that permeate archipelagic Southeast Asia. This background meant that the presentation of Malaysia as a source of fear took on a visceral element, at least for Singapore's Chinese majority. The inner circle of the Malaysian government even gave the Singapore government licence to foster the image of Malaysia as an enemy by helping to construct and perpetuate the myth that Singapore's exit from Malaysia had been a hostile expulsion. In fact it had been a negotiated withdrawal initiated by Singapore. Malaysia became something much more extensive and complex than just a source of fear. It became Singapore's 'Other': the sibling rival with whom Singaporeans liked to compare themselves to advantage. Malaysia continues this role, looming large in the Singapore psyche. Interestingly, Malaysia does not return the favour: consciousness of Singapore is very low except in Johor, where Singapore is a near neighbour. From around 2000 until the 2018 defeat of Malaysia's Barisan Nasional government, relations between the Singapore and Malaysian governments were at their friendliest since Separation, but for decades before that relations had been dominated by knowledge that Malaysia was the major source of Singapore's water. This particular source of insecurity dissipated as Singapore has edged closer and closer to full water security, utilising increased local catchment, imported water, reclaimed water (or NEWater) and desalinated water. The most celebrated of these innovations is the Marina Barrage, which has turned the Singapore Harbour into a freshwater reservoir; the least celebrated is the 'toilet-to-tap' NEWater programme.

In the heyday of hostile rhetoric, the imagery employed by the Singapore government was truly provocative: Singapore as a Chinese 'Israel in a Malay-Muslim sea'[47] and Singapore as a 'poisoned shrimp' that neighbours should avoid trying to swallow.[48] This rhetoric of fear and resistance – complete with its overtly racist subtext – proved to be the foundation for a systemic build-up of the Singapore Armed Forces into a professional army, navy and air force. It also underpinned the creation of a comprehensive National Service and Reservist system that would eventually become an inescapable social institution for boys and men, colouring what it means to be Singaporean.

The respective places of America and China in Singapore's fear-filled world of the 1960s and 1970s fit uneasily with the Singapore we know today, but between them they demonstrated the role of international vulnerability in the idea of Singapore in this period. China loomed large in elite imaginings, mainly because of fear that Chinese communism would appeal to younger Singaporeans who might mix ethnic identification with ideological commitment. This concern waned only in 1975 when Lee Kuan

Yew took his daughter with him on his first visit to China and, based on her reaction, decided that his fears were overblown.[49] The Soviet Union did not loom large, but fear of America – or at least mistrust – was a major feature of the Singapore government's discourse in the 1950s and the 1960s.[50] Commensurate with this phenomenon – but not actually connected with it – was fear of Western 'decadence' and Western liberalism. Each decade from the 1950s to the 1990s included a period in which there was a moral panic, whether it was identified as 'yellow culture', the 'hippy culture' or Western 'individualism'. The moral panics about the West easily outlasted the fear of China, but in the end even this conservative standby has drifted into history.

A MALAYAN SINGAPORE

These ideas of a small Singapore showing a defiant face to the world became the orthodoxy and have been taken as being 'normal' to the point where George Yeo's 'big Singapore' looks radical, but in fact they are not 'normal'. Even George Yeo's 'big Singapore' only looks 'big' compared to the previous idea of a very small Singapore. Most of the earlier ideas of Singapore were much 'bigger' and much more substantial than Yeo's national idea, which must almost inevitably contain the seeds of insularity simply by being a 'national' idea. I devoted a disproportionate amount of attention to George Yeo's idea of a 'big' Singapore because I want to use it to firmly establish the contrast between the insularity endemic in contemporary ideas of Singapore and the expansive openness that characterised earlier ideas of Singapore. Sadly, the only two points of time when the idea of 'small Singapore' dominated have turned out to be critical turning points that left Singapore isolated: the British decision at the end of World War II to separate Singapore from Malaya in order to retain control of its naval base; and the mutual agreement in 1965 between the governments in Kuala Lumpur and Singapore to 'expel' Singapore from the Federation of Malaysia. Yet these episodes are a major deviation from everything that is known about ideas of Singapore going back six centuries. Even the Japanese army of occupation envisioned Singapore/Syonan-To as part of the Malay Peninsula, seeing no significant difference between the two in either their invasion plans or the administration of their occupation.

Malaysia

In the first half of the 1960s the British Colonial Office, the Singapore elite and the Kuala Lumpur elite all thought of Singapore as part of a federated nation-state called Malaysia. It turned out, however, that the Kuala Lumpur and Singapore governments had very different ideas of the relationship between the two, a difference that carried the seeds of the idea's destruction: the Singapore elite saw Singapore as one state of a multi-racial Malaysia among 14 states of equal standing; the Malay-dominated elite in Kuala

Lumpur saw Singapore as a Chinese add-on to the existing Federation of Malaya. The Singapore elite envisioned a common market, porous borders and citizenship within the peninsula, with Singapore playing a leading role in Malaysia. The Kuala Lumpur elite feared a political and economic onslaught from the 'Chinese' island.

British Malaya and its Orphaned Children

From the late nineteenth century until the Japanese Occupation, Britain built a network of Malay polities on the Malay Peninsula that together were called and thought of as Malaya or British Malaya, even though neither term ever had any official standing or usage. The relationship between each of the polities and its colonial overlord was complex and varied and most of them barely had a relationship with each other. Singapore, Malacca and Penang were one colony (the Straits Settlements) and had no Sultan. They were under 'direct' British rule administered originally from Calcutta and, after 1867, directly from London.

The other colonies and protectorates had traditional rulers who enjoyed varying degrees of autonomy. Johor, Kedah, Kelantan, Perlis and Terengganu were each ruled indirectly by Britain on a strict hub-and-spokes model as the Unfederated Malay States, and the colonies of Selangor, Perak, Pahang and Negeri Sembilan were administered after 1895 more collectively as the Federated Malay States. Significantly for our history of Singapore, in the middle of the nineteenth century the Sultan of Johor was firmly established as the most powerful and autonomous traditional ruler – and remains so today. In addition, there were the indirectly ruled territories of British North Borneo (now Sabah), Brunei and Sarawak which, even though not physically part of 'Malaya', were treated by the British as affiliated to the same general cultural and economic construct. Between 1945 and 1963, they were all directly under Colonial Office rule and administered by members of the Malayan Civil Service.

The British construct of 'Malaya' became the default vehicle for the interaction of peoples, the conduct of commerce and the exchange of ideas and news. Singapore did not sit outside this construct any more than did any of the other colonies or cities on the peninsula. Furthermore, neither its island status nor its Chinese-majority population made Singapore unique. Kuala Lumpur itself was a Chinese-majority town, and Penang was both an island and a Chinese city. Throughout the nineteenth century and the first half of the twentieth century the inclusion of Singapore as part of Malaya was not a wilful statement of political or social identity on anyone's part – it was just a statement of how it was. The only people who had a different expectation were the radicals who thought Malaya should be part of a Greater Indonesia (Indonesia Raya).[51]

Not only was Singapore accepted as a natural part of Malaya, but it was also a city of particular importance, for several reasons. First and foremost, the Port of Singapore was the primary port for the peninsula. All the railway lines led to Singapore so it could export Malaya's rubber, tin and other goods to the world – mainly to Britain, but also to Japan and the United States. Second, Singapore was the administrative centre for British Malaya. Third, Singapore was the main urban centre on the peninsula, and – thanks to the port – the primary point of arrival and a significant point of reference for incoming migration and temporary visitors, who ranged from Chinese nationalists such as Sun Yat-Sen to Indonesian communists escaping Dutch security forces. It was a cosmopolitan centre with a higher level of connectivity with world events than the mainland.[52] It was natural, therefore, that without any deliberate effort it became the main seat of learning, communication and the fermentation and communication of ideas. It became the main base for Malaya's book publishers, newspapers, political movements, conferences and even film-makers.[53]

The Malay and Muslim communities were at the forefront of this utilisation of Singapore as a centre. William Roff wrote forcefully of this role:

> Singapore's reputation as a centre of Islamic life and learning in the late nineteenth century was widespread, though it rested less on possession of a school of religious thought (or even on particular teachers) than on its position in relation to the pilgrimage and Arab migration, and not least on its role as a publication and distribution centre for religious writings. Students from all over the archipelago … went either to Mecca or the Straits Settlements …. The city … formed the nucleus of an urban, mercantile society, with a way of life and thought significantly different … to that of either peasant or aristocratic Malaya.[54]

Singapore was particularly attractive to Malays and Muslims precisely because of the absence of a Sultan and the minority status of both the Malays and the Muslims: debates and exchanges could take place in the Chinese/British city that could never have been contemplated 'back home'. Even Britain's separation of Singapore from Malaya after the war did not quell the exuberance of Malay and Muslim activism in Singapore, though it totally reversed the Malay elite's presumption of support for including Singapore in a united Malaya.[55]

It was not just Islamic scholars and Malay ethno-nationalists who were drawn to Singapore. Aspiring middle-class liberals, socialists and communists met, communicated, wrote and often lived on the island. It is hardly surprising, therefore, that being 'Malayan' was the default self-descriptor for most locals, and they assumed without a second thought that Singapore's future was in a united Malaya.[56] The Malayan Communist Party (MCP), founded in 1930, followed Ho Chi Minh's model of a nationalist communist party, and for the MCP the 'nation' always meant Malaya, including Singapore.

The Chinese-educated population of Singapore and the peninsula also had a vision of a united Malaya, and across the entire political spectrum – from communist radicals to pro-business conservatives – local Chinese also described themselves as 'Malayans'. By the 1950s the Chinese-educated Chinese were numerically the largest community in Singapore (insofar as they could be considered a single community) and were also a substantial minority on the peninsula. Yet despite their numerical dominance, its members envisioned a multilingual society in which both Mandarin and Malay would be the dominant languages, with Malay (Bahasa Melayu) as the lingua franca. Hence in the 1950s and 1960s – even before Malay became a mandatory study stream – it was commonplace for students in Chinese high schools in Singapore to learn Malay.[57] And even in Nanyang University – the private Chinese university that was later closed down because it was supposedly a bastion of Chinese 'chauvinism' – students learnt Malay as a matter of routine, and the Malay language was part of the community's vision for its future.

Only when the British separated Singapore from the peninsula in 1946 and promised the Malay leadership in Kuala Lumpur a privileged political and social position in the newly democratic Malaya did the inclusion of Singapore in Malaya become a point of contention. Suddenly Singapore threatened a newly comfortable status quo on the peninsula, and its inclusion in the Malaya story became a subject of contention. Such was the tragedy of the Malayan dream.

RAFFLES AND THE STRAITS SETTLEMENTS

The long colonial period that preceded the Japanese Occupation is properly described in historical narratives as the period of 'the Straits Settlements'. This generic title refers to the peculiar set of administrative arrangements under which Singapore, Penang and Malacca were administered as one administrative unit, the Straits Settlements, directly from London from 1867 to 1942, and from Calcutta before that. The Straits Settlements formally came into being in 1826, two years after the East India Company established sovereignty over Singapore and seven years after Sir Stamford Raffles secured local agreement to establish a trading factory in 1819.

Singapore's historiography pays much more attention to 1819 than it does to the later dates that seem, on the surface, to be at least as significant. This choice is not accidental or incidental. It allowed the development of a simple narrative about yet another British hero like Clive of India, in which Singapore's 'first' 123 years (1819–1942) are presented as a modern myth: the progressive march of Raffles' initial vision of a free trade port to rival Calcutta; a port filled with traders and settlers from all over Asia who would flourish under British benevolence. Such was the possessiveness that Raffles felt towards 'his' creation that he wrote of it more than once as his 'child' – even his 'almost only child'.[58] This blessed project was a 'golden opportunity' to 'diffuse civilization' through the almost sacred vehicle of free trade.[59]

The creation of one colony out of three geographically separate settlements contains the superficial suggestion of a 'big', outward-looking Singapore that would accord with the theme that is being developed in this chapter, but that would in fact be misleading for there was nothing but rivalry between the three settlements. The Governor of Penang tried to stop Singapore being settled in the first place and then refused to send military reinforcements to deter a feared Dutch invasion. A year later the Penang merchants tried to get the settlement reversed. Penang's relationship with Singapore would have been even more fraught except that Singapore's growth came overwhelmingly from new business (mostly from looking east and to China) and Penang was able to grow independently by building existing business (mostly from looking west and to the Bay of Bengal) and by exploiting its small strip of land on the mainland (Province Wellesley) for agriculture. Half a century later the merchants of Penang were still jealously guarding their rights, on this occasion protesting the removal of Penang from the London-to-Singapore shipping run, and well they might be concerned. By that stage Penang had ceded to Singapore the roles of both administrative and financial capital of the Straits Settlements: it was a financially healthy but minor subsidiary of the Singapore economy. Perhaps even the word 'subsidiary' is too strong, since it suggests a level of integration that appears to have been absent, despite the best efforts of some Penang entrepreneurs.

Malacca had long since become a backwater under the Dutch, who saw Batavia as their main base. Even after Malacca was shifted from the Dutch to the British Empire as part of the Treaty of London in 1824, neither London nor Calcutta had much notion of what to do with it beyond keeping it out of Dutch hands. Its competitive advantage had already been stolen decades earlier by the establishment of Penang in 1786 and, after a few failed attempts to turn a profit, British Malacca slipped quietly into genteel poverty.

The Straits Settlements were thus little more than a convenient administrative unit. The real symbiosis in the Straits Settlements period was not between the British settlements, but between Singapore and Johor – a phenomenon that has been explored most thoroughly by Carl Trocki in his first book, *Prince of Pirates*, and which is presented in outline below.

SINGAPORE AND JOHOR

The relationship between Johor and Singapore in the first century of the Straits Settlements has turned out to be a virtuous cycle that has been key to the development of both polities and a model for the rest of Malaya. This was not so obvious at the time and even today it is not recognised in either Singaporean or Malaysian national narratives, but without Singapore, Johor as we know it would not exist, and without Johor, Singapore could not have been the success that it became. Indeed the Singapore experience was the point of articulation between the death of the old Johor-Riau Sultanate that succeeded the Malacca Sultanate, and the birth of the new Johor that is now a state of Malaysia. It should also be noted that when we talk of the idea of Singapore as the catalyst for the new Johor, it was a vision that was Singaporean but not British. It was a Malay idea that was embraced by local Chinese, spawned in Singapore, and financed and staffed from Singapore, but without much official colonial/British understanding or control.

The story starts in about 1844, when Singapore's newly thriving pepper and gambier industry began running out of arable land. At that time the most important Malay in Singapore was Temenggong Daing Ibrahim. He was a member of the traditional ruling family of Johor whose followers had earned their living patrolling and plundering the local seas, but who had been at a loose end since the arrival of the British. As land ran out in Singapore, the Temenggong jumped at the opportunity to transform his family business from saltwater piracy and extortion to farming, mining, land development and retail; from the sea to the land. In short, he started allowing the Chinese planters to settle and work his mainland possessions and ensured that he profited from just about every transaction that occurred in his lands.[60] As Trocki has explained:

> This laid the foundation for his own territorial state on the mainland and, at the same time, supplied him with an independent source of wealth. … [His] group of dependants … became bureaucrats who now learned how to administer the revenues of a Chinese agricultural system. … Their job was to encourage settlement in this hinterland of Singapore and, beyond this, to police the coastline and collect the Temenggong's revenues.[61]

Johor became an agricultural and mining exporter, and quickly established itself as a world leader in the production and export of its three key products: gutta-percha (used for coating submarine cables), gambier and pepper. And it all went through Singapore. (In the twentieth century Malaya would adopt the same role for the production of rubber and Singapore was also the point of export.) Such was the integration of the Singapore–Johor economies that, even as Johor was emerging as the major destination in the region for both Chinese capital and labour, its business model presumed the near-seamless integration of the island and the mainland.[62] Government, investment and Chinese secret societies all straddled both sides of the Johor Strait,[63] and the government of Singapore and the government of Johor formally shared the revenue from the sale of government monopolies in opium, liquor, gambling, prostitution, etc. The two economies were so intertwined that an economic downturn in Johor could cause a financial crisis in Singapore.

Furthermore, the management/government of Johor continued to be based in Singapore until 1858, when it was moved to present-day Johor Baru (New Johor). This shift was effected by Temenggong Ibrahim's son, Abu Bakar, who in his turn became an even more important figure than his father and pushed Johor to near-independence from both Singapore and Britain. (Johor involved itself in wars between other Malay kingdoms without deferring to the British and successfully declined to receive a British 'Adviser' until 1914.) The Sultan of Johor remains, even today, the most powerful and independent Sultan in Malaysia, building on the foundation laid by the Singapore connection in its first century or so.

MALACCA SULTANATE

This brings us to the end of this chapter, but not to the end of our exploration of ideas of Singapore. Long before the arrival of Raffles, there was already a firm idea of Singapore as the starting place of the Malacca Sultanate. Singapore, along with the islands and the straits that stretch directly south of Johor, plays a central, almost mystical role in the record of Malay history-cum-mythology. At the end of the fourteenth century the foundational Malay kings were driven from the region, having already shifted their base from the north coast of Sumatra to the island we now call Singapore. They escaped to Malacca where they established the Malacca Sultanate, which went on to become a major maritime and trading power. When the Portuguese chased them and their followers out of Malacca at the beginning of the sixteenth century they naturally returned to the southern end of the Straits of Malacca: Johor, Singapore and the islands of the Riau Archipelago. This region of sea and land is now divided between three nation-states – Malaysia, Singapore and Indonesia – but before this smallness was imposed, it formed one Sultanate that drew its wealth and power from control of the sea lanes. It never regained the greatness of Malacca, but it was, for a long time, a local power to be reckoned with. This sultanate in turn lay at the heart of a much bigger web of sea-based powers. This little stretch of sea thus assumes a surprising degree of importance in the region's history. Even the island of Singapore itself seems to recur with unwarranted frequency in the larger scheme of things, making the vision of a 'big Singapore' being proposed today seem, at least in some respects, understated. The reason for the centrality of this stretch of sea and this island is, simply, its place in the region and in the world. It is to this aspect that we turn in Chapter 3.

3

Singapore Central: The Role of Location in Singapore's History

Q. In what list would Singapore appear on equal status with New York, Sydney, Hong Kong, Hawaii, Tokyo and Cornwall? And by what justification could the old Singapore suburb of Katong – famous primarily for its eateries – appear on this same list alongside Hollywood and the Sydney suburb of Goonhilly Downs?

A. Singapore is one of eight global nodes of submarine fibre-optic cables, along with Hong Kong, Tokyo, Sydney, Hawaii, Southern Florida, New York/New Jersey and Cornwall. And Katong is one of the precise places within Singapore that talks to the world via submarine cables – along with Changi North, Changi South, Tuas, Hollywood and Goonhilly Downs.[1]

A consideration of Singapore's place in the global network of submarine cables may seem an odd opening for a chapter on the history of Singapore, but it brings home the pivotal role that geography has played in Singapore's place in history. As of early 2017, there were approximately 430 submarine cables in service around the world, most of them about the thickness of a garden hose.[2] Map 3.1 depicts this global cable system as it stood in 2015, based on a map produced by the consultancy firm, TeleGeography. The list of eight locations identified as major submarine cable nodes makes it obvious that the selection of these sites is based on a combination of geography and historical/commercial power. All are by the sea and most, including Singapore, have long histories as nodes of sea-bound transportation. All the sites except Tokyo are or have been part of the Anglophone world – and perhaps Japan's intimate post-war relationship with the United States, beginning with the post-war occupation, might even make Tokyo an honorary member of that club.

Since the invention of fibre optics in the 1980s, the submarine cable has become the preferred global carrier of electronic data, far outstripping its immediate technological predecessor, the satellite, by every measure: cost, reliability, speed and capacity. Today submarine cables carry around 95% of intercontinental data traffic, including Internet downloads and uploads at the rate of about 150 terabytes per second and the transfer of

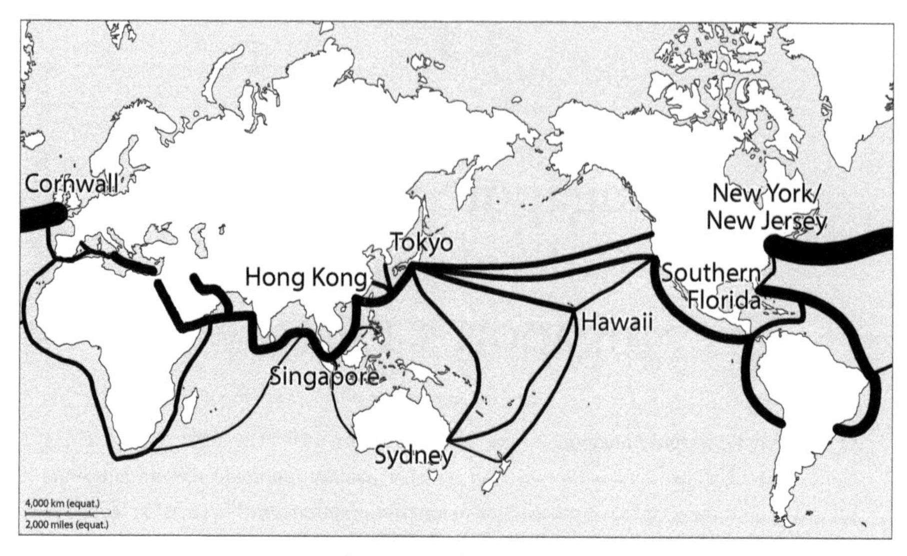

Map 3.1 Submarine cables and nodes, *c.*2015
The thickness of lines is indicative of the number of cables.
Source: TeleGeography, http://www.telegeography.com, accessed 25 June 2018.

money in the trillions of dollars per day. The cables run for nearly 1 million kilometres (600,000 miles), but each emerges from the sea into a shallow subterranean tunnel that leads to a landing station at some coast or other as fragile lengths of ultrafine, hollow silica, encased in an armour of steel, copper, polyethylene and nylon. The fragility of this network is demonstrated by the fact that most of the 498 cable breaks in the five years from 2008 to 2012 (i.e. an average of 100 breaks a year) occurred in less than 200 metres of water – mostly due to tangled fishing nets, mining operations and accidents with anchors.[3]

When a single cable is cut it takes an average of 10–15 days to get it fixed. Thanks to the capacity to reroute data, such incidents are not usually noticed by consumers. On the rare occasion when a cluster of cables is cut, it is a much more serious matter. Robert Martinage, a former undersecretary of the US Navy, tells us:

> In 2006 an undersea earthquake near Taiwan snapped nine cables. It took 11 ships 49 days to finish repairs, while China, Japan, the Philippines, Singapore, Taiwan and Vietnam lost critical communications links, disrupting regional banking, markets, and trade. In 2007 Vietnamese fishermen seeking to salvage copper from a defunct coaxial cable pulled up active lines instead, disrupting Vietnam's communications with Hong Kong and Thailand for nearly three months and requiring repairs that cost millions.[4]

It is no small matter, therefore, to note that Singapore hosts one end of 16 submarine cables that between them form a bottleneck for data traffic between the Pacific and

Indian oceans. Without the Singapore link, traffic gets diverted east and west across the Pacific, the Atlantic and the Indian oceans to reach its destination 'from behind' – assuming that the remaining lines can actually handle the extra traffic without crashing (a point that will hopefully remain moot).

LOCATION, LOCATION, LOCATION

There was nothing inevitable about Singapore being a global meeting point of submarine cables, but neither should it be a surprise. The island of Singapore sits astride the Straits of Malacca, which is the shortest, most placid and shallowest water route between the Indian Ocean and the Pacific Ocean – a waterway that connects everything west and north-west with the west coast of the United States, the whole of Northeast Asia, the Pacific Ocean countries of Southeast Asia, as well as Australia and New Zealand. It is also a safe geological zone, protected from the instability of the Sunda Trench by the long, large island of Sumatra (the Sunda Trench being the meeting place of the Indo-Australia Tectonic Plate and the Eurasia Plate, and the epicentre of the 2004 tsunami). The Straits are about 800 kilometres (500 miles) long and run north-west to south-east between the Indonesian island of Sumatra and the Malay Peninsula. Technically they start at the northern end at an invisible line that stretches between Phuket in Thailand and Banda Aceh on the northern tip of Sumatra, and, according to the formal delineation provided by the International Hydrographic Organization, they finish about 50 kilometres (30 miles) west of Singapore, at an invisible line that cuts through the Indonesian island of Karimun (see Map 3.2) In popular usage, however, the Straits are usually considered to include Singapore and Indonesia's Riau Archipelago, since there is no way out or in except by navigating past these islands. It is that latter usage that I have adopted in this book. There was no inevitability that Singapore would be the node in the submarine cable network, but it was obvious that there would be a node of some degree of concentration somewhere in that area. Geography dictated it. Singapore's island status and its convenient position right on the tip of the Malay Peninsula made it a prime candidate, and its political and social stability, reliable electricity supply, its hospitality to foreign professionals and its Anglophone history settled it. But it all started with its location.

This chapter is dedicated to understanding the role that physical geography has played and continues to play in Singapore's history – not just geography in a generic sense, but an appreciation of the strategic and pivotal roles that have been visited upon Singapore because of its physical location. Its relationships with the great powers in the northern hemisphere, with its immediate neighbours, its strategic importance, its economic well-being, and its vulnerabilities and strengths are all bound up to a considerable extent with its physical place in the world. This truth is wilfully ignored in the Singapore Story[5] and at best it usually hovers at the periphery of other iterations of

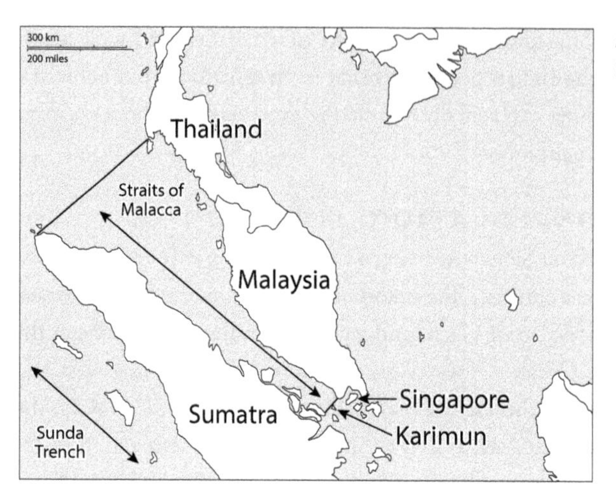

Map 3.2
Straits of Malacca

the national narrative,[6] yet the centrality of the role of geography in elite thinking was evident from the first days of independence, when Prime Minister Lee Kuan Yew returned repeatedly to the theme though a series of references to Fiji being in the middle of the South Pacific (meaning the middle of nowhere) and contrasting this with Singapore's place in the middle of Southeast Asia. Three times at the end of 1965 and once again in 1973, Lee singled out Fiji as the exemplar of an unimportant place and contrasted it with Singapore, yet on all four occasions he dwelt not upon the opportunities it opened, but upon the sensitivity and vulnerability of Singapore's location, in the middle of an area of contestation between larger neighbours and of interest to great powers. He and other leaders have also acknowledged the benefits and opportunities that come with Singapore's strategic location, but usually in passing. By contrast I argue that Singapore's position – sitting astride the Straits of Malacca, in the midst of Southeast Asia, near Northeast Asia – is the central element of independent Singapore's success, and that the leadership deserves full credit, not for overblown claims of transforming Singapore from a backwater into a global city and for taking the island from Third World to First, but for its successful exploitation of the advantages and opportunities that came with Singapore's historical position. By successfully husbanding these advantages, Singapore has positioned itself as the current successor of a long historical line of ports and port cities located in the Straits – and the modern Singapore 'miracle' is rooted at least as much in the successful inheritance of this mantle as it is in the internal workings of the city-state.

TWENTY-FIRST-CENTURY SINGAPORE

I opened with an insight into Singapore's global and trans-regional perspective from an unconventional starting point: submarine fibre-optic cables. I was making a point about the global and regional strategic significance dictated by the positioning of the island of Singapore. Before putting modern Singapore into its historical perspective, it is worthwhile dwelling for a few pages more on other contemporary manifestations of the extraordinary significance of Singapore's position in its current success. I resume with a map of global oil traffic (Map 3.3). The first thing to note is that, except for the complete absence of lines joining North America and East Asia, the global map of oil and petroleum traffic looks remarkably similar to the submarine cables in Map 3.1. The most notable feature of this map from the narrow perspective of the history of Singapore is the volume of traffic running past Singapore's front door through the short, narrow strip of water that is the focus of most of this chapter: the Straits of Malacca. At its narrowest it is less than 3 kilometres wide (about 1½ miles), but for more than half a century it has been the second-busiest thoroughfare for the transportation of oil and petroleum products in the world (after the Straits of Hormuz). In 2013, 27% of the world's maritime oil trade and 17% of the world's total oil production sailed through the Straits of Malacca, mostly on its way from the Middle East to East Asia. Ever since Japan began its post-war economic miracle the Straits of Malacca have been a choke point along the energy lifeline sustaining East Asia. Japan was initially the most strategically and economically important dependant on the Malaccan lifeline. Today China is by far the biggest, though certainly not the only consumer. Even with the slowdown of its rate of economic expansion in the wake of the global financial crisis, China is still the

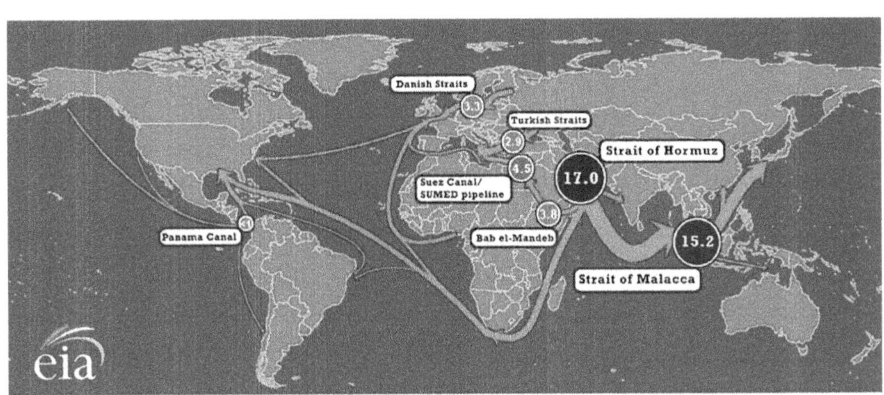

Map 3.3 Global shipping of crude oil and petroleum products, 2013
Source: Martime Executive, 'World Oil Transit Chokepoints', https://www.maritime-executive.com/article/world-oil-transit-chokepoints-2014-11-15#gs.j2fa2_w, accessed 8 July 2018.

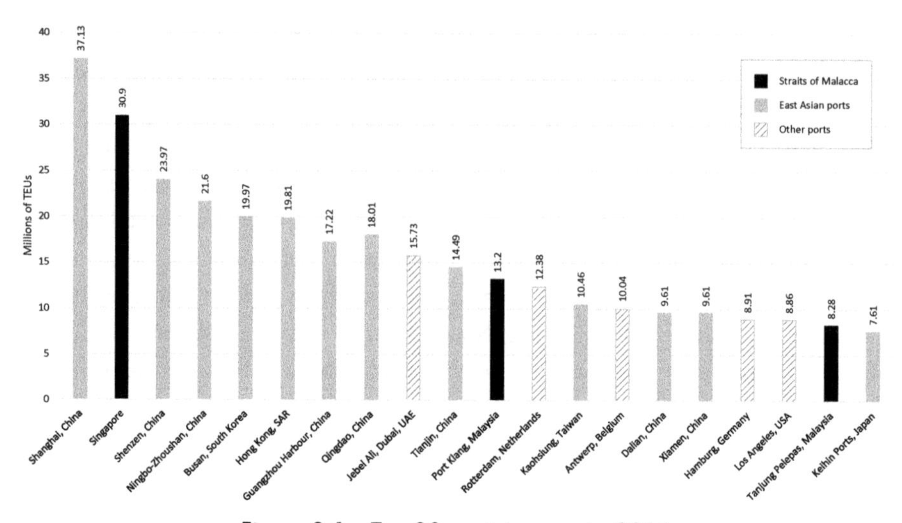

Figure 3.1 Top 20 container ports, 2016
Source World Shipping Council, 'Top 50 World Container Ports', http://www.worldshipping.org/about-the-industry/global-trade/top-50-world-container-ports, accessed 8 July 2018.

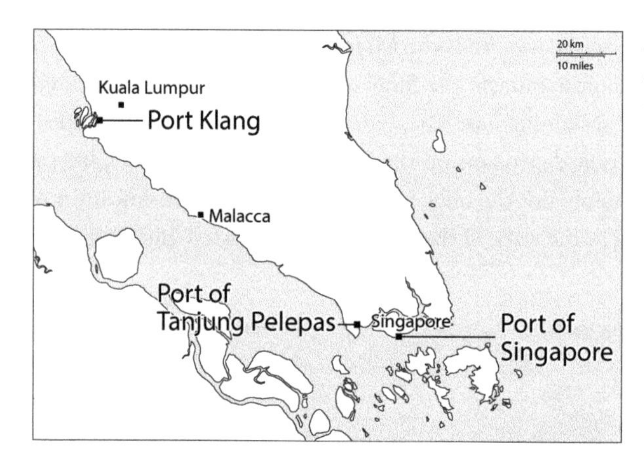

Map 3.4
Major ports in the Straits of Malacca

largest consumer of energy in the world (accounting for 23% of consumption in 2017) and oil is the second biggest component of its energy inputs (19% in 2017).[7]

Many vessels sail straight past Singapore without stopping on their way to Japan, China, Europe or the Persian Gulf, but a lot of them do dock at the island, contributing to the Singapore's status as one of the busiest ports worldwide every year since 1986. In fact, from 2005 to 2009 Singapore was officially the busiest port in the world, pulling ahead of Hong Kong. Only when we turn to northern China do we find ports comparable to Singapore: in 2010 the Port of Shanghai overtook Singapore as the busiest

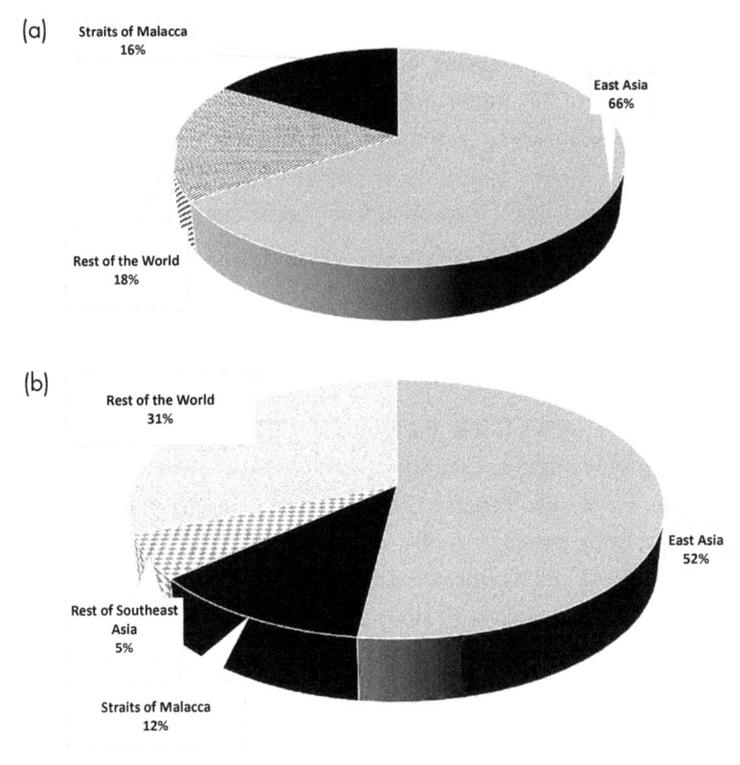

Figure 3.2 (a) Top 20 container ports by region, 2016.
(b) Top 50 container ports by region, 2016
Source: World Shipping Council, 'Top 50 World Container Ports', http://www.worldshipping.org/about-the-industry/global-trade/top-50-world-container-ports, accessed 8 July 2018.

container-handling port in the world, and held that position until Singapore took it back in 2016.[8]

If we make a systematic comparison with the world's busiest ports we find a narrative unfolding that returns this digression into port activities to the main point of this chapter: the role and importance of the place of Singapore in its history and development. Figure 3.1 shows the World Shipping Council's list of the top 20 container ports (as of 2016) and their volume of traffic for 2016. This chart identifies those ports by their region, but using an unusual classification of region: East Asia, Straits of Malacca and the Rest of the World. Map 3.4 shows the location of the three ports in the Straits of Malacca. The top panel of Figure 3.2 presents the same data as Figure 3.1. The bottom panel expands the scope to include the top 50 container ports, and adds a fourth unlikely 'region' to the list: 'The rest of Southeast Asia' (other than the Straits of Malacca).

When we consider that this chapter is interrogating the impact of the place of Singapore in the world, the story being told by these charts is every bit as fascinating as that of submarine cables. The importance of the proximity of a booming East Asia to the Straits of Malacca is borne out by the sheer dominance of East Asia in both the top 20 and the top 50 lists. A great part of the extraordinary prominence of the Straits and Southeast Asia more generally is because Southeast Asia forms part of a production hub that feeds into the factories of southern China,[9] but even this does not account for the dominance of the Straits within Southeast Asia, nor the dominance of Singapore within the Straits. There is a real sense in which Singapore is at the second epicentre of world trade: the first being in Northeast Asia. This dominance is not an accident.

NATURE PLUS NURTURE

Moving from Singapore's role as a seaport, we should also remember that it is a very successful air hub. If we could imagine Changi Airport being transplanted to America but retaining its existing passenger traffic, it would be America's fifth-busiest airport. Significantly the Chinese and Northeast Asian markets do not loom quite as large in its destinations as one might expect, with closer markets playing a much more significant role in Changi Airport's prosperity (Figure 3.3).

Yet impressive statistics and tables fail to convey fully the scale and extraordinary character of Singapore's achievement. Granted that we know Singapore is a hub, it is not entirely surprising that it is a major player in air traffic. The extent to which it has

	Changi Airport Top markets
1.	Indonesia
2.	Malaysia
3.	Thailand
4.	Australia
5.	China
6.	Hong Kong
7.	India
8.	Japan
9.	Philippines
10.	Vietnam

Figure 3.3 Top 10 markets for Changi Airport, 2015
Accurate as of July 2018. Source: Changi Airport Media Centre, http://www.changiairport.com/corporate/media-centre/newsroom.html#/images/changi2015-top-10-country-markets-516931, accessed 15 July 2018.

herded that traffic through its own gates, leaving rivals such as Kuala Lumpur in its wake, is a little more interesting, but it is nevertheless within the realms of the expected. We could perhaps say the same about container traffic, but what really brings home the nature and scale of Singapore's achievement is its performance in oil production.

Singapore has no oil reserves at all, but it has capitalised on its strategic position to turn itself into a regional hub of oil production. Since the beginning of the oil era at the opening of the twentieth century, the virtues of its harbour and its colonial-era infrastructure had made Singapore a major centre for the bunkering, storage and regional distribution of oil. Yet throughout the colonial era it was never more than a service centre, with virtually no profits or employment benefits accruing to the local economy beyond work in the port.[10] At the end of the 1960s, just a few years after separation from Malaysia, this began to change when Shell opened its first refinery on land that the government had cleared for the purpose at the western end of the island. This was to be the first of three refineries that opened in quick succession over the following decade, to be followed later by as many again.[11] In 2017 Singapore's total crude refining capacity stood at about 1.068 million barrels per day, which were processed on artificial islands to Singapore's south, with more than half of its exports going to Malaysia, Indonesia and Australia, despite the fact that Malaysia and Indonesia are themselves major oil producers.[12] Just as with the traffic through Changi Airport, the regional perspective turns out to be the key more than a Northeast Asian perspective. We will return to consider the development of Singapore as an oil-refining hub in Chapter 7, but for the moment let us just accept at face value that this could not have been possible if Singapore had not had its tremendous advantages of geography. It took human initiative to turn that advantage into a profitable enterprise, but without geography there would have been nothing on which to build.

BRITISH SINGAPORE

My attention to Singapore's geographic position is more intense and focused than is usual in the country's national histories, but in history itself it is very much a recurring theme. The island of Singapore was settled by the British early in the nineteenth century precisely because of its strategic location, both in relation to China and the more immediate region, along with Sir Stamford Raffles' obsessive drive to breach the Dutch regional hegemony. Yet let us note that it was not Singapore in particular that Raffles had targeted. Raffles initially wanted Britain to hold on to Java at the end of the Napoleonic Wars (having been minding the island as Lieutenant Governor on behalf of the Netherlands, who had been defeated in Europe by their mutual enemy, France). Failing that, he had ambitions to expand the tiny British presence on the west coast of Sumatra beyond its toehold in Bencoolen (of which Raffles was also Lieutenant Governor).[13] Indeed, even in the immediate aftermath of Raffles' success in establishing a British presence in Singapore, he justified his actions as the result of the failure of his plans for Sumatra.[14] At one time he even suggested a major development of British territory on the west coast of Borneo.[15] The first ambition (Java) was frustrated by high politics in London and the other two (West Sumatra and Borneo) were never serious options. Raffles was, however, able to convince Calcutta of the need to establish a trading post and factory at the southern end of the Straits of Malacca, both to supplement the small Penang base, which sat at the northern end of the Straits,[16] and to hem in the Dutch outpost in Malacca. Central to Raffles' concern was ensuring that British ships engaged in the China trade had a place for a speedy stopover that was not controlled by the Dutch. Late in 1818, Lord Hastings, the Governor General of India, instructed Raffles to travel to Penang and from there set out with his friend and colleague, Major William Farquhar, to negotiate an agreement with the Sultan of Aceh (which at the time was as powerful at sea as any of the European players in the region). Lord Hastings also instructed him to establish a presence at the existing port of 'Rhio' on the island of Bintan.[17] This island lies about 20 kilometres (13 miles) south-east of Singapore and across the middle of the extreme southern end of the Straits of Malacca (see Map 3.5). In the previous century Bintan and its neighbouring island, Batam, had been the political and economic centre of the Johor-Riau Sultanate, which included the island of Singapore. It was not the first time that a British expedition had set out to acquire a base in Bintan: in 1786 another Governor General of India – also called Hastings (Warren Hastings) – sent a mission to Riau, only to be thwarted by the Dutch.

When Raffles arrived in Penang at the beginning of 1819, the Dutch had already repeated their efforts of 1786 and negotiated a deal with the local Bugis leaders in Riau, so there was no point in continuing to Bintan. (And then the Governor of Penang frustrated the other part of his instructions by pressuring Raffles into postponing his plans to negotiate with Aceh.) With Riau off the table, the next option for settlement was not Singapore, but Major Farquhar's preference of Karimun – which is about the same distance from Singapore as Bintan, but further west, deeper in the Straits. Karimun is well placed strategically to monitor traffic in the Straits – a role it had been fulfilling for various powers for many centuries[18] – but unlike Singapore, it did not have a harbour. Karimun would have served Britain's immediate needs superbly without creating a rival for Penang, but without a harbour or the space for a settlement to grow, its prospects would have been limited. The problems of space in Karimun could perhaps have been overcome by expanding to the neighbouring island of Kundur, but the absence of a harbour in Karimun and the presence of a harbour on the south (seaward) side of the island of Singapore settled the matter in favour of Singapore. By

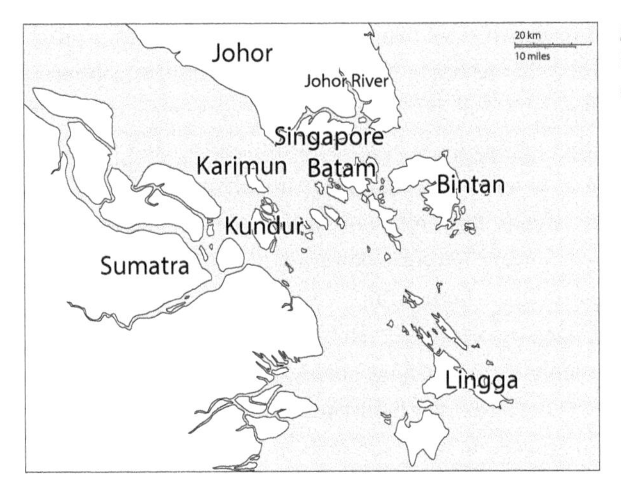

Map 3.5
Singapore, Karimun and Bintan

1819 the Johor River and Singapore had been adopted as the political and economic base for one of the contending factions in the Johor-Riau Sultanate's royal family (that of Temenggong Abdul Rahman and his ally, Hussain Mahummud Shah), with Riau being the base of the rival faction (that of Raja Ja'far and Sultan Abdul Rahman). The Dutch had already secured a treaty with the Riau faction, so the British approached the Johor faction, offering the Temenggong financial incentives and offering Hussain both financial incentives and the title of Sultan.[19] In the first instance Raffles was able to negotiate what was effectively the rental of a coastal strip to set up a factory on the island. This arrangement stayed in place until 1823 when John Crawfurd, as the British Resident, negotiated full sovereignty over the entire island except for two estates reserved for the Sultan and the Temenggong – though with the authority of all parties to the negotiations being so weak, it was a dubious foundation for a claim of full sovereignty.

In the context of the sense of inevitability that has been retrospectively generated by Singapore's national narrative it is tempting to ask why Singapore was not the first option all along, but the fact is that there was no particular reason it should have been. Singapore had not played a truly central role in anything for four centuries, and while it had many virtues as a base, they were not so overwhelming that they made the island an obvious choice ahead of Bintan, Karimun or even the Johor River. After all, Calcutta was not planning a second major presence in the Straits: the case Raffles put in Calcutta was merely to establish a way station for the China trade. Even this modest ambition was disowned almost immediately by London, though not soon enough to avert Raffles from fulfilling his ambitions. Furthermore the local colonial and commercial interests in Penang actively opposed the establishment of any significant rival settlement that might usurp its own role. Yet Raffles' vision, as we have already noted, had always been more ambitious and he hoped for much more than a way station. To realise his private ambitions for his new settlement he needed a harbour and an island of substantial dimensions – such as Singapore. By 1818 Raffles was already well acquainted with Singapore's particular virtues through his study of both British sources and the Malay records that have now come to be known as the *Malay Annals* – though we should note that when he first sailed within a stone's throw of the island in 1811, he went straight past without making any mention of it in any log, correspondence or report.[20]

Much has been made of the snippets from Raffles' correspondence that suggest he had set his heart on settling Singapore before he even left Calcutta. Such snippets are not hard to find, and they certainly show that Singapore featured in Raffles' thinking. A regular feature of this narrative is a letter that Raffles penned on 12 December 1818, a month before setting foot in Singapore and while still on board ship from England. He wrote:

> We are now on our way to the Eastward, in the hope of doing something, but I much fear the Dutch have hardly left us an inch of ground to stand upon. My attention is principally turned to Johore, and you must not be surprised if my next letter to you is dated from the site of the ancient city of Singhapura.[21]

This passage, and others, have been taken by some as evidence of Raffles' advance intentions to settle on Singapore,[22] but at most it reflects his intention to negotiate with the Malay powers in Johor-Riau,[23] for which purpose anchoring at Singapore was a logical and reasonable step, regardless of whether Singapore or Bintan was the objective. Even taking Karimun could not have been done without some interaction with the powers in Johor-Riau.

Leaving aside the unlikely scenario that Raffles already had a Singapore plan when he left England, it is nevertheless possible that he had a preference to settle Singapore by the time he left Calcutta late in 1818 – but even if he did, any such hopes would have been completely contingent upon securing a political settlement with an element of the fading and fracturing Johor-Riau Sultanate. Indeed John Bastin's study of Raffles' correspondence establishes beyond reasonable doubt that Raffles' principal immediate concern in selecting a site was not the virtues of the harbour, but the simple matter of availability. On 26 November 1818 Raffles wrote to his good friend Charlotte Seymour, the Duchess of Somerset, bemoaning the spread of the Dutch throughout the region. He hoped to 'obtain a Station at Rhio' but in his pessimism he conceded that his thoughts had 'turned towards Siam where I hope to have the field to myself'.[24] Siam. Not Singapore. Not even the Straits of Malacca.

A month of travel and consultations refined his thoughts somewhat and on 1 January 1819 – that is, just after he had been told that Riau was not available – Raffles told John

Bannerman, the Governor of Penang, that they needed 'to make a stand in some Port to the Eastward of Malacca where the Dutch may not have preoccupied' and complained that it might be difficult to find 'an Islet throughout the whole range of the Archipelago, to which they might lay claim'. Singapore was in his mind by this stage, but the letter presents it only as one of the preferred options: 'The Island of Singapura or the Districts of old Johor appear to me to possess peculiar & great advantages … The Carimon Islands have also advantages.'[25]

During his Penang stopover, Raffles sought out any news and intelligence he could about the indigenous politics and the local geography in the southern end of the Straits, drawing upon Asian traders and European 'Malacca old hands' such as his old friend Colonel William Farquhar, who had spent most of his working life in the region.[26] By the end of a week of consultations and research Raffles' thoughts had clearly turned towards Singapore. The earliest record of Raffles declaring his strong preference for Singapore was an official letter to Lord Hastings dated 8 January. Yet although he was certainly convinced of Singapore's natural advantages, he made it clear to Hastings that he was considering them alongside the more basic premise that the island might, with a bit of courage, be construed as being available:

> while we carefully abstain from an interference in any Island where the Dutch may be actually established or where the Dutch flag may fly, it may be questionable whether our own safety may not dictate the propriety of establishing ourselves in an advantageous position – even at the hazard of a subsequent claim being set up by the Dutch – They can set up no claim that cannot well be contested, and notwithstanding all we have heard of their Naval and Military Force there is no chance that they would attempt to dislodge any respectable Establishment.
>
> From every inquiry I have made I am fully satisfied of the value & importance of the island of Sincapore which commands Johor – There is a most excellent harbour which is even more defensible and more conveniently situated for the protection of our China Trade and for commanding the Straits than Rhio – it has been deserted for Centuries and long before the Dutch power existed in these Seas – There are about 2000 Inhabitants upon it (new settlers) under a respectable Chief – but it is probable the Dutch may say we have no right to go there as it forms part of the ancient Territory of Johor –
>
> I have mentioned to Mr Adam some particulars regarding this State & one object of Major Farquhar's Mission will be to obtain full information on the subject.[27]

Even a fortnight prior to his historic landing in Singapore River, Raffles was still making enquiries about the political situation in mainland Johor, Singapore and the nearby islands in order to establish what was 'attainable'. Furthermore, from his letter of 16 January to John Adam, Secretary to the Governor General, it is apparent that he was as much open to a settlement on the mainland as he was to a settlement on the island. He wrote:

> there does not seem to be any objection to a Station at Sincapore, or on the opposite shore towards Point Romania or on any of the smaller Islands which lie off this part of the Coast. The larger Harbour of Johore is declared by professional men whom I have consulted, and by every Eastern trader of experience to whom I have been able to refer, to be capacious & easily defensible, & the British Flag once hoisted, there would be no want of supplies to meet the immediate necessities of an Establishment.[28]

Local indigenous politics were also a major consideration because Asian 'native' sovereignty was fully recognised in European international law. Hence his letter of 16 January continued:

> we may possibly find at Johor or in its vicinity, a competent authority with whom to treat, and in this case, should that position be attainable in other respects, we shall have lost nothing essential by the preoccupation of Rhio by the Dutch.[29]

Upon securing the signature of the Temenggong, he wrote to his friend William Marsden:

> Most certainly the Dutch never had a factory in the island of Singapore; and it does not appear to me that their recent arrangements with a subordinate authority at Rhio can or ought to interfere with our permanent establishment here.[30]

Singapore's greatest points of attraction, therefore, were neither its harbour nor its particular position in the local waters (though both of these points were certainly strong pull factors in their own right), but the fact that the Dutch had never in history planted their flag there and that there were two members of the local ruling aristocracy (including a claimant to the title of Sultan) who might be induced to recognise the British presence on the island in exchange for the recognition of their own legitimacy.

With the exception of the local Malay politics, Raffles was well aware of all these factors before he left Penang for Karimun, yet there was never any certainty, probably even in his own mind, that it would be Singapore rather than Johor or some other island where he would end up. The point at which he ultimately established the viability of settling on Singapore was 28 January, when, fresh from Karimun, he landed on a small island (St John's Island) about 6 kilometres (4 miles) off the mouth of the Singapore River and sought news of the political situation from local Malays. They told him that Temenggong Abdul Rahman was on the island and the Dutch were not. Farquhar was separately able to assure Raffles that he knew the Temenggong and enjoyed his confidence, so they made straight for Singapore, dropped anchor in the river that same evening and came directly ashore to open discussions with the Temenggong.[31] Two days later, the 30th, they secured the Temenggong's signature on an interim treaty and raised the Union Flag.

The story of the settlement of Singapore is therefore a narrative about the region east of Penang – particularly the Johor-Riau stretch of sea – rather than about the island itself. The proximity to China was a critical point, as was taking a commanding position in the pathway to Southeast Asia, but there was no inevitability about setting up a factory on the island of Singapore in particular. Warren Hastings' preference in 1786 had been for Bintan. Lord Hastings' instructions of 1818 also targeted Bintan; Farquhar's preference was Karimun; London, as it turns out, would have been happier to have ended all such adventurism and stayed put in Penang. Raffles himself settled on Singapore only after every other option he suggested had been dashed.

Place per se was and is vital to Singapore's existence as a major centre, but when we say 'place' we primarily mean the region, not the island in particular. The island did have some distinguishing assets – primarily its well-positioned harbour – and these should not be dismissed lightly; but neither are they so important that all else pales before them. As we will see in the next section, the island itself (and particularly the channels around it) held critical strategic importance in the ages when sailors in frail boats hugged shorelines and placid waters whenever possible, and had incomplete knowledge of alternative routes, but by the time we reach the opening of the nineteenth century the intrinsic, natural advantages of the island itself were less important than its neighbourhood.

FURTHER BACK IN HISTORY

The historic importance of Singapore's neighbourhood is determined by a simple fact: from at least the fourteenth century onwards, the Straits of Malacca has been one of the principal sea routes from China to the rest of the world;[32] most immediately to the Indian subcontinent, but beyond that to what we now call the Middle East and Europe as well. In the age when ships could only sail with the wind, it was one of the better places to wait out the months between the summer and the winter monsoons while the winds reversed direction.[33] This meant that it was the turnpike for most of the world's transcontinental seaborne trade, commerce and cultural interchange for half a millennium before the British took much interest in the Straits. Even today it remains the most practical sea route between the West Pacific and everywhere west of the Straits, short of the Americas.

Looking more locally, the Straits sit comfortably at the south-west corner of a pair of local and relatively placid seas – the Java Sea and South China Sea (including the Gulf of Siam), which have been described collectively by several historians as being akin to the Mediterranean in terms of their facilitation of communication, trade and cultural exchange. If we include in our consideration two more navigable seas – the Indian Ocean/Bay of Bengal to the west of the Straits and the Banda Sea (home of the Spice Islands) to the east, we see that the Straits lay at the maritime conduit and choke point of a natural community of trade and civilisational intercourse.[34]

In the shifting fortunes of commerce and empire, the Straits of Malacca became a centre of regional trade early in the seventh century. By the beginning of the eighth century this commercial dominance was generating new centres of naval and political hegemony along the south-east coast of Sumatra, which eventually took the form of the Srivajaya maritime empire, based in the river-port city of Palembang.[35] This was a commercial empire, but really more of a maritime confederacy than an empire proper.[36] It was based on the ruthless exercise of naval superiority, which ensured that all trade passing through the Straits stopped in at imperial ports. A twelfth-century report of the Srivajaya method of doing business describes the reality, shorn of its gloss:

> If a merchant ship passes by [Palembang] without entering, her boats go forth to make a combined attack and all are ready to die [in battle]. That is the reason why the country is a great shipping centre.[37]

As with Singapore today, its fortunes were substantially tied to events in China and on access to China. China, of course, has been the economic powerhouse of the world for all historical periods up to the middle of the nineteenth century when it was brought to its knees by the British in the First Opium War. This military defeat was followed by indignity after indignity, culminating in the self-inflicted madness of the Great Leap Forward, the Great Famine and the Cultural Revolution, but until this period of ignominy and humiliation, China dominated the world in terms of luxury, innovations, food production, heavy industry, and manufactures. China was the El Dorado that attracted Marco Polo and Matteo Ricci from southern Europe, Ibn Battuta from North Africa and Genghis Khan from Mongolia.

The imperial rulers of Srivajaya proved adept at winning favour in the Chinese imperial court, and in the tenth century the newly enthroned Song dynasty made it a highly favoured tributary and trading kingdom.[38] The trade and wealth that flowed from China were vital to Srivajaya, but in 1025 the ships of their long-standing trading partners to the west – the Chola of southern India – arrived in the Straits in force as a navy and attacked no less than 14 Srivajayan trading ports, including its capital at Palembang. It seems likely that the root cause of the dispute was access to markets in China, though the primary sources are silent and ultimately we can only offer conjecture.[39] The attack effectively ended the original Srivajaya Empire, leaving the northern end of the Straits in Indian hands for about a century and the southern end

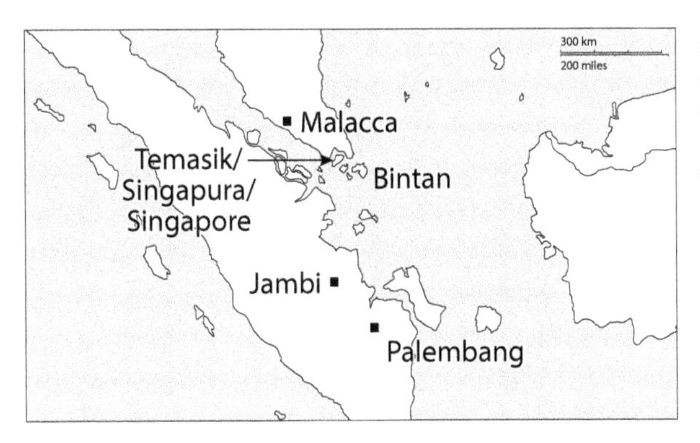

Map 3.6
Straits of Malacca, showing Singapore in relation to historical centres of power

under the looser domination of a collection of lesser local powers.[40] The most important of these successors to Srivajaya was based in a new capital at the Sumatran port of Jambi and it appropriated the Srivajaya name and tried to capitalise on it in later dealings with the imperial court in China (Map 3.6).

The next set of challenges for the powers in the Straits came in the first half of the twelfth century when imperial politics in China drove the Song to allow Chinese to engage in unrestricted external trade for the first time in China's history. It is of some interest to this history that one of the Chinese traders who was working in the Straits in this period had literary pretensions that led him to put quill to paper and write an extensive account of the region. According to Miksic, this trader, Wang Dayuan, writing in 1349, was the first person on record to identify Southeast Asia as a region in its own right. In his record of places of significance Wang made mention of the Malay Peninsula 14 times, including mention of Singapore twice. We know very little about Singapore specifically in the fourteenth century, but we know that it was important enough to send a tributary mission to China in 1325, and that it was attacked by Siamese forces in the 1340s.[41] We also know that in the mid-century Wang identified a 500 metre-wide stretch of water between Singapore's south coast and a little island later called Pulau Blakang Mati (now called Sentosa, made famous in 2018 for hosting the Trump–Kim Summit) as the gateway between the Indian and Pacific oceans – making him the first person on record to do so. In later European maps this would be known as Singapore Strait or Old Singapore Strait, but in Wang's time this little strait was called Dragon Tooth's Strait (or Dragon Tooth's Gate or *Longya men*/*Long Ya Men*) and it was a major base for pirates, suggesting that it was a busy thoroughfare (Map 3.7).[42]

With the slow decline of Sumatran kingdoms during the fourteenth century the Straits were open to new overlords. There was no shortage of candidates for domination of the Straits. Java, Aceh and China all had capacity and a history of interest in the region, but for reasons that are not completely clear, neither Aceh nor China showed

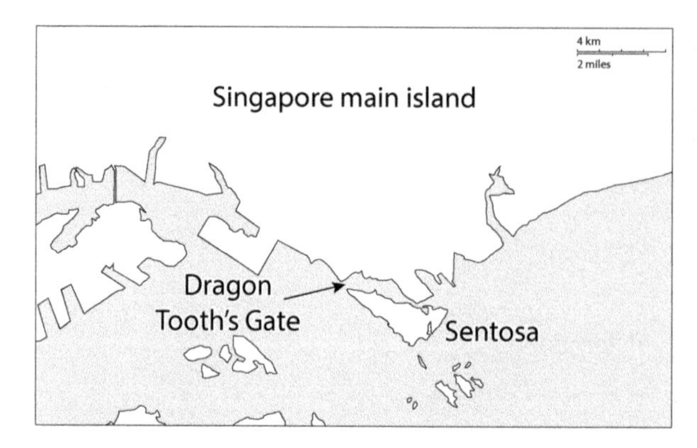

Map 3.7
Dragon Tooth's Strait/Gate, shown here after twentieth-century land reclamation

Figure 3.4
Two contemporary views across Dragon Tooth's Strait

any imperial or aggressive commercial interest in the Straits, and the way was clear for the rise of Java as the regional power. It extended its reach into Sumatra very quickly, taking 'the rump of Malay commercial and political power in south-eastern Sumatra' (to use Wolters' evocative words)[43] as a client state before turning its attention to the north side of the Straits of Malacca, including Johor and Singapore.

FROM PALEMBANG TO TEMASIK/SINGAPURA

The next stage of this narrative resumes a direct focus on the place of Singapore, but before moving on to this part of the story, a change of pace is required – and a word of explanation about sources. The following section sees a shift of power from Sumatra to the island of Singapore. It probably seems blindingly obvious that this landing on the shores of Singapore is an intrinsically important point in the history of Singapore, but in fact it would be of only incidental significance except for two points. First, it is a crucial element in the story of the rise of the Malacca Sultanate, which is the remote but most basic starting point in the foundation of modern Singapore. Second, the mythology that has been woven around the events of the landing and settlement at the beginning of the fourteenth century demonstrates the integration of the island of Singapore into its immediate region and the importance of place in Singapore's history and, by implication, in its present. Also note that knowledge of this period is not reliable in its details, coming to us from a mixture of archaeological remains, the contemporary and near-contemporaneous reports and maps provided by Chinese and Portuguese observers and participants, and the semi-mythical/semi-historical accounts given in an ancient piece of literature known today as the *Malay Annals*.[44]

The short version of the story is that the rise of the Majapahit Empire, based in northern Java, prompted resistance and some local rebellions as its reach spread, which in turn provoked reprisals from Java. One such rebellion and reprisal occurred in Palembang and it resulted in the *raja* of Palembang, Sang Nila Utama, fleeing with his navy to Temasik (present-day Singapore) somewhere around 1390. At that time Temasik was home to an established city that had already enjoyed about a century of prosperity as a trading port and a layover where sailors and traders could wait for the change of monsoons.[45] The new *raja* almost certainly killed the local ruler and suppressed the city's population before taking the island as his seat of power. His occupation lasted only for five or six years, however, and then he left again. The orthodox historical understanding is that he fled, though it is not clear from whom he was fleeing – Siamese? Pattani? Javanese? Based on the evidence of Portuguese records, however, Borschberg raises the possibility that he may not have fled at all: he may have just given up on his new domain and looked for greener pastures. In this scenario Temasik was already in decline when Sang Nila Utama and his navy arrived because of factors such as changes in the weather pattern (newly frequent storms and squalls), which were making the island unattractive as a port and layover.[46] Ultimately we cannot be sure of the level of prosperity of Temasik in 1390 or the cause of Sang Nila Utama's departure a few years later, but we do know that in 1396 or thereabouts the *raja* and his followers left for Malacca, leaving behind either a ruined and empty city or – more likely – one that just faded into relative obscurity and drifted out of history.

That seems to be about the full extent of our firm knowledge of these events – perhaps even moving past 'firm' knowledge. Beyond this account, the *Malay Annals* fleshes out the story in informative – if somewhat unreliable – ways to produce vignettes of history that undoubtedly convey much that is fact, but which is embellished and stylised to convey allegorical messages designed to establish the legitimacy of the subsequent rulers of the Sultanate of Malacca. One of the more interesting and plausible vignettes in the *Malay Annals* is that, on his way from Palembang to Temasik, Sang Nila Utama and his followers headed initially for the Riau islands, specifically Bintan, with a stopover in Lingga. These islands straddle the southern end of the Straits of Malacca so it should not be surprising that they were already home to large, powerful and prosperous seafaring communities that earned their living from a combination of trade and piracy. Bintan was the community's main base and there lived Queen Sakidar Shah, queen of the sea nomads (or *orang laut*, in Malay). She greeted the arrival of Sang Nila Utama and his followers with enthusiasm and immediately became his patron, making him her heir and placing at his disposal her full flotilla, which the *Malay Annals* describes as being 400 strong.[47] It is not clear why she was so generous. A later Portuguese commentator suggested that they were related through marriage and he (or perhaps his wife) was senior in the family hierarchy.[48] Winstedt's interpretation suggests that she knew him as the true *raja* and that she and her people were already in his service.[49] There is no contradiction between these lines of reasoning, and in any case the reason is less important than the outcome, whereby Sang Nila Utama found himself with a navy at his disposal and when he expressed a strong interest in one of the islands in the queen's kingdom – Temasik (present-day Singapore) – she gave it to him as a gift. Along with changing his own name to Sri Tri Buana, Sang Nila Utama also changed the name of Temasik to a similarly regal Sanskrit name – Singapura or Lion City – and established his new kingdom there.

The island's name change was supposedly prompted by the sighting of a lion on the island, but Miksic suggests that its real purpose was political: it declared the new importance of the island and signalled the shift of sovereignty and focus of the kingdom from Sumatra to the Malay Peninsula.[50] Borschberg has a more prosaic explanation: the name is derived from the Malay word *singgah* (break, interruption) which, if correct, refers simply to its role as a layover.[51] The *Malay Annals* recorded that, after the arrival of Sang Nila Utama, Singapura 'became a great city, to which foreigners resorted in great numbers so that the fame of the city and its greatness spread throughout the world'.[52] Wolters assures us this is a fabrication,[53] but it might be more precise to say that this particular claim is an attempt to bask in the city's former greatness. It seems unlikely that Singapore was ever a great city of 'world renown', but there is a wealth of archaeological evidence and early Portuguese reports that show it had been a city and port of some significance throughout the fourteenth century, so that it probably would have been known throughout the parts of the world that mattered to it.[54] Perhaps the greater import of the witness of the *Malay Annals* might be that it hints at the conclusions of the most recent scholarship on the subject, which is that Singapore was not suddenly deserted when the *raja* decamped for Malacca in about 1396, but continued as a city and functioning port into an indeterminate future.[55] Certainly, it remained the empire's main naval base during the Malaccan century, hosting not just a strong navy but also the Laksamana, or admiral of the fleet.[56]

The main point of the *Malay Annals* was to establish the genealogy and semi-divine legitimacy of the subsequent line of Malay *rajas*; it grants Singapore the status of the first great Malay port and the starting point of the Malacca Sultanate; and it claims intimate links between the Malay world and the *orang laut* of the Riau Archipelago. The point about the role of the *orang laut* was important in the context of the Malay politics of the sixteenth to the eighteenth century when the island of Bintan and the loyalty of the *orang laut* became pivotal in Malay and regional power politics.

JOHOR IN HISTORY

If we follow the Malays of Temasik as they escaped to Malacca in about 1396, we find that between the protection offered by its *orang laut* bodyguard and the tolerance of the Siamese regional overlords, the royal family was finally able to establish itself successfully in a base and build a new sultanate.[57] For the next four decades the Ming court chose to recognise the new sultanate and allowed it to pay tribute – a practice that repaid Malacca handsomely since it provided the basis of its China trade.[58] In 1436 the Ming banned all sea trade, but by then Malacca was already well placed to continue as a trading centre. Trade with India increased during this half-century (much of it via Indian Muslim traders) and Malacca was ideally situated to profit from that by becoming the main base for rendezvous, entrepôt trading, storage of goods, and hospitality for traders on layover (which could be for a year or two at a time).[59] Malacca formed a critical node in the new Silk Road of the Sea (to adopt Miksic's expression), but it was also a node in what might be called the Spice Road of the Sea, acting as an entrepôt and way station for pepper heading east from southern India, and nutmeg, mace and cloves heading west from the Spice Islands, which lay about 2,800 kilometres (1,700 miles) to the east as the crow flies. Singapore was part of the Malaccan Sultanate, but it was basically left to its own devices.

Return to Johor/Riau

After about a century of prosperity, Malacca received an unwelcome visit from a new, powerful force. In 1511, Alfonso de Albuquerque arrived with a fleet of 17 or 18 Portuguese warships and 1,200 men at arms.[60] Albuquerque was on a mission from the Portuguese throne to build a chain of trading and naval bases to reach the source of the spice supply that was currently reaching Europe through transcontinental Muslim networks. His passion for his mission was compounded by a vehemence born of religious nationalism: he arrived in Malacca just two decades after Portugal had violently expelled the last of the Muslims from its territory, and a time when Malaccans had mostly converted to Islam.

Thanks largely to treacherous divisions in the Sultan's government, Albuquerque was able to conquer Malacca in a month or so, after which Sultan Mahmud and many thousands of his followers abandoned the city. They made their way south, arriving very soon at the logical place from which to rebuild a sea-based empire: Bintan, close to where the Malaccan journey had started. From his base in Bintan Sultan Mahmud was able to confirm his rule over the Straits and Johor, but it was a highly contingent rule, always under threat from powerful neighbours such as the Acehnese and the Portuguese. The capital shifted relatively freely in these decades and in the following centuries between settlements on the peninsula and islands such as Bintan and Lingga, according to strategic needs, the vagaries of war and personal preferences. The most immediate beneficiary of the Portuguese capture of Malacca turned out to be the Kingdom of Aceh, which became a principal stopover for Asian traders trying to avoid Malacca. With its wealth and confidence growing, Aceh became a formidable commercial and naval force in the region,[61] able to send hundreds of boats carrying thousands of fighters into battle, just like Johor.

At around the end of the sixteenth century, a new European power, the Netherlands, arrived in the Straits. The Dutch were originally bit players in Asian affairs, but the Sultan of Johor recognised their potential as an ally against the Portuguese and the dreaded Acehnese. The Netherlands and Johor entered a formal alliance and laid many fruitless plans to retake Malacca from the Portuguese.[62] The year 1641 turned out to be a turning point in Johor's fortunes, when three independent events gave Johor a fresh start: a young and vigorous ruler succeeded to the Johor throne;[63] the Dutch finally took Malacca from the Portuguese; and the warlike Sultan Iskander Thani of Aceh died, leaving his kingdom in the hands of a line of more placid rulers.[64] Since the return of the Sultanate to the southern end of the Straits, Johor had faced nine Portuguese and six Acehnese invasions, often coming off the worst, but with Dutch friends in Malacca and no enemies in Aceh it felt safe and confident for the first time. The decades that followed were as prosperous as had been the century in Malacca – and the Malays in

Johor were running a much more profitable operation than were the Dutch in Malacca. This happy state of affairs lasted until the Johor branch of the Malaccan royal line died out in 1699 in an act of regicide that Andaya tells us completely destroyed the legitimacy of the Sultanate for ever.[65] Indeed, so dramatic was the break that scholars identify this point as the end of the Malacca-Johor period and the beginning of a new one that some call the Bugis-Dutch period or just the Bugis period.

At this point we are only a century away from the arrival of Sir Stamford Raffles in Singapore, and the main shifts that occurred in that century were the rising levels of intervention in the domestic affairs of the Malay Peninsula and Riau by new local powers (most notably the Bugis of South Sulawesi and Makassar, and the Minangkabau of central Sumatra) and by a third European power, Great Britain. Several decisive turning points can be picked out to track the pathway towards the nineteenth century. First, the Bugis forced their way into the government and economy of Johor and the Straits in 1722, pushing the Johor royals into the role of junior partners in their own Sultanate. The Bugis took Riau as their base and it rose to new eminence as a regional trading centre. Riau's new success was based on two primary factors: first, its ability to attract Chinese investors and labourers by the thousands to work on pepper plantations and to mine for tin for sale throughout the region; and secondly, its openness to British traders from India, who needed a non-Dutch port through which to distribute Indian opium throughout the region and through which they could buy Southeast Asia's collected produce, particularly its spices.[66]

The second turning point was the full reversal of all that had been achieved since 1722. In 1784 the Dutch drove the Bugis out of Riau, staking their own claim to the islands of the archipelago, but in the process destroying Riau as a viable commercial centre.[67] This had the direct effect of creating a double vacuum in the Straits: both the Malays and the British lacked a port city that they could use as a trading hub. The third turning point was Britain's response to the loss of access to Riau: it began its entry into Malay affairs by establishing a new settlement at Penang in 1786. This was followed nearly a decade later by the physical withdrawal of the Dutch from the Straits and Java due to the vagaries of the Napoleonic Wars being waged in Europe. The Dutch retained legal hold of their territories, but handed them over to the British to administer on their behalf. This effectively ended the Dutch treaty with Riau and might have prompted the English to rebuild Riau if they had not just swallowed their new possession in Penang.[68] If we were to consider the region more broadly, we might also add that by the opening of the nineteenth century, the Dutch had begun developing a new form of colonial exploitation in Java – large-scale agriculture. In retrospect this development marked the beginning of the decline of Dutch interest in the Malay Peninsula and prepared for the day, in 1824, when they would agree to give up all their claims on Malaya in exchange for a free hand in Java and Sumatra. Thus we arrive at the situation in the southern end of the Straits as it sat when Lord Hastings dispatched Sir Stamford Raffles from Calcutta to the Straits to establish a settlement in 'Rhio'/Bintan.

SINGAPORE IN THE STRAITS

The section above is a thumbnail history of the region from 1395 to 1819: a 424-year history in a few pages, taking us from Singapore to Malacca and back again. As such it is not a detailed account of the region, but it does enable us to see the regional context into which Sir Stamford Raffles was inserting the East India Company when he dropped anchor in 1819. The region was a dynamic but somewhat chaotic community of family, 'tribal' and colonial rivalries, in which everyone was vying for the same prize: a greater share of the interoceanic trade that was funnelled through the Straits of Malacca year in and year out. This was a source of fabulous wealth but it depended entirely on command of the seas and access to one or more good, well-placed ports – whether a seaport or a river port. Thus naval power was the main game of statecraft.

Singapore was an incidental feature of history over this period. The island continued to host a busy port and city, and probably a large portion of the Johorean navy for at least two centuries after the flight to Malacca,[69] and the Singapore Strait continued as the major thoroughfare for east–west traffic. It rates a handful of mentions in the main histories, yet essentially it was just one of several important ports at the southern end of the Straits of Malacca, along with Johor Lama (near the mouth of the Johor River), Batu Sawar (in the inner reaches of the Johor River) and Riau. Its significance was gauged according to the services it could perform for the main communities in the Johor-Riau Empire.[70] It was central primarily in a strictly geographical and strategic sense: as the cross-over point between the north–south line of Johor ports and the east–west trade between the Indian and the Pacific oceans.[71]

Little surprise, then, that throughout the latter part of the sixteenth century and the early decades of the seventeenth century – the beginnings of serious Dutch–Portuguese rivalry in the Straits – the European powers were paying close attention to the strategic importance of the area around Singapore. In the 1570s the Portuguese considered building a fortress either on Singapore or in the mouth of the Johor River before opting for the more manageable option of upgrading their fleet presence around the island.[72] The Portuguese revisited the idea of building fortresses early in the seventeenth century, but once again their ideas came to nothing. The Dutch actually took a firm decision to build a new fort along the Johor River in this same period, but in the end their determination waned and the project was diverted into nothing more than an upgrade of existing facilities.[73] The most substantive and decisive European intervention in this period came in the 1630s, when the Dutch identified three distinct strategic points at

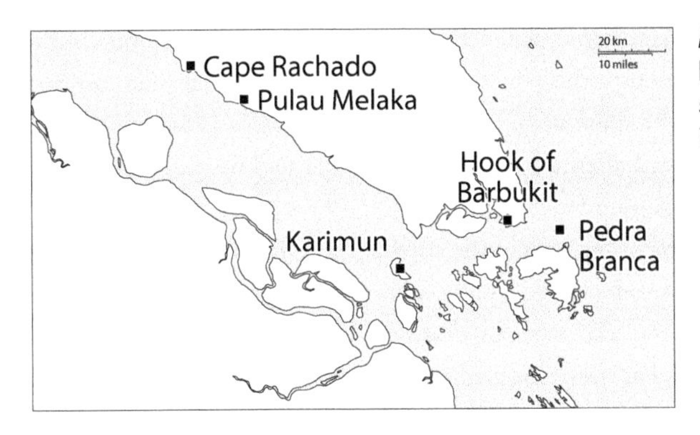

Map 3.8
Five strategic nodes secured by the Dutch in the 1630s

the southern end of the Straits of Malacca: a point of open sea near a small rock known as Pedra Branca, situated just beyond the east coast of Johor; the Hook of Barbukit on the eastern side of the mouth of the Johor River, looking south towards Bintan and west towards Singapore; and Karimun, 50 kilometres (30 miles) west of Singapore (see Map 3.8).[74] They did not build fortresses in these positions but they did rotate their naval presence through these areas on a seasonal basis. This in itself was not judged to be sufficient to guarantee their control of the traffic lanes between the Indian and Pacific oceans, but securing just two additional nodes further north – at a tiny island just out of cannon shot from Portuguese Malacca (present-day Pulau Melaka) and in the waters off Cape Rachado (near present-day Port Dickson) – completed the task and gave the Dutch the regional supremacy they sought.[75]

We must await further research to pierce the opacity of the situation in Singapore during the Malacca-Johor centuries – particularly the remaining mystery of why the island was severely and uncharacteristically depopulated when Raffles arrived in 1819[76] – but there is enough here to assure us that although Singapore was politically invisible, the island and its environs were strategically pivotal throughout the period. The Singapore Straits possessed a strategic importance that stood out even among the string of Dutch-identified choke points between Pedra Branca and Cape Rachado. Presumably it was this combination of political insignificance and strategic importance that prompted Sultan Abdul Jalil of Johor to offer the island to the British in 1703 at a time when he was desperate for allies.[77] This was a time of crisis for the sultanate: its legitimacy was in tatters following the murder of the previous sultan in 1699, the Dutch were flexing their muscles in the Straits and Abdul Jalil would probably have felt more secure knowing there were relatively friendly British nearby.

One of the fascinating features of sixteenth- and seventeenth-century Singapore is how little had changed strategically since Wang Dayuan wrote about Dragon Tooth's Gate as the gateway between oceans in 1349. For most of the sixteenth century the strait was still the major thoroughfare between the Pacific and Indian oceans. Even at the opening of the seventeenth century this was still the preferred route between east and west, though since the 1580s the more open route south of Sentosa was being used as a viable, though still not preferred alternative. By that time the two were known as Old Singapore Strait and New Singapore Strait respectively.[78]

With advances in technology – especially the capacity to sail independently of the wind – the need to seek placid waters and hug the shore has obliterated the significance of the Old Singapore Strait and also reduced drastically the significance of the New Singapore Strait. The old strait has been trimmed and tidied by Singapore's modern land 'reclamation' projects but it still survives, separating Keppel Harbour from the tourist island now called Sentosa. Today it is so insignificant that it is no longer dignified with a proper name on most maps (though Derek Heng identified it as Keppel Strait in a 1999 publication)[79] and the main danger comes in the form of cable-car accidents in the airspace overhead.

SINGAPORE AND MALAYA

The British passed up the opportunity to own Singapore in 1703, and in truth even in 1819 it was an accident of history rather than any grand design that drew the island into the British realm. Even when they had it, they were loath to spend any money towards using its strategic position to project – or even protect – British interests. Throughout the nineteenth century the British built a number of military establishments on the island, but they were too inadequately provisioned and manned to be of any practical use as a contribution to the security of the empire east of Suez, or even to the safety of British trade and subjects in the Straits.[80] As Hack and Blackburn neatly put it:

> For just over 100 years after Raffles secured Singapore for the East India Company, in 1819, its local defences remained more remarkable for their weakness than for their strength. Singapore's real protection had then come from the Royal Navy's global dominance, backed when necessary by the Indian Army.[81]

The attractions of Singapore's strategic position thus seemed to be wasted on the empire's military planners until they decided to build a naval base there in the 1920s. And even then it was not completed until 1938, just in time to be lost to the invading Japanese Army.

Yet it was a different story with the empire's capitalist entrepreneurs, and with the Chinese capitalists who, by the opening of the nineteenth century, had made themselves indispensable to European commerce in Southeast Asia. For these groups Singapore more than lived up to its promise as a trading hub. Most Indian-British opium was destined for consumers in China, but 'country traders' used Singapore as the hub through which they made bulk sales to local 'farmers' licensed by the colonial authorities. The 'farmers' in turn distributed it to perhaps a million Chinese labourers living and working in Southeast Asia at the turn of the century.[82] On both the return journeys to India and also on the onward journeys to China the produce of Southeast Asia filled those same ships to continue the trade network. Collecting this produce did not require another stop because Singapore was the regional hub and it handled the trade in all directions. Much of the produce in question was the result of heavy labour: tin and gold mining; gambier, pepper, rice, coffee, tea and sugar production. The labour was done mostly by the same Chinese labourers for whom the opium was intended, and it is fitting that a great many of them had also arrived in Southeast Asia through the port of Singapore.[83]

Flows of people came also from the west, as did flows of capital. India supplied convicts, labourers, soldiers and both native and European capitalists, along with their valuable capital. Much of Singapore's local trade in money was handled by Indians who gave their names to city streets and alleyways where they worked. In many cases the streets themselves were made by Indians. Natives from the Netherlands East Indies, the Malay Peninsula and further afield flocked to Singapore in the early decades of the settlement, and even though they were overwhelmed demographically by Chinese migrants later in the century, Singapore became a major centre of Malay and Islamic scholarly and political debate. With the Port of Singapore acting as the main commercial and migratory hub for the region, it was logical that it would eventually become the political hub for British Malaya, supplanting Penang. Singapore became the distribution point of Malaya's gambier and tin production in the nineteenth century and its rubber production in the twentieth century. Singapore's transformation into a hub for oil bunkering for both British and Dutch Southeast Asia towards the end of the nineteenth century is more surprising, but fits the pattern, as does the development of Singapore as a regional telegraph hub, education hub and, later, a key link in the air route to London.

This one-paragraph sketch of the flows into and out of Singapore in the nineteenth century do not remotely do justice to the century as a period in Singapore's history, but I hope it is sufficient to establish that Singapore's current role as a strategic hub is not peculiar to the twentieth century, let alone to the independence period. In later chapters we return to a more detailed consideration of many of the strands raised in the previous paragraph – as well as to related themes from the twentieth century – but I hope this is sufficient to allow me to conclude this chapter with some reflections relevant to the theme of 'place'.

ANOTHER SINGAPORE STORY

A substantial element of the mythology surrounding the Singapore Story lies in the implicit denial of the fundamental importance of Singapore's strategic location. The fact of the strategic location is never actually denied, but claims that Lee Kuan Yew took Singapore from Third World to First, or from a fetid swamp to a global city, attempt to bury its significance and damages the true story of Singapore's success – a story that may not be quite so spectacular, nor so hagiographic towards certain individuals, but which is impressive in its own right. Or it would be if it had a proper airing.

If we turn to the political economy of Singapore at the time of its independence, there is an exciting story to be told without need for embellishment. Upon independence in 1965, Singapore's government had no easy, safe or obvious options. The new microstate did start life with a significant number of advantages bequeathed by the former British colonial masters, but it faced many more problems. The country's main asset was clearly its strategic location, but how to capitalise on this was not obvious. And even insofar as the way forward could be plotted, this did not make it easy or simple from either a technical or a political perspective. The great achievement was clearly that the leadership did find a way to take advantage of Singapore's natural advantages.

There were many features that make the post-independence period distinctive – including changes in communication and transport – but the most distinctive and important one was surely that for the first time, Singapore was a city-state and an island-state. The dream of being part of a greater Malaya was ended. That idea of Singapore was dead. It was no longer a state of Malaysia, nor one colony among many, nor the de facto capital of British Malaya, nor one island among many in a regional empire. These challenges were genuinely frightening, hence the widespread characterisation of the post-independence years as being dominated by the 'politics of survival'.[84] There is a tendency among critics of the government to highlight the manipulation of the 'politics of survival' to facilitate and justify the descent into authoritarian rule, by implication downplaying what might be called the 'economics of survival'. Uncritical admirers of the regime conversely emphasise the economics at the expense of questioning the need for the harsh politics. In truth, both facets of the history have legitimacy and should be acknowledged. Unlike earlier generations of 'Singaporeans' (not that any of them would have recognised or used that term), the post-1965 generation really were on their own through no choice of their own. They mostly had nowhere else to go. For earlier British authorities, whether based in London or Calcutta, Singapore was a small place a long way away. There were bigger sources of concern and other promising sources of wealth. Not so for the first Singaporeans.

Earlier in this chapter I pointed to Lee Kuan Yew's focus on Singapore's central location in Southeast Asia in the immediate post-independence years, in contrast to Fiji which is in the middle of nowhere. Allow me to quote from just one of those speeches – delivered four months, almost to the day, after Singapore found itself as an independent city-state. In among much political hyperbole and some very mundane talk about exporting tyres to Australia and pyjamas to America were the following excerpts, which between them capture so many of the drivers that were now pushing the newly – and reluctantly – independent Singapore:

> with independence comes independence of action, opportunities to create the conditions for the eventual success of what we want: survival in Southeast Asia – a very turbulent part of the world – as a separate and distinct people, not absorbed or swallowed up by more backward hordes and bigger hordes.
>
> There are lots of bigger people than us who would like to absorb us, and I don't think that is good for us. We want to be ourselves – which means that we've first got to show everybody that we can look after ourselves. …
>
> And finally, what is all this for? For your future – yours and mine – so that a thousand years from now, we will be here, distinct and separate. …
>
> My job and yours is to ensure that the world's fifth biggest port becomes the world's fourth biggest port, and so on …
>
> How do we do that? I say, first, new markets. You see, it so happens that we are in an important corner of the world. If we were not, and we were all by ourselves like the Fiji Islands, it would have been the end of the works for us. Nobody would have been interested. But, as it is, a lot of people are interested in us; and I say we strike out (for) new markets.[85]

Lee's sense of superiority and his dismissal of Singapore's neighbours as 'backward hordes' reveal more about Lee than they do about Singapore or its neighbours, but they both feed the main point of his speech: Singapore needs to do whatever is necessary to take full advantage of its location and its harbour so that it can reach out to the world in pursuit of profit. Only if it can do so will it be able to make a living standing on its own feet, free of fear. And reach out it did – to the world and to the region. But in doing so, it was less breaking new ground than continuing a centuries-old function that might very easily have fallen to another port city in the immediate region.

CLOSING THE CIRCLE

The dominant theme of this chapter has been the importance of place in Singapore's history. It seems appropriate to conclude with some reflections on some of the latest developments that are affecting or might affect the significance of place in Singapore's future. Looking for storm clouds on the horizon, we might note several developments that threaten to reduce the importance of Singapore's strategic advantages. The first but least likely to be fulfilled is the Chinese aspiration to flatten a section of the Isthmus of Kra in southern Thailand and build a huge canal linking the Andaman Sea with the Gulf of Thailand. This would create a shortcut between the Pacific and the Indian oceans that would bypass Singapore. The second is the Chinese plan to build road, rail and pipeline links from south-western China to Gwada Port in Pakistan and to the Port of Kyaukphyu in Myanmar, each of which would also bypass Singapore. Any of these developments would diminish Singapore's traffic and importance, but none is such an immediate or direct threat as direct rivalry for Singapore's hub status, whether in shipping (Malaysia's Port Klang and Tanjung Pelepas; soon to be joined by yet another container port at Malacca), air travel (Dubai; Kuala Lumpur) or a myriad of other functions. Singapore built on the advantages of its geography when other potential players were struggling with nationalist, ethnic or ideological politics and were still trying to build the sorts of infrastructure that Singapore took for granted. In the twenty-first century the advantage of Singapore's location has not yet changed, but now there are competitors who share those advantages and are catching up: witness Port Klang's slow but steady climb up the rankings of the world's busiest ports in recent years.[86] This has created a sense of vulnerability in the ruling elite as they face the reality that, unless something drastic changes, competition with these new players will be nothing more than a perpetual effort to keep ahead: to be faster, better, cheaper. This is not a very endearing prospect to sell to a constituency on an ongoing basis.

Yet there is another, more upbeat side to the consequences of 'place'. For four-and-a-half centuries, from the fall of Malacca in 1511 until the separation of Singapore from Malaysia by the British in 1946, Singapore was part of a local economic and strategic community stretching from Johor to the Riau islands. The colonial separation of Singapore and Johor from Riau in 1824 impeded Riau's participation in this community without destroying it. The same point can be made about the administrative-cum-sovereign separation of Johor from Singapore.

The fascinating new development is that the economic and to some extent the social elements of this community are being rebuilt before our eyes. Singapore and Johor are now major investors in industrial and tourist developments in Bintan and Batam, while Johor has turned over an area three times the size of Singapore to serve as a joint development project, encompassing residential development estates, an airport, retirement villages, tourist and shopping complexes, and many industrial estates. It also includes Johor Baru, the capital of Johor.[87] The residential sections in the western end are inhabited by daily commuters from Singapore. The official name for this project is 'Iskandar', but to many Singaporeans it is known as 'North Singapore'. Since 1989 this development has been part of a larger project known in Singapore as the Singapore–Johor–Riau (SIJORI) growth triangle and to professional economists as the Indonesia–Malaysia–Singapore growth triangle (IMSGT), but under whatever name it has become one of the major production hubs in Southeast Asia.[88]

The new hub is directed primarily at manufacturing and other forms of production rather than trade and piracy, and there is no chance of obliterating the sovereign separation of each of the three components. But leaving these details aside, this new arrangement is effectively a modern recreation of the ancient, premodern Johor-Riau Sultanate. Having survived the threats from the 'backward hordes' in the local neighbourhood and established itself as global player in so many fields, it seems that a more mellow Singapore (working with a more mellow Malaysia and Indonesia) has wisely and profitably rediscovered a new way to maximise very localised advantages. This project of three-way co-operation is really about rebuilding economic and social relationships that have been obscured by artificial political divisions.

Mention of sovereign divisions leads naturally to a consideration of politics. Place and politics cannot be fully separated, and I must confess that my efforts to keep them apart in this chapter for the sake of building an analytical framework through the prism of 'place' has been only indifferently successful. It is appropriate, therefore, that this chapter finishes on a point where place and politics overlap and interact. This provides a tidy entrée to the following chapter, which begins a three-chapter sweep through Singapore's history explicitly through the prism of its politics.

4

Governance in Premodern Singapore

This chapter and the two that follow set out to study Singapore's long history through the prism of government and politics, beginning in the premodern era and finishing in the twenty-first century. The chapter structure follows an unconventional periodisation. This chapter's coverage of 'premodern Singapore' takes it up to 1867; Chapter 5 studies 'modern Singapore' from 1867 through to independence in 1965; and Chapter 6 considers 1965 onwards.

The periodisation generated by the Singapore Story runs somewhat differently from mine. In its purest form it runs thus: before 1819 nothing happened; from 1819 to 1942 was the British colonial era when the island filled up with industrious Chinese who flourished in Raffles' free port under relatively benevolent British rule; 1942–5 was the hardship of the Japanese Occupation; 1945–55 is generally dubbed Singapore's 'political awakening'; 1955–63 was the period of Singapore's internal communist threat; 1963–5 was the period of Singapore's membership of Malaysia; from independence in 1965 Singapore went from 'survival to progress' and thereafter flourished.[1] This, with slight variations, is the periodisation learnt by many cohorts of Singaporean school children. In the 2000s and 2010s, the Ministry of Education's curriculum designers began nuancing this simplistic account somewhat, but the essentials remain untouched. The current (2014) History Syllabus for Lower Secondary Schools offers the following periodisation:

- Before 1819 Singapore was a centre of commerce that had many connections to 'other countries' in the world. In this section 'students will … begin to recognise and see connections between Singapore's history and the Asian powers like China, India and the Middle-East that influenced Southeast Asia and dominated the maritime trade in this region prior to the coming of the Europeans in the 19th century'.
- 1819–1942 was the colonial period and the period of mass Chinese migration, though there is now more emphasis on the lives of the Asian population than there used to be.
- The third period is titled 'Towards Independence' and runs from 1942 to 1965, with special attention to the Japanese Occupation (1942–5) as a turning point but not a distinct period. The next turning point within the 'Towards Independence'

period is 1959, which is when the British gave the colony a reasonably high level of self-government – and when the People's Action Party (PAP) won office. The period of Malaysia's membership is swallowed into this period without much attention.

- The periodisation ends with a final entry titled 'Singapore's First Decade' (1965–75), which is characterised as the period of Singapore's great transformation into something close to that which is recognisable today.[2]

The most important common element of both of these Establishment-generated accounts – and indeed of virtually every account of Singapore's history – is the centrality of 1819 as a point where everything changed. This is the first and most basic point with which I take issue. In 1819 the British built a factory on the Malay island of Singapura. This was completely unremarkable in itself. It was not the first or even the second British factory to have been built in the Straits of Malacca. It was the third attempt, following the abortive establishment of an English factory in Kedah around 1670 and the successful establishment of a full colony at Penang in 1786.[3] Even using the simplistic measure of legal sovereignty, 1819 was no turning point. Britain did not even claim sovereignty over the island until 1823, and this claim was not recognised in international law until 1824. Unlike Raffles' treaties of early 1819, these events decisively and irrevocably shifted power relations on the island, but still not in any way that caused a breach with the Malay past or the principles on which the island's economy rested. During the first few decades after 1819, Singapore's economic activity and its population both increased under British protection, but the style of government remained basically the same: elite-driven and remote from the daily lives of most of the people impacted by it. In this it was not fundamentally different from the Malay era. And when the Temenggong started reconfiguring his traditional style of governance in the 1840s by developing his holdings in Johor (as was described at the end of Chapter 2), he and his family re-emerged as powerful figures in Singapore politics, underlining how little had changed politically, even as society and the economy were undergoing massive upheavals. Hence I argue that the early decades of Singapore's life after 1819 were not the beginning of modern Singapore in any meaningful sense.

This argument does not deny that 1819–24 marked a rejuvenation of the economic and social life of the island after a century as a backwater, nor that 1824 settled Singapore's legal status and its southern border, separating the island from the Riau Archipelago. Yet it does insist that the advent of a recognisably modern society, modern politics and modern economics came somewhere nearer the end of the nineteenth century, with its remote beginnings in 1867 on the transfer of the colony's administration from Calcutta to London. This is a precise turning point generated by an identifiable institutional change, but it also serves as a proxy for a more fundamental shift, since Transfer coincided loosely with a series of revolutions in transport and communications that ended Singapore's isolation. Not coincidentally, this was also the point at which Singapore's relations with the world and the government's relation with its own population began a decades-long process of incremental modernisation.

The abandonment of 1819 is key to reconstructing Singapore's modern history. It liberates the historian from the Singapore Story, and it does so with a decisiveness that the simple inclusion of the pre-1819 story as background lacks. It frames Singapore's history within the metanarrative of regional and global flows of people, trade and power, forcing it beyond the parameters of the British Empire and a couple of the 'Great Men of History'. The Empire and the 'Great Men' need to remain part of this narrative, but they should neither define it, nor bookend it.

BEFORE THE BRITISH

As we saw in Chapter 3, Singapore first appeared in history as a distinct polity for just a few years in the 1390s, when a Sumatran prince, Sang Nila Utama, fled Palembang and settled his followers on the island of Temasik (Singapore). Much of our knowledge of the politics and administration of this period is derived from the *Malay Annals* – which, it should be noted, is properly titled *Genealogy of the Malay Kings*.[4] This source is of limited value for settling precise details of chronology and events. It is, however, a priceless source for historians wishing to understand the politics of regime legitimation and the exercise of elite power in the centuries before the Europeans gained sufficient power to start changing the rules of the game in the southern end of the Straits of Malacca. In my case, the limitations of my own scholarship mean that the evidence of the *Malay Annals* is necessarily placed in the context provided by a number of classic studies of premodern statecraft in Southeast Asia written by those who know more about it – notably Anthony Milner, Anthony Reid and O.W. Wolters – along with a new revisionist work by Maziar Mozaffari Falarti.[5]

It has to be said that in the premodern era the pattern of politics was not recognisable to the modern eye as politics per se, and the level of administration was rudimentary to the point where the modern citizen would not recognise it as such. The era's politics was at its heart elitist, but this elite politics was always playing to a mass constituency of subjects – who might better be described as 'followers'. When the *Malay Annals* described the semi-divine origins of the Malaccan royal family and the magic transmutation of a rice crop into gold and silver, it was retrospectively building a myth of regime legitimation based on much more ancient Hindu myths. That the most ancient and remote forefather was named as the Quranic figure Iskander Shah (Alexander the Great) confirms that by the time the *Annals* was being written the Sultanate had embraced Islam, albeit one heavily suffused in Hindu imagery. According to the *Malay Annals*, late in the fourteenth century the founder of the Malaccan royal line, Sang Nila Utama, married a sequence of 39 beautiful princesses until he found one who was worthy of him. He was later adopted as heir by the powerful queen of the sea people (*orang laut*) who ruled and terrorised the seas between Sumatra and the Malay Peninsula. As we saw in Chapter 3, it was she who gifted Temasik to him, and he gave both the island and himself new Sanskrit names: Temasik became Singapura and Sang Nila Utama changed his name to Sri Tri Buana ('Lord of the Three Worlds'), by which title and royal diadem he claimed lordship over both the natural and the supernatural worlds:[6]

> And Sri Tri Buana became famous as a ruler; and all mankind, male and female, came from every part of the country to pay their homage to him, all of them bringing offerings for his acceptance. On all who came to present themselves before him Sri Tri Buana bestowed robes of honour.[7]

Thus wrote the chronicler of the genealogy of the Malay kings.

Sri Tri Buana may have taken Singapore as a matter of right as a gift from Queen Sakidar Shah of Bintan, but basing his conclusion on Portuguese sources, Miksic is fairly sure he had to kill the incumbent lord of the island, Sangesinga, and then subjugate the peoples with the aid of the *orang laut*. Sri Tri Buana seems to have subsequently fought off an attack from Java/Majapahit (using garfish or swordfish as weapons according to the *Malay Annals*),[8] but had to run for his life when allies of Sangesinga arrived to avenge his death.[9] They drove him and his followers to Malacca where they prospered until the Portuguese pushed them back to the vicinity of Johor/Riau a century later. The *Malay Annals* assures us that the Malaccan kingdom was so rich and so renowned that:

> When news reached China of the greatness of the Raja of Malaka, the Raja of China sent envoys to Malaka: and as a complimentary gift to accompany his letter he sent needles, a whole shipload of them. And when the envoys reached Malaka, the king ordered the letter to be fetched from the ship with due ceremony and borne in procession. And when it had been brought into the palace it was received by the herald and given [by] him to the reader of the mosque, who read it out. It ran as follows: –
>
> 'This letter from His Majesty Raja of Heaven is sent to the Raja of Malaka. We hear that the Raja of Malaka is a great *raja* and we desire accordingly to be on terms of amity with the Raja of Malaka. Of a truth there are no *raja*s in this world greater than ourselves, and there is no one who knoweth the number of our subjects. We have asked for one needle from each house in our realm and those are the needles with which the ship we sent to Malaka is laden.'[10]

This account is something akin to the phenomenon that Clifford Geertz, writing of nineteenth-century Bali, called the 'theatre state', whereby the elite claimed the loyalty of its mass of followers by divine or divinely bestowed authority, but which has to be earned and retained by the use of theatrical ritual that provides the evidence of divine approval.[11] In this case the Malaccan authority was not precisely divine in origin, but was certainly presented as – literally – awesome.

'Politics' in the Malaccan century and the Johor centuries that followed it consisted of a constant shifting of alignments within and across the elite families, but always with an eye to ensuring the loyalty of the followers/subjects. There were always plenty of siblings, sons and uncles to feed a pattern of court intrigue that was often deadly for losers, but for the whole of this period the important followers were consistently those who gave the *raja* mastery of the sea, particularly the *orang laut.* The sea was the only significant source of wealth and power in Southeast Asia. Land was often impassable (totally impassable within most of the Malay Peninsula) and not important except incidentally as a source of trading goods and some food and manpower. Hence domains were not demarcated by geographical land borders, but by the personal reach and alliances of *raja*s based in port cities, whether seaports such as Malacca or river ports such as Ayutthaya. Wherever they were found, sea power and wealth formed a self-reinforcing 'virtuous circle', and the decline of one would be followed by the decline of the other. It is a pattern of power identified by O.W. Wolters as the 'Mandala' system of outgoing waves of personal power emanating from the *raja.*

Perhaps the concept most pertinent to this chapter's study of governance is Milner's idea of the *kerajaan* (pronounced with four distinct syllables: ke-raja-an), the most radical (or non-modern) element of which was the subject's intrinsic tie to the person of the ruler (*raja*) with complete disregard for considerations of place and geographical land boundaries. In an effort to translate a term that has no translation, Milner defined *kerajaan* simply as 'the condition of having a ruler'.[12] It was related to, but different from, the Malay concept of *negeri*, which is akin to a modern country, complete with being tied to a place, but without the modern concept of sovereignty. (A *negeri* was more likely to be the subordinate outpost of a *raja.*) A *raja* was a *raja* initially by simply being born into and then acting the part, but to properly be a *raja* one had to have followers. If those followers were clustered in a number of places, then each one might be a *negeri.* The *raja* could establish his court in any of these places or somewhere new without ever diminishing the status of the *kerajaan.* Hence the *raja* of Palembang could decamp to Temasik and then again to Malacca, and his descendants and successors could return to the area they started from a century later without any loss of legitimacy. You could tell a *raja* by his clothing and jewellery and his place in ceremony. Hence sumptuary laws played a vital role in establishing social hierarchies.

Without followers *raja*s were sad objects, and so they lamented when their subjects left them for another *raja* (which was not an uncommon occurrence), and if need be they actively sought new subjects from the disgruntled followers of other *raja*s. Most of what passed for 'administration' in this period was court ritual, royal aggrandisement and public building programmes, though it was also absolutely necessary to ensure that between working the land (agriculture) and working the sea (trade, piracy, war and fishing) the population was fed and comfortable. Neglect of any of these elements would (and often did) bring about the decline of a *negeri* and ultimately a *kerajaan*. Assisting him in the exercise of these duties the *raja* had a full suite of councillors and executives with titles such as Bendahara, Temenggong and Laksamana. Little detail is known about these roles, but Trocki tells us that the Bendahara was a de facto prime minister and law giver, the Temenggong was in charge of the city as a combined mayor, police chief and chief justice, and the Laksamana was effectively an admiral, with direct charge of the kingdom's naval forces.[13] Some of the officials were little more than the Sultan's cyphers, but many of them exercised a considerable degree of independent power in their own portfolios or in their own *negeri*. Indeed it was a Temenggong who signed a treaty with Raffles in January 1819, initially without consulting any sultan.

Borschberg also identities a title that is of particular significance in our Singapore story: Shahbandar, or Harbour Master. This is important in the history of Singapore because it is clear from two independent pieces of contemporary testimony by European travellers that, as late as the early decades of the seventeenth century, the island of Singapore had a Shahbandar/Harbour Master subject to the 'King of Johor'. Furthermore the Shahbandar had vessels at his disposal, was the leader of the *orang laut* (under the title Sri Raja Negara) and was a significant political figure in the Johor sultanate in his own right.[14] Indeed one of these witnesses names Singapore as 'Isle de la Sahbandaria Vieja' (Island of the Old Shahbandar's Compound) and identified it as home to a port city. This evidence confirms that Singapore was a major port two centuries after the Sultanate fled to Malacca and two centuries before Raffles landed to negotiate a treaty with the Temenggong.[15]

Following the logic of the *kerajaan*, it should not be completely surprising that the most decisive historical watershed in the Malay world was not the flight from Singapura in the 1390s, or even the flight from Malacca in 1511. The *Malay Annals* makes it clear that these were setbacks rather than decisive breaks, let alone catastrophes. The turning point in this version of Malay history came in 1699 when Sultan Mahmud Syah of Johor was murdered by some subjects who had been pushed beyond the limit of loyalty by his barbarism and cruelty: particularly his routine practice of taking their wives for himself, only to mistreat and then discard them. The murder of a sultan was said to be unprecedented and no account of the unworthiness or brutality of the victim could mitigate

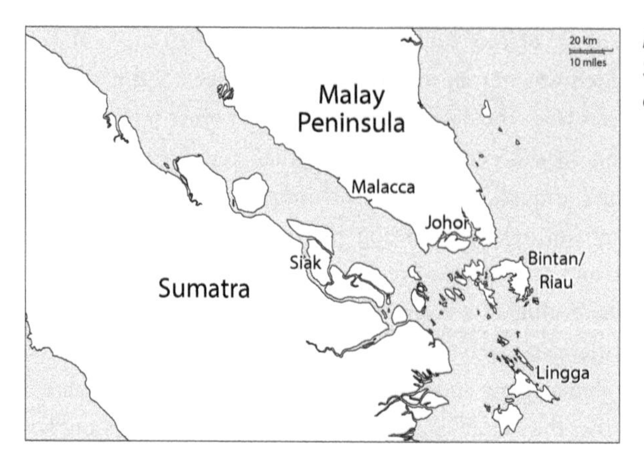

Map 4.1
Straits of Malacca, eighteenth century

the heinousness of the crime, nor restore the royal line to the throne. Despite one more failed attempt to restore the old dynasty to power by presenting a youth, Raja Kecil, as the son of Sultan Mahmud, born posthumously,[16] the regicide of 1699 proved to be the real end of the Malacca-Johor Sultanate. It was the end of an era, leaving the Malay legacy up and down the peninsula in the hands of rival royal houses that had previously been loosely in Johor's orbit.

A couple of decades into the eighteenth century a new power rose in Johor-Riau – the Bugis. As we saw in Chapter 3, they came from outside the immediate region. They were sea folk and it seemed logical that they would choose an island – Bintan – as their base, look to Lingga and other islands as their strongholds and build a Riau-Lingga Sultanate to replace the old Johor-Riau Sultanate (Map 4.1). The Bugis chiefs tried to cement their security both by a large-scale programme of intermarriage with local Malay royals and by imposing a treaty of amity upon Raja Kecil before sending him home to Siak (on Sumatra), where he founded a new, minor dynastic line. Despite these efforts, the Malays on the peninsula never accepted the Bugis, who quickly established themselves as not just the pre-eminent and wealthiest local Asian power but even as a serious challenger to Dutch interests. This proved to be a strategic mistake because the Dutch had hitherto been their allies, and by the 1730s Riau found itself utterly alone.

In 1756 the Bugis began engaging in intermittent open warfare against a Dutch–Malay alliance. In 1784 they laid siege to Malacca, only for the Dutch to push them back to their island strongholds in the south and defeat them utterly. The Dutch notionally reinstated the Malay royals to their former place of eminence in Riau, but in fact reduced the sultan to being a figurehead for a new Dutch Resident. The terms of the Dutch–Malay 'settlement' of Riau proved to be too humiliating for the newly installed Sultan Mahmud to bear and, instead of getting along with his Dutch masters, he organised a fresh invasion of Riau by a new group of outsiders, the Ilanun of Mindanao. These vicious pirates not only destroyed the Dutch garrison but also razed Riau to the ground – obviously acting far in excess of the Sultan's wishes. The next decade was disastrous for Riau: the Dutch reoccupied the island and the Sultan eventually negotiated his return to his nominal position as ruler, but the port's life as a commercial centre was dead forever. The island was left without much connection with either the European or Malay worlds, and its population of some thousands of Chinese gambier planters was left to look after itself.[17] Thus the stage was set at the end of the century for the entry of the British to fill the vacuum left by Johor-Riau.

BRITISH IN THE STRAITS

The British colonial presence in the Straits began in 1786 when the Sultan of Kedah signed over the island of Penang to the East India Company (EIC) in exchange for a defensive military alliance against Siam. The British had already been trading in the Straits for more than a century, briefly basing themselves in Kedah, where the Sultan allowed them to set up a factory at the end of the 1660s, but more recently using independent Riau as their trading hub.[18] In 1782, however, the Governor General of India, Warren Hastings, decided to establish a military base somewhere in the region after suffering an unexpected naval defeat at the hands of the French in the Bay of Bengal. He sought alliances with Aceh and Riau, but Aceh rebuffed British advances and the Dutch took Riau in 1784, before the British could act. It was with a certain amount of reluctance that Hastings finally agreed to risk involving the Company in local Malay politics by agreeing to help the Sultan of Kedah in exchange for the island of Penang. (Not that Britain ever did help the Sultan: having secured Penang, Britain abandoned the Sultan to his foes.)

Penang offered many advantages as a westward-facing port that could serve trade routes across the Bay of Bengal, but it was too far north (and there were too many Dutch bases to its south) for it to serve British interests in the South China Sea effectively. It was this shortcoming that Warren Hastings' successor, the Marquis of Hastings, set out to correct when he sent Raffles to establish a base at the southern end of the Straits at the end of 1818. Thus our narrative arrives at the birth of British Singapore on 30 January 1819, when an interim treaty was signed by Sir Stamford Raffles on behalf of the EIC and Temenggong Abdul Rahman, notionally on behalf of the Sultanate of Johor. As it happens, both claims to authority and representation made by the parties to this treaty were tenuous, if not tendentious. Unbeknownst to Raffles, the EIC had already overridden the instructions he had received from Hastings, and even Hastings was later to insist that Raffles had exceeded his authority by entering into this treaty.[19] For his part, Abdul Rahman held a position, Temenggong, which by this stage of history

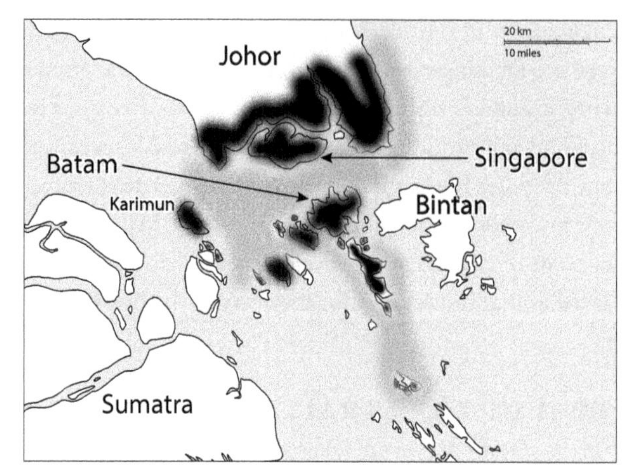

Map 4.2
The Temenggong's domain, by land and sea c.1818–23
Source: Trocki, *Prince of Pirates*, p. 60

had no duties or powers within the structure of the Riau sultanate. He was essentially a minor royal who had about 10,000 followers based in the rivers of Johor and many of the minor islands of the Riau Archipelago (Map 4.2), but who had fallen out of favour at court.[20] Raffles found him at Singapore because he had taken the island as his main base after decamping from Riau the year before.[21] Furthermore he signed the treaty as 'Ruler of Singapore, who governs the country in his own name and the name of Sree Sultan Hussein Mahummud Shah', but both he and Raffles were fully aware that his own claim as 'Ruler' was problematic in the eyes of both Riau and European law, and Hussain's claim to be sultan was not recognised by anyone except his own mother. 'Sultan' Hussain was indeed the eldest son of Sultan Mahmud of Riau-Lingga, who had died seven years earlier, but he had been passed over in favour of his brother, Sultan Abdul Rahman, who had since aligned himself with the Dutch. On 6 February Hussain fulfilled his role in Singapore by signing the final version of the treaty as 'His Highness the Sultan Hussain Mahomed Shah Sultan of Johore', thus accepting British recognition of his sovereignty over Singapore and Johor while providing recognition of the more modest British claims to the island. Considering that the British had earlier recognised the legitimacy of his brother's title of Sultan and implicitly of his claim over Singapore and Johor – and that the Dutch still recognised all these claims – it was a risky step on Raffles' part, and he knew it. Both Calcutta and London came close to disowning Raffles' claim to Singapore even after the deed was done, and the Dutch in Malacca came equally close to imposing a military solution – but in the end no party was quite willing to overturn the new status quo. Malacca hesitated just long enough for Calcutta to decide that they wanted to keep the island and for Hastings to order that the island be reinforced from Penang.

Trocki tells us that the Treaty of Singapore gave the three parties – the Temenggong, the Sultan and the EIC – joint and equal sovereignty over the island.[22] This description is accurate, but it tends to elevate an arrangement that was primarily commercial: the elements with immediate practical effect were the allocation of riverfront land to the EIC and the payment of large pensions by the EIC to the two Malay dignitaries ($3,000 per annum to the Temenggong and $5,000 per annum to the Sultan). In a neat inversion of the promises exchanged between the EIC and Sultan of Kedah, the Temenggong and the Sultan also promised to defend the island in the event of attack – but luckily this commitment was never put to the test.

Of less immediate practical effect was the nominal creation of a new state on the peninsula, independent of Riau and recognised by the British. Little noticed by most historians, but featured in John Bastin's history, is the fact that the interim treaty of 30 January actually referred to 'the Government of Singapore-Johore', something that had not hitherto been known to exist.[23] This new 'state' had ill-defined boundaries but it most certainly included Singapore and encompassed the southern end of the Malay Peninsula, stopping vaguely (and comfortably) short of Dutch interests in Malacca. Over the next half-century or so a distorted but tangible version of this notional state would become a reality, developing in a constant, intimate embrace between the island and the southern tip of the peninsula. The development of Johor is a vital strand of the story without which Singapore's history is not complete. It was studied in intense detail by Trocki in *Prince of Pirates*, but has been ignored in most histories of Singapore – even in the more recent revisionist histories that have consciously and deliberately diverged from the quasi-official national narrative. Such is the fixation on the 'national' element of the national history that even though my treatment of this relationship is basically derivative – synthesising scholarship that was published years, and even decades ago – its inclusion is likely to be questioned and dismissed by many who prefer to stop Singapore's history at the Strait of Johor.

Yet the development of Johor is still a few years in the future at this stage of our narrative. The most immediate impact of the treaties of January and February 1819 was more modest: the EIC gained its factory in the mouth of the Straits of Malacca, which was as much as it ever wanted – maybe more than it wanted. Raffles' tangible rewards were even more modest. He continued as Lieutenant Governor of Bencoolen and simply had the management of Singapore added to his responsibilities. He asked Lord Hastings for Penang as well, but this was denied him.[24] His powers in Singapore provided enough patronage to favour the financial interests of his brother-in-law, Captain William Flint, and to humiliate his personal rivals (most notably his former friend and ally, William Farquhar), but these were parsimonious rewards for what he considered to be his crowning achievement, akin to the arrival of his first-born.[25]

ANGLO-MALAY SINGAPORE, 1819–1824

The first five years of Singapore's post-Riau life was as an Anglo-Malay consortium. The EIC had control of the port and had permission to establish a factory along the north shore of a two-mile stretch of river, with the right to build within canon shot of the bank. Even within these limits, the British fiat was not absolute. The Temenggong claimed half the customs duties from the port, one-third of the proceeds of the opium, gambling and liquor monopolies, was recognised as the owner of all the land on the island, and was the formal source of all laws, such as they were.[26] On top of this he continued to receive 'gifts' directly from Asian traders passing through Singapore Strait (a privilege enforced by the thousands of his traditional followers who had flocked to the island after his deal with the British, and who generally spent their ample spare time getting into fights). The authority of the EIC, in the form of the Resident, Colonel William Farquhar, struggled to establish itself, even within canon shot of the river. The population grew quickly. Chinese from Riau and other parts, Indians and British traders from the subcontinent, Malays from both the offshore islands and the peninsula, and natives of what is now Indonesia made the island their home, all attracted by the rise of a rejuvenated local port offering new opportunities. Some newcomers were farmers or miners, but most in the early days were traders. The presence of British soldiers and sailors offered a welcome level of security – not an unimportant consideration on those lawless waters. The harbour was constantly filled with Asian trading craft and the population grew exponentially.[27] The Temenggong was delighted with this state of affairs. As Trocki tells us:

> to the Malays, [Singapore] was simply one more variation on a very old theme. Practically every Malay state known to history had been based on a trading city. In the maritime world, the entrepôt was the major political structure. If a ruler sought power, his aim was to control the port. The Malay chiefs at Singapore were fully aware of the significance of the port, and the treaties reflect the demands they must have made on the Europeans. The trading city had always been the focal point for the political forces of the Malay world. The Malay chiefs may not have foreseen the extent of Singapore's success, but they must have known that the city would soon dominate the region. From the beginning, it was their intention to have a share in its power.[28]

The British colonial authorities and British traders were also delighted with the commercial progress and the population growth, but not so enamoured of the continuing power of the Malay authorities – and no one was less happy than Raffles. Communication between Singapore and Bencoolen was problematic at all times, and there were months at a time when Farquhar was operating without advice or instructions. When Raffles did turn up he made it clear that he was displeased with the direction of the entire project. During his short stays he always tried to put the colony back on his intended course. Raffles' presence routinely caused Farquhar no end of problems; never less so than in 1823 when Farquhar was attacked and seriously wounded by a Malay, apparently driven to run amok by Raffles' newly declared ban on carrying weapons in the settlement. Raffles helped matters along by dragging the body of the perpetrator around the settlement after his execution and then leaving it hanging on a scaffold for three days. Suspicion that the incident might have been part of a power play by the Temenggong resulted in a direct military response involving at least 300 Company soldiers (mostly Indians) and 12 cannon, all of which pointlessly surrounded the Temenggong's empty house. For their part the Malays turned the attacker's eventual burial place into a shrine and a place of pilgrimage. Raffles would have loved to dispense with the Malays altogether, but he still needed them for the legal cover they provided against continuing Dutch protests at the British occupation. Despite his frustration, the most Raffles could manage was to buy off the Temenggong and the Sultan with yet more money. And so in a new agreement signed on 7 June 1823 the pair surrendered their control over the island and 'islands immediately adjacent' (leaving just their personal residencies in Malay hands), their share of port duties, their share of the tax farm revenues and their right to receive gifts from Chinese and native traders – all in exchange for their pensions being more than trebled.[29]

Questions of sovereignty and legality were left uncomfortably ambiguous but, as it happens, developments in London were moving towards a resolution of these problems. On 17 March 1824 the Kingdom of the Netherlands and the United Kingdom of Great Britain and Ireland signed the Anglo–Dutch Treaty (otherwise known as the Treaty of London). This treaty was intended to defuse Anglo–Dutch rivalry by dividing the Malay world between London and Amsterdam. Unfortunately for the Temenggong, the new border cut him off from his southern island territories, putting Bintan and everything east, west and south of it in Dutch hands. He was still master of his possessions on mainland Johor, but even these were formally declared to be part of the British sphere, along with the rest of the Malay Peninsula (Map 4.3). The Anglo–Dutch Treaty of 1824 was one of those turning points in history when cause and effect are clear and precise: following the end of the Napoleonic Wars in Europe, the major colonial powers decided to stop fighting each other in Asia and instead agreed to share in the exploitation of Asians. The Dutch gave up their now-faded hopes of retaining their position as the dominant European power in Asia, and in return for letting the UK turn the West Pacific and the Indian Ocean into a pair of British lakes, the Netherlands was given the undisputed right to impose its sovereignty anywhere in the Indonesian archipelago except part of Borneo. As it happens, this deal did not involve such a great sacrifice for Amsterdam because the Dutch East India Company (VOC) had declared bankruptcy in 1799 after losing most of its trading monopolies in its disputes with the British. The Dutch trading empire had

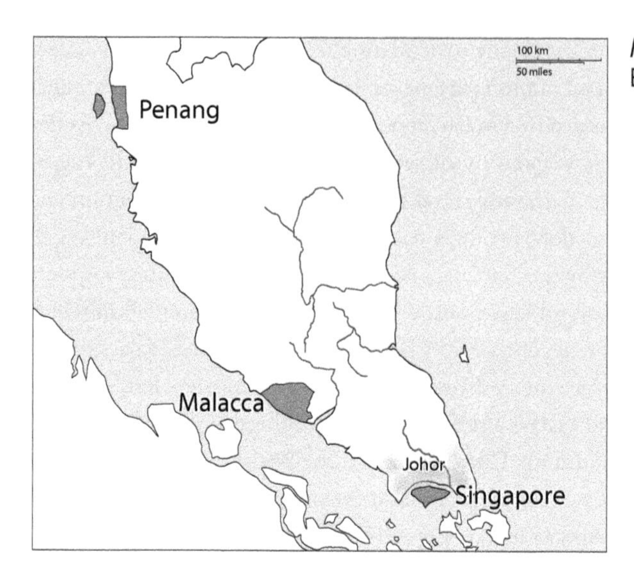

Map 4.3
British Malaya, 1824

already been winding down in the Straits of Malacca for half a century and, when the Dutch state took over the VOC holdings and was confirmed as ruler of Java and Sumatra by the Treaty, it simply completed the switch of Dutch imperial interests from seaborne trade to the land-hungry pursuits of industrial-scale agriculture and primary production.[30]

Britain would eventually follow the Dutch down the agricultural and mining path (and had already made a serious start with industrial-scale opium production in India),[31] but at this stage it was still a rising trading power, and so the Anglo–Dutch division of Asia was win–win – at least for the Europeans. For the Temenggong it was the end of his aspirations. The British now had a free hand to impose a Treaty of Friendship and Alliance on him, which he signed in August 1824. Under this treaty, the EIC paid the Temenggong and the Sultan even more money in exchange for formal sovereignty over Singapore and all islands within a 16 kilometre (10 mile) radius. Crucially the pair of Malay royals gave up all rights to have any overseas dealings. They were left with full sovereignty over their own (huge) residencies and the Temenggong was left with his vaguely defined territories on the mainland. This treaty marked the end of the brief Anglo-Malay period on the island.

BRITISH SINGAPORE; ASIAN SINGAPORE

Raffles found it easier to pension off the wounded Farquhar than he did the Temenggong. One of his final acts before his own retirement on 9 July 1823 was to appoint a former associate from his days in Java, Dr John Crawfurd, to replace Farquhar as Resident. Crawfurd's first acts were mostly concerned with unravelling the Raffles–Farquhar administration's ad hoc arrangements, which were of doubtful legality, and to dismantle their semi-corrupt patronage networks. Raffles was furious, but could do nothing about it. Indeed he should have been pleased on balance because Crawfurd also set about implementing much of Raffles' vision for Singapore, and doing so more effectively than Raffles ever could have managed himself. He arrived to office in fortuitous circumstances. The Malay, Dutch and sovereignty 'problems' that had plagued Farquhar's administration were well on their way to resolution; Raffles' retirement meant a second irritant was gone; and the Company took the opportunity of the change of personnel to cut Bencoolen out of the lines of communication and authority between Singapore and Calcutta. Singapore became an Indian Presidency, and as such it was institutionally equal to Penang in the eyes of the EIC and for the first time properly 'British'.[32]

Singapore lasted a remarkably short time as a stand-alone Indian Presidency. The 1824 Treaty of London not only ended Dutch claims to Singapore and gave the new Crawfurd administration the legal certainty it needed, but it also handed Malacca over to Britain. Malacca was already unprofitable by this stage, having suffered badly from Penang- and Singapore-based competition, so the EIC had no burning desire to own it, but it was theirs regardless. With Penang (well to Malacca's north) servicing traders coming in from the west and Singapore (to Malacca's south) now picking up the trade coming in from the east, Malacca was the Cinderella of the Straits.[33] Furthermore the Company had no interest in running three separate administrations, so in 1826 it amalgamated them into a single Indian Presidency called the Straits Settlements, with the specific intention of trying to get them to cover their costs.[34] In 1858 the British government wound up the EIC following the Indian Mutiny of the previous year and the Straits Settlements was transferred to Colonial Office rule (though still via Calcutta). Nine years later, in 1867, the Straits Settlements finally secured its independence from Calcutta, and became a Crown Colony administered directly from London. This change in the legal and administrative status slightly increased the indirect influence that the European community (and eventually the Asian communities) were able to exercise through an appointed Legislative Council. Its recommendations were not, however, binding on the Governor and it had no input into the composition of the Executive Council, so the administrative status quo was left basically untouched.

The Governor of the Straits Settlements based himself in Singapore from 1829 onwards, but Penang was the mother colony and for the time being remained both the major centre and the seat of government. Government was formally shifted to Singapore only in the late 1830s, but it was not a clean break, and the judiciary continued to be based in Penang until 1856.[35] The two former colonies never grew together as anything more than an administrative unit. The animosity that Penang's traders and its governor displayed towards Singapore in 1819 (see Chapter 3) never fully dissipated, and levels of economic co-operation, cross-investment and even social intercourse were much more restricted than one might reasonably expect of sister settlements. Meanwhile Malacca continued to wither: its river was left to silt up and the interior beyond the city limits remained basically unknown to Europeans.[36] Johor was closer to Singapore than either Malacca or Penang in every sense except that of formal administrative and sovereign ties. Johor was not a British colony, but its recognised sovereign ruler, the Temenggong, resided in Singapore on land over which he, and not the EIC, had sovereignty. He was a dependant of the EIC, and – as we will see later in this chapter – from 1840s ran Johor as a business from Singapore. Furthermore, the Temenggong was not the only one running a business in Johor from Singapore, for Trocki has shown that the economic ties between Johor and Singapore extended to the Chinese *towkays* (a Hokkien word meaning rich and powerful businessmen). In the 1820s and 1830s these economic ties were nascent, and if they had developed no further we would not be able to take them seriously, but with the benefit of hindsight we can recognise the emerging pattern.

We thus see two Singapores beginning to grow in the late 1820s. First there was a British Singapore that was tied to Malacca and Penang and which looked primarily west to Calcutta and London. It also looked east, but only for markets and trade. As late as 1860 there were only 466 people making up 'British Singapore', but they controlled the 60 or so European businesses in the colony, all arms of formal government and all the connections to Europe. They also contributed all of the Western engineering skills and machinery that were building Singapore's nascent industries, and would later in the century achieve what had never before been attempted – piercing and taming the jungles of the Malay peninsula.[37] This is the Singapore that dominates the purer versions of the Singapore Story.

Then there was an Asian Singapore that was much more heterogeneous and hundreds of times larger. Its members looked variously to Johor, the Malay Peninsula, southern China, southern India, the Dutch Indies (Indonesia), and even the region that today we call the Middle East. This Singapore has been accepted only recently and tentatively into the national narrative, but its story is now a mainstream element of Singapore's broader historiography. In subsequent chapters we will explore economic and social aspects of these two Singapores. For the moment, however, our focus is on governance, so it is sufficient to note the 'soft' inclusion of Johor in Map 4.3, and return our focus to British Singapore, where formal power lay for the next 118 years. It is tempting to think that Asian Singapore's main role was to pay for British administration through the taxes on its vices and purchases but, as we see below, there was more to it than this. British Singapore needed and often obtained the active co-operation of Asian Singapore in its administration of the Straits Settlements and Johor. So while the formal politics and administration of the island from 1823 until the Japanese Occupation looks like a very simple, British affair, in fact the real politics was more of an untidy Anglo-Asian regime.

ADMINISTRATION ON A SHOESTRING

The administration of Singapore was intended to run on minimal costs. Raffles had promised Hastings that it would not be a drain on the Company, but this was easier said than done. In 1823 the port stopped collecting duties in deference to Raffles' almost religious passion to run a free port, and there was also no income tax. Initially (until 1823) land could not be sold because it was unambiguously owned by the Temenggong – and soon after most of the profitable use of land by Singapore's entrepreneurs took place in Johor, which remained in the Temenggong's hands even after the British took full possession of Singapore.[38] Yet magistrates, civil servants, soldiers, bridges, roads and buildings all cost money – as do monthly payments to retired Malay aristocrats and their descendants. Farquhar's short-term solution to his financial problems was the exploitation of government monopolies, and this improvisation proved so successful that it was perpetuated as the long-term revenue source for the colony, lasting beyond the opening of the twentieth century.

For the most part, the monopolies were not taxed through any device as sophisticated as a sales tax on individual sales, or even on government ownership of products, but by auctioning monopolies to the highest bidder. The monopolies were called 'tax farms' or 'revenue farms' and the farmers' annual and monthly payments to the government were called 'rent'. This device was an effective means of extracting income from Singapore's Asian residents, who made up the bulk of the population. The farms 'taxed' all the vices, plus more: opium, prostitution, gambling, alcohol, betel nut, pawnbroking, pork, and local markets.[39] By far the most important of the tax farms was the opium monopoly. A river of opium had been flowing from the north and west of India past Singapore's shores on its way to China and other parts of Southeast Asia for decades before Raffles 'founded' Singapore. After 1819, the Singapore River replaced Riau as the point of local and regional disbursement. In all the years from 1820 until at least 1882, opium was the biggest single item in the colonial government's revenue stream. In nine of those 63 years it contributed more to government income than did every other source of revenue put together, and in another 19 of those years it contributed more than 45% of revenue. The government's reliance on opium continued into the twentieth century, with surges and dips in government revenues following faithfully the surges and dips in opium revenues right up to the end of the farm system in 1910.[40]

The Straits Settlements were run by a Governor who answered initially to the Governor General of India in Calcutta. The Governor's main task was not so much to run the colony, as to contribute to reducing the EIC's running deficits (which amounted to £3 million in 1825/6) by cutting costs and increasing revenue.[41] By the end of the 1820s a financial crisis in India and the forthcoming renegotiation of the EIC Charter in 1833 were turning the attention of the EIC's directors in London to matters of cost and profitability to an unusual degree. In 1830, as part of an effort to reduce expenditure, they downgraded the status of the Settlements from a Presidency to a Residency (nothing more than an administrative unit) attached to the Presidency of Bengal. As part of this move, they more than halved the civil service establishment from 19 'covenanted' officials (i.e. fully trained, white career officials, recruited as young men in London) to eight. They also abolished the key positions of Governor and Recorder and replaced them with a Resident based in Singapore and a Deputy Resident in each of Penang and Malacca. One immediate, if indirect effect of the 1830 settlement was that Robert Fullerton – formerly Governor, now Resident – became convinced that the legal basis of the local courts had been negated, so he closed them, thus pushing the colony into relative chaos until his ruling was overturned in April 1832. At that point they also restored the titles, though not the full powers, of Governor and Resident.[42] The cuts of 1830 contributed to the salvation of the Company, but it was a bitter-sweet victory. On the one hand, the Company's charter was revised and renewed, so it could (and indeed was obliged to) keep running the Settlements. On the other hand, the revised charter withdrew the Company's monopoly of the China trade. Since the EIC's only interest in the Settlements was to service the China trade, this left the Company in the uncomfortable position of being obliged to maintain a set of settlements in the Straits of Malacca that had never paid their way in any case, and now no longer served any clear purpose.

The changes of 1830 had already identified the Settlements as a backwater of the British Empire, but the loss of the Settlements' *raison d'être* set it on a seemingly irrevocable road to decay. After 1830 no ambitious company official ever wanted to be posted to the Straits, leaving the field to military officers and local civil servants engaged in a slow climb through the ranks, whereas the Settlements and Penang had previously attracted the best and most ambitious administrators. The supposedly plum position of Governor was particularly fraught because after 1832 the Recorders (who, among other roles, acted as judges) were better paid and more powerful than the Governors. They were also usually better educated, better qualified, and had better connections both locally and within the Company and were more difficult to remove from office.[43]

With the colony's precarious finances and parsimonious human resource practices, the government of the Settlements was not able to do very much. The colony's progress and success rested primarily on the efforts of the traders, entrepreneurs and workers – Asians and Europeans – who worked independently to make their fortunes. The main task of the colonial authorities was to stop piracy because it was bad for business. Beyond that basic task, the British built some infrastructure and provided a modicum of judicial certainty, but they were barely aware of or interested in the lives and trades of most of their residents, except those businesses over which the state had a monopoly.

Matters of public hygiene and health preoccupied the Europeans disproportionately because of their own vulnerability to vector- and water-borne disease,[44] and every now and again they would decide it was necessary to do something to regain some level of control of public and private space that had been effectively ceded to locals.[45] Security issues (crime and violence) sometimes became important too, but the Asian colonists lived and worked around the feet of an administration that was not much interested in them. For the most part the various Asian communities looked after their own affairs, utilising their own community leaders to act as their interface with the government. This practice was encouraged by the authorities except when it impinged on either commerce or public safety. Thus residential and vocational enclaves based on racial, religious and language identities developed into informal, and even formal, units of self-government.

It would be misleading to suggest that the British arrived at this form of governance as a conscious plan for avoiding responsibility. It would be fairer to say that they reflexively followed their usual colonial practice of minimising their interference in local communities, which led them to accept most of the pre-existing social structures. And despite the myth that Raffles started Singapore from almost nothing – 'a sleepy fishing village' is a common descriptor – these communal forms of self-government were already in place among the local Asian communities that migrated to Singapore. Trocki tells us that the thousands of Chinese who came from Riau brought with them their existing business and settlement structures, called *kongsi*. A *kongsi* was very much like a shareholder company, but it also provided social support and imposed local social discipline. The *kongsi* came to provide the foundations of the Chinese secret societies known as triads. Likewise, the Chinese from Malacca and Penang brought with them their communal power structures built around wealth, debt, *guanxi* (mutual-obligation networks) and gangster-like enforcers. They also arrived with a system of dealing with Europeans through a single strongman representing each community – a 'Kapitan China' – though this system lasted only a few years (until 1826) before the colonial authorities turned to Singapore's secret society leaders to act as their facilitators. The British worked through these conduits until 1890, by which time the secret societies had become so routinely violent that the British decided that they had to be extinguished.[46]

For their part, the Malays also had traditional structures, but the truth is that after 1823 their structures of governance seemed to be limping towards extinction. We have already seen that Temenggong Abdul Rahman had his followers, but after his death in 1825 his heir, Daing Ibrahim (Figure 4.1), and Sultan Hussain struggled to retain their loyalty, without which the Malay polity was basically dead. Yet the Temenggong's men were still living on the Temenggong's large estate in Singapore and they still took regularly to the sea. It was an indication of their importance that in 1835 Governor Samuel Bonham attributed a recent rise in the level of piracy to the Temenggong's death

Figure 4.1 Temenggong Daing Ibrahim

and Daing Ibrahim's failure to restrain his followers from resuming their traditional livelihood.[47] His solution, implemented a year later, was to increase Ibrahim's fortunes, authority and status in exchange for his active co-operation in suppressing piracy, that is, restraining his own followers.

With minimal aid coming from Calcutta, co-opting the Temenggong was probably Bonham's only reasonable course of action. It was no instant solution, but it worked eventually. The move made Ibrahim a de facto partner in government, increased his status with the regional Malay and Bugis networks, and set him on the first steps towards the establishment of Johor as an extension of Asian Singapore.[48] The deal also overshadowed Sultan Hussain and his impoverished death in 1835 brought the Johor 'Sultanate' to an end, leaving the Temenggong as the only local Malay ruler.[49] A few years later the Temenggong extended his advantage by opening a new and highly profitable business venture in Johor that occupied and enriched his people. This venture started with just one commodity – gutta-percha, which was needed to coat submarine telegraph cables – but by the late 1840s he had built a new commercial kingdom in Johor. Unlike earlier Malay trading empires it was based primarily on agricultural plantations, jungle products such as rattan and gutta-percha, pepper, gambier, mining and tax farms. In direct contrast to the British administrators in Singapore, the Malay administrators of Johor were intimately aware of the life and society of their Asian subjects/residents, most of whom were Chinese who had arrived via the Port of Singapore. The Temenggong did not share the Europeans' exquisitely modern penchant for taking a census every few years, but his wealth depended on his control of land: on everything that was grown on it and dug up from it; on everyone who lived or worked on it; and on everything that was bought, sold, imported and exported to, from and on it. So he made sure he knew what was going on in every part of his growing kingdom. His administrative units were the many rivers and capillary-like inlets that insinuated themselves throughout the coast-lands: each plantation and each business was centred on one of these and each had a Chinese headman – a *kangchu* – who was 'lord of the river' or 'lord of the port'. He was appointed by the Chinese owners of a tax farm (usually based in Singapore or perhaps Penang) and immediately answerable to them. Through this system, the tax farmer, together with the Temenggong, effectively owned the population of Johor. The *kangchu* system was an ancient variation of the *kongsi*/triad/Kapitan systems and was brutally effective in protecting the Temenggong's commercial interests thanks to two key facts: all trade passed through Singapore; and the most likely smugglers were already in the direct service of the Temenggong, working as his enforcers.[50]

The *kangchu* system in British Singapore-Johor-Penang rested on the foundation of the tax farm, creating a neat symbiosis between tax farms that grew nothing (but sold both the necessities and the vices that made life tolerable) and agricultural farms that, among other businesses, grew gambier and pepper. The Chinese labourers working and living on the farms served as both the exploited workers and the exploited consumers in this political economy. They also formed bodies of men who needed to be controlled and the revenue farmers thus became informal but absolutely vital partners with the Temenggong and the British colonial authorities in the governance of Johor-Singapore at a time when neither had much capacity to exercise direct sovereignty in Singapore, let alone in Johor. The concessions at the heart of the *kangchu* units became the primary keys to wealth and power for ambitious Chinese, and it became more and more expensive to win the concessions. As the price of concessions increased, so did the level of financial resources required to win at auction, along with the ruthlessness that winners and losers were willing to exercise. Control of the tax farms fell fairly naturally into the hands of elements comfortable with violent solutions and a willingness to skirt what passed for the law: Chinese secret societies or triad gangs. What is perhaps more surprising is the easy willingness of the colonial authorities to use the secret societies as their agents to control the Chinese population, though on reflection this complacency was just the onshore variation of British willingness to use the Temenggong's 'pirates' as government enforcers at sea.

The system was not without its problems. Much of the 'secret society violence' that bedevilled Singapore from the 1840s to the 1860s should be seen primarily as power struggles between rival farming syndicates as winners enforced their monopolies and losers smuggled to survive. These were popularly and officially regarded as law and order matters, but they were intertwined with matters of governance more directly than this label suggests: they were driven in large part by the colonial government's need to maintain a steady and increasing income stream in a colony that did not impose either excise duties or income taxes. The government was almost wholly dependent on revenue farms for its income throughout the whole of this period, and the secret society 'riots' were an outcome of this system. As the revenue farm and *kangchu* system was being installed in Johor in the 1840s the government profited not just from the expansion of the system but also from newly competitive auctions, thanks to wealthy outsiders joining the auctions and driving up prices. After the emergence of rival syndicates bidding for revenue farming licences in the early 1840s, secret societies became one of the vehicles through which rivals fought to make and protect their fortunes. Secret societies were substantially language-based, sometimes with an element of class solidarity thrown in, and had little regard for sovereign borders; their geographic spread stretched from Galang Island (south of Bintan) through Singapore and north to Johor and Penang. After that initial fillip in the 1840s the government routinely engaged in surreptitious manipulation of the auction system to force up the price of the licences, including imposing price hikes for the retail price of opium. This not only increased the cost of winning a licence and running a farm, but just as significantly it raised the cost of losing a licence, since most of the overheads – including maintaining the secret societies – were effectively fixed. Turf wars, shifting 'gangland' alliances and resort to smuggling thus became almost inevitable strategies, both to keep one's own business going and to undermine a rival.[51]

Singapore was the key to the whole system: Johor's exports and opium imports passed through the Port of Singapore; and the Temenggong continued to manage his empire from Singapore working hand-in-glove with the Chinese *towkay*s who provided much of the capital and who supplied, organised and disciplined the Chinese workforce. All of the Johor managers and entrepreneurs (*kongsi* stakeholders; triads; *towkay*s; and some Malays) were based in Singapore, and they usually ran their Johor businesses as an extension of their Singapore businesses. Yet this entire operation was invisible to the British. Not that they did not know it was there; this they understood very well. But it was invisible in the sense that they had even less idea of what was happening on the other side of the Strait of Johor than they had about the affairs of Asian Singapore.

The British are often accused of ruling heterogeneous colonial societies through a 'divide and conquer' strategy – and Raffles' master plan for dividing the city of Singapore into distinct ethnic residential zones provides evidence of such an approach. There is certainly some truth in this accusation, but it would be fairer to say that the British followed a line of least resistance in the colonies whenever their own core business and the welfare of Europeans were not at stake. It was the local communities themselves that reflexively turned inwards in pursuit of work, governance, security and social intercourse. Yet whatever judgement one cares to make about responsibility, the result laid the groundwork for the development of a socially fragmented 'plural society' where, as Furnivall and others have told us, people lived, worked and socialised alongside members of their own community, having few bonds with 'outsiders', including the state.[52] It also laid the groundwork for the highly racialised society that is modern Singapore today. In the twenty-first century, Singaporeans are no longer routinely sequestered into designated occupations or housing estates according to their race, but the government's management of Singaporeans' lives through the prism of race (and religion and language) continues openly, utilising racial and other communal designations that are direct lineal descendants of those that operated in the middle of the nineteenth century.

Singapore's formal politics during this period was basically non-existent. There was a free press serving the Europeans, but there was neither a representative assembly nor a formal channel for introducing initiatives or objections to government beyond petitions, which were easily ignored.[53] Furthermore, unless one had good personal or financial connections in London, there was little point in trying to appeal over the head of the governor because the Settlements barely featured in the consciousness of London or Calcutta. When everything was going well in the colony these limitations were accepted grudgingly, but between economic downturns, unpopular and ineffectual governors, rising secret society violence, and threats of tariffs emanating from London, such complacency became rarer as the decades rolled on. The first call for some level of direct popular representation in an official assembly was rebuffed by Calcutta in 1846. This episode provoked an escalation in the anti-Calcutta mood of the mercantile community, which quickly morphed into a movement calling for the transfer of the Straits Settlements from Calcutta to London. Two men led the charge. At the Singapore end was W.H. Read, a Straits merchant. The London end was anchored by John Crawfurd, Singapore's second Resident, long since retired and by then a strong critic of both the EIC and the Colonial Office. The grievances that kept the discontent alive were typical middle-class issues – law and order (secret society violence); taxes (the threat of tariffs); and the facilitation of commerce. Turnbull suggests that the critical factor in the success of the Transfer Movement, as it came to be known, was quicker and more reliable travel and mail between the Straits and London on the early generation of steam ships. This new technology facilitated the creation of a web of direct links between the colony's merchants and London that brought the affairs and woes of the Straits Settlements to the attention of Westminster in a way that Crawfurd had never been able to do, leading directly to the transfer of the Straits Settlements to the Colonial Office in 1867.[54]

The role of improved communications in the lead-up to Transfer was the beginning of a new pattern that transformed life in the colony. Steam technology continued to improve over the next few decades, reducing travel times and costs drastically. Transfer was also followed in short order by the opening of the Suez Canal in 1869 (which shaved even more time off a journey to London) and the laying of the first submarine telecommunications cable between London and Singapore in 1871 (which reduced communication time to a few hours and eventually a few minutes). These technological breakthroughs brought Singapore into daily contact with the city that was at the centre of global commerce.[55] By 1882 the Singapore telegraph office was handling around 10,000 messages a day, sent to and from all the major centres of the Anglophone world.[56] The submarine cable almost inadvertently ushered in a new age of communication, business and governance in Singapore and the Straits Settlements: for the first time the affairs of government and the bureaucracy started impinging upon the daily lives of ordinary residents, both Asian and European, and after 1869 there was no respite from supervision from London. One European merchant even complained that since the cable was laid, 'we might as well live in London as here; steam and telegraph bring us daily into communication with the old world. Our Sundays are not our own. By night and by day we are at work.'[57] And it was not only the telegraph that was tapping away; even the telephone was ringing. A single line was laid in 1879 between the port and the commercial centre, and by 1894 the European and business communities were well serviced by 256 telephone lines.[58]

As I indicated in the opening pages of this chapter, 1867 marked the quiet beginning of a decades-long process of modernisation in which government and its administrative agents gradually began intruding themselves into the daily lives of the great mass of ordinary residents, traders and visitors to the island. Transfer itself was not the key – and indeed it might even be considered a consequence rather than a cause. Having been launched in symbiosis with Transfer, modernisation was a creeping prospect rather than a reality, even as late as the 1880s. As Chapter 5 will show, it was not until around the end of the century that modernisation could be considered complete.

5

Governance in Modern Singapore, 1867–1965

For centuries, including the first half-century or more after Raffles' landing in Singapore, most Asian residents of the Straits had been able to live their lives without much direct reference to Europeans and their various colonial administrations. Turnbull put it neatly with specific reference to Singapore as late as the second half of the nineteenth century:

> When the India Office gave up Singapore in 1867, its government scarcely impinged on the life of the Asian population. An official commission reported in 1875, 'We believe that the vast majority of Chinamen who come to work in these Settlements return to their country not knowing clearly whether there is a government in them or not.'[1]

By century's end such a statement would have been false. By 1941 it would have been preposterous. The shift from a state of passive, almost absent government to something more intrusive began imperceptibly with the transfer of the Straits Settlements from the India Office to the Colonial Office. From this point – 1867, not 1819 – we can start looking at politics and governance in Singapore through something akin to modern eyes, with the full flowering of modern governance and modern society arriving not much before the turn of the century.

GOVERNING ASIAN SINGAPORE

The transformation of the Straits Settlements into a Crown Colony administered from London made no immediate difference to most Asian Singaporeans, who were able to continue in blissful ignorance of the existence of European government for at least another decade. If, however, we look at the situation two decades after Transfer, we find much of Singapore's Chinese population engaged forcefully and fully with government. In 1888 they were demonstrating in Chinatown against government efforts to clear them out of their ad hoc places of business (the verandas or 'five-foot ways' in front of the shop houses in which they lived and/or worked). The 'Veranda Riots', as they became known, marked the beginning of serious levels of government intrusion in the lives of Asian Singapore. A few years later, an entire field of private Chinese enterprise – the collection and sale of night soil – was first taken over by the state and then centralised into a new, modern sewerage system connected to domestic water closets.[2] By this stage, the government was also issuing directives to its Asian subjects on the collection and disposal of domestic garbage. By 1910 the Municipal Board was tearing down the back half of people's homes in Chinatown to create lane-ways at the rear.[3] The government's motivations for engaging in these activities centred ostensibly on concerns about the public commons, with public health, public safety and law and order being the most prominent. Of these, health and safety received the most attention in official statements, but in fact the urban reconstruction and regulation was substantially an exercise in snatching control of the city from the secret societies that had run much of it for decades. As we saw in Chapter 4, secret societies and their wealthy bosses had governed the Chinese communities on behalf of the colonial authorities throughout most of the nineteenth century, stepping into the role as unofficial partners of the colonial government at a time when the latter had little capacity of its own. It was a form of indirect British rule that had served both European and Asian elites well. The secret societies' governing role had grown from their original function as enforcers for the headmen who ran the revenue farms and the codependent gambier and pepper farms. The British sold localised monopolies of opium and other products and services to wealthy *towkays* and consortiums of Chinese investors on the clear understanding that, in return for the immense profits that came with the farms, they would keep 'their people' under control. In their dealings with colonial authorities the early revenue farmers were often represented by English-speaking Chinese gentlemen who wore western suits and whose ancestors had been living and working with Europeans in other parts of Southeast Asia for generations. They were known collectively as *baba* or *peranakan* Chinese and they were fully comfortable working for and with the British, and the British trusted them to understand the limitations of their roles as junior partners of the colonial establishment.[4] The real power, however, lay with tougher, wealthier Chinese who had little affinity with and less respect for the British and their laws. The egalitarian spirit of communal solidarity that imbued the early *kongsi* had also long since been bought out by new money.

By the time the Colonial Office took over management of the Straits Settlements, a new generation of Chinese leaders was running revenue farms and the *kongsi* had been transformed into secret societies. Their control of the workers was effective, if rather ruthless, and they were able to ensure that neither gambier and pepper productivity nor the government's monopolies were disrupted, which was the main concern of the colonial authorities. Violence was the ultimate sanction in the *towkays*' power relationships, but they had many more routine instruments of control. They also had many more workers in their control than just their direct employees. The secret society-cum-revenue farm bosses supplied most or all of the elements that made up the average 'coolie's' squalid daily life: work, debt, opium, liquor, prostitutes, housing and personal security.[5] These commodities also made substantial contributions to the *towkays*' income streams. The colonial authorities had qualms about this unsavoury arrangement, but they managed to ensure that they did not get in the way of running the colony.

War on the Triads: Moving Away from Indirect Government

The immediate post-Transfer period was relatively free from secret society violence, compared with what had gone before,[6] but it proved to be a short-lived respite. In the early 1880s rivalry between syndicates reached unprecedented levels. The short-to-medium-term result was a marked increase in the level of both secret society violence and opium smuggling – in short, the breakdown of the discipline that underpinned the usefulness of the secret societies to the colonial government. This degenerative process had been helped along by a new governor – Sir Frederick Weld – who tried to maximise profits for the colonial administration by both driving up the price of opium and playing favourites among the contenders. This was a standard government tactic employed across Southeast Asia, but the British were no match for their Chinese partners, for whom winning the contract was just a stage in the negotiations: they routinely forced the renegotiation of payments after winning contracts, thus depressing revenues. And so by the end of the 1880s the colonial government was thoroughly dissatisfied with its reliance on revenue farms and was setting out to bring them under tighter government control.[7] The government finally outlawed the triads in 1890. This latter move was intended to drive the secret societies out of business, but all it did was drive them underground, where they continued to flourish.[8] Two decades later the government was still trying to establish its authority over the city by opening up back alleys in Chinatown to remove the back doors and courtyard walls through which gangsters could come and go, invisible to the police. This was also when the government finally and belatedly brought the revenue farm system to an end, thus removing the prize for which the secret societies had been competing.

Managing the Other Communities

The Chinese communities had been singled out for special forms of governance because they were important economically and demographically – and difficult to govern. The war on the secret societies was an effort to rule the Chinese directly, but the rest of Asian Singapore had long since been governed by a variety of more routine structures that reflected their heterogeneity. Today the official designations for the non-Chinese communities have been collapsed into Malays, Indians and 'Others', but when we look at the nineteenth-century origins of these communities we find Bugis, Minangkabau, Javanese and other 'Indonesians' sharing the space that today is labelled 'Malay'. Today's generic 'Indians' were differentiated into Tamils, Malayalees, Punjabis, Bengalis and others. Of course there had always been Eurasians and Arabs in colonial Singapore, as there are now, but they were not collapsed into the soulless category of 'Other'. Chinese were not usually considered a single category, except in the most generic of conversations. Whether you were Hokkien, Hakka, Teochew or Cantonese probably determined where you lived and worked, and during periods of upheaval it could determine whether you lived or died. Even beyond this kaleidoscopic array of communal labels, Asian Singapore was further divided within and across ethnic communities by a variety of less recognised differences that, in a system of indirect rule, made a vast difference to one's relationship with government. Did you work in government service or the private sector? Were you daily rated or on a wage? Did you live in a *kampung* or the city? Differences in education, language, religion and, of course, gender made fundamental differences to how you were managed, much more so than is the case in a modern society. In some cases the impact was community-wide. Language was a key factor – not just the Asian language spoken, but the extent to which a person and a community was English-literate. A capacity to understand, speak, read and write English brought some groups (Eurasians, many Indians, as well as the *baba* Chinese) much more closely into the orbit of European governance than the rest. This entwinement was performed mostly through direct employment in the civil service, police and in European business houses (Eurasians, Malays, Indians, *baba* Chinese). The Chettiars from Tamil Nadu were distinctive as a community by their roles as money changers and financiers; they acted as bankers for Asian Singapore for the second half of the nineteenth century. Arrival patterns helped determine these outcomes as well: many Indians arrived already in the service of the colonial government (including as prisoners, soldiers and servants); others arrived to seek employment or to engage in commercial enterprise. Styles of township also affected the intensity of governance, with *kampung*s and squatter villages obviating most of the need for routine interaction between their government and their residents.[9]

Creeping Governance

The significant point for this study is that we see the same sort of governance creep in these communities in the post-Transfer period that we saw in Chinatown, even if it was not nearly as dramatic. New building and road-building programmes, an expanding trade economy with a commensurate expansion of port and docking facilities, a reformed and slightly more open civil service, and upgraded law enforcement agencies opened new opportunities for English-speaking and English-literate Asians to enter the orbit of government service and employment (or contracting) by European businesses. Yet all these groups – even English speakers – were drawn into the European orbit very slowly, and often on substantially their own terms. Malay civil servants working in the city still mostly returned to the *kampung* every evening, and there they were much less governable than someone living in the city. Not that the *kampung* was a fully 'traditional' phenomenon in Singapore. A century later, in the 1960s and 1970s, Lee Kuan Yew came to use the *kampung* as his symbol of the 'sleepy village' that he wanted to leave behind; a vestige of old Singapore to be discarded in the pursuit of modernisation. Yet the Singapore *kampung* was itself a direct product of the British colonial project and modernisation: it only became possible or even desirable to establish major new villages and towns thanks to Singapore's road-building programme. This roads programme had its substantial beginnings in the 1840s and gained pace later in the century as a deliberate part of the extension (almost literally) of government across Singapore. By the turn of the century, the economy and society were changing, and modern government was encroaching on every social fraction and every geographical space in Singapore.

BRITISH SINGAPORE

The immediate impact of the Transfer on the European population was even more muted than it had been for Asian Singapore, with the substantive changes also emerging slowly over the following decades. British colonists in the Settlements were, in fact, surprisingly ambivalent about the Transfer once it had become a reality. The European mercantile community in Penang was actively hostile, fearing (correctly) that London would sideline Penang in favour of Singapore. In strict terms of governance the main immediate change was the assertion of the powers and stature of the Governor and the creation of a dedicated Straits Civil Service recruited from London, complete with the provision of language training and a lifetime career path. An appointment to the Straits suddenly became an attractive career step for governors and lieutenant governors from other parts of the world and for young public school graduates seeking a career in the civil service.[10]

Yet regardless of the long-term impact of such improvements, remarkably little changed in Singapore in the short term. The introduction of an advisory Legislative Council added little value to a European and English-educated civil society that was already given a loud but mostly ineffective voice by an outspoken free press. The issues that concerned the civic leaders after 1867 were fundamentally the same as those that had occupied them before Transfer: law and order, taxes and the business environment. Intensified interest in public health issues in the 1890s varied the theme slightly – reflecting in part the fact that Singapore had a very high mortality rate, even by Asian colonial standards. Apart from upgrading the status of the Governor, and shifting the seat of government for the Settlements wholly to Singapore, the most easily identifiable reform in administration was the separation of rural and municipal Singapore into separate administrative units – but this did not make the local administration any more responsive to local voices. The Transfer did not even result in imperial recognition of Singapore's strategic importance or an increase in external funding of its defences.

The imperial status of the Straits – and Singapore in particular, as the main port – did improve in fact but only because the Straits benefited directly from the opening of the Suez Canal in 1869 and the growing prevalence of the steam ship in the decades that followed. (The opening of the Canal made the Straits of Malacca the only logical route from Europe to the Pacific – effectively removing the Sunda Straits from the map; steam engine technology enabled Singapore to export heavy and bulky produce, notably Malayan rubber and tin.) The importance of the Straits as a magnet for indentured Asian (particularly Chinese) labourers, prostitutes and of course traders and entrepreneurs increased with the expansion of the economy. This added to the colony's administrative challenges, but the reluctance of Asian subjects to come to the attention of government ensured that the level of official interaction was kept to a minimum. The little interaction that did take place was mediated mostly through police, health inspectors, dockyard officialdom and the like.

The post-Transfer period was in fact so calm on the surface that C.M. Turnbull opened her relevant chapter in *A History of Singapore* by quoting Thomas Carlyle's words, 'Happy the people whose annals are blank in the history books', saying they 'could well be applied to Singapore during the decades which followed the transfer to colonial rule'.[11] This is not to say that nothing happened. We have already seen that fundamental changes in community and governance took place, but it was just that most of the interesting developments were not very overtly concerned with the formal colonial administration and politics of the island.

'BRITISH' MALAYA

Some of the most significant developments in colonial governance in this period did not concern the island of Singapore per se, but rather the role of Singapore-Johor as the bridgehead for the British encroachment into the peninsula. The peninsula was vital to the economic prosperity of both Singapore and Penang, and the security of the Settlements as a whole. The Colonial Office and the local colonial establishments were in agreement that the myriad local Malay states suffered from constant problems of governance that were impinging upon profits and security, but they disagreed on how to respond. In the 1870s there were particular security problems in Muar (which at the time was independent of Johor) and in the nine statelets that make up present-day Negeri Sembilan. The leaders of these polities resisted all British advice and guidance and yet the Colonial Office refused for decades to countenance any moves to impose a solution, fearing a repeat of the imperial creep they had 'suffered' in India. The Straits governors who were confronted with the challenges of Muar and Negeri Sembilan (Sir William Jervois and then Acting Governor Sir Edward Anson) instead found a distinctively Malayan solution. They built up Britain's only ally-cum-dependant

Map 5.1
Malay states and Singapore

on the peninsula, Daing Ibrahim's son, Abu Bakar. He had inherited both the title of Temenggong and all the wealth of Johor upon his father's death in 1862 and the British had recognised him by the title 'Maharajah' since 1868. Jervois and Anson reasoned that if Abu Bakar was widely recognised as the senior Malay traditional ruler, they could call upon him to either impose solutions or at least to cajole his fellow royals to follow 'his' advice. Essentially they gave him Muar to add to his own kingdom (which settled the Muar problem directly) and then, from his new and clear status as the senior Malay ruler, he set about doing Britain's bidding in Negeri Sembilan. In return he was allowed to use Johor's proximity to and intimacy with Singapore to enrich Johor and establish himself as the pre-eminent Malay ruler – effectively as a partner of both the British and Singapore interests. His ultimate overt reward came in 1885 when the British recognised him as Sultan of Johor – a title that had been extinct for 30 years, and which had never belonged to his family in any case. Yet he could perhaps have been forgiven for taking just as much satisfaction from the events of the following year, when yet another governor, Sir Frederick Weld, tried unsuccessfully to curtail his powers and sovereignty by imposing a Resident in Johor, only to find himself outmanoeuvred and blocked. It turned out that the new Sultan of Johor had much better networks in both London and Singapore than did the new Governor of the Straits Settlements.

The Forward Policy

The later nineteenth century was marked by political battles between Singapore and the Colonial Office over what became known as 'the Forward Policy' – a policy of imposing British Residents/Advisers directly onto Malay rulers, as opposed to working through Johor. The advocates of the Forward Policy were ultimately victorious and Britain/Singapore came to rule the peninsula through British Residents. The central-western states of Negeri Sembilan, Selangor, Pahang and Perak were colonised in the late nineteenth century. Even though they were ruled as individual colonies, they were brought together as the Federated Malay States (FMS) for administrative convenience. The five northern states were formally colonised only in the early twentieth century and never joined the federation. Together with Johor, they were known as the Unfederated Malay States (UMS), though this label had no standing except as a matter of convenience in correspondence. Johor eventually accepted a Resident on the eve of World War I, long after Abu Bakar had died. The tipping point in the 'battle for Johor' turned out to be emblematic of Britain's Malaya policy over the previous half-century: Abu Bakar's successor, Sultan Ibrahim, made the mistake of thinking that he could defy British advice on a matter that went to the heart of British commercial interests – specifically their need to build a railway across Johor that would link the Port of Singapore with the rubber plantations of the peninsula.

MODERNITY COMES TO SINGAPORE

The decades that surrounded the turn of the century marked the modest beginning of an upsurge in government activity in Singapore, and the prosperity that came in the wake of the war confirmed that an era of modern government and modern government services had properly begun. Somewhere during this period we might say that modernity arrived in Malaya and its first stop was Singapore, where modern government (modernity from above) and modern modes of thought and social organisation (modernity from below) had already made the most substantial inroads. As is often the case, modernity from above and below were moving in very different directions.

From Above ...

Modernity from above was basically an extension of the colonial project. From the late 1880s, colonial officialdom was engaged in a steady intensification of its impact on Malayan and Singaporean society, much of which was designed specifically to replace the compromises that had been intrinsic to premodern colonial Malaya with direct colonial rule. On both the peninsula and in Singapore this meant marginalising those with whom the British had hitherto been sharing power – the traditional Malay rulers and the Chinese secret societies – and channelling political, economic and social power exclusively into the hands of government. On 1 January 1910 the government completed the most significant structural element of this task by de-privatising the opium industry, putting it in the hands of the Government Monopolies Department.[12] After World War I, public building programmes (hospitals, schools, a university, the General Post Office, City Hall and public housing) and public infrastructure programmes (roads, public transport, an electric power station, and reservoirs) transformed the face of the island and the character of Singapore society. For the first time in Singapore's centuries of history, government was routinely intruding into daily life and shaping the well-being of ordinary folk. In terms of administration, the interwar years were marked by incremental and half-hearted efforts on the government's part to nudge Singapore and Malaya closer to modern British ideals of representative and bureaucratic governance. In the 1920s Governor Sir Laurence Guillemard successfully broadened the pool from which he could draw municipal commissioners and expanded the number of unofficials in the Legislative Council (i.e. people who were not government officials) so that they made up half the chamber. He also tried to introduce income tax, but the Settlements' middle-class European community united to stop that, thus offering a sample of what representative politics meant in practice. In the 1930s Governor Sir Cecil Clementi pushed for a much closer form of union and more intense form of governance for British Malaya, but this came to nought when an investigator from the Colonial Office – Sir Samuel Wilson, Permanent Undersecretary of State for the Colonies – decided that the proposal faced too many obstacles to be viable, despite recognising the strong benefits that would come with union.[13]

From Below ...

It was hardly a coincidence that modernisation 'from below' was setting itself in opposition to state-based modernity. Both processes were facilitated by improvements in travel and communications that spread 'modern' ideas globally, and in the last half of the nineteenth century and the first half of the twentieth, many of those modern ideas were nothing short of revolutionary. As the main port city in the region, Singapore was the point of entry and the crucible, not only for the various forms of nationalism, but for almost every vestige of modern thought. So, for instance, avant-garde modern Islamic thinkers congregated in Singapore while traditionalists dominated Islamic thinking on the peninsula. More overt Malay nationalism was in the mix by the 1930s, often linked to attachment to Islam but just as often spiced with demands that the *rakyat* (the people/subjects) be empowered ahead of or alongside the Malay aristocracy. Some of the most important expressions of Malay nationalism – notably that of the pro-Japanese Young Malay Union (Kaum Melayu Muda, KMM), founded in 1938 – rejected the colonial boundaries set by the European powers and envisioned a union that included the Indonesian archipelago.

Chinese nationalism emerged throughout the same time frame as Malay nationalism, though in its case it was imported directly from abroad. The main Chinese political organisation in Malaya before World War II was the Malayan KMT (Kuomintang or Chinese Nationalist Party). The KMT had two primary enemies: communism (after the KMT in China broke with its communist allies in 1927) and the Japanese (after Japan's invasion of China in 1937). Its main immediate concern was always establishing and maintaining its political and organisational leadership of the Chinese population in Malaya.[14] Though illegal, it maintained a branch structure, was led by prominent members of the Chinese community, operated social and trade union organisations and raised a lot of money to support the mother KMT organisation in China. The KMT's focus was primarily on China rather than on Malaya, but the British were highly suspicious of its anti-imperialist message and did not trust it at all. After the Japanese invasion of China, the British allowed Chinese in Singapore to join the China KMT, but forbade them to organise locally as the KMT – a ban that the KMT was able to circumvent by working through more acceptable organisations such as the Chinese Chamber of Commerce, the Singapore China Relief Fund and the Malayan Patriotic Fund.[15] This tactic was so successful that Singapore became the Southeast Asian hub of Chinese support for defence of their homeland, and was the conduit for providing China with fortunes in money and volunteers by the thousands.[16]

The Malayan Communist Party (MCP) was substantially fishing in the same pond as the KMT, offering yet another radical form of modernity. During the interwar years the MCP never had the mass following among Malayan Chinese enjoyed by the KMT, but the Japanese Occupation changed that. The local KMT leadership consisted of respectable businessmen and community leaders, not suited for underground work or fighting. Many of them escaped Singapore before its fall along with the general exodus of rich Chinese and Europeans, and more were forced to collaborate with their new Japanese masters. The immediate result was the near-destruction of both the KMT and its cause in Malaya; this despite the continued resistance of small bands of KMT-aligned anti-Japanese fighters in the jungle.[17] The MCP survived and thrived because, on the eve of Singapore's fall, the British released their leadership from gaol, and they formed the largest group of armed anti-Japanese volunteers: the Singapore Overseas Chinese Anti-Japanese Volunteer Army. Under the banner of the Malayan People's Anti-Japanese Army (MPAJA), the communists fought a long-term guerrilla war on the peninsula against the Japanese in a close alliance with the British. They became nationalist heroes, recruiting tens of thousands of Chinese into the MPAJA.

The Anglophone community also voiced nationalist sentiments, though its members tended to be less sectarian and strident in their aspirations for equality and higher levels of self-government under the British.[18] In all of these movements, at all times (reaching back to the late nineteenth century and into the post-war period), Singapore (and Penang as well, in the case of the KMT) played a pivotal role: as a centre of publishing, a point of entry, a place of gathering, and as a seat of learning.

JAPANESE MALAYA

Despite the radicalism that was festering throughout Malayan society, the peninsula's political trajectory would probably have followed a fairly sedate path towards something like the type of future envisioned by the Anglophone community if it had not been for the disruption of the Japanese Occupation from 1942 to 1945. Respect for the victims demands an account of the main events, but the narrative flow of this book requires that I emphasise the impact of the Occupation period on subsequent history. I try to find a balance between both approaches below but, before even beginning that exercise, let us note that the history of the Occupation is properly written as a history of Malaya, not Singapore; a fact acknowledged frankly in the title of Paul Kratoska's history of the period: *The Japanese Occupation of Malaya: 1941–1945*.[19] Yet even within this framework, Singapore stood apart on numerous grounds. First, the Japanese made Singapore their headquarters and ruled the ten peninsular provinces from the island, a relationship that was underlined by the fact that Singapore was administered as a municipality with a mayor rather than as a province with a civilian governor. Second, it hosted the major port for the peninsula and third, it was at the end of the peninsula. Substantially because of the combined effect of the latter two points, by the time the Japanese Army arrived, the population of the island had been swelled by refugees driven south by the invading army, giving the island a civilian European population of around 3,000.[20] In a sense this European population was swelled even more by the occupier's subsequent choice of Changi Gaol as the place of incarceration for all the British and imperial soldiers (which included tens of thousands of Indians) who surrendered on the peninsula. Singapore was also distinguished by being an overwhelmingly Chinese island. This latter point did not make it unique, since Penang was also a Chinese island, but it was one more factor that helped determine the course of its treatment under Japanese rule.

Experiencing the Occupation

The experience of the Occupation varied dramatically according to one's race, one's willingness to co-operate with the occupiers and – perhaps most important of all – luck. The Chinese section of the population was subjected to the most graphic and spectacular of public horrors when the Japanese launched a systematic massacre of Chinese men between the ages of 18 and 50 on 17 February 1942, two days after they arrived. It was supposedly targeted at local Chinese who had collaborated with the British or supported the Chinese resistance to Japan in China, but the death toll of somewhere between

Figure 5.1 A full-size reconstruction of part of the 'Death Railway' in Thailand – the bridge over the River Kwai

25,000 (admitted by the Japanese Chief of Staff) and 50,000 (as later claimed by the Chinese community) indicates that it was a straightforward massacre of civilians. The survivors, along with Chinese women and children, lived under constant fear of arbitrary beatings or executions. As a community they subsequently suffered the humiliation of being forced to contribute $50 million to the Japanese war effort.

The community that suffered the highest proportion of incarceration was undoubtedly the Europeans. More than 3,000 civilians and many thousands of surrendered soldiers were incarcerated in Changi. Civilians were soon transferred to a compound in Sime Road where hunger and disease took a terrible toll. The soldiers remained in Changi for the duration of the war, except for those who died of starvation or of some other cruelty, and those who were transhipped to forced-labour camps in Japan, Taiwan or Thailand (to work on the infamous 'Death Railway', see Figure 5.1) along with locals. (One such local who was sent to work in a coal mine in northern Japan was David Marshall. He enters this history later in this chapter as Singapore's first Chief Minister.)[21]

The Indian prisoners of war were pressured to join the Indian National Army to make common cause with the Japanese to 'liberate' India from British rule; 25,000 prisoners of war (POWs) out of 65,000 did so. Those who did were trained in camps at Seletar in Singapore and at Seremban, Kuala Lumpur and Ipoh on the peninsula. They were joined by a regiment of nationalist women, whose passions had been stirred by the rhetoric and vision of Subhas Chandra Bose, a former president of the Congress Party who led Japan's overseas Indian nationalist movement from February 1943.[22] The POWs who refused to join the nationalist cause were sent to forced-labour camps in remote parts of the Japanese empire to work and often die in appalling conditions. When the war ended, 16,109 Indian POWs remained alive in Singapore and 2,664 on the peninsula.[23] The free section of the Indian community was cajoled by its Japanese-backed leaders to make its own donation to the Japanese war effort, emulating the reluctant example set by the Chinese community.[24]

The Malays had the most ambiguous relationship with the Japanese. The entire leadership of the Malay community had regarded the Japanese benignly at the outset of the Occupation because, like the Indian nationalists, they considered them as liberators from European colonialism. The Malays suffered measurably less than the other races from the directed cruelty of the Japanese and a much higher proportion of their schools were allowed to open than was the case for the Indians and Chinese. Yet they did not escape completely. Many ordinary Malays had fought the Japanese with the British, and some hundred or more of them were executed in the early days of the Occupation.[25] This episode marked the beginning of a deterioration in the relations between the Malay community and the Japanese administration that ran contrary to their generally favoured status and the consequences were far from trivial: they included thousands of Malay deaths in Japanese forced-labour camps in Thailand.[26] Most Malays kept their heads down during the Occupation, collaborating with the Japanese administration with varying degrees of enthusiasm. They were often at the front line of implementing Japanese forced-labour programmes and other repressive and unpopular measures, but many did what they could to protect their people. Such was the case of Tunku Abdul Rahman, the future Prime Minister of Malaya, who even acted as a recruiter for the British-led anti-Japanese resistance while he was working for the Occupation forces.[27]

Regardless of the ethnic group to which one belonged, everyone lived in fear of arbitrary death or cruelty, and by 1943 all communities (including the Japanese occupiers) were suffering the privations of food shortages. Indeed the island was short of almost every commodity for most of the Occupation because the Japanese lost control of the seas even before the end of 1942.[28]

Administration of Malai and Syonan-To

The administration of Malaya under the Occupation is a complicated and interesting field of study, but for the purposes of this history of Singapore it can be outlined in a few points extracted from Kratoska's intensive study of the subject. First note that

Malaya became Malai, and Singapore became Syonan-To (Light of the South). The four northern states of British Malaya were given to Thailand as a thank you for the latter's co-operative surrender. The main points of tension within the Japanese administration were between the military overlords and the Japanese civilian administrators. The main political technique of the administration was to manage the welfare of the population through ethnic self-help groups. The main political goal was to subjugate and 'Japanify' Malaya. Schools, media and mosques were all conscripted for this purpose.[29] Even the calendars and street signs were switched to Japanese forms, and – most idiosyncratically – clocks were moved forward by two hours to Tokyo time.

In the meantime the MCP and the MPAJA were in the jungle operating as a mass, mostly Chinese, partisan force. The MPAJA terrorised the Japanese occupiers in co-operation with the British guerrilla operation, Force 136. Their courage could not be doubted, but in the end the decisive factor that ended the Occupation was the American nuclear strikes on Hiroshima and Nagasaki in August 1945. This cut across the whole dynamic of the fight in the jungle at a stroke. Japan's unconditional surrender in the face of this awesome destructive force was so sudden that there was no authority or army in Malaya to receive their surrender or to marshal them. For several weeks – until the British Army finally returned – the MPAJA was the only militarised body of men in the country, and after it emerged from the jungle its units formed a ruthless makeshift government that meted out summary justice on any they judged to be collaborators or to have otherwise given offence.[30]

NO LOOKING BACK

Yet for all the suffering and disruption of the Japanese Occupation, the most lasting historical impact of the Occupation was much the same as it was elsewhere in Asia: it divided the twentieth century into two distinct halves. Before 1942, Asia was a world of European and Japanese colonies, with the Japanese empire expanding inexorably and the European portion engaged in a slow drift towards increased self-government and independence one day in the distant future. Maybe. After 1945, the Japanese empire was dead and the Asian elites (and many of their followers) were restless under the return of European rule. The elites may have spoken the language of the coloniser, and even travelled to the colonial metropole to go to university, but their overwhelming sentiment was hostility and resentment. Almost to a man, they wanted to end colonial rule, but for most this was just a first step to throw off much of the Europeans' associated baggage, notably capitalism, liberalism and racism – or at least white racism. In pursuing these agendas, the elites of Malaya faced a number of factors of recent history that made their situation distinctive.

First, the Occupation had bequeathed to Malaya a strong, legal, militarised and overwhelmingly Chinese communist movement that had formed the backbone of the anti-Japanese resistance in the jungles.[31] At the end of the war they were heroes, especially to their fellow Chinese, but also to the British, who literally pinned medals on their chests with full pomp and ceremony. This legacy provided a mass base for an ongoing populist movement that gave voice and force to militant anti-Western sentiment. This animosity persisted long after the MPAJA was demobilised in December 1945 and long after the MCP was declared illegal in June 1948. With 11,000 members in 1947, including nearly 1,000 in Singapore, it was truly a mass movement. At the same time the Kuomintang (KMT) still had over 27,000 members on its books, including 5,000 in Singapore.[32] Yet despite the differences in their numbers, the end days of the KMT in Malaya were approaching; the defeat of the Kuomintang in China in 1949 finally sealed it. By 1948, the MCP and the left more generically had become the default political vehicle for Chinese, peasant and industrial grievances across the length and breadth of Malaya/Singapore. Thanks to this historic shift, the MCP had a recruitment and support base and an associational network of disaffected Chinese that extended far beyond those who would regard themselves as communists, or even socialists. Turnbull reports that in Singapore alone it had a support base of around 70,000 in 1946.[33] After the movement launched its insurrection in the first half of 1948, this natural appeal was reinforced by a ruthless reign of terror, which helped make the MCP the most significant vehicle of oppositionist politics on both the peninsula and in Singapore until the opening of the 1950s.

Second, during the war the British lost confidence in the Malays and their sultans as their natural allies in Malaya. Instead they looked to build a modern, race-blind Malaya, drawing upon a broader range of educated elites in the quest for a new post-colonial order in Southeast Asia. They broke up the Straits Settlements into its three component parts, retaining Singapore as a stand-alone Crown Colony, but joining Penang and Malacca with the other former Malayan colonies with the plan of making them into a new Malayan Union. Thus, at the stroke of a pen, there was suddenly a clear distinction between Singapore and the rest of Malaya. For the first time Singapore was unambiguously distinct from every local centre with which it had ever been historically linked: Riau, Malacca, Johor, Penang and Bencoolen. It was distinct and separate, but still remained enmeshed in local relationships, certainly not an island entire of itself. Even in separation it still shared several important administrative functions with the Malay Peninsula: investments and workforces, currency, income tax, higher education, civil aviation, posts and telegraphs and immigration. And yet the damage was done: 'small Singapore' was born.

Crown Colony

The separation of colonial Singapore from peninsular Malaya was the forerunner for a deeper divergence, since the British planned to both lead the Malayan Union towards independence and retain Singapore as a Crown Colony, albeit without fully shutting the door to the possibility of reunification at some indeterminate time in the future. The Colonial Office's separatist approach to Singapore was adopted primarily for the sake of retaining the naval base at Sembawang, but it was also a gesture of consideration to the sensitivities of peninsular Malays who would have resented and feared Chinese dominance should Singapore have been retained in Malaya.

With this first separation, the political histories of the peninsula and Singapore diverged more decisively than they had at any point in the past and a sharper focus on the specifically Singapore end of the story is warranted. Yet at this point a complete separation of their two stories would be unwise because the Singapore and Malayan histories continued to intersect, and – as it turned out – there was to be a brief period of remerger less than two decades later before the parties settled on permanent separation. We do not need to plumb the details of the Malayan developments in the immediate post-war period, but we should note a few points of divergence that help us to understand later Singaporean history. Notably, Britain's attempt to impose a race-blind Malayan Union onto the peninsula failed. This misstep gave Malay ethno-nationalism the opening it needed to become the dominant force in Malayan politics through its new political vehicle, the United Malays National Organisation (UMNO). Furthermore, by the time the new Federation of Malaya was created by an act of independence from Britain in 1957, ethnic-communal politics had become institutionalised through the new Alliance Party – a governing party that housed UMNO, the Malayan Chinese Association (MCA) and the Malayan Indian Congress (MIC). The basis of the consociational arrangement that underpinned the Alliance was that the MCA and the MIC would acknowledge UMNO dominance and leadership along with Malay social/political hegemony.

A Shared Emergency

Perhaps even more important than the points of divergence, however, were the conditions that Malaya and Singapore shared – most notably their common colonial master and their common communist insurgency. The two features are themselves intertwined since it was the colonial master that determined and managed the response to the insurgency, which took the form of a 12-year (1948–60) counter-insurgency operation called the 'Malayan Emergency'. The impact of the Emergency on the future of Singapore proved to be dramatic – ultimately more dramatic than it was in Malaya. This was despite the fact that most of the real action and focus was on the peninsula and that the MCP in Singapore was, in the words of Richard Clutterbuck, 'a poor relation whose primary role was the support of the jungle war'.[34]

Following the end of the war, the MCP was a legal political party and it pursued a 'united front' strategy of making common cause with other nationalist and progressive forces. Unbeknownst to the comrades, it was also being led by a British agent, Lai Teck, who had a parallel agenda of stifling revolutionary capacity as part of his deal with the British. In Singapore the party set up a myriad of trade unions, youth and student organisations, and a political party comprised of English-speaking activists – the Malayan Democratic Union – all under the direct control of a small central body, the Singapore Town Committee.[35] Suffice to say that the colonial establishment's post-war rapprochement with the MCP did not outlast the exposure and sudden disappearance of Lai Tek in March 1947. After a couple of years of relative quiet and civility both in Singapore and on the peninsula,[36] Chinese squatter and peasant associations, industrial unions and plantation unions (led variously by the MCP, KMT and triads) started becoming more aggressive and militant in pursuit of redress of a wide range of grievances. Sometimes they directed their attacks against employers or the British, but more often they fought each other as part of a protracted turf war for control of towns and regions.[37] The colonial officials had been treating strikes gently in deference to the Labour Government in office in London, but the violence brought forth harsher restrictions on strike activity and draconian rules that set out to control the lawless Chinese squatter-peasant settlements on the peninsula. The MCP was now led by a former guerrilla commander who operated under the alias Chin Peng. He responded with an escalation of strikes and violence. This set the MCP on a path towards the launch of full insurrection that was planned for September 1948. Alas, the colonial authorities did not wait for September but declared war in everything but name and legal form with a preventative set of mass arrests over 18–20 June.[38]

RADICAL POLITICS IN SINGAPORE

While guerrilla warfare festered in the Malayan jungle, the residents of Singapore continued to shape a city around themselves – though with very limited agency. In 1947, just a couple of years after the end of the Occupation, Singapore had a population of over 900,000, of whom three-quarters lived in the city area.[39] Ten years later three-quarters of Singapore's population of 1.45 million still lived within 8 kilometres (5 miles) of Raffles' landing place.[40] Beyond the inner city both Chinese and Malays lived overwhelmingly in unplanned and unregulated *kampungs*, which sprang from nowhere by the dozen, fed by both a high birth rate and a steady flow of Chinese migrants from China and Malaya. Built of timber and whatever scraps of building material could be bought or found, this is where the new generations of families lived – even if many of the breadwinners still worked in town.[41]

Meanwhile the city proper was crowded and pockmarked with slums. A 1947 government survey reported 25% of the municipal population to be living in acutely overcrowded conditions, and another 33% living in conditions that were merely overcrowded (but not acutely so). Chinatown and some other locales were noted for the predominance of rooms that had been subdivided into residential cubicles, many of which did not even have windows to the sky.[42] When Barrington Kaye performed a more intense social survey of Chinatown's Upper Nankin Street over 1954–6, he predictably found the situation on the ground to be much worse.[43] The colonial government was ill-equipped and unwilling to systematically address these problems and in fact it did not have an arm, board, trust or authority that was responsible for housing as such. The Singaporean Improvement Trust (SIT) is generally considered to have this mandate, and it did engage in building programmes that suggested that it was responsible for housing. Yet the Colonial Secretary made clear in 1953 that this was not the case. The SIT was responsible for slum clearance, not 'to undertake housing schemes'.[44] Even when the government loaned the SIT $100 million for housing development, it did not accept theoretical responsibility for housing.[45] The reason is clear: the housing situation was deteriorating because of the high rate of population growth, and accepting responsibility for housing would have involved making an undefined financial commitment.[46]

Singapore had in fact become overwhelmingly a city of families, which is why there were cohorts of school children and school-leavers ready to complain and challenge the colonial authorities in the 1950s and 1960s. Between 1947 and 1957 Singapore's population grew by 54% (507,800, from 938,000 to 1.45 million), and 78% of that growth (395,600) was natural increase.[47] In 1957, 43% of the population (619,000) was under the age of 15.[48] With such a population profile living mostly in a crowded and unplanned city recovering from a hostile occupation, health was a constant challenge. Malnutrition and serious communicable diseases including measles, tuberculosis and smallpox afflicted the young. The government's modest network of clinics and (mainly military) hospitals, along with a small army of nurses recruited after the war, did what they could, but in 1960 the infant mortality rate was still two per thousand live births (albeit down from eight per thousand ten years earlier). Singapore's last smallpox epidemic was as late as 1959.[49] Children and families meant schooling, but the building and running of schools was left mostly in private hands, leading to the flourishing of a network of ethnic-/language-based schools that exaggerated the social silos that already seemed natural in colonial Singapore. As a city, Singapore was suffering from severe neglect, and this created a dynamic and fertile environment for radical politics in the mid-1950s, though it followed a very different script from that which was being followed on the mainland.

Figure 5.2 Kampung Baru Nilai, an old 'New Village' in Negeri Sembilan, Malaysia

On the peninsula the Emergency was a fully militarised struggle where the most effective tool proved to be a mass resettlement of 1.2 million ethnic Chinese into around 600 garrison towns known as 'New Villages' (Figure 5.2). These compound-like settlements were intended to deprive the communist 'bandits' of the Malayan National Liberation Army of intelligence, shelter, medicine and – most importantly – food.[50] Many peninsula Chinese fled to Singapore rather than live in the New Villages, thus feeding the island's 1950s population surge.[51] In Singapore the frontline colonialist force in the Emergency was the Special Branch rather than the army, and the determining parameters were centred on politics rather than the food supply. Politics on the island was played out in the context of a free but compliant English-language press, a free and fiercely independent Chinese press, the Legislative Council, and a suite of colonial officials who held all the real power. The Legislative Council was notionally representative of social and sectional interests but was in fact fully appointed by the Governor until the first elections were held in 1955. Long before these elections, in a series of raids and arrests spread between May and December 1950, the MCP in Singapore was all but destroyed as an operational entity, leaving it isolated and leaderless for the next three or more years.[52]

The sweep of 1950 took out the entire Singapore Town Committee of the MCP, along with most of its members. It had the unplanned effect of giving the radical nationalist and leftist movements in the island's trade unions and Chinese schools the chance to grow almost from scratch without much contact with or direction from the communists. After 1950 the MCP was left with about 20 full cadre members in Singapore, who organised themselves into an industrial branch, a student branch and an assassination branch. They also set up a branch-cum-front organisation called the Anti-British League (ABL), which by its peak in 1954 had built a network of supporters about 2,000 strong. None of these branches was subject to effective discipline, though C.C. Chin tells us that the ABL became the de facto leading branch and played something of a central planning and organisational role in several of the pivotal events of the mid-1950s.[53] The MCP did what it could to restore its fortunes, but the emerging grass-roots coalition of radical interests and passions was proving itself to be thoroughly undisciplined, populist and answerable to no one. The most prominent and charismatic grass-roots leader in this period was a trade union leader by the name of Lim Chin Siong who emerged to prominence in the mid-1950s. The description of Lim by the British Deputy High Commissioner to Singapore in July 1962 confirms the picture of an undirected movement:

> while we accept that Lim Chin Siong is a Communist, there is no evidence that he is receiving his orders from the CPM, Peking or Moscow. Our impression is that Lim is working very much on his own and that his primary objective is not the Communist millennium but to obtain control of the constitutional government of Singapore.[54]

By the time the Singapore Town Committee had been reconstructed and was poised to resume leadership of the movement in 1954 (just as both Lim Chin Siong's and Lee Kuan Yew's stars were rising), it found itself dealing with a generation of radicalised youths that was used to operating without either party discipline or outside direction.[55] In those years the MCP was not so much trying to install its personnel as leaders in the grass-roots movements, as it was trying to recruit promising activists into the party.

The Communist Party Tries Again

After a disastrous set of riots in 1956, in which the MCP lost control of events completely, it made a serious effort to bring the Singapore operation under proper discipline, placing it in 1957 under the command of a three-man Singapore Working Committee safely based in Riau. The Committee succeeded in imposing an imperfect chain of command, but after years of disruptions, arrests and deportations by the Special Branch, all that this shift achieved was to place the local operation in the hands of an overly young, naïve and grossly inexperienced youth – Fang Chuang-Pi, otherwise known as 'The Plen'. He walked into all the strategic cul-de-sacs and traps being laid by the MCP's newest, albeit undeclared adversary, the radical young lawyer-cum-politician, Lee Kuan Yew (Figure 5.3).[56] Years later Fang confessed that he was so naïve that he did not even realise

Figure 5.3
A young Lee Kuan Yew, shown on a poster hanging in the Singapore National Museum, June 2015

that when he was proving his 'good faith' to Lee, he was in fact 'surrendering all his winning cards in the first hand': in a series of meetings beginning in March 1958, Fang agreed to cut off ties with all political movements other than Lee's new People's Action Party (PAP), leaving the MCP totally exposed and completely reliant on Lee's good faith.[57] Looking back with the benefit of hindsight, Fang was adamant that he had no practical option other than to work with Lee – such was the MCP's weakness and Lee's strength – but he regretted his incapacity to recognise that he was being played. (Chin Peng made a parallel apologia in 1999 when he insisted that as Secretary General of the MCP he was ultimately responsible for the mistakes of 1958, but this can be dismissed as a magnanimous gesture: at the time the decisions were taken Chin Peng was holed up in southern Thailand, lacking adequate lines of communication with Singapore and fighting a war on the peninsula that was going very badly.)[58]

MCP Death Throes

The MCP's acceptance of Lee's deal in 1958 was, very obviously, a function of its weakness and diminished assets – both in Singapore and on the peninsula, where the insurgency was in full retreat following failed negotiations in 1957 that had been aimed at ending both the insurgency and the Emergency.[59] If confirmation of this reality is needed, it was recorded in a confidential report sent to London in 1962 by the Acting High Commissioner to Singapore, Lord Selkirk: 'The Singapore Special Branch have virtually failed to identify directly any communists during the last three years.'[60]

By the time of the PAP's election victory in 1959, organised, disciplined communist activism was all-but dead. Speaking as prime minister of the newly elected government, Lee Kuan Yew himself told the tripartite (British, Malayan and Singaporean) Internal Security Council that MCP membership was down to around 40 and membership of the ABL was down to around 80. He also confirmed that their activities were 'uncoordinated' and that cells operated 'without either lateral or vertical contact'.[61] Yet this did not stop him driving a high-profile public campaign to vilify his opponents as leaders, pawns or collaborators in a tightly organised conspiracy that he knew did not exist. Over the next couple of years British and Australian diplomats and officials routinely expressed their dismay – both to Lee directly and also to their superiors in London and Canberra – about Lee's 'unsavoury' plans to detain his political opponents, using security as a pretext.[62] In his 1962 report, mentioned above, Selkirk warned:

> Evidence on which to base repressive action is almost entirely lacking. … I must, however, warn you that Lee Kuan Yew is quite clearly attracted by the prospect of wiping out his main political opposition before the next Singapore elections. I think therefore that you will find him advocating a policy of provocation on Lim Chin Siong and his associates with a view to forcing them into unconstitutional action justifying their arrests.[63]

British High Commissioner Philip Moore was indignant, arguing to his superiors in London that it was wrong 'to be party to a device for deliberate misrepresentation of responsibility for continuing detentions in order to help the PAP government to remain in power'.[64] Yet despite British and Australian reluctance, the threatened 'repressive action' did take place. By the end of 1962 the Singaporeans, British and Australians were fully committed to merging Singapore into a new Malaysia (see below), and a major round of detentions was seen (probably correctly) as an absolute precondition, both to keep Lee in power and the Malayan leadership in Kuala Lumpur aboard. The British and Australians clearly decided that, regardless of the case against particular victims, Lee's political survival was more important than principle.[65] The repressive action took the form of a security sweep that began on 2 February 1963, and went by the code name 'Operation Coldstore'. Lee had been pressing to arrest around 1,000 people[66] and, after the British gave up trying to stop him altogether, they pushed for a target of around 70 before settling on a figure of 'around 180'.[67] In the end the full list of detainees contained the names of 183 people, of whom 53 escaped, leaving 130 victims in detention.[68] Those detained included nine identified members of the MCP. The rest were mainly left-wing activists from trade unions, student unions, rural associations and the like,[69] but to this list Lee Kuan Yew had personally added a number of new names, including opposition members of the Legislative Assembly.[70] Three of these elected politicians were from the conservative United People's Party. By no stretch of the imagination could they have been considered a security risk and targeting these men only served to convince the British, Australians and Kuala Lumpur that Lee was primarily interested in politics rather than security issues.[71] Unsurprisingly the subsequent interrogation of the prisoners revealed virtually no intelligence,[72] but the myth of the communist threat lives on in the government imagination, even today.[73]

HEADING FOR SELF-GOVERNMENT

The politics of the left provides a necessary context in which to study the more formal expression of political and administrative developments from the late 1940s to the mid-1960s. The left was a force to be reckoned with, initially as a unified, disciplined mass movement with a small terrorist wing; in the mid-1950s as a dynamic but totally undisciplined mass movement; and by the late 1950s as an increasingly conventional political movement with diminishing claims to a mass following as it bled supporters to Lee Kuan Yew and his team.

The Cold War Sets the Stage

The degeneration of the left was played out against a backdrop of British power and British strategic agendas in the context of the Cold War, Singapore's choreographed drift towards constitutional self-government, the rise of a conservative Malay-dominated government on the peninsula, and the rise and rise of Lee Kuan Yew. It would be unwise to try too hard to separate these four factors from each other, or from the politics of the left because they feed off and into each other, but differentiating them at the outset helps us understand the whole. The Cold War setting has two dimensions. The primary one is that throughout the late 1940s, the whole of the 1950s and most of the 1960s, the British thought they needed to keep their naval base in Singapore at all costs. The matter was further complicated by the Chinese Communist Party's 1949 victory in China, which not only invigorated Chinese communists in Malaya a year into the Emergency, but also generated an upsurge of ethno-nationalist pride among most sections of Singapore's Chinese communities – whether they were communist or not. The tone was set on 10 October 1949, ten days after Mao's declaration of the People's Republic, when about a hundred Chinese associations and middle schools welcomed the 'birth of a new China', and celebrated Mao's victory in the presence of two huge communist flags.[74] The communist victory represented hope and pride to both impoverished and wealthy Chinese in Singapore.

With the Sino–Soviet split still a decade away this development raised the fear that Chinese Singaporeans might act as cyphers for a communist state. These premises built upon the reality of the strength of the MCP in the late 1940s, but ignored its slippage in the 1950s. It generated the narrative that Singapore's trajectory was a problem for Britain. In March 1956 the British Chiefs of Staff put it thus:

> self-government would inevitably lead to the domination of Singapore by Chinese in close touch with Peking. Whether these would be Chinese national[ist]s or Communists is immaterial. ... It is not too much to say an independent Singapore run as an outpost of China would significantly affect the world situation. ...
>
> We are emphatically of the opinion that under no circumstances must Singapore be given its independence except possibly as a member of the Federation [of Malaya].[75]

Thus we see the narration of the skeleton of a Singapore Story wherein the island's future was seen against the backdrop of the West's Cold War. It was into this narrative that Lee Kuan Yew so cleverly inserted himself, as the Chinese the British could trust and who could keep 'the Chinese' under control. At the same time he convinced the MCP that he was their only viable partner in their campaign against the British.

Singapore Politics Goes Off-Script

From this starting point the British offered Singaporeans elections in 1948 and 1951, but only for a minority of the Legislative Council, with no determining effect on the Executive. Furthermore, the franchise was restricted to the small minority of residents who were British subjects. This gave the colonial officials the chance, or so they thought, to nurture and train their preferred heirs – English-speaking British subjects who had organised themselves into the Progressive Party (PP). The PP was founded in 1947 by leaders of the Straits Chinese British Association and the conservative Singapore Association to protect the political and business interests of British subjects in Singapore. Its three foundation members, John Laycock, C.C. Tan and N.A. Mallal, were all London-trained solicitors, and all three were mono-linguistic Anglophones who were very comfortable in colonial Singapore. They were in no hurry at all to win self-government, let alone independence.[76] Their main electoral rival was a mildly left-of-centre Labour Party and a few ethnic parties. In the tiny pool of enfranchised Singaporeans of 1948 and 1951 the British-backed PP was supreme, but this supremacy had a very fragile base. As soon as the franchise was expanded to include a sizeable portion of the Chinese population – that is, in the 1955 elections – two parties of the left reduced the PP and the other parties of the right to a rump in the legislature. This was significant, not only because it showed that the wind was blowing to the left, but it was the first election in which executive positions in government were at stake – even if power still ultimately rested with the Governor and his officials.

David Marshall's Labour Front won the most seats (10 of 17 contested) and formed a government in de facto coalition with a minor right-wing party, supported by the colonial officials and two of the Governor's nominated unofficials. Marshall became Chief Minister based on this untidy arrangement. He would have preferred to have formed a coalition with Lee Kuan Yew's PAP, which had won three seats out of four contested, and which also had the automatic support of a notional independent who was aligned with the PAP. This option was not, however, on the table because Lee preferred to keep his anti-colonialist credentials pristine. Lee's caution proved to be wise, for it gave him billing as opposition leader rather than a junior coalition partner. It also allowed him to undermine support for Marshall and the Labour Front, which found itself compromised politically by its routine co-operation with the colonial administration. Often overlooked in the PAP's narrative of this period is the fact that even as he was being outflanked on the left by Lee, Marshall was doing Lee's work for him: he was engaged in a high-stakes game of brinkmanship with the governors – first Sir John Nicoll, and then Sir Robert Black – and successfully insisted that the Governor be obliged to accept the advice of the Chief Minister in virtually all matters that did not pertain to security, thus single-handedly transforming the role of Chief Minister from a piece of theatre into administrative reality.[77] Left-wing militancy – both among Chinese school students and in the trade unions – was Marshall's greatest problem in office.[78] This issue bedevilled his administration, but in fact it was beyond his power to solve because he had no control at all over the British troops in Singapore and no formal jurisdiction on security issues. Yet his greatest asset was the presence and prevalence of these same radical students and unionists in the opposition PAP. This gave Marshall serious leverage in his dealings with the Governor, since, as Turnbull tells us, 'the British feared that Marshall's departure would open the way to a more radical and irresponsible government'.[79]

Marshall's Brinkmanship Goes Off-Script

Alas, Marshall's attempt to repeat his brinkmanship in London did not go so well. He pulled off a coup by bringing the British to the negotiating table in 1956 to discuss self-government and independence, but raised the bar too high by threatening that his government would resign if all his demands were not met. They were not, so upon returning home from inconclusive negotiations in London, he resigned – only to be disappointed when the rest of his government declined to follow suit.[80] Marshall went on to found a new political party, the Workers' Party, which ultimately became the new centre of gravity for opposition politics. Later he served his country as an activist solicitor and defender of human rights and then as Ambassador to France,[81] but his record in government came to an abrupt end in 1956. His role as Singapore's first Chief Minister is glossed over in Singapore's national narrative, which instead focuses on Lee Kuan Yew's role as the first Prime Minister. Marshall's high principles and his exuberant temperament did not make him a natural politician, but we can only wonder how well he might have grown into the role if he had been just a little more circumspect in 1956, or if his government had had more real capacity to act. Nevertheless, he should be credited with laying the foundations for Singapore's multilingual education system. He was primarily interested in finding a way to meet the grievances of rioting Chinese school students, but the recommendations of his All-Party Committee on Chinese Education almost inadvertently provided the cornerstone of the Singaporean ideal of multiracialism.[82]

After Marshall's political demise the Labour Front administration continued, but under very different leadership. Chief Minister Lim Yew Hock not only had no problem agreeing to British plans for the detention of militant students and trade unionists on security grounds, but also did not have a problem in early 1959 with trying to orchestrate the detention of Lee Kuan Yew for no better reason than political expediency. It was primarily thanks to the high principles of David Marshall that Lim's plans came to nothing: Marshall refused to have anything to do with it and, since he still possessed the standing to scupper such an action, Lee was allowed to go free.[83] Lim was desperate because his administration and his party – by then called the Singapore People's Alliance – had lost its entire base of support and had degenerated into corruption and ineptitude. According to one of its own former ministers, it had come to rely upon secret society gangsters to intimidate the PAP and left-wing unionists and upon highly suspect financial donations to keep the party alive.[84] Lim Yew Hock's main achievement was securing Lee Kuan Yew's control of the PAP by detaining almost all of his most senior opponents in a series of actions over 1956 and 1957.[85] (Lim's real objective was not to save Lee, but to end the communist threat. The two specific triggers for Lim's actions were some of the 'riots' and strikes referred to in Chapter 2, and a successful left-wing push against Lee's group that was mounted from within the PAP in 1957.) Lim can also take some credit for the successful 1957 negotiations with the British over Singapore's demand for self-government – but since the British had already written off Lim Yew Hock from their medium-term calculations, most of the credit for this really needs to go to Lee Kuan Yew, to whom the British were already turning as a safer pair of hands.

Lee Tries to Write his Own Script

Lee's star began to rise in Whitehall during the negotiations in London in 1956. His strengths as a serious and intelligent politician were on display in London, as were his disarmingly familiar English manners. At close quarters, in both official meetings and

Figure 5.4
Lim Chin Siong, 1950s

informal gatherings, Lee was able to convey the message that he was not the wild radical militant that they had assumed him to be. From then on, Colonial Office officials began moving to the conclusion that Lee was their natural choice – probably their only choice – to inherit Singapore.[86] Back home, Lee was still in opposition in this period, and his attention was set firmly on his goal of forming a majority government after the next elections, in which the franchise was expected (correctly) to encompass the entire adult population for the first time. If all went well, this would put Lee in charge of an administration that was completely free of British officials and almost completely free of the heavy hand of the Governor's veto. He managed to achieve this goal handsomely in the 1959 elections (winning 43 seats out of 51), but what he could not do was take complete control of his own party.

Through the first two years in government, Lee and his group of confidantes (who would later come to be known as the 'Old Guard') continued to share control of the PAP with populists on the left and the right. The leftists were led by Lim Chin Siong (Figure 5.4), who was indefatigable and fluent in both Mandarin and Hokkien, the latter being the language most commonly spoken by Singapore's Chinese population. At the time of the PAP's election victory in 1959, Lim – along with most of the senior public leadership of the left – had been in detention since late 1956. Yet such was the importance of the electoral appeal of the left leadership to the PAP that Lee Kuan Yew made the release of the most prominent detainees a precondition for accepting office. All became important political players upon their release, but it was Lim Chin Siong who was able to stir the Chinese crowds and draw on the loyalty of dedicated activists. He was also a crucial player on the left in the split in the PAP in 1961 that resulted in the formation of the breakaway left-wing party, Barisan Sosialis (Socialist Front).

Right-wing populism came in a very different form – and indeed it was so free of ideology and real commitment to principle that we might doubt the appropriateness of applying the 'right wing' label at all. Much of the PAP's momentum in opposition derived from the party's stunning success in the December 1957 City Council elections. Led by the Hokkien orator and crowd-pleaser Ong Eng Guan, the PAP swept into office and then Mayor Ong used the platform to confirm the PAP's credentials as the leading anti-colonialist party. Unfortunately for Lee and his group, Ong had no notion of playing a subordinate role to Lee – nor did he have much notion of administration. This was of only incidental consequence while Ong was just running the City Council, but after the elections he was Minister for National Development and an integral part of the administration. After two acrimonious years he fell out with Lee and his close allies (especially Finance Minister Goh Keng Swee) in 1961 and took several colleagues with him to form a new party, the United People's Party (UPP). The difficulty for Lee was that both Lim and Ong had mass followings – and Lim was, in any case, part of a broader mass movement with an organisational base. Their power was unanswerably demonstrated in two separate by-elections, both in 1961, where the PAP lost both seats. The detentions of 1963 in Operation Coldstore were directed primarily at Lim and his allies on the left but, as we saw above, Lee personally intervened against British opposition to ensure that the list included three members of Ong's UPP.[87]

Ong's departure prompted a burst of heightened government activity on the municipal and urban development front. The *kampung*s in the urban fringe were sanitation hazards, fire hazards and – for the government – political hazards all in one. Perhaps just as offensive to the government's sensibilities as the direct political risk of these towns was the simple fact that they were ungovernable. They shared with the labyrinth of shop houses in Chinatown the dubious honour of being almost unmapped and unnavigable by officials, so unplanned were they in their construction and so insulated were they from government.

The danger and reality of fire had long been part of *kampung* life, and avoiding and fighting fire served as a focus of communal co-operation. But a massive blaze in Bukit Ho Swee in 1961 changed the established pattern irrevocably. From the night of that fire, the government prohibited any unapproved building on the sites of burnt-out *kampung*s, and instead accelerated beyond any reasonable expectation the high-rise housing programme for which the state has since become famous. The residents of Bukit

Ho Swee were not allowed to rebuild. Instead they were given makeshift emergency accommodation and, barely nine months after their *kampung* was razed, they moved into new high-rise flats built almost literally on the ashes of their old homes. This new pattern provided the basis of a new wave of modernisation. The ways of the *kampung* – living rent-free and running backyard businesses and keeping livestock and chickens to supplement low-paying jobs – were becoming a thing of the past[88] as Singaporeans entered a new world of rents, conservancy fees and ordered, numbered houses that were very much in the gaze of officialdom. By 1966, 23% of the population had been moved into more than 55,000 such modern flats, with residents forced out by fires or by police arriving in Black Marias.[89] It also helped that breaking up *kampung*s often also dispersed recalcitrant communities that were less than enthusiastic about the PAP's modernist vision of their future and who tended to support opposition parties.[90] The PAP government's urbanisation plans were thus part of the key to achieving long-term political hegemony and remaking Singapore as a node of modernity. They were not, however, much help in facing immediate political challenges.

INTO MALAYSIA AND BACK

The PAP's first by-election loss of 1961 – Ong's victory in Hong Lim constituency in April – had an immediate but totally unexpected effect: it scared Tunku Abdul Rahman, the conservative UMNO Prime Minister of Malaya, into declaring his support for the idea of absorbing Singapore into Malaya. He saw this as the most practical way of stabilising Singapore and ensuring that the island just a mile south of Johor Baru would not fall to the communists. The Tunku wanted Singapore to become the New York of Malaya and not 'a second Cuba'.[91] This idea of the reunification of Singapore and Malaya had been floating in public discourse since the end of the war. Notwithstanding the fact that it was the British who separated Singapore from Malaya in the first place, it also fitted neatly with Britain's master scheme for a long-term post-war settlement for Southeast Asia because a greater Malaya might also absorb Britain's three orphaned colonies on Borneo – Sarawak, Brunei and North Borneo (Sabah). The problem, however, was that the conservative Malay leadership in Kuala Lumpur wanted none of it because such a merger would have brought another million Chinese into Malaya, putting Malay hegemony at risk. Not even the UMNO's Chinese partner – the conservative Malayan Chinese Association (MCA) – was supportive because a million new Chinese Malaysians with no loyalty to the MCA would have put its place in government at risk. For both of them the rise of the left-wing PAP as the main party in Singapore, led by that difficult personality Lee Kuan Yew, simply made the proposition preposterous. Yet anti-communism was a basic tenet of the Tunku's politics and that of his Malay constituency, and there was no doubt in the Tunku's mind that the only winners in any collapse of the PAP government would be the communists. Such was his loathing of this prospect that it outweighed his dread of bringing both a million Chinese and Lee Kuan Yew into Malaya, and so just a month after the Hong Lim by-election he announced that he was open to the idea of a merger between Malaya and Singapore, providing it included the Borneo territories to offset the new Chinese voters in Singapore.

The left wing of the PAP around Lim Chin Siong regarded this announcement as treachery on Lee Kuan Yew's part. Despite being notionally in favour of a united Malaya, they knew perfectly well that this merger could only spell their political destruction, if not their personal detention. Lee Kuan Yew had assured them that there was no prospect at all of such a merger, and when the Tunku made his grand gesture they refused to believe that Lee did not know about it in advance. In fact the Tunku seems to have caught everyone off guard, including his close friends in the British establishment, so Lee was probably being truthful. Regardless of the facts, however, the left was convinced that it had been betrayed and in the second by-election of 1961 – in Anson constituency, in which David Marshall was the candidate for his new Workers' Party – it withheld its vote bank from the PAP, leading to the loss of the constituency to Marshall. After these events it was only a short step to a split in the PAP, with the left forming Barisan Sosialis and the PAP being left with a majority of just one in the Legislative Assembly.

Lee Pushes Singapore Into Malaysia

Lee pushed forward with a high-profile political campaign to take Singapore into this new greater Malaya – to be called the Federation of Malaysia, and which would include Sabah and Sarawak (but not Brunei, which decided not to join). The high point of the campaign was a plebiscite in September 1962 offering three options – all of which were a vote to join Malaysia. As Deputy Prime Minister Toh Chin Chye put it decades later:

> The ballot paper was crafted by Lee Kuan Yew. Whichever way you voted, you voted for merger. There were three choices: A, B, or C. But frankly, they were all votes for merger. And we moved in the Referendum Bill that [even] spoilt votes will be counted as votes for merger.[92]

This referendum remains one of the ongoing peculiarities of the official national narrative. The government's preferred option won 75% of the vote, and Singapore duly entered Malaysia as a constituent state in September 1963. It is still officially presented as a great achievement for Singapore, whereas in reality it proved to be an unmitigated disaster. Goh Keng Swee became disenchanted with Malaysia soon after merger,[93] and in the end Lee himself only narrowly avoided detention by the Central Government in Kuala Lumpur. Lee's problem in 1961 was that he was desperate. He was fending off a broadly based political tsunami led by Lim Chin Siong and Ong Eng Guan and wanted to use the security services against them, but without getting his own hands dirty. Hence he needed Kuala Lumpur to detain his political opponents, just as Lim Yew Hock had detained them in the mid-1950s. In pursuit of this he was ready to give away almost everything that he held either dear or strategically important: the common market and equal citizenship in Malaysia; control of the police and education; and jurisdiction over the trade unions. He ended up successfully retrieving education and the trade unions, but only after he was pressured by Deputy Prime Minister Toh Chin Chye and Finance Minister Goh Keng Swee to stand his ground. So desperate was Lee to join the Malaysia club that he even agreed that Singapore would have a smaller representation in the Federal Parliament than that to which it was entitled based on its share of the total population; and then accepted an instruction from the Tunku not to run PAP candidates on the peninsula in the forthcoming federal elections (though in the end he did contest a few seats, seemingly without considering it a gross breach of trust). Lee's security sweep of 1963 (Operation Coldstore) was the final, humiliating concession: the Tunku insisted that Singapore would enter Malaysia with its left wing already under lock and key, whereas for Lee, a major purpose of merger was to have someone else take the blame.

Goh Pulls Singapore Out of Malaysia

Singapore's membership of Malaysia turned out to be a disaster from beginning to end, in part because Lee's successful 1963 sweep of the 'communists' meant that the Tunku's main motivation for suggesting merger in the first place was no longer applicable. By the time Malaysia was formed, Singapore already had the status in Kuala Lumpur of a barely tolerated stepsister rather than a welcomed brother. Lee appears to have genuinely thought he was entering a new era of progress and prosperity when he took Singapore into Malaysia, but it turned out to be two years of frustration and disappointment. The common market sought so keenly by Goh Keng Swee never eventuated, and in fact Goh felt that Kuala Lumpur was acting in 'utter bad faith' from the start, treating Singapore as an economic rival to be crushed, rather than as a constituent state of Malaysia.

The Tunku treated the PAP with suspicion, and Lee personally was treated as an enemy by critical elements in the UMNO leadership, including Deputy Prime Minister Tun Abdul Razak. The more Lee tried to heal the growing rift, whether by conciliation, compromise or confrontation, the worse it became. The stress of this period took its toll on Lee in highly visible and destructive ways. He found it increasingly difficult to exercise self-control in front of a microphone, and he developed a pattern of making outrageous and inflammatory speeches, which Toh Chin Chye later characterised as anti-Malay. When Lim Kim San, a key Cabinet minister during the period, was asked by Melanie Chew decades later whether he had counselled Lee to tone down his speeches, he replied: 'Oh yes! We did! But once he got onto the podium in front of the crowd, paah, everything would come out. Exactly what we told him not to say, he would say!'[94]

It was therefore with a sense of desperation that Goh Keng Swee opened secret negotiations with the leadership of the UMNO in mid-July 1965 to arrange a tidy departure of Singapore from Malaysia. He wanted to avoid a round of mutually destructive rancour that would leave both Singapore and Malaysia compromised. The final formula centred on the creation of a lie that would become the foundation of Singapore's nation-building mythology: the story that the Tunku expelled Singapore from Malaysia against its will.

The 'expulsion' of Singapore shocked just about everyone: ordinary Singaporeans and Malaysians of course, but also the second tier of the UMNO leadership; the Singapore Cabinet; the leadership of Sabah and Sarawak (to whom Lee had made substantial commitments); the British High Commissioner and Colonial Office; and the Australian High Commissioner, Lee's good friend Tom Critchley. As a coup it was the perfect crime. It was kept secret for three decades, and even the emergence of the truth in 1996 has not been allowed to disturb the established mythology that has formed the centrepiece of Lee Kuan Yew's *Singapore Story*.[95] This myth-making was a face-saving measure for the Singapore leadership, and a way to avert Lee Kuan Yew's detention at the hands of the Kuala Lumpur police. Just a fortnight after Goh's initial moves in Kuala Lumpur, Singapore was theatrically 'expelled' from Malaysia and faced the world as an independent republic.

6

Governance in Independent Singapore

One of my favourite stories from the Lee Kuan Yew press wars dates to the late 1980s when Singapore had cut *The Asian Wall Street Journal*'s circulation to 400 copies a day from about 5000. The cuts were in retaliation for the paper's refusal to print two long letters from the Monetary Authority of Singapore. The government ordered that many of the approved copies go to government or quasi-government libraries.

One day the phone rang at the *Journal*'s bureau in Singapore. The Prime Minister's Office wanted to know where Mr Lee's subscription was. Yes, we know that your circulation has been restricted, the caller said, but surely this doesn't apply to the prime minister? The *Journal* representative replied that if the prime minister valued the *Journal*'s reporting and commentary, he had the same option that was available to all Singaporeans who were deprived of their newspaper. Go to the library.

Melanie Kirkpatrick, 22 March 2015[1]

The place of politics in present-day Singapore is something of an enigma. According to the narrative of the Singapore Story, politics is hardly practised at all. Once every four or five years, a general election is held across the country, and the parliament and the government are elected in a secret ballot. Presidents are elected less frequently. The campaign periods for these elections are generally no longer than the mandated minimum of nine days, including a 'cooling off day' in which there can be no campaigning. During official campaign periods, rallies can be held and speeches given. This is the designated time for 'politics'. The rest of the time is for governing, for administration and for 'leadership'. In this configuration, governance, administration and even leadership are somehow disconnected from politics so that the actions and words of members of the government are above politics, but the actions and words of government critics are 'political'. Journalists, academics and bloggers who support the government are not 'political' but the journalists, academics and bloggers who are critical of the government are. By the same token, foreign newspapers, researchers and non-governmental organisations (NGOs) that praise the Singapore government are reported widely, while foreign newspapers, researchers and NGOs that criticise the Singapore government are dismissed as interfering foreigners. The explicit assumptions behind these approaches are that 'politics' places the stability and prosperity of the country at risk, and it must be contained to its designated place so that the government can get on with its job. This view of politics suits the country's ruling elite very nicely, and from the mid-1970s until the end of the century it was also internalised and accepted with varying degrees of enthusiasm and fatalism by most journalists, academics, civil servants, courts and voters. Foreign newspapers and magazines held out against this consensus until the end of the 1980s, but even they succumbed to government pressure. Since the opening of the new century, however, this ideal configuration has given way in incremental and small steps to new realities dictated by factors such as a relatively free Internet and an increasingly restive electorate.[2] The firewall between 'politics' and 'not politics' is no longer as clear-cut as it used to be, and yet it still underlies the projection of political norms into the media, schools, academia and most areas of civil society.

I adhere to a completely contrary view: that independent Singapore is a hyper-politicised space; that politics has permeated every aspect of society; and that politics provides the core to understanding most aspects of society. This applies to the corporate sector, housing estates, the media, the military, the churches and religious communities, the legal profession, universities, think tanks, schools, trade unions, business associations, banks and ethnic associations. Even multinational and overseas corporations that do business in Singapore have been integrated into the ruling elite's political space.

◆ ◆ ◆ ◆ ◆

In the previous chapter we left Singapore at the point of its birth as an independent republic, which is a point of periodisation that this narrative shares with that of the Singapore Story, even if I invest it with significantly different meaning. In institutional terms, the transfer of sovereignty changed very little. The constitution rolled over almost unchanged. Lee Kuan Yew (Figure 6.1) continued in his third iteration as Prime Minister of Singapore (initially Prime Minister of the Crown Colony of Singapore, then Prime Minister of the Malaysian State of Singapore, and finally Prime Minister of the Republic of Singapore). Even the transformation of the legislature was seamless: the final Legislative Assembly of the Crown Colony of Singapore had already been rolled over as the Legislative Assembly of the Malaysian State of Singapore, and in 1965 it continued as the first Parliament of the Republic of Singapore. So little changed on the surface and yet, in reality, every dynamic of government was transformed by independence.

Singapore was now a self-contained political and legal entity, with an executive able to act domestically free of most checks or balances. The myth of Singapore's expulsion is at the heart of the Singapore Story and provided the main basis of the nationalist narrative of solidarity in the face of overwhelming odds. This was a partisan and hyper-politicised

Figure 6.1
Lee Kuan Yew in the 1970s, shown on a poster hanging in the Singapore National Museum, June 2015

foundational myth that successfully rallied most of the populace behind the government, in the process permeating the whole of government, the judiciary, the trade union movement, the press and the housing estates. It injected a sense of perpetual crisis into public discourse, as it was designed to do. The larger landscape on which this mythology was painted was initially that of the ongoing Cold War and the American-sponsored Bretton Woods international economic system, and more recently the emergence and rise of neo-liberalism and the opening and rise of China. After an early misdirection,[3] Singapore aligned itself firmly with the United States as one of its best friends (though never a formal ally) in Asia,[4] making the American connection an integral element of both its domestic and international politics.

Yet despite the unremitting logic and power of the forces arrayed against them, there remained elements of Singapore society that were unwilling to surrender fully to the government's vision. For many ordinary Singaporeans, the benefits of the government's master plan were over-the-horizon promises that failed to ameliorate the immediate effects of constant change that was making their lives harder and much less pleasant.[5] In the face of such resistance the government could not have succeeded in its developmental path without strong coercive powers – at least it could not have done so in quite the same way or with the same speed. In the early 1970s, the Singaporean political scientist Chan Heng Chee gave the ethos and this period a name that was so apt that it has survived 50 years of scholarly revisionism: 'the politics of survival'.[6] She also gave the system of governance a name which did not capture the spirit of the times quite so well, but is nevertheless useful: 'the administrative state'.[7]

This chapter unpacks the political history of independent Singapore using these two concepts as starting points. The first – 'survival' – offers a narrative of functional economic and social achievement by the nation: what Lee Kuan Yew called going 'from Third World to First'. The second – 'the administrative state' – is the starting point of a narrative of a different sort of achievement, one that has turned Singapore into a prototype of a new and impressive political form which Garry Rodan has called 'consultative authoritarianism'.[8]

These political and the socio-economic profiles are closely intertwined and codependent, with political imperatives being the primary driver in the relationship. Yet there is one other factor that must be considered in some detail before turning to either 'survival' or the 'administrative state' motifs, and that is Singapore's new-found intimacy with the United States. This developed initially in the context of the Cold War/Bretton Woods paradigm, and then continued to flourish in the post-Cold War era of neo-liberalism. This international context provides the essential backdrop to the domestic politics and economics, so it is here that we resume the story.

LOVING YOUR HEGEMON

Immediately following Singapore's 'expulsion' from Malaysia in August 1965, Prime Minister Lee Kuan Yew became involved in a shouting match with the US foreign policy establishment. As part of his megaphone diplomacy Lee threatened, among other things, to invite the Soviet Union to Singapore to provide a regional balance against China.[9] This was a surprising move for a man known as an Anglophile and one of the more pro-Western of the 'non-aligned' post-colonial leaders. The US was keen to bring Lee and Singapore into its orbit, but the relatively young and inexperienced Lee was having none of it – not until the British government forced his hand. The decisive turning point was November 1967–February 1968, when the British Labour Government devalued the pound by 14% with immediate, devastating effect on Singapore's foreign reserves. It then announced that it was closing the Singapore Naval Base almost immediately, in 1971. These developments shocked Lee, who regarded them as tantamount to betrayal. As soon as he had done what he could to manage the problems created by the British decisions he took off for the US – for a sabbatical at the John F. Kennedy School of Government (Institute of Politics) at Harvard University. According to Lee's memoirs, the Kennedy School made him 'an honorary fellow and arranged breakfasts, lunches, dinners and seminars' so he could meet up with 'a host of distinguished scholars'.[10] In November that same year he was back in New York telling an 800-strong crowd of decision makers at the Economic Club of New York about the virtues of investing in Singapore. In December he was back again, addressing another gathering at the Economic Club.[11] In fact over the next year or so Lee was such a frequent visitor to New York and the Kennedy School that the website shows the period of his fellowship as concluding in 'Spring 1970'.[12]

This was the beginning of a close relationship between Lee and the American political and business establishment. The most startling confirmation of the new intimacy is the fact that only a few years later his son and heir, Lee Hsien Loong, arrived to study at the US Army Command and General Staff College at Fort Leavenworth. Lee Hsien Loong studied at the Staff College from 1978 to 1979, after which he followed in his father's footsteps by enrolling in a Master of Public Administration at the Kennedy School, where he studied from 1979 to 1980. He was, at the time, a senior officer and a rising star in the Singapore Armed Forces (SAF). Two years after his return to Singapore, Lee Hsien Loong became Chief of Staff of the General Staff in the SAF, after which he retired from the army and entered politics, in 1984. He became Singapore's third prime minister 20 years later.[13] Since the elder Lee's initial sojourn in 1968, around 200 Singaporeans have studied at the Kennedy School.[14] Significantly, as of July 2018 this figure included not just Prime Minister Lee Hsien Loong, but also Deputy Prime Minister Teo Chee Hean, Deputy Prime Minister Tharman Shanmugaratnam, and another three ministers who between them make up nearly a third of the Cabinet (six out of 19). On top of this, four more members of Cabinet are graduates of other American universities.

The pattern intimated at Cabinet level flows down even more strongly into the upper levels of the ministries. Of the 25 positions of permanent secretary in the Singapore Civil Service (as of June 2017), 11 were held by graduates of the Kennedy School of Government, including all of the key centres of power: Prime Minister's Office, Defence, Education, Home Affairs, Trade and Industry, Finance, Manpower, Foreign Affairs, and Environment and Water Resources. Another six permanent secretary portfolios are held by graduates of other American universities.

Study in Britain also features prominently in the CVs of many senior members of the political and administrative elite, but the interesting thing is how often the US element has entered elite CVs as an afterword to professional education – as a Master's degree, often taken after a person has established himself or herself as a candidate for the elite. The pattern of treating the US as a 'finishing school' began with Lee Kuan Yew and Lee Hsien Loong, both of whom did their main tertiary education at Cambridge and only crossed the Atlantic years afterwards. Indeed the Kennedy School of Government, which has featured prominently in this analysis, does not even offer primary degrees.

Singapore has never formally entered an alliance with the US, but Tim Huxley describes the relationship as a 'quasi-alliance'.[15] In 1969 (the same year that Nixon declared that he was scaling back American military commitments in Asia), the US Navy opened an office in Singapore to co-ordinate the by then regular ship visits (for maintenance, resupply and 'rest and recreation' functions) during the Vietnam War. In the 1970s Singapore and the US began conducting small-scale joint naval exercises. The US became Singapore's main defence supplier during the 1970s and in the early 1980s the US Air Force began using Singapore as a quasi-base for its operations in the Indian Ocean.[16] The defence relationship continued to intensify in the 1990s and in 2007 the US opened its Navy Region Center in Singapore – the naval base you have when you don't want to call it a base. Today Singapore is singled out by scholars such as Natasha Hamilton-Hart as 'the most consistent and unequivocal' country of Southeast Asia in its support of US foreign policy.[17]

Clearly, Lee Kuan Yew's extended sabbatical at Harvard at the end of the 1960s marked the beginning of a beautiful friendship. From that point, Singapore invested unreservedly in an American-sponsored future – not just in the military and diplomatic domains. It also joined America's post-war economic world. In 1968 this was the world of the Bretton Woods agreement, but that collapsed almost immediately after Singapore's entry when with Nixon revoked the gold standard in 1971. Without hesitation, Singapore stuck with America as it negotiated its way through the 1970s and 1980s towards what we now call the age of neo-liberalism.[18] The fundamental difference between Bretton Woods and neo-liberalism was the balance of power between capital and social goods. On the one hand Bretton Woods set out to regulate and curtail the power and mobility of capital in order to maintain social goods such as full employment (at least in the First World) while still retaining a liberal international order.[19] Neo-liberalism, on the other hand, regards the empowerment and mobility of capital as a primary social good in itself – and places 'other' social goods, such as national sovereignty, employment, welfare and even essential services at a discount.[20] The most important common link between them is the significance of the US as the central player in both systems, and it should be recognised that Singapore embraced America rather than either of the systems it sponsored. The Singapore government strove to profit within the prevailing system but it was never as concerned with the distribution of wealth and social goods as was implied in the Bretton Woods ideal; nor was it ever as disregarding of welfare or its national interests as neo-liberalism expects. It has successfully gone a considerable way down the neo-liberal path, for instance by favouring international capital over labour, especially over cheap foreign labour. At different times it has tried to go further in its disregard of the distribution of social goods, only to pull back under domestic public pressure – notably in the 1980s when it tried to unravel completely the system of almost-free hospital wards on which most Singaporeans depended.[21] Yet ultimately it was a variation of the Japanese model that Singapore followed and continues to follow rather than any Anglo-American model: a *ménage à trois* of strong state, strong bureaucracy and big business, all manufacturing goods for external markets, ideally without losing sight of the welfare and politics of domestic constituencies.

Throughout all of these developments, it was the ongoing pivotal role of the US that held Singapore in thrall. Having placed a huge bet on America as the key to the country's prosperity, the Singapore government had to play to win. Even China's emergence as a new generator of wealth, which began about a decade after Nixon's dollar default, has not shifted the centrality of America for the Singapore elite: Singapore's relationship with China has developed within the context of the Singapore elite's ongoing devotion to America, and the attachment and tangible connection with America has proved the mainstay of Singapore's relationship with the world. In a different way it also underpinned its domestic politics, with the Cold War providing the backdrop for the Singapore government's distinctive and home-grown style of repressive politics, at least for the first few decades of its life.

It is ironic that one of the major challenges facing Singapore today has been generated by the American strategy that had served it so well for the country's first four decades. When you have a graduate of the US Army Command and General Staff College as prime minister, and around a third of your cabinet and 40% of your permanent secretaries educated in America's premier school of government and international relations, how dispassionate is the government likely to be in its attitude towards America? The American connection has served Singapore very well, but America has not been the only power in East Asia for some time. Not only is China a new economic powerhouse, but it has engaged in active push-back against both American military hegemony and the sovereign claims of its more immediate neighbours in the South China Sea.

Singapore's relations with China had been grounded in deliberate ambiguity under Lee Kuan Yew and Goh Chok Tong. Lee Kuan Yew started visiting China in the 1970s – 15 years before Singapore formally recognised it – and he emerged as a prominent figure in smoothing China's entry into international society throughout the 1980s and 1990s. He also set Singapore on the path to profit from China's rise,[22] and yet he had never had any great love – and certainly not much trust – of the Chinese regime. His memoirs and the books written in his old age make these points crystal-clear – and also demonstrate the centrality of the United States in his thinking.[23] Under Lee Kuan Yew and Goh Chok Tong after him, Singapore's relations with both China and the United States had their ups and downs, but always within well-defined limits that minimised offence to China while securing the American relationship. Relations with China have been openly self-serving, with only a superficial level of sentimentality. Singapore is currently the largest foreign investor in China and its third-largest supplier of services, while China is Singapore's largest trading partner, so Singapore has a lot to lose by a misstep.[24] The current leadership is clearly aware of China's importance and is making a long-term investment in building a China-literate leadership. Since around 2004 the government has invested heavily at the school, junior college and tertiary level within Singapore to produce China-literate entrepreneurs, and since 2008 it has been offering targeted incentives to encourage winners of overseas government scholarships to study in China.[25] Yet the relationship is currently under stress, and not just because China is becoming more assertive as it becomes more powerful.

An important element in facilitating the China relationship has always been, in the words of John Wong and Lye Liang Fook, that 'there are no outstanding issues and no areas of open conflict between them'.[26] Even today, Singapore is the only member of the Association of Southeast Asian Nations (ASEAN) with a coast facing the Pacific that is not in conflict with China over its claims in the South China Sea. So with nothing directly at stake and so much to lose, why did Singapore take a leading role within ASEAN on the South China Sea issue in 2016? This was a particularly bad year for Singapore's relations with China, and most of the damage was self-inflicted. In quick succession the Prime Minister upset the Chinese leadership by enthusing a little too passionately about its American connection during a visit to the White House and then engaged in a high-profile attack on Chinese claims in the South China Sea. The Chinese blow-back came at the popular level through the nationalist *Global Times* newspaper, at the diplomatic level through carpeting the Singapore Ambassador in Beijing, and finally quasi-militarily through impounding nine SAF armoured vehicles in Hong Kong for several months, as they were on their way back to Singapore from Taiwan (of all places).[27] To suffer attacks as part of a quest is one thing, but in this case the suffering seems to have been prompted for no purpose and it is difficult to escape the conclusion that the elite's personal attachment to the American Establishment is getting in the way of hard choices.

Furthermore, we know independently that the only reason Singapore's armoured vehicles were even landed in Hong Kong was because earlier in the year the government had sold off its national shipping line, Neptune Orient Lines (NOL), due to a downturn in the shipping industry.[28] Then it put the transport of its military hardware up for commercial contract. It beggars belief that either Lee Kuan Yew or Goh Chok Tong would have sold NOL just because of a downturn in the shipping industry: they would have recognised that as an island-state, dependent on access to international trade routes, Singapore needed a national shipping line for strategic reasons. As we return to a more domestic focus and also return our narrative to 1966, we are left to ponder whether the foreign policy behaviour exhibited in 2016 is an aberration, or the beginning of a new pattern of behaviour.

1966: SURVIVAL AND THE ADMINISTRATIVE STATE

In late 1966, as Singapore faced the world as a sovereign state, the challenges facing the country were serious and existential. Singapore had been cut off from its hinterland (Malaysia), and did not yet have any reason to be assured that the military and diplomatic threat from Indonesia's Konfrontasi had ended. Furthermore it had very little industry and exports, and a polyglot and youthful population with a high unemployment rate. The new 'Singaporeans' had never before thought of themselves as Singaporeans, and many did not particularly wish to be Singaporeans. The police patrolling the streets were Malaysian police and the soldiers in the local army barracks were members of the Malaysian Armed Forces. Furthermore, it was not clear that anyone would recognise the new republic. Singapore had good friends in the UK, Australia and New Zealand but, as we saw in the previous chapter, Lee had gone behind their backs in order to see Singapore cleanly out of Malaysia. Lee and Singapore had more friends in the Third World, but would they 'stick', or would Sukarno's anti-imperialist Konfrontasi rhetoric hold sway?

Yet all was not lost. Singapore was blessed by Britain's 1921 decision to build a huge naval base in Singapore, which in 1965 was providing direct and indirect employment and income to about one-fifth of the island's workforce. Singapore had fully functional administrative and judicial machinery, an educated elite, a vibrant capitalist class and a world-class harbour. And no matter what else happened, the island was still sitting at the southern end of the Straits of Malacca, the gateway between the Indian and Pacific oceans. At this particular juncture of history, this put it right in the pathway of the newly emerging economic giant of Northeast Asia – Japan.

These assets were sufficient to provide a strong base from which to move forward, but only with some luck, much ruthlessness and considerable nimbleness in governance. International friends proved relatively easy to assuage and retain, thanks in large part to Lee's successful retention of his government's socialist credentials. Lee and his colleagues had started out as anti-colonialist leftists, and despite their drift from these roots they had assiduously cultivated the semblance of this political profile. This stood them in good stead as they toured the Third World and non-aligned states seeking recognition for the fledgling country. Meanwhile it turned out that the Labour Government in the UK and the conservative governments in Australia and New Zealand were all willing to support the new country at a time when it desperately needed such support.

The government successfully imposed an economic revolution in the country, substantially through an intensification of Goh Keng Swee's 'bulldoze and build' model of export-oriented industrialisation, whereby tracts of land (especially at Jurong in the west and on the smaller southern islands) were flattened to make way for factories and oil refineries purpose-built for multinational companies.[29] Note the element of ruthlessness implicit in this strategy. It certainly would have been possible to engage in such a programme without slipping into authoritarian habits – especially since Jurong was a mostly uninhabited 'lost region' of the island[30] – but there can be little doubt that the need to clear land and build infrastructure to order lent itself to impatience with checks and balances, planning regulations, trade unions, residents *in situ*, an undisciplined press and political opposition. By the time of independence the government was well practised in such methods, not just from the development of Jurong Industrial Estate and the parallel expansion of high-rise public housing, but also in overt acts of political oppression such as those we considered in Chapter 5.

The government framed the frenetic devotion to expansion of the young country's industrial base in more basic terms than prosperity or economic development: it was about survival as a nation. Lee Kuan Yew was typically rousing and rhetorical in his exposition of this point:

> [T]he touchstone of our policies is survival. There are people who believe – and this is the reason they booted us out – that by booting us out, they would have the squeeze on us. … Meanwhile, this is a lesson of survival. Forget all about bonuses and this, that and the other for the next two years. We have really got to pull ourselves up by the boot straps. … It means that until you break through, you can't have your labour running around doing foolish things.[31]

Writing contemporaneously, the political scientist Chan Heng Chee described it with less passion, but giving more attention to the bigger picture:

> The most striking feature of PAP thinking after separation … is the party's unshaken belief that the survival of Singapore will depend on the willingness and ability of the Singapore citizen to adopt a new set of attitudes, a new set of values, and new set of perspectives; in short, on the creation of a new man.[32]

On the trope of survival hung a radically new set of premises that impacted the whole of society, going far beyond mere politics. Continuing the same sort of apocalyptic logic that justified Operation Coldstore a few years earlier, Lee Kuan Yew presented Singapore with a Manichaean choice between survival and destruction. Destruction of the new nation was the challenge; surviving by any means was the national response. At this time Lee was heavily influenced by his reading of Arnold Toynbee's *A Study of History*, which contains a theory of civilisational development through the mechanism of elite responses to existential challenges. This idea appealed to Lee as a political and social model. He routinely framed politics in terms of this dialectic, effectively creating a national ideology that paralleled Marxism–Leninism, complete with himself and his associates as the vanguard of the revolution.[33] All was subordinated to 'survival': religion, trade unions, sexual mores, education, ideology, language, ethnic associations, universities, the press and politics. Indeed 'politics' was equated with fruitless contention bordering on sedition, and more than anything else had to be subjugated to the demands of professional managerialism – the 'Administrative State'.[34]

1970s: CONSOLIDATING REPRESSIVE POLITICS

With politics itself subordinated to 'government', the late 1960s and the entire period of the 1970s became a dark period for freedoms, as the press and unions and every other vehicle of political expression were pulled into line using a combination of co-option, coercion, replacement of personnel, replacement of entire institutions, and partisan implementation of regulations. When it was considered necessary it included the detention of key personnel without trial, sometimes for years. The most critical period in party politics was the late 1960s when the People's Action Party (PAP) established itself as the only party in parliament, first by detaining and chasing out of Singapore all remaining opposition MPs, and then by winning every seat in the 1968 general election. The ruling PAP was notionally just one political party among many, but politics was such an uneven playing field that a contemporary political scientist described Singapore as 'a dominant party system'.[35] Many years later another approvingly described the PAP of this period as 'the national party'.[36]

Yet party politics was just one small piece of the picture. The entire story is too detailed and complex to recount in its entirety here,[37] but if we just consider, ever so briefly, the institutional takeover of the media and the trade unions, we can see the pattern. The media was brought into line in two major steps: 1971 and 1974, when the government ended the independence of the press and transformed a diverse ecosystem of newspapers in many languages into a single entity with multiple outlets, but just one voice.[38] The trade unions followed a similar trajectory. Militant trade unions and trade union leaders had already been mostly replaced by PAP-aligned unions and leaders in the early 1960s. This task was completed in the late 1960s and early 1970s, and then those local PAP leaders themselves were supplanted by hand-picked 'professionals' appointed by the government from the end of the 1970s. These emasculated unions were then brought into a tame, corporatist relationship with capital and the state through the tripartite National Wages Council.[39] Even local businesses and banks were elbowed aside to make way for multinational companies and also for a new type of entity that would become ubiquitous: the government-linked company (GLC), through which the government could interpolate itself directly into the heart of local capitalism.[40] The judiciary was not treated in a comparable way to the other arms of society, and yet even so, its record of decision making rarely disturbed or challenged the government.[41]

Throughout this critical period the biggest constraint on the effective imposition of the government's will was not political opposition, but administrative incapacity. At

Figure 6.2
Dr Goh Keng Swee, 1967

independence, the government inherited a functioning civil service that was eminently satisfactory for running a colony, and may have even been good enough for running an ordinary government, but was inadequate to facilitate the hyperactive managerialism displayed by Cabinet ministers such as Prime Minister Lee Kuan Yew, or Deputy Prime Ministers Goh Keng Swee (Figure 6.2) and Toh Chin Chye.[42] The fact that the government intended the civil service to run businesses heightened both expectations and disappointments. Such was the administrative ambition of Lee and his colleagues that they had to suffer decades of frustration until they did something decisive to fix it in the 1980s when they started to build a new type of civil servant, which we might call the 'uber-technocrat'.

THE NEW TECHNOCRATS

Lee Kuan Yew launched independent Singapore with a deep-seated conviction in the universal applicability of 'talent' to any situation, and he transformed this conviction into the basis and legitimating rationale of the Singapore political system. He was convinced that the secret of good governance lay in the identification of those people with a genetic and almost tangible quality called 'talent'. Finding 'good men' and giving them power was the key to good governance. The mechanism by which a society finds and funnels such people to the top is just a question of means, not principle. In its late-colonial phase Singapore had already been running a modest system of elite schools and Public Service Commission (PSC) university scholarships for outstanding students. The top echelons of the civil service – the Administrative Service – had long since been recruited from these pathways, and after it came to power in 1959 the PAP government continued and intensified this practice. Prime Minister Goh Chok Tong was an early product of this system. Goh was recruited straight into the Administrative Service directly from doing his MA in Economics at Williams College, Massachusetts in 1967. This was also the year in which Lee Kuan Yew began his practice of taking a close professional interest in PSC scholarship award holders. He followed their careers and received confidential reports on their work, regarding these cohorts of bonded government scholarship winners as the government's routine source of professional executives and the ruling party's longer-term source of political leaders. A few years later, in 1971, Lee personally intervened to establish a new superclass of scholarships available only to new recruits entering the officer corps of the military: the Singapore Armed Forces (SAF) Overseas Scholarships. This initiative was designed to create a new type of elite officer corps. The SAF was the direct beneficiary of this initiative but it also created a new pool of military-trained personnel who began moving into both the civil service and politics in the mid-1980s. At about the same time, in 1982, Lee Kuan Yew announced that he was streamlining the management of the civil service by adapting the staff review and promotions system used by the Shell oil company. He also began harvesting the fruit of his long-standing practice of combing the civil service and the military for talent to be drafted into politics. This resulted in Cabinet becoming utterly dominated by people recruited from the public sector from the early 1980s onwards. With the foundations of the contemporary, professional civil service in place by the mid-1980s, the pace of change slowed to that of a slow drip until a shake-up occurred in the mid-1990s. It was at this point that the Singapore elite's technocratic logic blossomed to the point where it began to smell of conceit – providing early hints of the more recent claims of Singapore's exceptionalism as showcased in Chapter 2. These elites – especially those who came through the military – were drawn almost exclusively from the same upper-middle-class, English-speaking Chinese social background; they went to the same schools; many of the military scholars had served in the same officer corps of the army; they competed for and won the same scholarships. And when they returned from study they joined the same clubs, attended the same postgraduate finishing schools, and engaged in the same structured socialisation and bonding exercises.[43]

1980s: A PIVOTAL DECADE

The long decade of the 1980s (from *c.*1978 to *c.*1992) was a turning point for Singapore, substantially because the international environment was changing. The rise of Margaret Thatcher in Britain and Ronald Reagan in America ushered in an ideological shift in the relationship between labour and capital – and indeed between nation-states and capital. The Bretton Woods era of regulation and the curtailment of the power of capital gave way to the Washington Consensus: neo-liberalism's doctrine of the supremacy of capital over labour and the unfettered mobility of capital between jurisdictions. This shift presented great opportunities for Singapore as a provider of cheap labour and low-cost infrastructure, but if it continued down this path its leaders knew they would be sentencing Singapore to a permanent place in the lower reaches of the international manufacturing production chain. Rather than settle for this future, the government set out in the late 1970s and early 1980s to move up the production ladder to become a high-technology centre. In the early 1990s it took the next logical step and set out to move to the other side of the table: to become an international source of capital (see Chapter 7 for more details). Neither decision was unproblematic, but the shift of the late 1970s in particular was poorly handled and caused a high level of economic and social pain that compounded political problems that were emerging independently.

This chapter is concerned with politics and administration, and politics was indeed the central locus of the pivot of the 1980s: the reinvention of Singapore's education system and the politics of language (which are explored in Chapter 8); the reinvention of the relationship between the Singapore market and the foreign media (which is the subject of the quotation that opens this chapter); and the professionalisation of the civil service (referred to above). By the opening of the 1980s Singapore had been independent for a decade-and-a-half, and the PAP had been in government for two decades. On the PAP's watch the economy and society (housing, education, languages spoken, factories, community centres, and the physical landscape of the island) had been transformed beyond recognition. The forced pace of building very basic and utilitarian high-rise housing estates was an early and very visible sign of the physical and social transformation of the island in the 1960s and the first half of the 1970s, and they caused massive short-term dislocation and unhappiness. By the time we get to the 1980s the pace of building had slowed and considerably more thought was being given to using the housing programme to create geographic communities, and trying to provide proximity to work, worship and recreational facilities.[44] The social elements of this programme were never fully successful, but this became a moot point because at the same time the government began laying train lines across the island. In the process it created new logics of physical association that disregarded proximity.

The upshot of these building programmes was the systematically organised destruction of communities and the uprooting of families as homes were razed and populations dispersed to new centres. Even as late as the period from 1979 to 1985, 44,574 'squatters' were relocated and rehoused by the government – and this does not count residents with legal leases or tenure who were shifted, nor the thousands of businesses that were relocated to Jurong.[45] There is a tendency to think that the physical transformation of Singapore in the PAP period was completely innovative, and

Figure 6.3 Housing and Development Board living

that the economy and society took off from a standing start. This habit of mind is a natural consequence of the dominance of the Singapore Story, but in fact Singapore's post-1965 launch had strong precedent in the colonial, and especially the late colonial period. The Lee Kuan Yew government increased the pace and tightened the focus of Singapore's urban makeover, but it did not invent it. Long before independence, the Singapore Improvement Trust and the Municipal Authorities had bulldozed and rebuilt some of the most densely occupied parts of the city, albeit in small pockets. Factories, mosques, temples and schools had been built, shifted and rebuilt, as one would expect in a growing city constructed on a small island. Indeed, reading a recently published account of the vicissitudes of an obscure Chinese temple as it was pushed from one location to another by encroaching development, I was struck by the fact that the forced relocations and the intrusion of bureaucracy predated 1965 by decades.[46] Yet as Peter van der Veer demonstrates in a separate publication, the post-1965 migration of Chinese and other temples is distinctive in that it has been much more centrally and deliberately directed by the government through the mechanism of restricting temples to leaseholds of 30 years – which means that every generation they need to renew them at commercial rates. This simple device has driven many temples out of the central and residential areas and into the cheaper industrial estates at the fringes of the island, often forcing several religions to share accommodation in the interests of economy.[47]

In among the dislocations of the 1960s and 1970s, the PAP government rightly took credit for the identifiable successes and achievements as light became visible at the end of the tunnel, and as the 1980s approached, talk of 'survival' gradually shifted to talk of 'success'.[48] But Singaporeans did not yet feel rich and the modernisation of the economy was itself causing social and economic dislocation and hardship that hit some fractions of society very hard – especially manual workers and older workers. The contrast between the new prosperity being enjoyed overall and the patchy effects of economic development stretched the political loyalty of some groups to breaking point. One such group was the dock workers. They found their voice by voting an opposition candidate – J.B. Jeyaretnam of the Workers' Party – into parliament in a 1981 by-election, thus breaking the PAP's monopoly on parliamentary seats. This achievement was followed by a second opposition candidate – the Singapore Democratic Party's Chiam See Tong – winning another seat in parliament in the 1984 general election. The rise of even such a poorly represented parliamentary opposition raised many people's hopes that there might be a lightening of the repressive hand of government but, as we shall see later in this chapter, such optimism was misplaced.

The 1980s was a decisive decade in Singapore's history in many ways, but none was more pivotal than the high politics in Cabinet. This was the time when Lee Kuan Yew emerged from the relative humility of being first among equals in a Cabinet of his strong-minded peers. After the retirement of Goh Keng Swee in 1984, Lee was left as the unchallengeable patriarch in a Cabinet comprised of much younger men. Politics and even Singapore as a nation became increasingly personalised around Lee Kuan Yew in the 1980s, and for the first time he was able to act much as he wished, giving immediate force to his ideological and personal whims, at least in the first instance. Once the adverse political consequences of some of his more extreme initiatives started to become obvious in the context of a rejuvenated parliamentary opposition, even Lee was forced to slow down the implementation of some of his dreams. Nevertheless the scope of his imagination and the seriousness of his purpose ensured that most of his dreams survived in some form. The most notable strategic retreat was in the field of eugenics, when he had to abandon his elaborate plans of providing incentives to encourage well-educated women to marry and have more children.[49] The next most significant setback was much less dramatic and has already been mentioned in passing – he had to reverse his programme of closing the cheapest hospital wards.[50] Yet notwithstanding these hesitations, within the space of just a few years Lee had set in train a phalanx of reforms that revolutionised Singapore's education system, its practice of multiracialism and multilingualism, its housing system and its health system. For the most part, these reforms were driven by his elitism (education), his Chinese supremacism (education, language, multi-racialism), his personal hostility to welfare (health), and his determination to dilute the Malay community's political power (by introducing racial quotas into housing estates).[51]

THE REINVENTION OF AUTHORITARIANISM

The 1980s also featured the invention and implementation of a newly sophisticated form of authoritarian rule. From Operation Coldstore onwards, Singapore had combined elections with authoritarian practices that inhibited free speech, a free press, the redress of government actions by courts, independent unions and the free operation of opposition political parties and civil society. The government's scare from seeing the election of a mere two opposition candidates to parliament in the first half of the 1980s prompted a major recalibration of the political rules and institutions that left even less to chance.[52] Perhaps one of the more interesting and innovative measures was the introduction in 1984 of a pretend opposition into parliament, whereby some of the best-performing losers among opposition candidates to parliament were appointed as Non-Constituency MPs. This initiative was followed in 1990 by the creation of yet another class of MP appointed by parliament – the Nominated MP. These new classes of MPs were designed to meet the acknowledged popular demand for alternative voices in parliament, but to create the perception that it could be achieved within the PAP's authoritarian ecosystem – no need to vote for the opposition. Together with a multiplicity of government-managed feedback mechanisms introduced in the 1980s and refined thereafter, these devices were also intended to feed alternate and constituency views to the government in a nonconfrontational, non-threatening manner, something that Garry Rodan has identified as a 'consultative authoritarian regime'.[53] Rodan argued:

> While their emphasis on *consultation* is meant to limit the boundaries and conduct of political conflict, this is also informed by a view of politics as a principally problem-solving rather than normative exercise that can usefully harness relevant information and expertise.
>
> Consultative authoritarianism, then, is distinguished from other forms of authoritarianism by the emphasis on state-controlled institutions to increase political participation. Political suppression and intimidation remain integral to these regimes [but] new social and economic interests generated by capitalist development are increasingly engaged through various creative mechanisms of consultation in an attempt to obviate greater demand for independent political space.[54]

The underlying logic at all times rested on technocratic elitism: the myth that Cabinet ministers and senior bureaucrats truly brought professional standards and best practice into government. For decades the presumption of competence that derives from the rationale of elitism provided members of the government with a high level of immunity from accountability and scrutiny. This immunity rested not just on the presumption that members of the elite are highly competent but also on the presumption that they are exceptionally virtuous and can be trusted without close scrutiny. The presumptions of trust, virtue and competence were widely accepted by the general population until recently, and they cocooned Cabinet from serious critique. The very fact that Singapore law and administration has no concept of conflict of interest is indicative of this presumption.[55] A legal reality of comparable significance is the jurisprudential approach to the 'fundamental liberties' provided in the constitution: there are no rights to be upheld by courts, only liberties that are gifted upon Singaporeans by the government and parliament.[56] The continuing existence of these liberties is therefore contingent upon the goodwill and the good character of government. This is a wilfully benign reading of the nature of those who hold power and would collapse if it were widely thought that the powerful could not be trusted. The presumptions of virtue and competence are therefore intertwined, and have been entrenched in public discourse as the default assumption of government.[57]

The second half of the 1980s provided an object lesson in what happens to Singaporeans who refrain from extending uncritical trust to the government and who choose to go outside the government's feedback and tamed opposition framework to act on their convictions. I refer to the detention of 22 social activists under the Internal Security Act in 1987 – activists who were mostly associated either with the Catholic Church or with alternative theatre. According to a confidential assessment made by Lee Kuan Yew at the time, they were naïve 'do-gooders who wanted to help the poor and the dispossessed'. They were nevertheless arrested (though never charged or tried) based on fanciful accusations that they were planning the overthrow of the Singapore government with the objective of imposing a communist dictatorship.[58] The detentions of 1987 emerged as yet another turning point that made the 1980s a climacteric in Singapore's modern history for two distinct but related reasons. First, the optimism of the early 1980s disappeared overnight (literally). Second, the purge was ostensibly conducted by the so-called 'second generation' of Cabinet ministers, who had been presenting themselves as being gentler and more open than the Lee Kuan Yew generation. The public faces of the detentions were Deputy Prime Minister Goh Chok Tong, Minister for Home Affairs S. Jayakumar and the newly arrived junior minister, Lee Hsien Loong. Also fully implicated in the decision were other up-and-coming ministers such as the future Deputy Prime Minister and President, Tony Tan.[59] If a development in which nothing changed can be properly considered a 'turning point', then this one was decisive – confirming that the continued use of repression against independent political activism would continue as the government's ultimate backstop, underpinning the Singapore version of governance.

Only now, with this template secure and his successors fully implicated in what he called 'knuckleduster' politics, was Lee ready to step down from the prime ministership and hand over to Goh Chok Tong in November 1990. Not that Lee stepped very far down: he stayed in Cabinet as Senior Minister and retained his office in the Istana (the palace where the Prime Minister's Office is located). He maintained a light-touch rein on general political developments while reserving complete freedom to intervene in the minutia of administration whenever he thought it warranted his attention. Such high-handed interventions were not necessary very often, but when they were 'warranted' they were always decisive. During this period Lee Kuan Yew retained his position as Chairman of one of the government's two sovereign wealth funds, the Government of Singapore Investment Corporation.[60] Also note that his final act before stepping down as Prime Minister was to make Lee Hsien Loong a Deputy Prime Minister with 'special responsibility for the economy and civil service matters', placing him at the crossroads of the corridors of power.

THE GOH CHOK TONG INTERREGNUM

Viewed strictly through the prism of elite politics, the defining narrative of the 13 years from the end of 1990 began with the appointment of Goh Chok Tong (Figure 6.4) as Prime Minister in what was expected universally to be a caretaker role until it was Lee Hsien Loong's turn. This scenario was transformed in the blink of an eye when Lee Hsien Loong was diagnosed with cancer late in 1992. Lee Hsien Loong stayed on as Deputy Prime Minister, but without a portfolio until he was formally cleared of cancer in 1996, whereupon he resumed his trajectory towards the prime ministership.[61] Goh

Figure 6.4
Goh Chok Tong, 1990s

brought a different style and freshness to the office of prime minister, and on his watch the government took on a more consultative feel. A space was provided in Hong Lim Park (near Chinatown and the financial district) for limited airing of non-government views in public, and he made some efforts to break down the rigid ethnic silos that his government had inherited from Lee Kuan Yew. He presided over efforts to reduce the content-driven rote learning character of schooling and to emphasise creative thinking.[62] During the second half of his prime ministership he devoted a lot of energy to developing Singapore's ties with India, the Middle East and other parts of the world that had not been a major focus to date.[63] And yet at the end of 13 years as prime minister, his greatest achievement was to hold off the rise of Lee Hsien Loong for that long – something that no one expected.

THE SON RISES

Lee Hsien Loong (Figure 6.5) became Prime Minister in 2004, having been Deputy Prime Minister since 1990, and yet despite his long apprenticeship – or perhaps because of it – he remained in his father's shadow for several years. Even the decision to retain Lee Kuan Yew in Cabinet as 'Minister Mentor' was taken and announced by Lee Kuan Yew himself, not by Lee Hsien Loong.[64] It did not help that in 2006, in the first general election after Lee Hsien Loong became prime minister, the PAP vote dropped by several points, and dropped particularly badly in Lee's own constituency. As the years passed, small but noticeable signs of differences between father and son began emerging, but it was only after the next general election – in 2011 – that Lee Hsien Loong was finally able to establish his authority.

The 2011 elections have a complex legacy. It was Lee Hsien Loong's second general election as prime minister and it came off the back of two previous general elections in which the PAP vote had already been declining. Most significantly, the government was suffering in the wake of a series of administrative and political failures that for the most part had been avoidable: politically unsustainable levels of immigration (foreign workers), the rising cost of living, health care and housing, an inadequate supply of housing, inadequate transport infrastructure, and even the escape of a terrorist from gaol (by climbing through a toilet window and then hiding with his family disguised as a woman!).[65] Popular discontent over the parsimonious nature of Singapore's social welfare measures was also reaching new heights. As a consequence, opposition parties were swamped with new volunteers and were in a state of unrealistically high expectation in the months leading up to the poll.[66] In the event, the PAP did do poorly in the 2011 poll, though not as badly as the opposition had hoped. The PAP received its lowest vote since independence (60%) and the Workers' Party sent a record six elected MPs to sit in a parliament of 87 elected members.

Figure 6.5 Lee Hsien Loong, 2007

Yet Lee Hsien Loong was able to use this worst-ever election result to establish his own authority. He achieved this by a clever and desperate exercise in self-effacement. In the last days of the campaign he apologised for policy and administrative errors and promised to do better. Then, in the aftermath of the election he forced the retirement of three underperforming ministers, as well as that of his father and of Senior Minister Goh Chok Tong.[67] The apology has been generally accepted as the turning point of the campaign, averting a disastrous result for the government and providing a base from which the PAP was able to rebuild significantly in the 2015 general election: Lee Hsien Loong restored its vote to 70%, though without winning back the seats lost in 2011.

The full implications of the 2011 elections are not, in my view, found in the government's relatively poor showing in the vote, but in Lee Hsien Loong's apology. Since the 1980s, the ruling elite had been justifying its monopoly on power by reference to its exceptional performance as a government – which reached its high point in Lee Kuan Yew and Lee Hsien Loong's claims of Singapore's exceptionalism (see Chapter 2). Now such boasts are being greeted with considerable scepticism and the government has had to reconfigure its self-justification downwards.

The 10% swing the government received in the 2015 general election suggests that it has succeeded in lowering the expectations of the electorate to mere competence and yet

Rodan suggests that even these more manageable expectations could be unsustainable without a more drastic and fundamental adjustment to the nation's political economy.[68] In his analysis, the political problems facing the government rest fundamentally on contradictions that are 'inherent' in Singapore's model of capitalism, particularly those elements that rely upon cheap foreign labour (including cheap skilled foreign labour). This reliance is the inevitable outcome of Singapore's ongoing subordinate role in the international production chain and Singapore's embrace of the neo-liberal international order, but its debilitating effects include the depression of local incomes, magnified income inequalities and the disempowerment of local agency – including local elite agency. Taken together, these are all issues that underpinned the government's political challenges in 2011 and continue to worry it as this book goes to press in 2018.

As well as quick fixes on issues such as housing supply and transport infrastructure, a major element in the government's recovery in the 2015 general election was the introduction of social welfare measures – particularly for the elderly – alongside a significant reduction in the inflows of foreign workers, in other words a retreat from the neo-liberal accommodation of international capital. But the details of these measures raise doubts about their long-term viability: most of the social welfare measures have sunset clauses, and the reduction in the inflows of foreign workers is both slowing the economy and drawing complaints from capital investors. While acknowledging the government's 'impressive' capacity to manage the political implications of such social contradictions, Rodan goes as far as suggesting that the challenges between the politics and the economics are ultimately irreconcilable.[69]

Time will tell, but I end this chapter on this note from Rodan because it serves as a link between the political and the economic chapters of this book. Looking backwards, it returns us to a consideration of the importance of the international context that I canvassed at the beginning of this chapter – notably the tensions arising from Singapore's place in the contemporary neo-liberal order. Looking forward, it foreshadows some of the themes raised in the following chapter, which is a brief study of Singapore's economic history.

7

The Economy: Singapore, Still at the Centre

There has been an uninterrupted succession of commercial emporia in South-East Asia belonging to a system of intra-regional and international relations that is more than 2,000 years old, and the Republic of Singapore inherits precisely its functions from this succession of state organisations based on the typical economic structures of an emporium.

Philippe Regnier,
Introduction to *Singapore: City-State in Southeast Asia*[1]

The economic success of Singapore – remarkable, though not a 'miracle' as sometimes suggested – is explicable on two counts. One is that Singapore started from a high base. The other is the favourable international economic forces on which Singapore capitalized.

W.G. Huff,
Chapter 1 of *The Economic Growth of Singapore*[2]

More than any other aspect of Singapore's story, its economic history has been a captive of its geographical place in the region and the world. The large island sitting at the mouth of the Johor River has had a rich history as a fulcrum of traffic and trade travelling between two great oceans. At most times in its history it has been a functioning harbour, plying trade and engaging in commerce on a trans-regional scale, sitting as it does between the giant economies of East Asia, the Indian subcontinent and what we now call the Middle East. Singapore itself has not usually been the main centre of commercial or political power, but somewhere in the region there has always been such a centre, and control of the island and its surrounds has always been an important element in exercising control over the southern mouth of the Straits of Malacca. This has been the case regardless of where political power resided: in Riau, Malacca, Johor, Sumatra, Java, Siam or in Singapore itself – or in London, Amsterdam or Lisbon for that matter.

One of the items in Peter Borschberg's collection of Dutch documents from the beginning of the seventeenth century reveals the Singapore Straits as a favoured place to wait for valuable goods to arrive from China so they could be waylaid and pilfered.[3] Another warns of the difficulties and dangers of dealing with the 'king of Johor': it might be more dangerous to cut him out of a deal than to include him, but the trouble is that when he is included, he 'would want to shear the sheep and let us shear the pigs'.[4]

Much of the current Singaporean regime's economic success has involved its imaginative, ruthless and overwhelmingly successful exploitation of Singapore's place. The remote historical background necessary to appreciate this argument has already been explored extensively in Chapter 3, and this paragraph presents a précis of that account, with a sharper focus on the economic history embedded in the politics. We have seen that the island of Singapore had already enjoyed two distinct periods of prosperity before the British arrived at the beginning of the nineteenth century. The first was the century or so before Sang Nila Utama (Sri Tri Buana) took over the island in around 1390 and renamed it Singapura, only to flee with his followers to Malacca a few years later. Sang Nila Utama invaded with a navy consisting of hundreds of boats, subdued an existing community and probably killed its leader. It may have been already in decline by the time he landed, but it is clear that Sang Nila Utama occupied an existing city that had been an important trading centre during the whole of the fourteenth century. The island's second period of prosperity was the sixteenth and seventeenth centuries when the Sultan returned to the southern end of the Straits after the fall of Malacca to the Portuguese. As far as we know, Singapore was never the centre of political or economic power during this period, but thanks to its harbour and strategic location it was an important centre of activity. It serviced commercial traffic travelling east and west, was the base for much of the Johor navy, and at least some of the time was home to the Laksamana, or admiral of the fleet. This period of prosperity ended with the murder of the last Sultan in 1699, after which Johor and Singapore seem to have been mostly deserted for a century.[5] If we look beyond the island to consider Singapore's broader heritage, we can also identify the Malaccan century (*c.*1400–1511) as a period of magnificent prosperity, and we should also note that when Riau was under the rule of the Bugis in the middle of the eighteenth century, it enjoyed some decades of prosperity acting as an entrepôt and a hub for Asian and British vessels.

This thumbnail sketch brings us to the cusp of Singapore's third period of economic prosperity, which had its beginnings loosely around 1819. In 1811, Temenggong Abdul Rahman established a base in Singapore and set about building the island's economy as a commercial harbour and a centre for gambier and pepper farming.[6] In 1818 he abandoned the court at Riau and made Singapore his primary residence.[7] By this stage he had thousands of his followers fully established in a city on the island, along with several *kongsi* of Chinese gambier and pepper farmers who had relocated from Riau at the Temenggong's invitation over the previous decade. When Raffles landed in January 1819, supported by the familiar figure of William Farquhar, the Temenggong recognised it as a brilliant new business opportunity and happily allowed the East India Company

(EIC) to set up a factory by the Singapore River. Chinese and native migrants, particularly from Riau and Malacca, began relocating to the island immediately upon hearing news of a British free port and British protection. In 1823 the Malay royals signed away their sovereignty over the island to the EIC and in 1824 the Treaty of London recognised Britain's sovereignty. This final step ended years of uncertainty and placed the trajectory of the 1810s on a firm, long-term footing.

There is a fuzziness in this timeline that stands in sharp contrast to the certainty found in most scholarship that 1819 is the beginning. My approach is unusual, but not unprecedented. When Carl Trocki titled his 1990 book, *Opium and Empire: Chinese Society in Colonial Singapore, 1800–1910*, his choice of 1800 as the start date rather than 1819 was no accident. He was consciously rejecting 1819 and he was, I think, the first scholar to do so.[8] Trocki's focus was on Chinese and local Asian society in Southeast Asia. He traced both the lines of continuity in local Chinese business enterprise – the *kongsi*, the *kangchu* and the Chinese Kapitan system – and the lines of royal descent and power among the local indigenous peoples – Malays, Bugis and *orang laut*. He tracked these business and family histories forward to late-nineteenth-century Johor and back as far as the opening of the eighteenth century.[9] In such an Asia-focused approach to history, the arrival of the British is a new development, not a starting point. Peter Borschberg's more recent scholarship studies Singapore's economic history over the *longue durée*, taking an even longer perspective than Trocki. He identifies the island's third period of economic prosperity as beginning variously 'around 1800' and 'at the end of the Napoleonic Wars' (which implicitly points to the Treaty of London as a decisive marker).[10] None of us deny that British protection and presence was crucial, but all three of us insist that this single action be considered in context, for without the context there was nothing for the British to protect and no vehicle through which it could operate.

In this economic history chapter, I am therefore taking a more expansive view of Singapore's history than either the Singapore Story or the Turnbull story. Thanks to the ground covered in earlier chapters,[11] however, it is sufficient to expand the 1819 time frame by only half a century or so. This is the point at which we can see – at least in retrospect – that the Dutch hegemony of Southeast Asia's seas, especially the Straits of Malacca, was beginning to give way to the reach of the British Navy and the EIC. Throughout this century, new economic units and relationships – notably the *kongsi* among the Chinese – were also emerging and consolidating throughout the region, developing hand-in-glove with European colonialism. The Europeans were part of these developments, but the relationships could never be categorised as being European. The dynamic mixture of European, indigenous and Chinese inputs, whether as workers, rulers, investors, traders, sailors or consumers, provided the key to Southeast

Asia's political economy in the nineteenth century, and the key to the development of Singapore as a new centre.

When Raffles arrived in Singapore in 1819, he was very much aware of the existing dynamics in the region, beginning with the historical role of Johor-Singapore-Riau as the centre of Asian 'native' empires, and the Straits' place at the fulcrum of trans-oceanic trade. He wanted the EIC to be part of this operation and so was desperate to find some speck of land on which he could plausibly argue that the Dutch did not have a prior claim. If it had a decent harbour and was on a major sea route, so much the better. Singapore was both a last-gasp chance to (barely) meet the political-legal threshold at the heart of this formula (no Dutch) and also, as it happened, a near-perfect selection to meet the geographic and strategic criteria. He would have happily settled for setting up a factory at Riau or somewhere on the southern end of the Johor mainland – perhaps just across from present-day Changi, where the Dutch had fruitlessly sought Johor's permission to build a fortress two centuries earlier. Singapore had a unique combination of natural advantages: position, harbour and a substantial size. Yet the deciding factor was that he could mount a barely plausible argument to say that the island was not a Dutch possession.

A FREE PORT; A BRITISH PORT

The most decisive feature of the new British settlement on Singapore was Raffles' unilateral introduction of free trade. British protection was the second feature. Between them, these two points proved to be magnets for Asian entrepreneurs throughout the immediate region. Upon Resident Farquhar sending word to Dutch Malacca that the British were in Singapore, much of the non-European population began loading their boats and heading south. Not even a Dutch blockade of its own port could halt the exodus; they could only watch as the repopulation of Singapore sped Malacca's slide into irrelevance.[12]

Prominent among the earliest immigrants were Chinese pepper and gambier farmers and labourers from Riau and, like those that had already migrated to Singapore under the Temenggong's rule, they transplanted *in toto* the economic and self-governance system of the *kongsi*. So all the newcomers needed to do was occupy vacant land away from the major settlements, set up a simple workshop and recruit workers. This latter task was accomplished through Chinese clan and other networks that reached not just to other parts of Southeast Asia, but also into villages in southern China. The *kongsi* became a basic unit of the Singapore economy, but it was never an independent one. The men who ran them quickly formed partnerships with the other type of 'farmer' in Singapore: the revenue 'farmer' who ran a revenue or tax 'farm'. As was explained in Chapter 4, the 'tax farm' was basically a licence giving an entrepreneur – or more commonly a syndicate of wealthy investors – the right to profit from a government monopoly. The 'farm' was an early form of outsourcing government and social services in exchange for a rent that was determined at a public auction. The 'services' in this instance focused primarily on the vices that could be monetised (opium, prostitution, alcohol, etc.), but also included pork, candles and a wide range of goods and services needed for daily life. Both the *kongsi* and the revenue farm required capital and both benefited from the 'protection' offered by the criminal and semi-criminal aspects of the *kongsi*'s life, and so the two modes of business spread to other enterprises. The linkages between the *kongsi* and the syndicates holding revenue farms began declining in the 1890s, partly because pepper and gambier (mainly used for tanning leather) went into decline and competition among revenue farmers reached new and unsustainable levels.[13]

Despite Raffles' keenness to establish a new way station to service the EIC's China trade, this role was short-lived. It came to an end when the EIC lost its monopoly on the China trade in 1833, only 14 years after the Singapore factory was founded. When we use the terms 'China trade' and 'China monopoly' we need to be clear that these are euphemisms for the opium trade and the EIC's opium monopoly. Indian opium went east, while Chinese silks, porcelain, jade and tea went west. Furthermore it was not so much a way station for supplies that the EIC needed as much as a base to provide security for vulnerable merchant ships. Lower on the list of needs was a regional hub for the transhipment of Southeast Asian products for sale in Canton and India, but after the loss of the China trade this sideline became the colony's main function. Singapore as a colony continued to rely on opium revenue derived from local consumption and revenue farms right up to the opening of World War I,[14] but the EIC's profitability was fatally damaged in 1833 and the whole purpose of building settlements in the Straits of Malacca had disappeared along with the China monopoly.

As an investment that was expected to deliver the EIC a return on capital, Singapore never at any time lived up to expectations. As a going concern for private entrepreneurs, however, it was a real winner. European (mainly British) capitalists and traders began arriving and settling in Singapore in the early 1820s, setting up trading companies (known as 'agency houses'). These men risked their capital, but they had very limited control or understanding of the operation they were notionally heading. Their contacts and networks were with Europe and European colonies, which gave them downstream access to markets. Without much or any Chinese language or many Chinese contacts, they had no direct access to upstream producers. For this they were reliant upon a cascading network of Chinese *towkay*s and Kapitans, Chinese labourers, and a combination of Chinese and native sailors/traders and producers, which was bonded together in what Trocki has called a 'pyramid of debt and exchange', with indentured labourers at the bottom of the pyramid.[15] Many of the leading figures among the early *towkay*s had emigrated from Malacca upon Singapore's foundation, and they brought their local and regional operations with them as going concerns.

Singapore's place as a pivot of trade was an entirely traditional role for the island. Penang was also a natural meeting place for traders, but it looked to the northern end of the Malay Peninsula and westward to Aceh and across the Bay of Bengal. It was too far 'up' the Straits to catch the Southeast Asian trade that moved from east to west. This was especially so because Dutch Malacca stood to Penang's south and caught everything heading north, but even without Malacca as a neighbour, the piratical *orang laut* in Riau, Johor and Singapore were active deterrents to carrying valuable goods into the Straits from the east. The narrow straits and often treacherous weather around Singapore made it a very attractive base for waylaying passing trade. Once Singapore became a safe base rather than a place of danger, it was transformed overnight into a magnet for Asian traders from across the Indonesian archipelago as well as north towards China and Japan. Trocki puts it simply:

> [Singapore] acted as a gathering point for the products of Southeast Asia: the sea products of the islands and coasts, and the rice, pepper, spices, forest produce, tin and gold of the inland areas. These commodities, many of them unique to tropical Asia, found markets throughout the world.[16]

Ten years after Raffles established a factory on the island, Asian vessels accounted for 90% of vessels and half the tonnage passing through the Port of Singapore. If we extend this survey to include the following two decades, we find that during this period Asian vessels still outnumbered the European vessels engaged in intra-Asia trade by an average of 7:1. The European ships were square-rigged vessels and carried much bigger loads than the small Asian boats, but the sheer number of small Asian vessels meant that they still accounted for 45% of the intra-Asian tonnage passing through Singapore over this period.[17] Singapore's entrepôt role survived the end of the EIC's China monopoly in 1833, finding new purpose when the Dutch opened Makassar and the British opened Hong Kong and other Chinese coastal cities as free trade ports. In the 1850s the British and the Americans continued the trend by forcing free trade on Siam and Japan respectively. These acts certainly created competitors to the Port of Singapore, but they also created newly active trading partners and broke open massive markets from which Singaporean traders could profit, pushing the value of Singapore's trade to more than double that of the early 1840s.[18]

Since Singapore was a free port, all this profitable activity took place at the EIC's expense, but to the benefit of the European trading houses and Asian entrepreneurs throughout the region. The local mercantile community in Singapore was asked to pay for very little, and even those projects that it did help with were mostly self-serving.

One such recipient of mercantile largesse was the Horsburgh Lighthouse, which was constructed by the colonial government with financial aid from the local mercantile community to secure a safer passage for shipping. Built in 1851 by Chinese, Malay and Indian labour, Horsburgh Lighthouse was part of a chain of new-generation British lighthouses that lit the global trade routes for the empire. It still stands (and operates) today on Pedra Branca, a lonely rock about 87 kilometres (54 miles) to Singapore's east, where the Straits of Malacca meet the South China Sea.[19] By the time it was constructed, most of Singapore's trading goods were being carried on European ships, but Europe was not yet the primary destination: three-quarters of that trade was still being conducted within Asia.[20]

In the early decades, Singapore's role as a regional trading hub was the primary source of the colony's wealth, but in the 1840s it began transforming itself into a gateway to the Malay Peninsula. This had originally been envisioned as British Penang's given role but, as we saw above, it was restricted to looking north-east and west because the Dutch had been sitting in Malacca, to Penang's south. Penang continued to dominate trade with the Malay kingdoms at the northern end of the peninsula, but Singapore opened a new gateway through Johor, as was explained in Chapters 2 and 5. I mentioned above that pepper and gambier farming went into decline in the 1890s, but long before that Singapore had run out of room for the expansion of gambier and pepper farming. In the 1840s, about 600 gambier and pepper plantations employed about 6,000 Chinese labourers on the island. This proved to be maximum capacity – the soil was being exhausted from overproduction and there was little arable land left to be cleared. Furthermore the colonial government in Singapore was opening up the interior of the island through a road development programme, which brought many benefits but also limited the scope for this type of entrepreneurship by bringing land usage across the island under the gaze of government officials.

It was at this point that the Temenggong, Daing Ibrahim, began opening up the southern end of Johor for development. His initial venture in exploiting his holdings on the mainland was triggered in 1843 by the discovery of gutta-percha, which was necessary for the production of submarine telegraph cables. He exploited this discovery with uninhibited zeal, and exhausted the supply of the product in Johor completely in just a single, highly profitable year. He immediately sought new ways to maintain his flow of income and turned his attention to opening up Johor's river lands for gambier and pepper production, using his newly acquired capital to fund the initial administration of his new state.[21] In the second half of the nineteenth century, hundreds of thousands of Chinese passed through the Port of Singapore on their way to Johor, where they joined *kongsi*, hoping to make their fortunes. Singapore planters regarded this very simply as a new capital investment and seamlessly expanded their businesses to the mainland.

The revenue farming syndicates likewise expanded their operations to Johor without giving up their still-lucrative holdings in Singapore. Indeed the *kongsi* and the tax farm syndicates were so integrated and interdependent by this stage that it would have been remarkable if they had not moved together. Apart from being substantially run by the same people, they drew on the same capital and exploited the same cohorts of Chinese labourers for their businesses. Thus developed a new pattern whereby revenue farm syndicates straddled both jurisdictions.[22]

Daing Ibrahim also diverted his traditional followers from their usual 'piratical' occupation of harassing local shipping and turned them into the enforcers of his monopoly on all the goods coming from and through Johor (including ongoing gutta-percha production in other parts of the peninsula). Thus the Temenggong not only built robust reserves for his new state, but also transformed himself into a person of respectability and influence in the Singapore business community. In 1845 there were 50 gambier plantations on four rivers in Johor. By the time of Daing Ibrahim's death in 1862, his agricultural settlements straddled the banks of 38 rivers and creeks in Johor, and the Johor state was on a firm footing.[23]

The Temenggong's entrepreneurial successes transformed the politics and the economics of the Malay world. In 1840 the Temenggong had been one traditional Malay ruler among many: in the aftermath of the Johor-Riau Sultanate there seemed to be sultans to spare on the peninsula, and Daing Ibrahim was not even a sultan. By 1850 he was easily the most powerful, wealthiest and best-connected Malay in the world. Yet at every point his business operation was integrated with and dependent upon Singapore – and Singapore was becoming increasingly integrated with his business interests and dependent upon him.

RUBBER AND TIN

By the last quarter of the nineteenth century, Singapore's fortunes were increasingly intertwined, not just with those of Johor but with the Malay Peninsula more generally (which by then was known as 'British Malaya'). Singapore became rich along with Malaya. This was, to a considerable extent, the natural consequence of the integration of the peninsula into the British sphere following the Treaty of London in 1824. Beyond this imperial logic, two more specific developments reinforced this pattern and perpetuated it into the early twentieth century: the gradually increasing use of steam ships from 1845 onwards; and the opening of the Suez Canal in 1869. With these two technological changes, shipping to Europe became quicker and more reliable. It also expanded the type of goods that could be carried. Bulk heavy goods – whether grains, textiles, tin or rubber – could now be transported to Europe reliably and profitably. Furthermore, steam ships burnt coal and needed refuelling stations straddling their shipping routes – places such as Singapore.

Global demand for the primary products that Malaya and the region could produce increased dramatically in the late nineteenth century and the early years of the twentieth century, generating an unbroken economic boom for Singapore and Malaya that lasted from the 1870s until the Great Depression of 1929.[24] In the 1870s the production, storage and transportation of tin and rubber replaced the earlier trade in gambier and pepper as the staples of the Singapore economy.[25] Tin-mining on the peninsula and in other parts of Southeast Asia predated the spread of British rule by centuries, but technological change, plus easy access to British markets, transformed it into a major industry from the 1870s onwards.[26] Indeed, technological change was at the heart of this part of the story. Global demand for both tin and rubber increased exponentially as a direct consequence of Karl Benz's patenting of the motor car and Nikolaus August Otto's invention of the petrol engine, both in 1886, and John Dunlop's invention of the pneumatic tyre a year later. These developments created a huge market for rubber, even before Henry Ford opened his first assembly line in 1913.The invention and popularity of the motor car assisted Malaya's economy initially by contributing to a massive upsurge in global tin consumption, since tin was needed to make barrels in which to transport petroleum. By 1899 Malaya produced half of the world's tin.[27] The high point of tin production followed just a few years later – in 1905 – after which production began to lag as Malaya's reserves thinned. Throughout this period Singapore smelted most of Malaya's and nearly all of present-day Indonesia's tin, and its production stabilised at about one-third of global production.[28]

The exponential increase in the global market for rubber was driven by the same technological change that drove up the market for tin and, as luck would have it, Malaya's capacity to produce rubber took off just as tin was beginning its slow decline. The critical technological breakthrough in rubber production was a local Malayan development: in 1897, after nearly a decade of trial and error in Singapore's Botanic Gardens, Henry Ridley perfected modern rubber tree planting and tapping, making it suitable for plantation-scale production for the first time.[29] Commercial rubber production began on a small scale in Singapore in 1896 and emerged as a sunrise industry on the peninsula a decade later. Initially plantation owners were casting around for an alternative crop to replace coffee, which had become uncompetitive thanks to competition from Brazil, but rubber became much more important to the economy than coffee had ever been.

In the first decade of the twentieth century about a million acres were planted and rubber became easily Malaya's most important product.[30] Between 1905 and the outbreak of World War I – itself a major stimulus for the consumption of rubber – Malaya was producing around half the world's rubber, and most of that was exported through Singapore. Tin mines were originally small-scale, low-capital operations relying on Chinese labour and capital, but became more capital-intensive and European-dominated by the century's end. The rubber plantations were by definition large-scale, capital-intensive operations that quickly came to rely upon imported Indian labour. They were predominantly European-owned from the beginning. Both industries turned mainly to Singapore for sales and distribution of their Malayan output, but from almost the foundation of the commercial rubber industry the Singaporean arms of British firms set about turning Singapore into a regional hub for both rubber and tin sales.[31] The long-term importance of these arrangements is evident from the impact of the mini-boom in tin and rubber that was generated by the Korean War (1950–3): it temporarily doubled colonial government revenue on the peninsula and trebled it in Singapore.[32] The island of Singapore itself was the home of neither rubber plantations nor tin mines during this period, but Malaya and other centres of production in the region used Singapore as their conduit to global markets, confirming the interdependence of the island and the region.

Note that by the 1930s the demand for Malayan goods was global, not just British or European. The disruptions of World War I had created an opening for Japan and the United States to expand their trade relations with Singapore and Malaya from a very low base. Both Japan and the United States were rising economic powers – especially America, which was by this stage the largest economy in the world. Furthermore, they were both a lot closer geographically to Singapore than was the UK. Unsurprisingly, the colonies were not inclined to surrender these new markets after the war, just because Britain was once again ready to give them her attention. So in the lead-up to World War II, we find that the share of Malaya's exports that went to the US was more than double what it had been in the lead-up to World War I, and Japan's share of its exports had more than tripled.[33] Imports were a different matter, and Singapore and Malaya's immediate neighbours supplied most of its imports – particularly the Netherlands East Indies and Sarawak, which fed the colonies' need for raw materials for processing and re-export.[34] It needs to be acknowledged, however, that this was only importing in a technical sense. As we shall see in the section immediately following, the regional production lines crossed Singapore, Malaya, Sarawak and Netherlands East Indies without much regard for colonial borders, reflecting the unregulated flows of the ancient world more so than the rigidly demarcated silos of modern international relations. These patterns of trade – both regional and extra-regional – were totally disrupted by the Pacific War, but were resumed and extended after the United States assumed its post-war role as hegemon of the Asia-Pacific region and Japan became its ally and business partner.

OIL

Oil is the only product of the trio of core colonial Malayan staples that remains important to Singapore in the twenty-first century, making Singapore the third-largest oil exporter in the world and accounting for 11% of its total export earnings.[35] Its origins of course lie in the same technological breakthroughs that drove the rise of tin and rubber, but it stands apart from those commodities because it still makes a major contribution to the Singapore (and Malayan) economy. Today Singapore is the centre of oil production, processing, pricing and distribution to Southeast Asia and Australia, but its association with oil started rather humbly in 1892 when the London-based company, M. Samuel and Co. (which became Shell Transport and Trading Co. in 1897), established a bunker for the storage of Russian kerosene on Pulau Bukum, which sits just off Singapore's southern shore, between Sentosa and Jurong islands.[36] The British and the Dutch were sitting on huge oil reserves in Borneo and Sumatra, and when the British started production in Borneo in 1897, Pulau Bukum became their storage facility. By this stage the Royal Dutch Company had already established a storage facility 16.5 kilometres (10 miles) to the south-east at Pulau Sambu. The Dutch island is much smaller than Pulau Bukum and when the Dutch and British companies merged in 1907 to form Royal Dutch Shell, Pulau Bukum naturally became the primary base for storage and distribution – to be managed from Singapore through its subsidiary, the Asiatic Petroleum Company. For the purposes of storage and distribution, Singapore and Pulau Bukum offered all the advantages of geography that have been discussed at length in this book, to which was added the advantages of proximity to a major, modern city and a magnificent harbour that offered a remarkable level of freedom from the burden of safety regulations. As a bonus it also provided an entrée to global markets via the British imperial network just as the world was turning to oil as the fuel of choice for transportation both on sea and land.

Figure 7.1 Pulau Bukum, 2015: view from the southern shore of Sentosa

At Pulau Bukum, Shell stored and blended petroleum from the Netherlands East Indies (mainly Sumatra and Borneo) and British Sarawak, and during the interwar years consistently sold more than half of it within the region (to Australia, New Zealand, Japan and Southeast Asia). Singapore became home to British, Dutch and American expertise in bunkering, marketing and transporting petroleum products, and its southern islands became crowded with oil tanks.[37] Singapore did no oil refining at this stage, but in 1962 Mobil, which had been operating on Singapore's Pulau Sebarok since 1931, approached Singapore's Economic Development Board (EDB) with a proposal to expand its operation. The two key leaders in the EDB, Chairman Hon Sui Sen and Director E.J. Mayer, saw a larger opportunity and convinced Mobil to invest in an oil refinery, offering an attractive combination of tax concessions, free land, infrastructure, few regulations and a compliant workforce. Mobil was open to persuasion, partly because it had already been conscious of the need for a regional centre in Southeast Asia, but also because it was concerned that Sukarno might nationalise its existing facilities in Indonesia.[38] The opening of Mobil's refinery in 1966 marked just the beginning of a long series of major investments in oil refining and related industries by oil companies that has in turn emerged as a major contributor to the Singapore economy, both directly and through ancillary industries.[39] It is significant that by this stage the new investment was American rather than British or Dutch: the United States had long since overtaken Britain as the hegemonic economic and military power in the Pacific, and Singapore was at least as well placed geographically to serve the New World as the Old.

Beyond the investments, the multinational oil companies also brought their technical and managerial personnel, just as they had done earlier in the century, confirming a pattern whereby foreign technical and managerial expertise routinely accompanied foreign capital to Singapore. To a certain extent this development was an inevitable consequence of encouraging foreign direct investment (FDI), but in fact the government and its agencies consciously targeted industries that would require high-level experts and managers to relocate to Singapore, rather than just send lowly factory supervisors. They hoped to learn techniques from them, and at the same time develop Singapore into a regional hub for what was to become known as 'foreign talent'.

The major spin-off industry spawned by oil was ship maintenance and repair. Oil bunkering and distribution of course involves shipping, and ships need to be maintained and repaired somewhere – preferably somewhere that is already on the major shipping routes. Singapore's shipping industry had its remote origins in 1829, but started to get serious only in the 1860s, when it installed modern, steam-powered equipment for the construction of ocean-going steam ships. The shipbuilding industry was overhauled and modernised in this period, thanks to the injection of private capital and an influx of engineers from the UK (mainly Scots), who ran both the shipbuilding and ship-repair industries, and the dockyard and shipping industries. The development of New Harbour (now Keppel Harbour) to the west of Singapore River began in 1864 as well, with the Tanjong Pagar Dock Company investing heavily in the building of a brand-new dock facing the Old Singapore Strait. The electrification of the dock in 1886 doubled New Harbour's throughput. It nevertheless struggled to keep pace with the volume of traffic because Singapore was now well established as a major point of not just repair but also refuelling – thanks to the now-ubiquitous steam engine's insatiable appetite for coal. In the short term, Singapore's rise as a coaling station in the 1850s had cemented its place on global trade routes. In the long term it marked it as a logical site for the development of an oil bunkering and refuelling industry once oil started to replace coal as the fuel of choice half a century later.[40] By the latter part of the century, Singapore had established itself globally as a centre for the construction, maintenance, fuelling and handling of large, ocean-going vessels and was the British Empire's key port in 'the East', but it was barely coping, partly due to the primitive state of the land transport connecting the harbour with the city (dirt roads; no railway), but also due to the reluctance of the dock company to invest and modernise at adequate levels. In 1905 the colonial government responded by taking over the entire dockyard, including all four dry docks. It established the Singapore Harbour Board in 1912 and only two years later Singapore had become the third busiest port in Asia, behind Hong Kong and Colombo.[41] The Harbour Board upgraded the dry docks explicitly to prepare for the new age of oil – not just bunkering and supplying oil, but repairing oil tankers. In 1913 it built a fifth dry dock designed to serve the Admiralty, and then the Admiralty itself built a floating dock in 1928. This was followed by the construction of a graving dock in 1938. Singapore's ship repair and maintenance industry fluctuated with external factors such as war, demand for oil, the Great Depression and straightforward competition from rivals in other parts of Asia, but by the mid-1930s the Harbour Board's commercial ship-repair industry was a major going concern, and most of its business came from the Asiatic Petroleum Company.[42]

FROM STAPLE PORT TO MANUFACTURING

Huff argues that from the 1870s right through to the 1960s, Singapore should properly be studied as a 'staple port'.[43] Favourable geography is the first and most basic element of a successful staple port, but beyond that it needs five distinct features to prosper: a conducive entrepreneurial culture that facilitates investment and professional management; sophisticated financial services; efficient processing of the staples; effective marketing; and the close involvement of business interests in the port with production in the hinterland.[44] Thanks to the combination of British overlordship, British and Asian (Chinese and Malay) capitalists and capital, and Asian workers (mainly Chinese, but also many Indians), Singapore and its Malayan hinterland possessed all these features from the opening of this time frame.

Yet notwithstanding its ongoing success and importance, the oil industry is atypical of independent Singapore's economic narrative, since Singapore's future turned out to lie in manufacturing and services rather than staples.[45] When the People's Action Party (PAP) won government in 1959, it was already a successful colonial city. It had one of the busiest ports in the world, a fine airport, and was a regional centre for education, and for rubber and oil sales.[46] It did, however, also face serious short-term economic problems, which most notably centred on providing gainful employment for the island's legions of new school-leavers: in 1957, 43% of the population was under the age of 15 and had to be absorbed into the workforce over the next few years.[47]

The PAP government had hoped to perpetuate Singapore's historical relationship with Malaya so that it could continue exporting its rubber and other primary products to the world. It also hoped to sell Singapore's manufactures on the peninsula. Unfortunately politics got in the way of both these hopes. As late as the end of the 1950s, many of the old synergies with Malaya were still operational: Malaya was still producing 41% of the world's natural rubber and most of that was still being exported through Singapore. Yet the two-year experiment of merging Singapore into the new Federation of Malaysia (September 1963–August 1965) did not just fail, it created such ill will that the post-Separation relationship between the former colonies was fraught beyond reason. One of the many sticking points during the Merger years was the refusal of both the Malay and the Chinese wings of the central leadership in Kuala Lumpur (the United Malays National Organisation and the Malayan Chinese Association, respectively) to facilitate the economic integration of Singapore and the peninsula. It should not be surprising, therefore, that after Separation the situation did not return to the rather benign *status quo ante*. Rather, tit-for-tat spite and imprudent speeches by leaders escalated petty grievances into minor crises. In this environment, Malaysia and Singapore gradually introduced barriers, penalties and permit systems that made it more difficult to access each other's workers, newspapers and products, even as the two sets of leaders were managing an orderly separation of their assets (notably airlines and shipping lines), currency and the armed forces.

With the Malaysian market effectively lost, the Singapore government was left with only one viable economic strategy: manufacturing for export. And it worked. Unemployment in the 1960s was mostly around 8–9%, but just a few years into the 1970s Singapore's unemployment problem had been transformed into a labour shortage problem,[48] thanks mostly to the government's strategy of building a new manufacturing sector hungry for waged labour. Manufacturing had been the primary economic development strategy for the PAP since before it won government in 1959. This is confirmed both in articles to this effect published in the late 1950s in the PAP's journal, *Petir*, and by the fact that the decision to clear Jurong for factories was taken almost as soon as it took office, in 1960. The Economic Development Board (EDB) was started in 1961, charged with the twin tasks of enticing FDI and literally preparing the ground (i.e. clearing the land and building the factories, etc.) to pave the way for the arrival of multinational corporations.[49] While there had been a chance of forming some sort of economic union with Malaya there was some ambiguity in the government's thinking over whether the domestic market might play a significant role in the government's manufacturing strategy, but this dream died even before the experiment with Malaysia was ended.

The government's economic agenda was led by Finance Minister Goh Keng Swee, who was aided and advised by people such as Hon Sui Sen (Chairman of the EDB and later Minister for Finance), and by Dr Albert Winsemius, a Dutch economist who began advising Singapore in 1960, initially on behalf of the United Nations Development Programme. Dr Winsemius continued as the government's economic adviser until 1984, and is justly given credit for many of Singapore's economic achievements. Among other milestones, Lee Kuan Yew credited him with having been the prime mover of the government's policy of attracting high-level technological and managerial expertise from overseas (1961), and of its decisions to position Singapore as a financial centre (1968) and to containerise the port (1969).[50]

With the direction of Singapore's economy set, the main challenge was to raise capital. This had been at the forefront of Goh Keng Swee's mind since before the PAP won government, and featured prominently in *Petir* even before the 1959 elections. There were two distinct aspects to the need for capital: for public investment and for private investment. It had long been Goh's intention to use the capital in the Central Provident Fund (CPF) – a compulsory retirement fund for Singaporean waged and salaried employees – as a vehicle for industrial and infrastructure investment, and Goh had planned to begin raising the rate of contributions into the fund after they won government.[51] In government he and his successors pursued this plan, systematically raising the monthly contribution levels from the 10% of income they inherited in 1959 to an unsustainable high of 50% in 1984.[52] Yet even at these extraordinary rates, the CPF was only a partial solution for Singapore's capital needs. Another source of capital was the three Chinese banks based in Singapore: they were told to hand over nearly half their capital to the new, government-owned Development Bank of Singapore (DBS), which then used its rivals' capital to make itself the biggest commercial bank in Southeast Asia, pushing the original Chinese banks into the shade.

The CPF and DBS, along with a few other resources (e.g. government reserves, Post Office Savings Bank deposits) made an impressive contribution to Singapore's capital requirements, but they did not solve the need for massive and immediate job-creating investment in manufacturing. Private investment was needed to fund that, and there were severe limits to how much private investment could be raised on the island. The government's answer was to do everything possible to entice multinational companies to move their manufacturing operations to Singapore, applying a more generalised version of the model that led to Mobil opening its refinery on Pulau Bukum and shifting its regional operation to Singapore.

The quest for private capital took Singapore's business emissaries to the same doorsteps that their predecessors had been opening in the first half of the twentieth century: America, Japan and Europe (including the UK, but with the Netherlands and Germany emerging as major investors in electronics). Early efforts to entice Japanese investment met with only limited success, and it was not until the 1980s that Japan assumed significance with a massive investment in the petrochemical sector.[53] Nevertheless, even by 1975 the rising rate of Japanese investment was already at a level that made it comparable with the UK's declining rate of investment. Clearly Singapore was expanding its field of vision far beyond its traditional comfort zone (see Figure 7.2).

The major prize was the United States. America was both a land of mass production and mass consumption. It was also underwriting the post-war capitalist economy on a global scale and by the 1970s Singapore had established itself comfortably as part of its network of friendly Asian governments. Building on the contacts and the favourable impressions that Lee Kuan Yew made during his sojourns at the Kennedy School of Government from 1968 to 1970 (see Chapter 6), the EDB dispatched officers to the US, knocking on doors, proposing business plans and promising the world – or at least cheap, compliant labour, tailor-made modern factories, a modern port and extensive tax holidays.[54]

Thus, the government started down the path of developing its own distinctive developmental model, whereby international capital and the Singapore state worked together to turn Singapore into a key, albeit subordinate, node in intercontinental production cycles based and financed in places such as New York, Tokyo, London and Amsterdam: a relationship between dominant, mostly Western capital and subordinate, Asian labour, which political economists described as being part of the New International Division of Labour (NIDL).[55] Singapore's strategy focused on manufacturing parts for inclusion in more complicated products such as computers and electronic devices, but Singapore's oil and ship-repair industries can be considered as different dimensions of the same transnational strategy. The success of this model was dependent on the simultaneous presence of many factors: easy and timely accessibility to Singapore from the important centres of world capital in the New World, the Old World and Northeast Asia; local access to raw materials; the use of fast, reliable and cheap seaborne transport for the movement

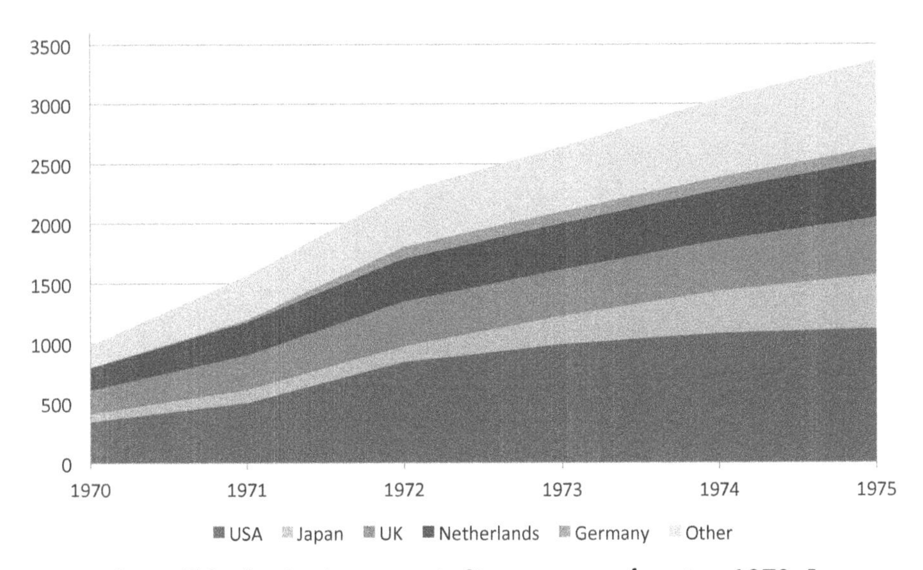

Figure 7.2 Foreign investment in Singapore manufacturing, 1970–5
Source: Garry Rodan, *The Political Economy of Singapore's Industrialization*, Table 4.5, p. 122.

of manufactured goods to and from distant factories and markets; high-quality infrastructure and world-class port facilities in Singapore; a cheap, reliable Singaporean workforce with enough sophistication to deliver goods to demanding specifications; and a stable political system with minimal sovereign risk. The most critical new element in this scenario was the advent of fast, cheap transportation of bulk goods by sea, which suddenly made Singapore competitive as an exporter of manufactured goods to the US and Europe – a point whose importance was explained in detail to Lee Kuan Yew in 1968 by Ray Vernon, a Professor of Business at Harvard University.[56]

These factors are the leading and most obvious characteristics that explain the success of Singapore's developmental model, but beyond these, a number of less obvious factors needed to be in play. First, potential rivals had to be either slow to join the race (China, India, Indonesia and Malaysia in the early decades) or be turned into partners (America and Japan in the early decades; China, India, Indonesia and Malaysia more recently). The importance of the early partnership with America and to a lesser extent Japan cannot be overstated. It was this articulation of interests that drove the Port of Singapore's decision to convert itself into a container port in 1969. Japan and the west coast of America were leading the world in containerisation, and between them they were among the world's major markets for both consumption and manufacturing inputs.[57] If Singapore was to be their partner in Southeast Asia, it needed to be able to accept their ships and handle their containers. In essence, Singapore successfully rode

Figure 7.3 Cranes for containers, Port of Singapore

the first wave of the shipping container revolution that began on 26 April 1956 in the Port of New Jersey and which transformed intercontinental transportation, manufacturing and consumerism on a global scale. Hence, in 1972 Singapore became the first commercial Asian port outside Japan to containerise, successfully staking its claim as the hub port for Southeast Asia.[58] Today, when every major port is containerised, Singapore retains its edge by having a higher capacity and a much lower 'dwelling time' (time spent in port waiting, unloading, waiting, loading, leaving) than its neighbours.[59]

Second, state management of commercial enterprises needed, above all other considerations, to be professional. Achieving this was not a simple matter, and in the early years government ministers were very much feeling their way, placing relatives, friends and old school chums into positions of great trust: men such as Ngiam Tong Dow (the self-described 'first PAP civil servant' who later became Head of the Civil Service),[60]

J.Y. Pillay (later head of Singapore Airlines and the Development Bank of Singapore, among other roles), Cabinet ministers S. Dhanabalan, Hon Sui Sen and Lim Kim San, and Goh Chok Tong. Only gradually did the government develop more systematic and relatively impersonal approaches to recruitment and management.[61] Initially the state operated through companies and statutory boards fully owned and directly managed by government ministries. By trial and error the government eventually settled on its preferred model, which was based on the government-linked company (GLC). These were partially or fully government-owned companies that were given enough independence to act like a business in day-to-day affairs, but with more than enough government control to make them reliable instruments of state policy and political patronage. In 1974 most of the GLCs were consolidated into two holding companies: Sheng-li Holdings (later Singapore Technologies and now ST Engineering) for the GLCs owned by the Ministry of Defence; and Temasek Holdings for the rest. In 1981 the management of the Singapore government's direct overseas investments was consolidated into the Government of Singapore Investment Corporation (GIC) and in 1994 Singapore Technologies was moved under the umbrella of Temasek Holdings, leaving Singapore with two sovereign wealth funds: Temasek Holdings and the GIC. By its nature, this arm's-length management entailed surrendering real managerial power to trusted delegates, but even today one of the most distinctive features of 'Singapore Inc.' is that power and the lines of command are very personal. No instrument of power – economic or otherwise – is allowed to drift out of the leadership's orbit. Hence both Temasek Holdings and the GIC have always had members and trusted friends of Lee Kuan Yew's family firmly embedded in the most senior levels of management, and between them these two bodies have become the country's most important tools of patronage and power.[62] Despite its flaws and many false steps, the system has attained a high level of professionalism to the point where scholarship specialising in such matters regards Singapore Inc. as being the most efficient form of state capitalism in the world[63] – seemingly having found a 'sweet spot' that balances modest levels of public and commercial accountability on the one hand, and centralised, long-term leadership on the other, all with relatively low transaction costs. Whether this record can be maintained in the absence of its architects remains to be seen but, as of the mid-2010s, this record is justly a source of national pride.

Third, both state and international capital required a quiescent labour force. The most basic requirement in this programme was a stable, reliable and useful body of people who needed regular paid employment. Such a workforce could not be taken for granted, since Singapore had long had a large underbelly of unemployed, underemployed, self-employed and daily rated workers who were barely part of the money economy at all. They might have been single men renting part of a room in Chinatown,

Figure 7.4
From zinc and atap to high-rise: Singapore in the 1960s

or families living rent-free or squatting in a *kampung*, or in one of the many atap- or zinc-roofed villages, perhaps fishing or raising a few animals or chickens or growing some vegetables to help get by. Such workers had no more utility charges to cover than the cost of a bit of kerosene for cooking and lighting. No longer. As part of the government's housing programme, *kampung* dwellers and squatters were systematically moved into high-rise government flats where rent and utility bills had to be paid and there was no room for animals or chickens (Figure 7.4). They needed steady wages.[64] Hence the workforce participation rate (the proportion of the adult population in regular paid employment) climbed in a spectacular fashion in these early years of development, as not just school-leavers and hitherto unemployed or underemployed men went to work in factories, but they were also joined by women.

To be useful, this putative workforce had to be given sufficient training to suit them for the new sort of repetitive unskilled and semi-skilled work that was likely to be on offer in factories, and they had to be socialised into being meek and compliant employees. Much of the government rhetoric in the late 1960s and throughout the 1970s was directed at fostering just such attitudes, but the most important work was done at the level of the factory floor itself by the newly compliant trade union movement. Critical in this process in the 1960s and 1970s was C.V. Devan Nair, a charismatic and hard-working former left-wing union leader who switched his allegiance to Lee Kuan Yew in 1960. A year later he formed the PAP-aligned National Trades Union Congress (NTUC) as a rival to the left-wing Singapore Association of Trades Unions, and successfully led the government's campaign to destroy the latter. By the end of the 1960s the left had been destroyed, both in the trade unions and in other walks of life, and there was hardly a union in the country that was not affiliated to the NTUC and run by leaders sympathetic to the government.[65] One of the many roles of the new-look trade union movement was that of working with the government to organise and promote a seemingly endless stream of training and retraining programmes for workers. Separately to such short-term adult training programmes, the entire education system was overhauled to produce cohorts of graduates suitable to work in Singapore's rapidly changing economy. This was a much more significant and transformative investment.

There was also an entirely separate workforce that was vital to the Singapore enterprise: low-paid foreign guest workers from poorer countries in South and Southeast Asia. Transient workers had long been integral to Singapore's success, whether as indentured labourers, plantation workers, gambier farmers, or sea nomads who followed a Temenggong. When Singapore found itself independent and economically vulnerable, the government began turning a stony face to foreign workers as it sought to protect the jobs of its citizen workforce, but once its unemployment problem was transformed into a labour shortage problem, foreign workers once again became an asset to be sought. In the mid-1970s there were up to 200,000 foreign workers; in 2004 there were 621,400; 900,800 in 2008; and as of December 2017, there were 1,368,000 foreign workers, comprising nearly 40% of the population.[66] Until the mid-2000s, low-paid foreign workers were overwhelmingly unskilled or semi-skilled, but today they also include skilled workers and professionals who are competing more directly with Singaporeans for jobs.

The contributions of low-paid foreign workers have been severely underplayed in Singapore's economic history. Writing in 1994, Huff devoted only three sentences to the topic:

> The job security of Singapore nationals was, in part, underwritten through hosting ... guest workers ... who could be sent home, and so bore much of the risk of unemployment in an economic downturn. In 1985 there was a net reduction of 96,000 jobs, but over three-fifths of those affected were foreign workers. These workers thus came to fulfil a function similar to that of recently-arrived immigrants from south China before World War II.[67]

In fact the contribution of low-paid foreign workers is much more extensive than Huff suggests – and much more fundamental than is suggested by economists such as Abeysinghe and Choy, whose analysis never moves past considering their impact on Singaporeans' wages, salaries and employability.[68] Foreign workers have built Singapore's factories, schools, skyscrapers, roads and railway lines. They drive the buses, work in the factories, cook and serve the food, clean the toilets and public buildings, and – perhaps the most basic of all – provide seemingly unlimited domestic service so that middle-class Singaporeans can work extremely long hours, knowing their flats and houses are being cleaned, their meals are being cooked and their children raised by cheap hired help. It is no exaggeration to say that Singapore's reliance upon cheap, vulnerable foreign labour has been at least as important to the country's economic development as more celebrated aspects of the political economy, such as its highly educated citizen workforce.

On top of these essential elements came a piece of singular good fortune: the economic boon provided by the Vietnam War. Singapore's role in America's war in Vietnam not only converted Lee Kuan Yew's 'American turn' of 1968 into immediate profit, but in the long term it also won a favoured place for Singapore in the American view of Asia. Singapore's development strategy may have succeeded even without the input from the Vietnam War, but it certainly would not have enjoyed such a quick and successful launch. The oil-refining and ship-repair industries were the big winners, with other manufactures also expanding or establishing themselves in the Southeast Asian boom generated by the war. Oil exports increased manyfold as Singapore fed off military-generated demand in Vietnam and Thailand. By the time the wartime bonanza came to an end in 1975, Singapore was well placed to feed the oil demands of Japan's manufacturing industry.[69] The latter was not a direct consequence of the Vietnam War, but if not for the war and the American connection, Singapore may not have had the refining capacity to meet Japanese demand, and without the common connection with America, Japan may not have turned to Singapore so readily.

TWO CHALLENGES

The economic machine that the new state built was single-minded in the pursuit of economic development. According to the latest figures at the time of writing, Singapore's gross domestic product (GDP) increased at an average rate of 6.67% per annum from 1976 to 2018.[70] Overall, Singapore's economic achievements have been considerable although, as Huff points out, it is certainly not the 'miracle' that many have identified (see his quotation at the opening of this chapter). There have also been missteps, including many egregious losses by GLCs (counted in the billions of dollars) for which no one ever seems to be held to account, as would happen in truly private enterprises. More fundamental than individual losses, however, are the two basic challenges facing

Singapore's economic growth: increasing productivity; and overcoming the constraints of Singapore's small land mass. The historical record has been problematic for both, though the future looks more promising for the latter than the former.

Productivity

The challenge of increasing Singapore's productivity (total factor productivity, TFP) as the key to expansion and healthy growth has long been recognised by Singaporean authorities. A strong statement of the importance of productivity can be found in a 2010 speech by Ngiam Tong Dow, a former permanent secretary in the Prime Minister's Office, the Ministry of Finance and the Ministry of Trade and Industry:

> In my view, raising TFP is the core function of the CEO of a company. For the government, the prime minister is the CEO.
>
> The CEO has to own the whole process. He cannot simply delegate it to others. Performance bonuses have to be tied inextricably to TFP.
>
> Expansion has to be differentiated from growth. Expansion occurs when the input–output ratio is unity. One new unit of input produces one unit of output. Growth occurs when one unit of input produces two or more units of output. The input–output ratio has to be more than one before performance bonuses kick in.[71]

This excerpt leaves no doubt that the challenge of productivity is known in government, but perhaps Ngiam's explanation of the nature of productivity per se might be a little abstruse for those who are coming to the question for the first time. In layman's terms, productivity is the measure of the value created by a worker in a set measured time. For instance, a farmer putting individual crop seeds into the ground one by one contributes a certain value to the economy. But if it is practical for the farmer to plant seed by casting a handful at a time, then introducing this simple innovation will increase productivity dramatically. To take another example, a factory worker assembling a Samsung smartphone on a production line probably contributes more value to the economy in an hour of work then the farmer, no matter which method of planting is utilised. But an engineer or scientist who introduces a significant and successful innovation to the design of that smartphone has contributed much more value than the production worker, partly because this contribution has increased the value of an hour's work on the production line. Productivity is not simply a matter of mechanising or upscaling. Such steps can play a part, but the farmer who uses a tractor to sow seeds has not necessarily increased his or her productivity because the work being measured is not that of a farmer, but that of a farmer-plus-a-tractor-plus-diesel, etc. All the inputs need to be included in the calculation. If nothing more changes than the volume of inputs, then a blunt tool such as mechanisation might even reduce the value of an hour of the farmer's work.

It seems that Singapore has had a problem increasing its level of productivity. The situation has been disguised by increasing the volume of the inputs – the number of workers, the number of hours worked per worker, the volume of capital investment – but the reality is that for most of independent Singapore's life, the increase in the actual value contributed by workers as measured by the value of an hour worked has been negligible, especially when compared with places such as South Korea, Hong Kong and Taiwan.[72] This is the problem that Ngiam is addressing in his 2010 speech.

Independent Singapore's first really major economic misstep was the direct result of trying to increase productivity at the end of the 1970s. The government's plan was to force an increase in productivity by pricing Singapore out of the low end of the market and improving incentives for foreign investment in higher-end manufacturing that required higher technical skills. This was also the government's first attempt to shift Singapore further up the hierarchy of the NIDL. Unhappily this sudden structural shift in the local economy – which was known officially as the 'Second Industrial Revolution' – seriously damaged Singapore's competitiveness across most sectors. Not only did it raise costs dramatically and universally, but the new FDI it attracted competed with local enterprise both for business and for the very small pool of local technicians, scientists and managers, without sharing much technology or offering much training in return.[73] To make matters worse, it coincided perfectly with a global downturn in the shipping business whose effect was compounded by the opening of rival dry dock facilities in other parts of Asia. Between them, these factors led to a generalised recession in the mid-1980s with a particular concentration in the docks, where the throughput of Singapore's ship-repair business was halved in a year.[74] It was not the government's finest moment, and the domestic discontent it generated laid the foundation for a new, albeit modest, opposition presence in parliament. Apart from the issue of timing, the other problem with the Second Industrial Revolution was sequencing. The wage rises became effective immediately by government fiat, beginning in 1979, but five years later Singapore was still waiting to see new sunrise industries in place. (According to Ngiam Tong Dow, the recession of the 1980s was entirely 'self-inflicted': the direct result of 'rising wages and an appreciating currency', which between them cut Singapore's international competitiveness.)[75]

When the Nobel Prize-winning economist, Paul Krugman, spectacularly accused Singapore in 1994 of failing to improve productivity, Lee Kuan Yew did not dispute the charge: he just argued that the future would be different. It is worthwhile quoting Krugman at some length because he also captures in vivid imagery the undisputed essentials of the Singapore success story from 1965 until the mid-1990s:

> the [Singapore] miracle turns out to have been based on perspiration rather than inspiration ... The employed share of the population surged from 27 to 51 percent. The

> educational standards of that work force were dramatically upgraded ... Above all, the country had made an awesome investment in physical capital: investment as a share of output rose from 11 to more than 40 percent.
>
> ... all of Singapore's growth can be explained by increases in measured inputs. There is no sign at all of increased efficiency. In this sense, the growth of Lee Kuan Yew's Singapore is an economic twin of the growth of Stalin's Soviet Union – growth achieved purely through mobilization of resources.[76]

Since the publication of Krugman's article, economists have argued about whether the situation has improved, searching for a clarity that has not been aided by the opaqueness of many government statistics.[77] Perhaps more indicative of the true state of affairs are those words of insiders that belie the claims of government-friendly economists. Returning to Ngiam Tong Dow's speech referred to above, the ultimate insider appears to be in full agreement with Krugman:

> Singapore's GDP increases of the last twenty years were due largely to expansion rather than growth. Import of large numbers of foreign work permit holders enabled the economy to expand at GDP ratios of 6–8 percent. Productivity stagnated at one percent. In some years it was negative.
>
> This is the Achilles' heel of the Singapore success story. We expanded but did not grow.[78]

In contrast to scholars and other commentators, Ngiam had full access to the raw data as well as command of several teams of civil service economists whose day job was the management and study of these figures and factors. Hence, his words cannot be easily dismissed. Nor can the official statistics issued by the Department of Statistics, which show the average of Multifactor Productivity Growth in Real Terms from 1974 to 2017 as a neat zero. This means that the Singapore workforce is no more productive today than it was in 1974; there are just more workers and they are utilising capital equipment of much higher value.[79]

Size

The government's efforts to overcome the limitations of Singapore's small size have been more successful than its efforts to raise productivity, though it has also had plenty of disappointments. The practice of importing cheap foreign labour was part of the effort to compensate for the small population base, but if we just restrict our consideration in this section to the problem of Singapore's small land mass, we see that the government has engaged in numerous and diverse enterprises to overcome the problem – and despite some disappointments, many have been successful. The most basic efforts began in earnest in the 1960s, with land extension projects (usually misnamed land 'reclamation' projects) that have increased the country's land mass by nearly 25% at the expense of the surrounding waters. In the process, small islands to Singapore's south have been joined together to make bigger islands for industrial (and especially oil) sites, and the mouth of the Singapore River has been extended into the sea and converted into a freshwater reservoir. It is also the site of the iconic Marina Bay Sands resort. Entire residential estates and highways on the southern shore now sit on land where there used to be sea (pictured in Figure 7.5). The old western tip of the island now plunges 15 kilometres (9 miles) south in a long hook-shaped extension that hosts the Tuas industrial estate. Tuas' length and land surface will be doubled again by the time the government's

Figure 7.5 Land extensions for work, rest and play
Roads (top left), a housing estate (top right), a sports facility in a community centre (middle left) and a casino (middle right), all built on 'reclaimed' land. Bottom: oil bunkering and refineries build on enlarged islands.

extension plans are completed, creating an artificial peninsula that will, among other services, consolidate the five sites that currently make up the Port of Singapore into one huge facility with double its current capacity.[80] At the eastern end of the island, half of Changi Airport also sits on 'reclaimed' land and Malaysia's Johor River now opens onto a bloated Singaporean island (Pulau Tekong) that is about twice its natural size and is going to double in size yet again with further land extension.[81] And Beach Road is now a very long walk from the water! An odd consequence of half a century of terraforming is that maps of the southern shoreline and southern islands are now dominated by straight lines, right angles and geometric shapes that are never be found in nature.

Land extension is the most basic element of overcoming the problem of space, but it was only the beginning. In 1993 the Singapore government set forth to breach the bounds of its geography in another way: outward foreign direct investment (OFDI), including in industrial estates in other countries.[82] This was called 'growing a second wing' and it was Singapore's second effort to move beyond its subordinate role in the NIDL – by becoming an investor in underdeveloped economies, rather than just the recipient of capital investment. Less directly, this was also a considered response to the new mobility of capital that was ushered in with the neo-liberal international order: if capital is supreme, then let us deploy our capital to greatest advantage. In fact Singapore's growing capital reserves had already been restless for more than a decade, which is why the government established the Government of Singapore Investment Corporation (GIC) in 1981. This, however, was different: now Singapore was going to be buying businesses, building industrial parks and integrating them into the country's production and service networks.[83]

The EDB, the GLC sector and to a lesser extent Temasek Holdings were all charged with reinventing the Singapore public business sector as international entrepreneurs, seeking both greenfield investments and going concerns. The major targets (at a time when China had not yet opened up) were Southeast Asian countries, followed by the newly industrialised economies of East Asia, then Europe and America. As China opened up in the 1990s it became a major recipient of Singapore investment (18.8% of the total by 1998) as well as a major trading partner, shifting Singapore's Northeast Asian focus away from Japan. In 2007 China overtook the United States as a trading partner[84] but it only overtook the Association of Southeast Asian Nations (ASEAN) states as the largest recipient of Singapore's OFDI in 2010 (including Hong Kong as part of China).[85] As of 2016, China (including Hong Kong) received 22% of Singapore's OFDI compared with ASEAN's 18%. Distinguishing between China and Hong Kong, Singapore's investment in China is mostly in manufacturing and its investment in Hong Kong is mostly in financial and insurance services. China/HK was also the market for 27% of Singapore's exports.[86] Yet Singapore's more immediate neighbours remain a major focus of Singapore's second wing to this day, with ASEAN still attracting more OFDI than mainland China (excluding Hong Kong).[87] The main industries in which Singapore invests overseas, measured by the size of investments, are finance, followed by manufacturing, commerce and real estate respectively.[88] The composition and rankings of the lower-order investments have changed and shifted over the intervening decades, but finance has continued to dominate, accounting for around half of all OFDI at all times, followed much further behind by manufacturing with 20–25%.[89]

This has been very different from the domestic economy, where manufacturing has led at all times.[90] The Singapore government has made massive investments in the service and education sectors and in new technologies in yet more efforts to develop its economy beyond its traditional place in the international production networks. It has had some successes, but much has ended in embarrassment, such as its abortive alliances with Warwick University and the University of New South Wales in the 2000s,[91] or in good money chasing bad, such as seems to be happening with its efforts to develop a biotechnology industry.[92] The essence of the problem in the government's approach is its misplaced faith in the power of money as a source of attraction. Goh Chor Boon has explored this problem in his book, *From Traders to Innovators*, and at one point isolated the problem the government faces in a quotation from an unnamed scientist he interviewed:

> If you don't have the scientific culture it is hard to get good people … And money is not everything. You will never be able to get top-ranked scientists because they think that when they come to Singapore they are not going to progress very much in their scientific achievements. So I don't think salary is the real issue.[93]

Compounding over-investment in rented research talent, the government has also under-invested in home-grown talent by every measure – punching well below its weight in research training and investment compared with rivals such as South Korea and Taiwan. As a direct consequence, it has failed to create a critical mass of innovation in any of the new technologies.[94] According to data released by the Department of Statistics in 2016, the ranking of industry sectors in the domestic Singapore economy (based on their contribution to GDP) has been unchanged for the 15 years up to 2014: manufacturing first, followed by wholesale and retail trade, then business services, finance and insurance, transportation and storage, and finally construction. (The rankings are unchanged, but in fact manufacturing has slipped from a high of 27.7% of GDP in 2004 to 19.2% in 2017, and is now only fractionally ahead of wholesale and retail trade and of business services.[95] The strength of business services reflects in part the presence of 7,000 logistics companies employing more than 9% of the Singapore workforce – a very sensible and successful effort to capitalise on Singapore's natural comparative advantage as a global hub.)[96]

Manufacturing traditionally has a special role in newly industrialising economies as a mass employer. This sector certainly played this role in the early decades of independence, but from the 1980s onwards the government has deliberately steered the economy away from this path. It has focused instead on replacing domestic labour in the manufacturing sector with new technology funded mostly by foreign capital, and then turned to low-cost foreign labour for the parts of the manufacturing sector that cannot avoid being labour-intensive.[97] This strategy makes narrow economic sense, but in the new century it has imported the social and political problems of neo-liberalism into Singapore by encouraging the government to focus more on the needs of foreign capital and its hunger for foreign workers than it has about the needs, comfort and aspirations of Singaporeans. This trajectory reached a tipping point in 2005 when, fearing an economic downturn, the government launched a drastic increase in the rate of immigration – mainly low-cost foreign workers on work permits – to the point where five years later nearly 40 percent of people in Singapore were foreigners. To make matters worse, no provision was made for increased infrastructure on the island to accommodate a million extra people, nor was any thought given to social integration or political backlash. This provoked the government's electoral setbacks of 2011 and put it on the defensive for the next four years – until it managed to recover somewhat in the 2015 general election (see Chapter 6).[98] The ongoing problem for the government is that even though it is managing the politics of immigration satisfactorily, the basic problem has not gone away: it is suffering for its failure to break out of the Krugman dilemma. Despite decades of trying, it has still not succeeded in finding a way forward except by increasing inputs so as to increase outputs.

We saw earlier that one of the most distinctive features of Singapore's domestic political economy has been the dominance of state-owned and state-linked enterprises. Likewise, state enterprises dominate Singapore's OFDI strategies, with the state-linked DBS leading the way in the provision of financial services to facilitate this programme. The track record of these overseas direct investments has been very mixed, with some major missteps and investment duds among its many solid performers, but overall the initiative is producing results that are at least satisfactory – certainly better results than its efforts to boost domestic productivity. Perhaps the most extraordinary feature of the second wing strategy is not its overall success, but the fact that by far the most promising long-term venture has turned out to be building a new version of the economic relationship that underpinned both the old Johor-Riau Sultanate and the Johor-Singapore symbiosis of the nineteenth century.

Johor, Singapore and the Riau Islands of Bintan and Batam are divided by fixed boundaries establishing the sovereign limits of Indonesia, Singapore and Malaysia, but government-to-government and business-to-business relations have been flourishing

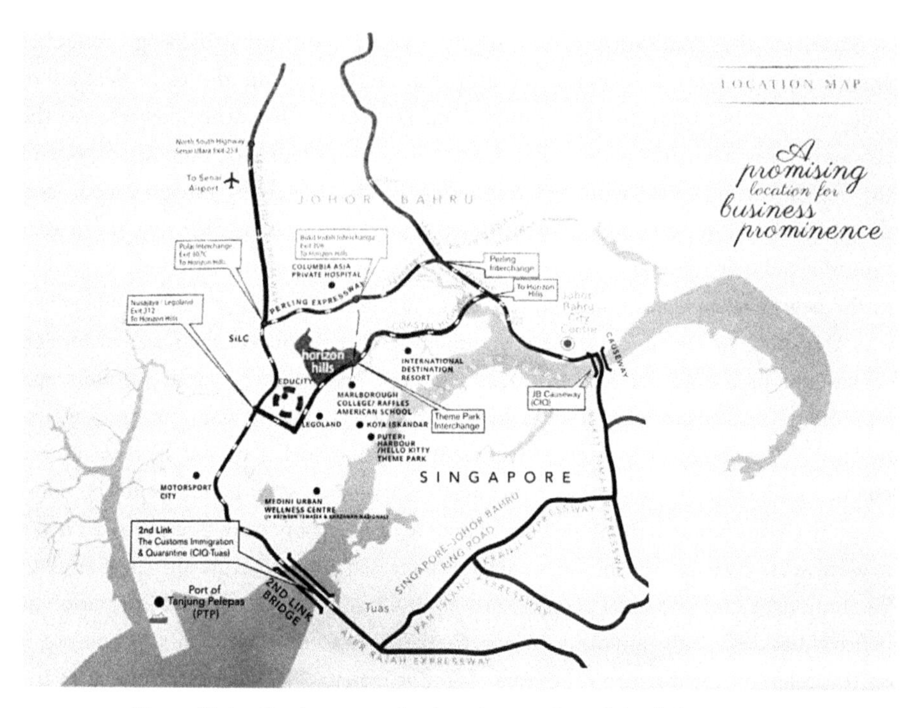

Figure 7.6 Real estate sales brochure selling 'North Singapore'

since the humble beginnings of the Singapore–Johor–Riau (SIJORI) growth triangle in the 1980s. Singapore capital and management is the cornerstone of this co-operation, with the other partners primarily providing a de facto hinterland for the city-state. Bintan, Batam and some associated islands comprise the Indonesian component. They host two airports, several industrial parks, a major tourist resort and a collection of ferry terminals that connect them to Singapore. Yet the real dynamism in the tripartite relationship is on the Johor side, where the Malaysian and Johor governments have set aside an area three times the size of Singapore for joint development. It is officially called the Iskandar Development Region but is known colloquially among many Singaporeans as 'North Singapore' (Figure 7.6). After some false starts it took off in a big way in 2006 and since then has been attracting escalating levels of Singaporean, Chinese and American investment. Iskandar includes not just industrial estates, but also gated communities for Singaporeans, an airport, a commercial port (Tanjung Pelepas) and two bridges to Singapore. It is becoming to Singapore what Shenzhen has been to Hong Kong: a land platform providing room to work, live and invest. The optimism about the future of Iskandar is palpable. It will never substitute for global investment, but it has one thing to offer Singapore that no one else can match: local land to spare. Of course this future is substantially dependent on the maintenance of close relations between the government of Singapore and the governments of both Malaysia and Johor, but with so much money to be made it seems unlikely that a change of heart or change of regime would be allowed to become more than an inconvenience.

PLUS ÇA CHANGE

At first glance it seems extraordinary that after having successfully brought Singapore 'from Third World to First' (though it is doubtful if it was ever really Third World), invented and refined a new and innovative form of state capitalism, and set itself up with one of the busiest ports and airports in the world, the way forward forged by the country's ruling elite should include elements that are so local. And yet it should not surprise. At all times in its history, Singapore's centrality in the immediate region and in the surrounding oceans has been the *raison d'être* for interest in the island. Its very success as a modern economy in both colonial and particularly post-colonial times has been based on the intense and successful exploitation of the regional and extra-regional relationships that it inherited from the pre-colonial millennia. In the late nineteenth century Singapore was a port city of considerable significance globally and of primary importance in its own region. Today it ranks somewhere in the top six for most city-based indices of global business significance and connectivity.[99] The development from the former to the latter is both logical and predictable. It is also unremarkable, except for the extent of its success. Less impressive has been its efforts to reach beyond this paradigm and to turn itself into something more than a hub.

8

Making Modern Singaporeans: People, Society and Place

> There is some implicit assumption that technology, nature, economy, culture, and power come together to form the city which is then imposed on its dwellers as given. … It is our view that … citizens have created cities. … By analysing the interaction between cities and people in a historical perspective, we should be able to detect some basic mechanisms underlying the social production of urban life and forms.
>
> Manuel Castells, *The City and the Grassroots*, 1983[1]

At one point in James Warren's pioneering social histories of Singapore, he recounted the story of an Englishman, Bruce Lockhart, who was a regular visitor to Singapore in the first quarter of the twentieth century, and who paid a 'nostalgic' visit in the late 1930s. Warren tells us he 'took one last rickshaw ride into yesteryear – a trip that invariably was meant to end in Malay Street'. Malay Street at that time contained the brothels of choice for Europeans. In his account, Warren mapped the brothels of the early twentieth century by tracing both the racial profiles of the prostitutes and those of their client bases. Japanese prostitutes served Europeans in Malay Street, Malabar Street and Trengganu Street while Chinese prostitutes served Chinese clients in Chinatown.[2] Nothing has remained as it was. Since 1995 Malay Street has been a pedestrian, air-conditioned, indoor street full of retail outlets. It now sits on top of an interchange between one of the oldest Mass Rapid Transit (MRT) lines (the East–West Line; first stage opened in 1989) and one of the newest (the Downtown Line; first stage opened in 2015). On a recent visit to Singapore I arranged to meet my wife there after she had spent the afternoon having tea and cake with friends in the rather posh Intercontinental Hotel, which opens onto Malay Street. Chinatown is not yet air-conditioned, but most of the brothels have long gone, as have most of the traditional Chinese eating and retail places. The death of Chinatown as a place serving local Chinese Singaporeans was sounded by the opening of an MRT station there in 2003. Land values jumped and rents began soaring in the whole area as new businesses increasingly catered for well-heeled tourists rather than working-class Chinese. The traditional Chinese businesses followed the brothels to suburban Geylang, a few miles to the east, and so Chinatown is now the place for foreigners to enjoy boutique beer from all over the world, buy knick-knacks, T-shirts and other examples of Chinese and Singaporean kitsch, visit some historical temples and other sites of interest and sample the 'authentic' tastes of Singapore – all without moving more than a few blocks from the train station. It also hosts Southeast Asia's only Tintin Shop. In 2015 Chinatown Station became an interchange between the North-East Line and the new Downtown Line. Its near neighbour, Outram Park Station, is slated to become a three-line interchange in 2021, so Chinatown's upmarket trajectory will inevitably continue.

In Chapter 2, I opened a line of thought that highlighted Singapore's identity as a city, as opposed to its identity as a state or a nation. Over the subsequent chapters this theme has never been very far below the surface. 'Singaporeans' of the nineteenth and twentieth centuries arrived from many places and societies and the primary thing they had in common – and their only point of interest to this book – is that they came to the island and helped build a city. And, yes, it was substantially settlers rather than the colonial authorities that built the city. James Warren's account of Bruce Lockhart's last rickshaw ride to Malay Street, and my own personal associations with the new Malay Street, brought home to me the intimacy of the relationship between people and locale. The history of the people of Singapore is a history of streets, alleys, highways, railways, farms, factories, docks, islands, shop houses, *kampungs*, shanty towns, bungalows, slums, high-rises, mosques, temples, churches, schools and ethnic enclaves. These are all mappable real estate.

Place and people feed each other as cause and effect, so the history of the people as society is effectively a history of the city as host to society. This is why so many social histories and sociological studies of Singapore actually use place or urban geography as the primary identifier,[3] and it brings particular poignancy to one of the many elements of contemporary Singapore that seems to be universally regretted by Singaporeans: that the landscape and markers have changed so far beyond recognition that the sense of connection with a local past has been lost, just like the Malay Street and the Chinatown of old. There are still historic buildings maintained for tourists and also a few areas of the island that retain their old-world charm – notably in cute eastern suburbs such as Katong and parts of Serangoon Road in Little India – but not many adults can visit their old primary school, or any building or public space (for instance a cemetery) with which they or their families have a historical connection. They have mostly been shifted, rebuilt or simply obliterated from the map.

Even contemporary neighbourhood lineages are mostly overwhelmed by the impersonal character of high-rises and by the tyranny of commuting imposed by the MRT. There is a sense in which the Singapore versions of modernisation and development are at war with civic intimacy. This is not just a Singaporean phenomenon, of course, but it is particularly strong in today's Singapore, and it means that, from the perspective of social history, the importance of locale has slid away as the city has eaten itself, a process that started in the late colonial period. New developments are oddly dislocated and aloof from local history, local wishes and local initiative. They are centrally driven and follow established patterns, meaning that housing estates, shopping centres, underground retail malls, and hubs for transport, research and industry are reproduced across the island, with all the variety of a blancmange. The old Malay Street was unique; the new Malay Street is just another mall. Some urban developments have a more particular significance – and several of these have already been canvassed. It is, however, of marginal importance or interest that the Biopolis Biomedical Research Hub and Fusionopolis One have been built in Buona Vista, rather than in some other part of the island, or that Farrer Park, near Little India, has become a medical tourism hub. In any case such initiatives come and go, like the old airport at Kallang which was superseded by Changi Airport even before its last upgrade had a reasonable chance to get dirty.[4]

With this dissonance in mind, I have approached the later part of Singapore's social history through a different lens from that which I apply to the nineteenth century and the earlier decades of the twentieth century. I approach the first century of Singapore's history as a city through the conventional lens of a social historian, but for its second century I allow the civic perspective to fade and instead use the history of education and language as a proxy for social history – a device that I hope provides a manageable 'road map' through the social development of modern Singapore, and one that enables me to unpack the title theme for this chapter: making modern Singaporeans.

Of all the themes explored in this book, social history is the one tied most closely to civic history, and yet in contrast to a study of Singapore's economy or politics – and obviously in contrast to Singapore as a place or an idea – it is not appropriate to track society before the most recent foundation of the settlement; not the 1819 of the Singapore Story and the Turnbull story, but around 1811, when the Temenggong started developing the island.

KAMPONG GLAM (GELAM)

Temenggong Abdul Rahman was the founder of nineteenth-century Singapore. He was a Malay royal who was intimately bound up in the palace intrigues in the Malay-Bugis court in Riau. Like all Malay and Bugis royals, his legitimacy depended on his lineage, his fortune and his followers, and the three were inseparable. His lineage was the prerequisite for his royal status; he needed his followers to build and maintain his wealth; and he needed wealth to retain the loyalty of his followers. As a royal he had his own fiefdom within the broader geographical domain of the Sultanate, with a collection of islands and coastlines that he considered his property, of which the neglected island of Singapore was one (see Map 4.2). In about 1811 he took a business decision to redevelop

Singapore as a farm.[5] He wanted to take a slice of the pepper and gambier industry that was doing so well in other parts of the Straits and so he invited Chinese gambier farmers from the Riau islands, and several hundred of them accepted his invitation – not as individuals, but collectively as *kongsi* (see Chapters 4 and 7). To make the offer more palatable, he offered protection in the form of a settlement of his followers, several thousand of whom relocated from other islands to Singapore.[6] For the Temenggong's followers, this shift meant little more than mooring their boats in a different harbour: they continued in their established professions as traders, pirates and the Temenggong's enforcers, and gave his new farms all the protection they needed just by their physical proximity. We do not have much notion of where these early gambier and pepper farms were, but they would have been relatively isolated in the jungle, safe from both the pirates who were protecting them and from others that might be passing by boat. We do, however, know exactly where the Temenggong's followers lived: Kampong Glam (Kampong Gelam in the old spelling). Today, after two centuries of land extension, Kampong Glam stands about 400 metres (about a quarter of a mile) to the west of the Kallang Basin, but in 1811 it was on the water's edge. Kampong Glam would have looked much like any number of port-side *kampungs* of its day: bamboo, rattan, timber and atap constructions, built on stilts and facing dirt roads or walkways.

In 1818 the Temenggong found himself on the losing side of palace politics in Riau. He had aligned himself with the eldest son of the late Sultan Mahmud, but in that year the Dutch settled the succession by recognising his younger brother as Sultan. Deciding that there was no future for him at court, he retreated to Singapore and made it his place of residence and his primary base.[7] It was into this world that Raffles and the Temenggong's friend, William Farquhar, sailed in January 1819.

THE SINGAPORE RIVER

The beginnings of Singapore's redevelopment thus started on the banks of the Singapore River, and that is where it stayed for a century. Thus a study of the history of the city must begin and stay with the Singapore River, the original port and focus of both Malay and European activity. Writing specifically of the European period, Stephen Dobbs made this point in the opening pages of his social history of the Singapore River:

> For many years after the establishment of the British settlement in Singapore in 1819, to speak of Singapore was to speak of the river. … The river and settlement of Singapore are largely inseparable throughout this early period of the island's development.[8]

This assessment downplays the role of the Malays and Chinese who were already living further along the coast or who had established themselves inland, but it certainly captures the dynamic heart of the new Singapore – and in any case even the subsequent inland farmers and workers entered through the port. As we have already noted, after 1819, Chinese came from Malacca and Riau and other parts of Southeast Asia, attracted by the new British port. Indian financiers and convict labourers were also among the early arrivals. It was not long before Chinese started arriving in large numbers directly from southern China, but for most of these migrants, the port was just the entry point to the Malay Peninsula or other parts of the Straits.[9] There were also many 'Malay' migrants,[10] from places such as Riau, Sumatra, Sulawesi and Java, but only eight years after British settlement the Chinese were already the largest racial group in a population of less than 16,000.[11] The colony's population continued to grow, but the rate was uneven, whether measured by percentages or in raw numbers. The period up to 1860 had very high growth measured as a percentage (between 4 and 8% per annum), but this was because it was starting from a low base. Only in the 1881 census did the population break through the 100,000 mark and begin a steady climb, decade on decade. It still took 66 years – to 1947 – to approach the 1 million mark, despite decades of high growth in terms of raw numbers. In this long period there was no decade with less than 43,000 net increase and in just the 16 years from 1931 to 1947 the population increased in excess of 380,000. This post-1881 period of growth was all the more impressive because, for the first 40 years, the natural increase was in the negative by tens of thousands, and so migration had to make up for this loss before beginning to contribute to growth.[12]

Behind such bald figures lurk human stories of misery and loneliness: the 'natural' growth rate was negative because of the combined effect of an imbalanced sex ratio among the Chinese and Indian populations and a high rate of premature deaths due to factors such as work-related accidents, vector-borne diseases, opium abuse, venereal disease, malnutrition, unsanitary living conditions and sheer exhaustion. Many of the social histories mentioned earlier are littered with such stories, particularly Warren's two books, which use coroner's reports to reconstruct the lives and social environs of Singapore's Chinese rickshaw pullers and Japanese prostitutes.[13] The rickshaw pullers were the lifeblood of urban Singapore's streets from the 1880s until the bus, tram and car overwhelmed them in the 1930s. In the half-century during which the rickshaw puller was the raggedy king of the road, many tens of thousands of men worked themselves to death providing rides for Europeans and better-off Asians. Without them, the city would come to a halt – as indeed it did on the rare occasions when they went on strike.[14]

The commercial and trading centre of the island sat at the mouth of the Singapore River, which was not the cleverest site for Raffles to choose: the river was short and shallow; the left bank consisted of useless mudflats that were underwater at high tide; the mouth was dangerous due to its direct exposure to the sea, to which was added the complication of a semi-submerged breakwater. The Temenggong was almost certainly a bit canny in signing away some of his rights to the Singapore River to the British while keeping the better ports for himself: his personal royal port at Teluk Belanga (present-day Keppel Harbour) a few miles to the west, and Kallang River, a few miles to the east.[15] The inadequacy of the Singapore River as a port turned out to be a significant force shaping Singapore's social and urban development. The south bank had to be filled in and reinforced straight away to make it of any practical use, and this was achieved by flattening a hill that stood at the current Raffles Square and using the soil and rock as fill (thus also providing flat ground for the financial district, both at the time and today). This exercise in terraforming the river has continued in fits and starts for the last two centuries, culminating in 2008 with the fulfilment of Lee Kuan Yew's dream of extending and enclosing the mouth of the river to create a freshwater reservoir. After the opening of New Harbour (now Keppel Harbour) in 1852, the Singapore River's importance as a port gradually declined, but it was still busy in the 1980s and did not finally cease to function until the 1990s.[16] In the meantime, however, its inadequacies were directly responsible for producing and sustaining generations of Chinese and Indian lightermen: labourers who performed back-breaking and often dangerous work on small, wide, shallow boats called lighters, shifting cargo between the quays on the banks of the shallow river and the large trading vessels that had to anchor outside the river (Figure 8.1). As unskilled labour goes, it was prestigious and well-paid because it was difficult and highly responsible work, with a single lighterman carrying weights of perhaps 200 kilograms (440 pounds) or more on his back.[17]

The river was Singapore's front door and the lightermen and the bobbing fleet of lighters that dominated the river for considerably more than a century were both a symbolic and an actual point of entry into the colony, supplemented by the presence of clerks, officials and Chinese middlemen who 'welcomed' and processed the human cargoes that were disgorged nearby. With only slight local variations, this scene was typical of ports the world over in an age when port cities were emerging as a newly important node in the global economy. As the German historian Jürgen Osterhammel wrote in his history of the nineteenth century:

> [this] was the golden age of ports and port cities. ... Seaports were what airports became in the second half of the twentieth century: the key transaction points between countries and continents. The first things that arriving travellers saw from the sea were the quays and buildings, a harbour front; the first local people they encountered were pilots, longshoremen, and customs officials. As steamships, freight loads, and crowds of intercontinental migrants multiplied in size and number, sea travel acquired a significance it had never previously had.[18]

In Southeast Asia, and indeed in Asia more generally, the port city was already ancient as a centre of commerce and power, with connectivity primarily oriented towards other Asian

Figure 8.1 Ship to shore: lighters and lightermen at Pasir Panjang, 1993

ports. One of the new features of this scene in British Singapore was the extension of its connectivity so that it was truly global. Yet for most of the century the vast majority of the trading vessels plying Asian waters were Asian. The bobbing gaggle of lighters jostling in the river were the key, visible point of articulation in Singapore's core entrepôt trade, carrying bulk goods onshore, and local products offshore. Many migrants and sojourners moved into the growing city but others continued east and west along the coast and north into the interior of the island, generally without official sanction and often without official knowledge; such were the limits of colonial governance. Traders and their crews also came. They mostly stayed for no more than a few weeks or months at a time, but they came in such numbers – by the thousands – and with such regularity from places such as Java, Sulawesi, Sumatra and China that they also became very much part of Singapore. In the 1840s the movement inland was overwhelmed by the new phenomenon of through traffic that arrived at the front door from southern China and went straight out the back door to Johor, with Singapore picking up a minority who stayed behind. Social networks among all the races except the Malays were dominated by public face: their place of work and their place in their public social hierarchies. These public social settings took precedence over domestic social arrangements because they did not really have domestic settings thanks to the fact that, until well into the twentieth century, there were very few families. Singapore's sex ratio was completely distorted by the near-total absence of women among the Asian colonists. At one point – in 1836 – there were more than 14 Chinese men to every Chinese woman. In the same year there were nearly 10 Indian men to every Indian woman, which was actually a slight improvement from a few years earlier.[19]

COMMUNITY AND HYBRIDITY

Not that the Chinese or Indians thought of themselves primarily in such terms. Chinese were Teochew, Hakka, Cantonese or – in most cases – Hokkien, according to which Chinese language they spoke. Teochew dominated the gambier and pepper farms, Hokkiens dominated business, Cantonese took most labouring and trade/artisan positions, and Hakkas dominated tin-mining in the region.[20] The social segmentation was both the result of a natural desire for familiarity and the impenetrability of most of the many languages beyond their own communities – an impenetrability that operated for the most part between the various Chinese languages as well as between Chinese and others. It was also an unnatural function of British colonial policy, which had very fixed prejudices about the commercial and social functions of the different races – complete with derision of the 'lazy' Malays, admiration for the zeal and industry of Chinese and dismissal of Indians as being unsuited to anything more than repetitive hard labour. (The prejudice about Indians was imported directly from the subcontinent, as were the Indians themselves, who mostly arrived in the colony as state-sponsored indentured or convict labourers.) As was mentioned in Chapter 4, the colonial authorities also preferred to manage the Chinese through their 'natural' community leaders. All of these factors meant that economic and social interaction exaggerated intra-communal commonality and intercommunal differences. In 1822, just three years after the foundation of the colony, the government established a committee to plan the geographical segregation of the communities along racial lines, which was then extended without conscious decision to segregate language-based communities within those designated areas. Phyllis Chew has provided an account of this segregation, going right down to the racial composition of individual streets:

> The Caucasians were mostly found in Tanglin, the Malays along the Rochor River and in Geylang, the Arabs in Arab Street, the Bugis in Bugis Street and the Chinese in Chinatown. As for the Indians they were concentrated in Chulia Street, High Street, Market Street and the naval base in Sembawang, the railway/port areas of Tanjong Pagar and the Serangoon Road area. The Eurasians were allotted space in Kampong Glam between Waterloo Street and Queen Street, and later to Upper Serangoon Road as designated by road names such as Lange, Richards, Aroozoo and de Silver.
>
> … within each racial category were further subdivisions based on the geography of regional origin and language. For example, the Teochews made Hong Kong Street their base, while the Cantonese occupied Kreta Ayer or Chinatown, and the Hainanese the North Bridge Road area.[21]

With such a beginning it should not be surprising that the vocational determinism of language/race/community became more pronounced and finely tuned as the century wore on, forging new colonial stereotypes and refining old ones. Once again, we turn to Phyllis Chew's scholarship for a concise and evocative depiction of developments, this time for a choice quotation from English visitors writing in 1883:

> Then there are the native Malays, who … besides being tolerably industrious as boatmen and fishermen, form the main body of the police. The Parsee merchants, who like our rule, form a respectable class of merchants here …. The Javanese are numerous and make good servants and sailors …. The washer men and grooms are nearly all Bengalees. Jews and Arabs make money and keep it … [and] the Klings [Indians] make splendid boatmen.[22]

Among the Chinese, one's language-cum-communal grouping also determined allegiances during the many riots and secret society wars that plagued colonial Singapore over its first century or so, so it was no trivial matter. On a more benign note, as late as the first half of the twentieth century, Catholic parishes and the Chinese Catholic Mission were also organised along language lines (Hokkien, Cantonese, etc.), as was the Chinese Methodist Church.

Some of the more financially successful Asians settled in Singapore for the long term – or at least until they were ready to return to their homelands in their old age. Many of the more successful Chinese who wanted to settle down integrated themselves into local Malay society, often marrying local Malay women. Such pioneers fed the development of the distinctive Chinese–Malay–Western cultural mix known loosely as *peranakan* Chinese or *baba*s, following a pattern that had already been established in British Penang, Dutch Malacca and Dutch Batavia (Java).[23] The *baba*s emerged as a new elite in both Penang and Singapore. They generally had little or no Chinese language, but had excellent English, which won them significant niches in the colonial economy as employees and interlocutors of European agency houses and colonial departments. The men were resplendent if rather sweaty in their Western suits and the women were gorgeous in their distinctive *nyonya* batik and Chinese-style dresses, pant suits and sarongs.[24] Singapore's *baba*s were routinely well-to-do, though not necessarily wealthy, and they usually lived in spacious bungalows with ornate furniture that reflected Chinese, Malay and Anglo influences. *Peranakan* Chinese as a community were products of colonialism per se, owing their very existence and identity to hybridity. The same could be said of the Eurasians, who were mostly Catholic descendants of Portuguese and Indian unions. Down the generations, the *baba*s became increasingly distinctive and isolated from the mainstream Chinese communities, who tended to be dominated and organised by newer arrivals. The leaders of the latter group overtook the *baba*s in terms of wealth and raw power, and they generally clung more tightly and overtly to their Chinese culture. In fact, after the 1860s they assiduously used the clannishness and hierarchy embedded in Chinese temple, clan and other grass-roots associations to augment and even to underpin the social and economic power that came with their role as wealthy revenue farmers, traders, employers and/or bankers.[25] They even invented a brand-new type of 'traditional' Chinese association – the same-surname association – to provide a new channel of patron-client relations when loyalty to the *kongsi* was under stress in the 1860s.[26] These Chinese were generally known as Straits Chinese, and the wealthy entrepreneurs and headmen among them were known by the Hokkien term, *towkay*. As a social and economic group, the Straits Chinese fully overshadowed the *peranakan* at every level – except for social acceptability in European circles. This situation lasted until the eve of independence in the second half of the twentieth century, when a *baba*, in the person of Lee Kuan Yew, emerged as the new headman.

After 1819, Singapore quickly emerged as the cosmopolitan centre of a region that was already well established as a cosmopolitan hub. The *peranakan* and Eurasians were the personification of cosmopolitan openness and hybridity, but every immigrant group, especially the British, maintained flows of trade, communications and personnel beyond Malaya and mostly beyond Southeast Asia. As we have seen, however, this openness did not extend to immediate neighbours within the city, since residence, work and social intercourse was heavily segmented according to class, language, religion and a myriad of other criteria. Yet even in the classic Furnivallian 'plural society' of social segmentation, most workers had daily, or at least frequent, contact with people from other communal groups. By necessity they all engaged in at least superficial and transactional cross-cultural, cross-lingual exchanges as a matter of course (see Figure 8.2).[27]

Perhaps the most powerful indicator of the cosmopolitan nature of the society was not the immigrants from outside the region, but the Malays, who are indigenous to the region and not usually associated with hybridity. Yet they were. Writing of the late nineteenth and early twentieth centuries, Joel Kahn described Malay culture in the most forceful language of hybridity that he could find:

> hybridity exists at the heart of Malay culture and the Malay community, not just at its borders. …
>
> Although it will doubtless scandalise Malay cultural purists to suggest it, surely Malay culture, at least as it has evolved over the last century, is the ultimate *peranakan* culture. This is literally the case for the descendants born in Peninsular Malaya of the large numbers of other Malays who came to the Peninsula from the late 19th century onwards from insular Southeast Asia. Although they were never called *peranakan*, the term is entirely appropriate to describe them. If, moreover, the meaning of *peranakan* is pushed beyond its literal meaning to take in connotations of hybridity and cultural flux, then Malay-ness might be described as *peranakan* culture par excellence.[28]

This hybridity flowed through the whole peninsula and much of the surrounding seas and lands, and Singapore was the fulcrum. By the late nineteenth century, the port and city of Singapore was the meeting place of Malay and Islamic intellectuals and reformers as they forged a Malay-Muslim communal identity and ultimately a nationalist political programme.[29] It is important to note, as Carl Trocki did in his 2006 history of Singapore, that this hybridity and openness was not at all extraordinary in its day. This melting pot of races, languages and creeds was the norm in a 'traditional Indian Ocean port society'. Only in the age of nation-states and nationalism is such diversity considered unusual, or even a problem to be managed.[30] Significantly the compartmentalisation imposed by spoken languages had less impact in the printed media. English-language newspapers began soon after the foundation of the colony, as did Malay papers. The Malay newspapers reached out to traders and immigrants from across the Malay/Straits region and, in a classic application of Benedict Anderson's thesis, arguably played a significant role in building a self-aware Malay and Malay-Muslim identity, not just in Singapore, but throughout the peninsula.[31] Chinese newspapers did not get their start until 1881. Although their focus was overwhelmingly on events and politics in the motherland,[32] they did facilitate the building of a local identity because the mutually

Figure 8.2 Meeting in the marketplace: a plural society in a port city, 1910s

unintelligible Chinese spoken languages shared the same written script. Thus the fluid and diverse newspaper establishments, which began as early as the 1820s and continued until the Japanese Occupation in 1942, offered both a modest bridge across Singapore's social silos and fed a moderately active civil society.[33]

BUILDING A CITY

A city is both bricks and mortar and flesh and blood. The two components are closely related, since people are needed to both build and to fill urban environments. In the case of Singapore, the bricks and mortar got off to a slow start because so few of the Europeans treated the island as anything more than a source of short-term profit. There was an official building programme launched after the establishment of the Straits Settlements, with Indian convict labour supplying the muscle. These men – more than 1,000 at any one time – were, literally, the builders of Singapore. They not only

Figure 8.3 Indian road builders in the nineteenth century

constructed government buildings, but they also converted swamp and sea into dry land, and built roads and bridges (Figure 8.3).[34] Yet even so, in the 1830s official colonial functions were still being carried out in ad hoc accommodation and the colony's putative first school (the Singapore Institution, later the Raffles Institution) was still standing half-finished. By the end of the 1830s the city was starting to look like a city and the island was starting to look like a colony, thanks to roads that were opening up the interior.

Singapore's economic fortunes were intimately tied to global fortunes (as indeed they are today) but at that stage the fortunes of Johor and the Malay Peninsula were the primary drivers in population growth and the evolution of the city. Yet the distinction between Johor and the world as drivers is less significant than might appear at first glance, since Johor and the peninsula's development was in turn driven by world trade, and by the revolutions in shipping and technology that were considered in Chapter 7. The second half of the nineteenth century was the great period of transformation of Singapore and by the century's end modernity was in evidence everywhere. Frost and Balasingamchow date the arrival of 'modern times' proper loosely from the 1890s:

> On the face of it, the arrival of modern times in Singapore was heralded by a series of new and highly visible technologies. In 1896, the first motorcar drove down the city's streets; in 1915, the first aeroplane took off from Farrer Park, and in that same year, the first wireless

station began operation. By 1906, the town centre had been electrified, a development that made possible electric street lights … and electric fans [in offices].[35]

It would be fruitless to dispute exactly when Singapore 'became modern', but if we wanted to identify the absolute latest date, we could perhaps, at least symbolically, say 1903–4. The reasons for singling out these years are a trifle whimsical, but between them they convey a picture of entry into a recognisably 'modern' society. The year 1903 is chosen because it was when an expatriate Australian, Deburgh Persse, established the Cold Storage company. Capitalising on Singapore's central location in Southeast Asia and on its world-class port facilities, Cold Storage became a manufacturer and exporter of ice in the interwar years. Today it is an iconic supermarket chain in Singapore, but back in 1903 its goal was simply to import and sell frozen foods – meat, fruit, vegetables and butter – from Australia, primarily so local expats could enjoy a familiar meal.[36] In 1904, Singapore's last tiger was shot in the wild – or rather in Orchard Road, outside the newly built Goodwood House (what is now the Goodwood Park Hotel).[37] Certainly somewhere around the turn of the century seems a reasonable choice as a divider since, apart from aeroplanes, cars and electricity, that last decade of the nineteenth century and first decade of the twentieth marked loosely the foundations of its modern economy.

A MODERN CENTURY

By the turn of the century, the effects of another major change that had begun gestating in the 1860s was transforming society in fundamental ways. The movement of people out of southern China for Nanyang (South Seas) really began with the opening of the Treaty Ports in China in the 1840s, but the 1860s was a turning point as the decade in which the Qing dynasty brought its ban on emigration to a practical end (though it was not formalised until decades later) at the same time as the horrors and disruption of the Taiping Rebellion were driving young men in southern China to seek their fortunes elsewhere. These drivers not only opened Singapore's front door to the mass migration of male labourers that Singapore and Malaya desperately needed, but it also became much more practical for successful Chinese men to send or travel 'home' for a wife. Other young women arrived to join family members or to enjoy the relative freedom from traditional expectations that came with being an *amah* (maid) for a European family.[38] Numerically, the emigration of women was still dominated by illegally imported prostitutes (often kidnapped or sold into virtual slavery)[39] and the gender imbalance was still about 7:4 as late as the early 1930s. It did not come close to being even until the 1950s,[40] but Singapore's slow shift towards becoming a normal, sedentary society had begun – in rough parallel with the settlement's creeping modernisation.

EDUCATION AS PROXY

With families came births and children, followed by the need for schools. The colonial authorities had no interest at all in the education of the great majority of Asian children and they certainly did not want to provide mass English-language education for fear that the Asians might start getting above themselves. They did show some interest in providing an English-language education to a small number of those who already had a workable knowledge of English, but even in the case of this exception to the rule, it was left to a group of merchants to revive Raffles' plans to build the Singapore Institution in the 1830s. Nevertheless, with the number of children increasing noticeably, the Asian communities – both the immigrant communities and the Malays – along with a large number of Christian missionary societies, established many schools in the second half of the nineteenth century. Some of these schools had modest levels of state support, but many were entirely self-sustaining and between them they offered a bewildering variety of curricula and standards. A collection of these Christian schools still exists today as state-supported 'mission schools' – such as St Joseph's Institution (founded in the 1850s) and the Methodist Girl's School (founded in the 1880s). Yet only at the opening of the twentieth century did the colonial authorities begin taking much interest in education. In 1902 the government made modest commitments to provide English-medium education to Asian children and in 1903 it resumed control of Singapore's first school, Raffles Institution, eight decades after Raffles initiated the project and seven decades after private beneficiaries finished the building and opened the school. The government continued to ignore Chinese and Indian schools but, in a gesture towards the region's indigenous population, it did build some Malay-medium schools. Ironically this gesture does not seem to have done the Malays any favours in the long term, since it set the community down a path that led it to successfully resist the introduction of English-language education in the 1950s. And indeed the Malay language seemed to be on the ascendant culturally as well as politically in the 1950s and 1960s, complete with a flourishing film industry that was churning out racy Malay-language films from studios in Singapore.[41] This victory laid the foundations for the community's later economic and social disadvantage when the government turned English into the language of economic and political empowerment.[42] (The leadership of the Chinese communities also resisted the introduction of English-medium education in the 1960s, but with less success.)

Education provides a fair proxy for Singapore's social history in the twentieth century. This was the 'modern' century where ordinary people were beginning to matter globally in ways they had not in the past – as industrial producers, consumers, professional soldiers in standing armies, voters, taxpayers and eventually as investors (whether directly or through pooled funds). Asia was a late starter in the modernisation project but it has not been a laggard. Indeed Asia spent a century or so frantically catching up with the West and by some measures is now setting the pace.

Mass education was a key component in this project everywhere. In the case of twentieth-century Singapore it provides a particularly valuable key to understanding many aspects of social development, impinging as it does on issues of language, community, religion, loyalty and identity, social and economic inclusion/exclusion, and pathways into the elite. Between them, such factors account for most of the critical areas of social inquiry. Yet even 'education' is a relatively broad canvas, and I suggest that by focusing on language issues we can be even more nuanced in seeking a lodestone by which to navigate Singapore's twentieth-century social history. In Singapore, the medium of instruction in schools was a nodal point in social navigation, and it became increasingly important as the century moved forward. This created a strong line of continuity with the social history of the nineteenth century, where, as we have just seen, spoken and written languages provided much of the basis of both segmentation and hybridity, even without education being in the mix in any significant way.

ENGLISH VS VERNACULAR

In Singapore, the language of the twentieth century was English. The mission schools and the state between them provided English-medium education for small but important segments of the child population. In the early decades, the main beneficiaries were the sons and daughters of *baba* Chinese and Singhalese because both communities were particularly open to having their children exposed to English. When I say these communities were important, I mean that their command of English created niches for them that made them important. In the case of the Singhalese, it also created new divisions. Most of these Anglophone boys and girls learnt their English (and how to be a Victorian 'Gentleman' or 'Lady') at mission schools and then many converted to Christianity. This created a gulf between English-speaking Singhalese Christians and Singhalese-speaking Singhalese Buddhists. By the 1930s the reach of English education had breached the old boundaries and a significant though still small number of Straits Chinese (not just *baba*) and Indian boys and girls attended mission schools as a means of learning English and getting a Western education. Their parents put them on this course simply because this was the path to getting a better job, but one of the effects was to break down the binary division between English-speaking *baba* Chinese and Chinese-speaking Straits Chinese.[43] By the 1940s, bilingual Straits Chinese had emerged as a major social group in Singapore, albeit one that was not generally recognised as distinct. It should also be noted that without a second thought, textbooks and teachers in English-medium schools built and passed on racial/communal stereotypes that are the very stuff of colonial hegemony. Much of this stereotyping was then confirmed in the minds of the young men when the English-speaking boys entered government service or a profession, or became a clerk with a European company or trading house. They were setting out on a path towards middle-class comfort while their non-Anglophone neighbours took ill-paid jobs as factory or farm workers, drivers or the like, with the most enterprising likely to go into business or perhaps journalism.

As late as 1957, only 22% of the population over the age of 15 spoke English (35% of Indians, 23% of Malays and 18% of Chinese),[44] despite more than half a century of privileging English as the medium of education. This does not demonstrate a failure of colonial education policy. Rather, it points to its extremely limited reach into society, reflecting a basic disinterest. The 1947 social survey conducted by the Department of Social Welfare found that 45% of household breadwinners in the city area had no education at all, and only 14% had any English-medium education.[45] The figures suggest that younger workers had slightly higher rates of English education and education per se, but not so much higher that it could be regarded as a firm trend. The translation of these low levels of English-language education (and education in general) to employment and housing is direct and startling.

Restricting ourselves just to those Chinese, Indians and Malays who were born in Singapore and therefore received any schooling they may have had in Singapore – and staying with the 1947 social survey – we find that only 2.5% of Chinese, no Indians and 1.7% of Malays worked in professions and big business. By contrast 81.5% of Europeans and 10.8% of the Anglophone Eurasians worked in professions and big business. The equivalent figures for semi-skilled and unskilled workers stand at 40% for Chinese, 38% for Indians, 63% for Malays, 1.5% for Eurasians and zero for Europeans. The full figures are shown in Figure 8.4, complete with its anachronistic terminology.

The linkage between language, race and education flowed through into housing as well. Europeans, Eurasians and *peranakan* Chinese overwhelmingly lived in free-standing, airy bungalows, and the rest of the population lived in anything from pleasant *kampungs* to squalid, dirty, smelly, airless, overcrowded cubicles above shop houses in Chinatown. Options such as atap- and zinc-roofed squatter villages lay somewhere between these two extremes. The interwar influx of immigrants, particularly from southern China and Malaysia, overwhelmed Singapore's housing infrastructure, sanitation systems, water and electricity supplies, and health care, along with the government's attempts at urban reform and family planning. In any case, many of the government's efforts in these fields were interpreted by their intended beneficiaries as colonial intrusions designed to interfere with their lives and independence – which was basically true – and they found many ways to resist. Brenda Yeoh's *Contesting Space in Colonial Singapore* is substantially an account of the cat-and-mouse games between

Percentage Distribution of Wage-Earners in the various Race Groups according to the Occupation Groups The Chinese, Indian and Malaysian Wage-Earners are further sub-divided into the Immigrant and Indigenous Components

Occupation	RACE GROUPS									
	Chinese		Indians		Malaysians		Euro-peans	Eura-sians	Others	All Races
	Immi-grants	Indi-genous	Immi-grants	Indi-genous	Immi-grants	Indi-genous				
	%	%	%	%	%	%	%	%	%	%
I. Highest Professionals & Big Business ..	1.1	2.5	1.7	—	.9	1.7	81.5	10.8	8.3	2.1
II. Medium Business ..	2.4	1.7	1.9	1.2	—	—	—	—	—	1.9
III. Minor Professions ..	3.7	5.8	4.2	1.2	.6	3.2	6.9	18.5	22.9	4.3
IV. Clerks	4.1	16.3	6.8	34.6	1.7	10.5	2.3	50.8	43.7	8.5
V. Shop-Keepers & Shop Assistants	18.6	13.1	15.7	6.2	1.7	1.7	—	3.1	4.2	14.9
VI. Overseers, Foremen .	.7	1.4	.6	4.9	.9	5.2	9.3	3.1	2.1	1.2
VII. Skilled Workers ..	9.5	16.1	4.9	11.1	4.7	12.2	—	7.7	—	10.5
VIII. Semi-Skilled Workers	39.6	27.2	30.0	33.3	68.2	48.3	—	1.5	10.4	36.8
IX. Unskilled Workers ..	18.5	13.4	32.5	4.9	18.3	15.1	—	—	6.3	17.7
No Occupation	1.9	2.4	1.7	2.5	2.0	2.3	—	4.6	2.1	2.1
TOTAL ..	100.0	100.0	100.0	100.0	100.0	100.0	100.0	100.0	100.0	100.0
Number Classified	3772	1661	527	81	343	344	43	65	48	6887
Number Unknown & Un-classified	69	29	7	1	9	14	3	2	2	133

Figure 8.4 Table reproduced from the 1947 social survey of the city of Singapore
Source: Department of Social Welfare, Singapore, *A Social Survey of Singapore*, p. 52, Table XVI.

the Municipal Authority of Singapore and the urban Asian population from the late nineteenth century until 1930. It was a contest between:

> on the one hand, municipal attempts at imposing social and spatial control to create a city after the colonial image – orderly, sanitized, racially divided, hierarchical – and on the other, Asian agency in wresting concessions and asserting its own view of urban life.[46]

In Chapter 4 I suggested that from 1819 onwards we should distinguish between British Singapore and Asian Singapore as subjects of study. If this were true of the nineteenth century, it was more so in the first half of the twentieth, but with a difference that was even more basic than one of mere degree. In the nineteenth century, the two worlds could and substantially did ignore each other. British rule over Asian Singapore was indirect and ineffective, and the only Asians who gave much thought to their colonial masters were the elites that had to deal with them. Even for the elites, the relationship was primarily transactional.

The twentieth century was a very different world, especially in Asia. It was a century of nationalism, communalism, socialism, communism and anti-colonialism. The impact of these inherently modern forces – along with rebellions, invasions and wars

– was neither consistent nor evenly spread, but from the opening of the century the twin vectors of new technologies (particularly the telegraph, fast ships and aeroplanes) and the slow spread of education ensured that Asian Singapore was in touch with and highly sensitive to all these disruptive forces. Singapore was a cosmopolitan centre of news, ideas and printing. Radical ideas of nationalism, modernism, identity politics and Asian resurgence being generated in Japan, China, India and Java consequently flowed freely through Asian Singapore. Philanthropists such as Tan Kah Kee poured money into Chinese education, founding such iconic institutions as the Chinese High School, but not for the sake of promoting traditional Chinese education. He and others like him were modern Chinese and they wanted to build modern Chinese schools with modern curricula: science, history, geography and a full appreciation of and identification with the nationalist, modern aspirations of the motherland. This included a new appreciation of Mandarin as a both a nationalist tongue and a unifying language for Singapore's Chinese community. The same Tan Kah Kee who was seeding Chinese education was also meeting Sun Yat-Sen and raising money for the Kuomintang, and by the 1930s, when the motherland was being carved up by a rising and newly militarist Japan, the Singapore Chinese communities were ferociously nationalist.[47]

The other Asian communities went through their own modern disruptions, though not necessarily with education playing such a prominent role as it did for the Chinese, and not with the same mass impact on the community as a whole. Indian soldiers mutinied against their British officers in 1915 in an explicit act of nationalist identification with their homeland,[48] but life and work and the English-medium education of many of their children continued. Malay nationalism and modern ideas of Islam swirled through both the Malay schools and the coffee houses of Arab Street and Kampong Glam, though its full impact was ultimately felt more on the peninsula than in Singapore. By the 1930s, leadership of the Malay community in Singapore was firmly in the hands of an English-educated elite comprised of journalists, civil servants and merchants, and their primary concern was working with the British to defend Malay interests against the rising tide of Chinese assertion. Turnbull paints a portrait of everyday Malay life in the 1930s that prefigures many of the problems and challenges it was to face after the war:

> Even if their work took them to the city as civil servants, clerks, drivers or labourers, urban Malays could preserve some of their traditional way of life in Singapore in the 1930s, living in peaceful surroundings in kampong-style houses in almost exclusively Malay districts such as Kampong Melayu and Geylang Serai. Some small Malay communities were able to resist modernization almost entirely. …
>
> In the southern islands and at points along the north and east coasts of the island, Malay villages remained almost untouched by modern progress. …

Figure 8.5
Malays in a *kampung*, c.1911

Official educational policy encouraged Malays to cling to their accustomed way of life. With the growth of urban opportunities, the city's pull became stronger, but it was not yet irresistible.[49]

The local-born Anglophone Asian communities were not immune from nationalism either, but theirs was a much more genteel form than that of the numerically dominant Chinese-educated or Chinese-speaking Chinese communities. Like the Malays of the 1930s, their aspirations were firmly set within the context of Pax Britannica. Many identified themselves as 'Malayans', signifying their conviction that Malaya and not China or India was their home. They were overwhelmingly middle class and were growing in both numbers and prominence, only to see their world fall apart with the Japanese Occupation in the first half of the 1940s.

THE OCCUPATION

The three-and-a-half-year occupation of Malaya and Singapore by the Japanese army disrupted continuity so severely that there is a tendency to ignore the content of the Occupation itself and put it primarily in the context of what came afterwards. Indeed, Barbara and Leonard Andaya, in their *A History of Malaysia*, collapse their several pages on the Occupation into a totally forward-looking chapter titled 'Negotiating a New Nation, 1941–69'.[50] Three years is certainly a short time frame compared with those that predominate in the rest of this book, in which history is mostly measured in decades and centuries. The social framework of Malaya and Singapore during the Occupation is outlined over several pages in Chapter 5, and there is no need to revisit this. It might be worthwhile noting, however, that the cruelty and capriciousness of the occupying forces should not disguise the underlying rationality and purpose of the Occupation: the search for oil, tin, rubber and other commodities required for Japan's war economy.[51] The only element of the project that was illogical was the search for a food supply, since Malaya had never been self-sufficient in food production in the first place. The Japanese efforts simply created a food shortage, not only for the locals but even for the occupying forces themselves, resulting in runaway inflation of the cost of all food products. The price of 500 grams of rice went from $0.60 in December 1941 to $75 by August 1945, while the same weight of pork went from $0.48 to $280. A single egg cost $35 by 1945.[52]

Other exports fared much better, at least in the short term, as Malaya's entire export industry was diverted to serving the Japanese war effort – often through the mechanism of the forced relocation of labour to far-flung islands. The actual export of primary products slowed dramatically as Japan began losing control of the seas after the Battle of the Coral Sea and the Battle of Midway in mid-1942, but this did not stop the push for production. Slavish working conditions imposed on an underfed and cruelly treated workforce continued unabated, resulting in useless stockpiles of goods and totally unnecessary human hardship.

In my study of twentieth-century Singapore I have been using education as a window through which to follow such aspects of social history as language, communalism, identity politics and nationalism. The Occupation is a short disruption in this metanarrative and yet, even within this frame, education continues to serve as a useful prism for the study of society more broadly. In fact, it is remarkable how closely the Japanese education policy paralleled the pre-war colonial education practice, once soft words of good intentions are stripped away. With an emphasis on technical instruction and on the cultivation of an attitude of what the Japanese called 'respectful labour', they set about promoting only the most basic levels of education in the vernacular languages. They closed higher education completely in the first instance (the Raffles Institution and the King Edward VII Medical School), eventually replacing it with some basic post-secondary technical training colleges. Malay-medium primary schools were the first to reopen after the British surrender, but standards were low and the teaching of history and religion was forbidden. Mission schools were allowed to function but, as with the Malay schools, without history or religion. The messaging was simple. Locals were being prepared to play low-level roles in the economy and the emphasis was on instilling subservience in the workforce. Little surprise that when the food shortages became acute in 1944, attendance rates plummeted as parents kept their children home to help grow food. English-medium schools were a partial exception to the general disregard for education. They were converted into Japanese schools and – as with the elite English schools that they displaced – had a much more comprehensive and academic curriculum designed to provide a proper modern education for a small number of children.[53]

The elements of comparison with pre-war education are strong, providing one does not push the analogy too far. The similarities are obvious: reinforcement of communal identity through language; the provision of very basic and poor-quality schooling in vernacular schools; and something passing for elite education in the schools that used the colonial language. Yet we should note that the British were moving imperfectly in the direction of improving and broadening education, whereas the Japanese were decisively winding it back and dumbing it down. Whether a long-term Japanese Occupation might have resulted in a more forward-looking and positive education policy – such as that imposed on colonial Korea after 1910 – we will never know, but certainly in the short term the Japanese education policies were entirely destructive, as was every other aspect of the Occupation.

FROM SCARCITY TO QUANTITY; FROM MULTILINGUALISM TO ENGLISH-PLUS-ONE

After the Japanese surrendered in August 1945 the British returned to a new Malaya and a new Singapore – though they did not recognise this immediately. They were welcomed with fanfare upon their return because life under the Japanese had been so terrible that anything was an improvement, and failed to realise that the mystique of the superior white man had been shattered. This realisation came very slowly, but in the meantime there was much rebuilding to engage a new occupying army. The docks and railways had been bombed, the harbour and construction industry were not functional and food was still in short supply – and none of Malaya's pre-war suppliers had surpluses to spare for Malaya. Hospitals had little medicine and disease was rife due to an upsurge of unsanitary housing (much of it unregulated squatting) and the near-total destruction of public utilities. Corruption had settled into the business and working cultures and the police force was so tainted by alleged collaboration with the Japanese that it needed protection from the public. The British retained Singapore as a Crown Colony, separate from peninsular Malaya, but had no focused plans for the reconstruction or the running of the island. They nevertheless restored the city's most critical losses as a matter of priority, and – happily for the education-focused theme of this chapter – one of those immediate priorities was reopening the schools. Schools were not a priority just for the colonial authorities. While the British Military Administration (BMA) was busy reopening the Malay and English schools with state resources, the Chinese communities were rebuilding Chinese education, substantially with private resources. By the end of the year, 66 Chinese schools, 37 English schools and 21 Malay schools were functioning, and by March 1946, 62,000 children were attending school.[54]

Strictly in terms of social standing, this was a good time to be Chinese – and more precisely, it was a good time to be a Chinese-speaking and left-wing Chinese. As a community the Chinese were still struggling and poor, but they had the status of being both the most prominent victims of the Japanese occupiers and also of providing the most prominent heroes of the resistance. Both suffering and valour were much too widespread among the different races of Malaya for the Chinese community to make exclusive claims on either, but their prominence in both classes was indisputable.[55] The Chinese communist leaders of the Malayan People's Anti-Japanese Army (MPAJA) were lionised as war heroes by the returning British, and they were even invited to nominate three representatives to sit on the BMA itself.[56] The mythology of their special role could have easily become a central and divisive element of nation building in independent Singapore, leading to Chinese conceit and non-Chinese resentment, except that Lee Kuan Yew's government insisted that all corporate memory and memorials commemorated the dead and the heroes of all four of Singapore's official 'races' – Chinese, Malays, Indians and 'Others'. This insistence prevailed even when it was the Chinese community that raised the funds and organised the commemoration.[57]

There was a serious level of tension between the conservative and the leftist elites of Singapore's Chinese communities. The conservatives were heartily capitalist – *towkays*, bankers and businessmen – mostly working through the Chinese Chamber of Commerce and traditional Chinese associations.[58] The leftists were a mixture of ideological communists, former fighters, left-wing militants and radical students working through unions, farmers' groups, schools and sectional interest groups. Yet even the conservatives were China-oriented nationalists, anti-colonialists and uncompromising defenders/promoters of Chinese language, education and 'culture', and a lot of the leftists were budding entrepreneurs who were fighting for their right to prosper under capitalism and free trade. The distinction between the two groups was thus less clear than is suggested by neat labels such as 'conservative' and 'leftist'. In the battle for hearts and minds, the leftists had the upper hand in the early post-war years, especially after Mao's victory in 1949 when communism became intimately identified with Chinese nationalism. Hence rich conservatives led and substantially funded the reconstruction and expansion of the Chinese education system that became the main recruiting ground for the leftists. The most famous of these relationships did not involve a school, but a university: Singapore's Chinese-medium Nanyang University (known as Nantah), which opened in Jurong in 1958. The fundraising and building of Nantah was driven by Singapore's most famous post-war *towkay*, Tan Lark Sye, and the university was intended as a bastion of Chinese language, culture and scholarship in Nanyang. Tan was no leftist, but he was a champion of Chinese identity politics. The campus he founded immediately became a lightning rod for ethnic Chinese causes and grievances, and its student body became increasingly militant and radicalised.[59]

In the midst of this swirling mix of ethnic pride and anti-colonialism, the returning British were making the most cavalier of assumptions about the future of their colony. They presumed that small, incremental gestures towards limited self-government would be acceptable. In this they made a serious misjudgement, essentially because they mistakenly assumed that the British-trained Asian lawyers and businessmen with whom they were familiar and comfortable would be accepted by the rest of the population as their natural leaders. This was never going to happen and it bred bitter resentment in much of the population – most spectacularly among non-English-speaking Chinese and working-class Indians. This resentment brewed in the midst of a newly swirling sea of anti-colonialist and nationalist energy. The Chinese community's reactions in particular were substantially channelled through the politics of education and schools.

The turmoil in Chinese schools reflected a much broader contest between rival visions of the new nation: an Anglo-colonial social and educational agenda that presumed that English was the language of the future, at least for the elite; a Malaya-oriented nationalist agenda that hoped Bahasa Melayu (the Malay language) would be Singapore's lingua franca, even if not its primary language; and a Chinese nationalist agenda that passionately set out to preserve Chinese education and language. These divisions were not mutually exclusive or consistent, either in principle or in leading personnel. In 1946 the colonial authorities proposed letting vernacular primary schools continue without English, provided they accepted full government support and a government curriculum.[60] Chinese nationalists commonly upheld the centrality of Bahasa Melayu and so they learnt and spoke the language.[61] Nationalists such as Lee Kuan Yew shifted seamlessly between championing Bahasa Melayu, Chinese education and English as need be. Yet despite these overlaps and shifting agendas, the social cognition of the inhabitants of the different worlds of Singapore had very little in common – English-educated Asians and colonialists saw a world of communist Chinese mayhem and conspiracy, while Chinese-educated workers and students saw colonial plots to subordinate them and deprive them of their culture and language. Put in these terms, the rest of this narrative up to the 1980s is the story of the selection and victory of English as the language of the elite and the main language of social mobility – and the utter defeat of the social forces behind both of its rivals.

If we turn to Chinese schools as our guide to social issues, we find that the schools were not only at the centre of the politics of language, but also the key to class conflict and consciousness. The problems and frustrations were endemic and the linkage between education and communal issues was headlined in the realities of life, whereby education for most children in Chinese-medium schools ended at the end of primary school for lack of Chinese middle schools. The alternative path was to switch to the English stream, which usually led to a frustrating middle-school career of being barely able to follow lessons or read textbooks. No wonder there was such a divergence in the career and life pathways between Chinese and English speakers.

The school students engaged not only in the politics of education and language, but in industrial disputation and the politics of robust nationalism (both China- and Malaya-oriented nationalism). This was in some senses a 'natural' progression, but in practice it was facilitated by some radical Chinese trade union leaders – notably Lim Chin Siong and Fong Swee Suan – who had influence far beyond their institutional bases.[62] Under leaders such as Lim, mobs of school children provided the frontline 'troops' in support of striking workers until 1955, when the strike at the Hock Lee Bus Company turned violent and the students mostly retreated to issues that concerned them directly.[63] Industrial action had never been their main focus in any case, though it should be noted that their solidarity with bus drivers shows that the students were fully aware of the career and educational limitations that came with a Chinese education in colonial Singapore. The other activities touched more directly upon central elements of the contestation between the differing visions of Singapore's future, flanking the Hock Lee bus strike: the 13 May 1954 petition seeking deferral of National Service until after graduation from school, and the 1956 protest against the deregistration of the Singapore Chinese Middle School Students' Union and the expulsion of 140 students. Thirteen people were killed in the latter incident so they were not trivial matters.[64] Based on little more than a good imagination, the government and the *Straits Times* accused the protesting students of both episodes of being operatives of the Malayan Communist Party (MCP) and the Chinese Communist Party – even though Special Branch itself confirmed that by 1954 the MCP was almost non-functional; that the MCP operatives were specifically trying to avoid an insurrectionary situation; and that the Party leaders were young, inexperienced and not remotely in control of the situation in the schools. Far from being in charge, they were as surprised as anyone else at the various turns of events.[65]

Figure 8.6
David Marshall, 1950s

In among this upheaval, Singapore was moving towards self-government, and in 1955 a general election turned decisively against the colonial government's favoured set of candidates and instead swept David Marshall into office as Chief Minister under the new, temporary constitution that instituted very limited self-government in Singapore (Figure 8.6). Marshall is important in Singapore's story for many reasons, but the main point of interest in this chapter is his input on schools, language and security policies. After independence, Singapore developed a version of multiculturalism that it has called multiracialism. This form of social organisation had its origins with David Marshall's presumption that Singapore's future lay with assimilating its various ethnic cultures into a dominant hegemonic culture, and his attempted political settlement of what he described as the Chinese education 'situation' in 1956.

Marshall was trying to construct an inclusive society built on Singapore citizenship, multilingualism and mutual respect between communities. Faced with a groundswell of student protests and strikes that sometimes escalated into violence, Marshall set out to neutralise what he viewed as legitimate concern about the future of Chinese education in the hope that this would facilitate rational discourse by segregating highly sensitive issues from each other. At the same time, he faced less strident but still important calls from the Malay community to raise the standard of Malay education (which already had significant state support) by teaching English, and bringing its curriculum and teacher salaries into line with those of the English schools.[66]

In response to these disparate and contradictory pressures he established the All-Party Committee on Chinese Education to investigate the issues. The Committee's solution was the creation of a quad-lingual educational system, whereby each of the main languages of Singapore – English, Mandarin, Malay and Tamil – would be treated equally, and parents could choose any of these options for their children. The intention of this move was to dissipate communal tensions and facilitate nation building, and it seems from the reaction of the Chinese and Tamil press that the moves were welcomed on both counts in those quarters, though the Malay press was much slower to accept the good intentions of the government.[67] Unfortunately, the move also provided the long-term basis for reinforcing and perpetuating the sense of communal separateness that had been long established. In contrast, another recommendation took Singapore a step down the path of assimilation. The Committee recommended the revision of all textbooks used in all language streams to ensure their content encouraged a Malayan consciousness (as opposed to consciousness of a distant 'homeland'). The Malay language was also encouraged for use as Singapore's lingua franca. The initiatives of the All-Party Committee did not end the violence or resolve the Chinese school 'situation' but, together with Marshall's successful advocacy of multilingualism in general, they did place Singapore on the path that we now recognise as 'multiracialism', complete with its ongoing tensions between communal separateness and assimilation. When the People's Action Party (PAP) assumed power in late-colonial Singapore in 1959, it continued to pursue a policy of tolerant assimilation but, in an effort to seduce Malaya into forming an economic and political union, Malay culture and language were given fresh emphasis. This Malaya-centrism seemed to bear fruit when Singapore and Malaya (with Sarawak and Sabah) joined to become Malaysia in 1963, but it came to an abrupt end with the acrimonious separation of Singapore from Malaysia in August 1965.

Separation from Malaysia left Singapore as an independent republic, almost by accident, and the Singapore government was in the hands of the PAP, minus its left wing. It had no use for a Malaya-centred assimilation, but little confidence that a merely Singapore-centred focus could subdue ethnic pride and separatism (or even worse, a primordial loyalty to the ethnic 'homelands': China, India and Indonesia/Malaysia). In a supreme effort of nation building, the Minister for Culture, S. Rajaratnam, forged a government programme of forceful assimilation directed both at building a 'modern' society and at keeping potentially troublesome social forces in check through programmes of monitoring, control and/or marginalisation. The groups affected most by the hot breath of government included: the Chinese communities, including Chinese small and medium-sized enterprises (SMEs); the print media; trade unions; and the Malay-Muslim community. The level and style of state intervention varied: the government set out to marginalise Chinese social associations by imposing its own;

SMEs were starved almost to the point of extinction in favour of state and foreign enterprises; the print media was harassed and then tamed; troublesome trade unions and trade union leaders were replaced slowly, over a period of years; the government took direct control of the administration of Islam by creating a statutory board (the Islamic Religious Council of Singapore) to run it; and Lee Kuan Yew successfully co-opted the leadership of the Malay community.[68] The textual symbolism of the official nation-building project in the 1960s and 1970s was thoroughly inclusive and Singapore's success was routinely attributed to the 'industry of the various races' – to use Minister Ong Pang Boon's words of 1969.[69] This situation was not without its tensions and blemishes, but it lasted until the early 1980s and is still remembered with nostalgia by members of the minority races as a little golden age of tolerance and respect.[70]

In this initial decade-and-a-half, the government brought every existing school on the island into the national system and concentrated on expanding the education system so that schooling was genuinely universal. It continued with Chinese, Tamil and Malay schools, but shifted the focus to technical, maths and science education in line with the needs of a newly industrialising economy. It also did what it could to push students into engaging with English through three techniques: encouraging them to enter English-medium schools; pushing English-plus-one bilingualism; and interpolating English elements (notably in the science and maths curricula) into vernacular schools. The push to enrol children in English-medium national schools went well because the tangible benefits of an English education were clear to many parents, but the other two elements – which between them amounted to imposing bilingual education on monolingual students – were disastrous: they widened the education outcomes between the English-educated and the vernacular-educated students.

FROM BREADTH TO CALIBRATED DIFFERENTIATION

By the opening of the 1980s, the effort to see that every child in Singapore was going to school was all but complete. Schools may have routinely educated their pupils in two shifts (morning and afternoon), there may have been confusion and dissatisfaction over languages, and most of the teachers may have been poorly trained and poorly paid, but at least nearly everyone was at school and following the same curriculum. Now it was time to decide upon the next step, and with Lee Kuan Yew approaching the height of his power (see Chapter 6), there should be no surprise that the agenda was driven by him (in consultation with Goh Keng Swee, as Minister for Education). It should also not be too surprising that it was integrated into a much broader social vision that presumed the special importance of elites and Chinese. The government's approach henceforth continued to improve mass education, but this was just one part of a carefully calibrated programme that sought different outcomes for different groups: special treatment for 'elite' English-medium schools and 'elite' children; special primary schools and preschools for Chinese children; special help and special programmes for 'elite' Chinese schools; and a generic effort to lift the standards of 'neighbourhood' schools.[71] Significantly, however, gender was not a decisive point of differentiation and well-educated, well-paid professional women have become ubiquitous in the new Singapore. These changes in the education system were at the vanguard of subsequent history and have given us the Singapore we have today: highly educated; highly pressured; English-speaking, but with imperfect English-plus-one bilingualism; hierarchical; diminishing levels of social mobility; Chinese-dominated, with diminishing levels of intercommunal interaction; and uncompromisingly materialist. If your parents had money and were Chinese and your English and Mandarin were good, your goal after the 1980s was to go to an elite school, win a government scholarship to study overseas and return as a member of the 'scholar' class who would enter the higher levels of the civil service or the officer corps of the military and be set for life. If you had all these attributes but were not Chinese, you still had some chance of becoming a 'scholar' and being set for life, but you were at a major and statistically measurable disadvantage. For poorer children with good English, the most likely pathway was through a neighbourhood school and the most likely endpoint was entry into a local university or a polytechnic (though still allowing for the realistic possibility of doing better). If your English was not good, you were more likely to end up in an Institute of Technical Education at best. By the 1990s, English was king in Singapore and Mandarin was queen, and both were comfortably middle class. Singapore's subsequent social development has continued along this trajectory, with increasing levels of wealth and standards of education.

In the midst of Singapore's wealth and success, however, outcomes for different social strata of Singaporeans have been as diverse as they ever were. The wealthy are very wealthy indeed, while the poor are so poor and prevalent that income inequality has emerged as a serious social issue. For those in the middle, the cost of living and housing has made it relatively commonplace for families to rent out a room to make ends meet, especially if there are children to educate or aged parents to support. This combination has produced prosperity but has given Singapore and Singaporeans a frantic edge. The one thing that seems to unite everyone is that life in Singapore has become uncomfortably crowded, frightfully expensive and above all, unrelentingly busy. Foreign maids have provided the invisible hands that have kept working families going; often substituting for the maternal figure in children's lives as professional couples and small business holders struggle to find time for family life. Until the government's scare at the 2011 general election, the only area where there had been some relief from frantic pressure was in education, wherein some incremental reforms introduced since 2004 had eased some of the more extreme pressures on school children – especially, but not exclusively, regarding the need to master a second language.[72] Since then, the government has been working overtime to ease some of the pressures on housing, transport and other areas, but 'busyness' nevertheless remains as ubiquitous.

As the country moves forward, the government is setting itself an agenda of social reform to smooth some of these sharp edges in economic and social policies to make Singapore a more comfortable place to live and work. The problem it faces is that most of these elements are not so much the unintended consequences of policy decisions: they *are* the policy decisions.[73] It remains to be seen, therefore, if the government can remodel the economy and society to make it gentler without also removing the central drivers that generate the prosperity.

Afterword

Reflecting on the place of Raffles and 1819 in Singapore's history, I continue to be dismayed that the political elite of an Asian nation as replete in rich historical legacies as is Singapore, should decide to build the country's foundation myth on the arrival of an English imperialist. One can understand why the British colonialists might want to dismiss Asian contributions to the Singapore story – they wanted to claim the credit for themselves – but why did the Asian nationalists do so? Were the early English-educated elites so brainwashed in their colonial schools and British universities that they knew no better? Were the Chinese among them so prejudiced against the Malays that they could not bear to acknowledge their contribution? Or is the explanation as simple as political expediency: the temptation to build a simple narrative about two 'Great Men of History'? Then again, why would the sons and daughters of these early nationalists insist on perpetuating these myths? Are they afraid of having such weak legacies of their own that they need to rest on the laurels of dead men? I am confident that there is some truth in all of these explanations, but none is entirely satisfactory. Fortunately, this is not a set of questions that I need to answer today.

As I conclude this book, I return to a point I made in Chapter 1. I set out to make 1819 a punctuation mark, not a headline in Singapore's story. I doubt that I will have convinced everyone, but I am confident that I have made a strong case. This should not, however, be taken as a complete dismissal of 1819. Even punctuation marks are important, and the period around 1819 – loosely from 1811 to 1826 – really was very important in Singapore's history. Nevertheless, this period was not the beginning of its history, nor the beginning of modern Singapore.

The reality is that Raffles still sits squarely in the founding mythology as it is taught both in Singapore and internationally, and this mythology is part of the legitimising narrative of the country's current ruling elite. When Raffles is bookended with Lee Kuan Yew, so that they are presented as the men who 'founded' and 'shaped' Singapore respectively,[1] this mythology is being drafted into the political service of the Lee family. Whatever the future may hold for Singapore, we can be reasonably sure that the aura of being Lee Kuan Yew's eldest son will continue to sustain Lee Hsien Loong's political hegemony for some years to come. His government has been going through a difficult time since he took the prime ministership in 2004, and yet we need to recognise that the elite has been too successful at reproducing itself – and in crafting the next generation of elites – to be dismissed.

Note that when we talk of the ruling elite, we are not just talking about the people who happen to be in Cabinet at the time of writing, let alone the PAP MPs. We are talking about an entire ecosystem of elite reproduction and elite formation that stretches through a handful of powerful families, through a substantial clutch of elite schools, and through the officer corps of the military and the upper levels of the civil service.[2] It is riven with weaknesses and flaws, but it also offers compensations that other systems cannot – stability, purpose and a high level of administrative competence. This elite, crafted and formed by Lee Kuan Yew and a few hand-picked colleagues, deserves credit for taking Singapore from being a successful colonial port city to being a successful global city. Such achievements are not to be thrown away lightly.

The current elite is here to stay and I would be very surprised if the Singapore Story does not continue to determine the national narrative, albeit in a more mature form than the original. Even before I started writing this book the narrative had already been expanded to include the perspectives of Asian colonists, and now there seems to be some official willingness to include Singapore's pre-colonial past as part of the Singapore story. This new version of history is not yet interfering with the national elite's self-serving accounts of Singapore's success, but at least the history is emerging from the shadows into the light of day. I cannot be as sanguine about recognition of the pivotal contributions to Singapore's prosperity of Johor and its 19th century rulers. This was a major theme of my book and I live in hope that other scholars will continue this research trajectory.

At the time of writing there is every sign that in one form or another, the Singapore Story is being extended to benefit Lee Hsien Loong's branch of the family. If confirmation of the ongoing centrality of Lee Kuan Yew in the mythology of the nation is needed, it came a week before the first anniversary of Lee Kuan Yew's death, when the Ministry of Culture, Community and Youth issued guidelines regulating the use of the former prime minister's name and image, explicitly saying that they 'may be used for purposes of identifying with the nation'.[3]

The Lee family has become a brand and has been effectively identified as such by the founder and patriarch, who towards the end of his life expressed mock concern that his grandchildren might 'degrade the Lee name' if they go into politics and are not good enough.[4] Now that the baton has been passed decisively from the patriarch to the eldest son, and there is a third generation waiting in the wings, it has become clear that the Lee name is not just a political brand, or just a domestic brand. At least for the foreseeable future, brand 'Lee' now equals brand 'Singapore'. And the Singapore Story lives on.

Notes

PROLOGUE

1. Benedict R.O.G. Anderson, *Imagined Communities: Reflections on the Origin and Spread of Nationalism*, London: Verso, 2006 (1983).

CHAPTER 1 LET'S TALK ABOUT 1819: REORIENTING THE NATIONAL NARRATIVE

1. H.F. Pearson, *Singapore: A Popular History*, Singapore: Times Books International, 1985 (1961), p. 1.
2. Nassim Nicholas Taleb and Gregory F. Treverton, 'The Calm Before the Storm', *Foreign Affairs*, January–February 2015, p. 90.
3. Ibid., p. 92.
4. See Ministry of Information and the Arts, *The Singapore Story: Overcoming the Odds*, CD-ROM, 1999. A National Education Project by the Ministry of Information and the Arts, this CD-ROM has been widely distributed to school children as part of a package entitled 'The Singapore Story: A Choice Collection'. Also see Lee Kuan Yew, *The Singapore Story: Memoirs of Lee Kuan Yew*, Singapore: Prentice Hall, 1998; and Lee Kuan Yew, *From Third World to First: The Singapore Story: 1965–2000. Memoirs of Lee Kuan Yew*, Singapore: Singapore Press Holdings and Times Editions, 2000.
5. The History curriculum was just one small part of the National Education programme, which also embraced Civics, Moral Education, Social Studies and language studies.
6. Discovery Channel, *The History of Singapore: Lion City, Asian Tiger*, Hoboken, NJ: John Wiley & Sons, 2010. Also see the documentary itself on YouTube.
7. Ernest Koh, *Singapore Stories: Language, Class and the Chinese of Singapore 1945–2000*, Amherst, NY: Cambria Press, 2010, p. 2.
8. Kwa Chong Guan, Derek Heng and Tan Tai Yong, *Singapore: A 700-Year History from Early Emporium to World City*, Singapore: National Archives of Singapore, 2009, p. 7.
9. Koh, *Singapore Stories*, p. 2.
10. T.N. Harper, 'Lim Chin Siong and the "Singapore Story"', in Tan Jing Quee and Jomo K.S. (eds), *Comet in Our Sky: Lim Chin Siong in History*, Kuala Lumpur: Insan, 2001, p. 6.
11. C.M. Turnbull, *A History of Singapore 1819–1988*, 2nd edn, Singapore: Oxford University Press, 1989 (1977), p. 1.
12. Singapore History Project Team, *History of Modern Singapore (Secondary 1)*, Singapore: Addison Wesley Longman for the Curriculum Development Institute of Singapore, 1984–94. The Lower Secondary textbook carried the same front cover except for substitution of 'Lower Secondary' for 'Secondary 1'.
13. Karl Hack, 'Framing Singapore's History', in Nicholas Tarling (ed.), *Studying Singapore's Past: C.M. Turnbull and the History of Modern Singapore*, Singapore: National University of Singapore Press, 2012, p. 18.

14. Kumar Ramakrishna, *'Original Sin'? Revising the Revisionist Critique of the 1963 Operation Coldstore in Singapore*, Singapore: Institute of Southeast Asian Studies, 2015.
15. See Michael D. Barr, 'Review of Kumar Ramakrishna, *"Original Sin"? Revising the Revisionist Critique of the 1963 Operation Coldstore in Singapore*', *The Developing Economies*, 54(3), 2016, pp. 260–3.
16. Philippe Regnier, *Singapore: City-State in South-East Asia*, Honolulu: University of Hawai'i Press, 1987.
17. Carl A. Trocki, *Prince of Pirates: The Temenggongs and the Development of Johor and Singapore 1784–1885*, Singapore: National University of Singapore Press, 2007 (1979); and Carl A. Trocki, *Opium and Empire: Chinese Society in Colonial Singapore, 1800–1910*, Ithaca and London: Cornell University Press, 1990.
18. James Francis Warren, *Rickshaw Coolie: A People's History of Singapore 1880–1940*, Singapore: Singapore University Press, 2003 (1986); and James Francis Warren, *Ah Ku and Karayuki-San: Prostitution in Singapore 1870–1940*, Singapore: Singapore University Press, 2003 (1993).
19. John N. Miksic, *Archaeological Research on 'Forbidden Hill' of Singapore: Excavations at Fort Canning, 1984*, Singapore: National Museum of Singapore, 1985; and John N. Miksic, *Singapore and the Silk Road of the Sea, 1300–1800*, Singapore: National University of Singapore Press and National Museum of Singapore, 2013.
20. Kevin Blackburn, 'Mary Turnbull's History Textbook for the Singapore Nation', in Tarling (ed.), *Studying Singapore's Past*, p. 76. Prof. Wang made essentially the same point to me two decades later when he was advising me at the beginning of my research for *Constructing Singapore: Elitism, Ethnicity and the Nation-Building Project*. To drive his point home, he cited the absurdity of a book on Belgium that he had once browsed in a bookshop, in which Belgian 'national' history has supposedly been tracked back 80,000 years using geological data – as if Belgium's current borders gave the nation-state a claim on everything that happened within and below the land down to the centre of the earth.
21. According to his LinkedIn page, Borschberg has native fluency in German, professional working proficiency in Portuguese, Dutch, French, Spanish and Italian, and limited working proficiency in Malay.
22. For a representative sample of his work, see Peter Borschberg, 'Singapore in the Cycles of the Long Durée', *Journal of the Malaysian Branch of the Royal Asiatic Society*, 90 (Part 1, Number 312), 2017, pp. 29–60; Peter Borschberg, *Hugo Grotius, the Portuguese and Free Trade in the East Indies*, Singapore: National University of Singapore Press, 2011; Peter Borschberg, 'Malacca as a "Sea-Borne Empire" – Continuities and Discontinuities from Sultanate to Portuguese Colony (Fifteenth and Sixteenth Century)', in Peter Borschberg and Martin Krieger (eds), *Water and State in Europe and Asia*, New Delhi: Manohar, 2008, pp. 35–71; Peter Borschberg, *The Singapore and Melaka Straits: Violence, Security and Diplomacy in the 17th Century*, Singapore: National University of Singapore Press, 2010; and Peter Borschberg, 'Security, VOC Penetration and Luso-Spanish Co-operation: The Armada of Philippine Governor Juan de Silva in the Straits of Singapore, 1616', in Peter Borschberg (ed.), *Iberians in the Singapore-Melaka Area and Adjacent Regions (16th to 18th Century)*, Wiesbaden: Harrassowitz Verlag; Lisbon: Fundação Oriente, 2004, pp. 35–62.
23. Peter Borschberg, in conversation, April 2012. Since that conversation, Borschberg has gone to print with firm evidence that, at least until the end of the seventeenth century, Europeans thought of Singapore as being an island in the Johor River estuary, with the strip of water between Singapore Island and the mainland identified as a branch of the river, rather than as a strait. See, for instance, Peter Borschberg, 'Singapura in Early Modern Cartography: A Sea of Challenges', National Library Board, *Visualising Space: Maps of Singapore and the Region: Collections from the National Library and National Archives of Singapore*, Singapore: National Library Board, [2015], pp. 22, 25.
24. Hack, 'Framing Singapore's History', p. 20.
25. Curriculum Planning and Development Division, Ministry of Education, *Singapore: The Making of a Nation-State, 1300–1975*, Singapore: Star Publishing, 2014.
26. 'New Sec 2 History Textbook to encourage Thinking Skills', *Today*, 29 May 2014.

CHAPTER 2 THE IDEA OF SINGAPORE

1. George Yeo, 'Renewing the Sap: Civil Society Rejuvenates the Singapore's Public Sector Banyan Tree', interview with Dr Albert Bressand and Catherine Distler, 17 May 2001, National Archives of Singapore Online.
2. Government of Singapore, *White Paper: Salaries for a Capable and Committed Government*, Singapore: Government of Singapore, 10 January 2012, Introduction, p. 9.
3. Michael D. Barr, 'Ordinary Singapore: The Decline of Singapore Exceptionalism', *Journal of Contemporary Asia*, 46(1), 2016, pp. 1–17.
4. Jon S.T. Quah, *Public Administration Singapore Style*, Talisman: Singapore, 2010, dust jacket.
5. Goh Chok Tong, 'Speech by Mr Goh Chok Tong, Minister for Health and Second Minister of Defence, at the Singapore General Hospital (SGH) Nite 1982', 6 March 1982, National Archives of Singapore Online.
6. 'Chok Tong is First DPM', *Straits Times*, 1 January 1985.
7. Yeo, 'Renewing the Sap'.
8. George Yeo, 'Between North and South, Between East and West', speech at The SGH Lecture, 29 April 2001, National Archives of Singapore Online.
9. Lee Hsien Loong, 'Prime Minister Lee Hsien Loong's 2004 National Day Rally Speech, Sunday 22 August 2004', National Archives of Singapore Online.
10. '4 shifts in Singapore's approach to healthcare, outlined by PM Lee', *Channel NewsAsia*, 10 February 2015.
11. Lee Hsien Loong, 'Transcript of Prime Minister Lee Hsien Loong's May Day Rally Speech on 1 May 2015', http://www.pmo.gov.sg/newsroom/transcript-prime-minister-lee-hsien-loong-may-day-rally-speech-1-may-2015, accessed 25 June 2018.
12. Han Fook Kwang, Zuraidah Ibrahim, Chua Mui Hoong, Lydia Lim, Ignatius Low, Rachel Lin and Robin Chan, *Lee Kuan Yew: Hard Truths to Keep Singapore Going*, Singapore: Straits Times Press, 2011, p. 99.
13. *World History*, 'John O'Sullivan and Manifest Destiny', https://worldhistory.us/american-history/john-osullivan-and-manifest-destiny.php, accessed 8 July 2018.
14. Eric Hobsbawm and Terence Ranger (eds), *The Invention of Tradition*, Cambridge: Cambridge University Press, 1983.
15. C.M. Turnbull, *A History of Singapore 1819–1988*, 2nd edn, Singapore: Oxford University Press, 1989 (1977), p. 131.
16. 'Singapore seen as New York of the Nation', *Straits Times*, 30 July 1962.
17. S. Rajaratnam, 'Singapore: Global City', in Kwa Chong Guan (ed.), *S. Rajaratnam on Singapore: From Ideas to Reality*, Singapore: World Scientific and Institute of Defence and Strategic Studies, 2006, pp. 227–237.
18. Selvaraj Velayutham, *Responding to Globalization: Nation, Culture and Identity in Singapore*, Singapore: Institute of Southeast Asian Studies, 2007, Chapter 3.
19. See Kenneth Paul Tan (ed.), *Renaissance Singapore? Economy, Culture, and Politics*, Singapore: National University of Singapore Press, 2007.
20. See, for example, Jean E. Abshire, *The History of Singapore*, Santa Barbara, CA: Greenwood, 2011, Chapter 1, 'A Globalized City-State'; and Karl Hack and Jean-Louis Margolin, with Karine Delaye (eds), *Singapore from Temasek to the 21st Century: Reinventing the Global City*, Singapore: National University of Singapore Press, 2010.
21. Anthony Reid, *Southeast Asia in the Age of Commerce, 1450–1680, Volume Two: Expansion and Crisis*, Chiang Mai, Thailand: Silkworm Books, 1993; and O.W. Wolters, *History, Culture, and Region in Southeast Asian Perspectives*, rev. edn, Ithaca, NY: Southeast Asia Program Publications, Southeast Asia Program, Cornell University, 1999 (originally published 1982 by the Institute of Southeast Asian Studies, Singapore).
22. Philippe Regnier, *Singapore: City-State in South-East Asia*, Honolulu: University of Hawai'i Press, 1987. Also see Garry Rodan, *The Political Economy of Singapore's Industrialization: National State and International Capital*, Kuala Lumpur: Forum, 1991 (1989).

23. Ross King, *Kuala Lumpur and Putrajaya: Negotiating Urban Space in Malaysia*, Singapore: National University of Singapore Press; Copenhagen: Nordic Institute of Asian Studies, 2008.
24. Daniel A. Bell and Avner de-Shalit, *The Spirit of Cities: Why the Identity of a City Matters in a Global Age*, Princeton and Oxford: Princeton University Press, 2011.
25. Yeo, 'Between North and South'; and Yeo, 'Renewing the Sap'.
26. Yeo, 'Between North and South'.
27. Ibid.
28. Hong Lysa and Huang Jianli, *The Scripting of a National History: Singapore and Its Pasts*, Singapore: National University of Singapore Press, 2008, Chapter 9.
29. Edgar H. Schein, *Strategic Pragmatism: The Culture of Singapore's Economic Development Board*, Singapore: Toppan with The MIT Press, 1996; and Chan Chin Bock *et al.*, *Heart Work*, Singapore: Economic Development Board and EDB Society, 2002.
30. Michael Leifer, *Singapore's Foreign Policy: Coping with Vulnerability*, London and New York: Routledge, 2000.
31. Editorial, 'An incident that should not have taken place', *Nanfang Evening Post*, 14 May 1954; Editorial, 'Students–Police clash, an unfortunate incident', *Chung Shing Jit Pao*, 15 May 1954; and 'Eleven Students of call-up age whose appeals were rejected openly state that they will not report for training', *Nanyang Siang Pau*, 13 October 1954. All cited in the Colony of Singapore, *Weekly Digest of Non-English Press*, 1954.
32. The excitement and spontaneity running through the crowds of school children involved in many of these 'riots' of the mid-1950s – many of whom were overage due to the interruption to their schooling caused by the Occupation – is conveyed by several oral histories reported in Kevin Blackburn, 'Family Memories as Alternative Narratives to the State's Construction of Singapore's National History', in Loh Kah Seng, Ernest Koh and Stephen Dobbs (eds), *Oral History in Southeast Asia: Memories and Fragments*, New York: Palgrave Macmillan, 2013, pp. 35–9.
33. Geoff Wade, 'Operation Coldstore: A Key Event in the Creation of Modern Singapore', in Poh Soo Kai, Tan Kok Fang and Hong Lysa (eds), *The 1963 Operation Coldstore in Singapore: Commemorating 50 Years*, Petaling Jaya: Strategic Information and Research Development Centre; Kuala Lumpur: Pusat Sejarah Rakyat, 2013, pp. 55, 60–2, 68.
34. C.C. Chin, 'The United Front Strategy of the Malayan Communist Party in Singapore, 1950s–1960s', in Michael D. Barr and Carl A. Trocki (eds), *Paths Not Taken: Political Pluralism in Post-War Singapore*, Singapore: National University of Singapore Press, 2008, p. 72. Also see Thum Ping Tjin, '"Flesh and Bone Reunite as One Body": Singapore's Chinese-Speaking and Their Perspectives on Merger', in Poh *et al.* (eds), *The 1963 Operation Coldstore in Singapore*, p. 112. The widespread expectation of a security sweep in the weeks leading up to Operation Coldstore is confirmed by detainee Lim Hock Siew, in Lim Hock Siew, '"I would never lift one finger to justify my own detention"', in Poh *et al.* (eds), *The 1963 Operation Coldstore in Singapore*, p. 224.
35. Lee Ting Hui, *The Open United Front: The Communist Struggle in Singapore, 1954–1966*, Singapore: South Seas Society, 1996; Kumar Ramakrishna, *'Original Sin'? Revising the Revisionist Critique of the 1963 Operation Coldstore in Singapore*, Singapore: Institute of Southeast Asian Studies, 2015; and Chin, 'The United Front Strategy'.
36. Ramakrishna, *'Original Sin'?*, p. 3.
37. Chin, 'The United Front Strategy', p. 72. Chin's article is more akin to testimony than research. In the debate about the validity of the communist threat of the 1950s and 1960s, Chin confirms the reality and the political/industrial strength of the communist movement, but insists that by 1963 the MCP had long since lost control of the forces on the ground.
38. Michael D. Barr, 'Marxists in Singapore? Lee Kuan Yew's Campaign Against Catholic Social Justice Activists in the 1980s', *Critical Asian Studies*, 42(3), 2010, pp. 335–62.
39. Chan Heng Chee, *Singapore: The Politics of Survival 1965–1967*, Singapore and Kuala Lumpur: Oxford University Press, 1971; Chan Heng Chee, *Politics in an Administrative State: Where Has the Politics Gone?*, Singapore: Department of Political Science, University of Singapore, 1975; and Chan Heng Chee, *The Dynamics of One Party Dominance: The PAP at the Grassroots*, Singapore: Oxford University Press, 1976.

40. See, for instance, 'Barisan MP and 40 others are held', *Straits Times*, 4 July 1966; 'MP to stand trial for unlawful assembly', *Straits Times*, 5 July 1966; and 'Two Barisan leaders arrested on sedition charge', *Straits Times*, 16 April 1966.
41. See, for instance, 'Arrests made "to foil repeat of riots"', *Straits Times*, 9 October 1963; and 'Month's jail for eight: Dr Lee and Chan acquitted', *Straits Times*, 10 August 1963.
42. For an account of the anti-Barisan Sosialis roots of the 1966 Vandalism Act see Jothie Rajah, *Authoritarian Rule of Law: Legislation, Discourse and Legitimacy in Singapore*, Cambridge, UK: Cambridge University Press, 2012, Chapter 3, 'Punishing Bodies, Securing the Nation: 1966 *Vandalism Act*'.
43. See, for example, the following articles and editorials that were chosen more or less at random from a perusal of the government's weekly summary of the non-English press: 'The Future Political Situation of Singapore as Viewed from the Recent By-Elections', *Sin Chew Jit Poh*, 4 March 1966; 'Singapore By-Elections', *Tamil Nesan*, 3 March 1966; 'How to Deal with Opposition Parties and Political Prisoners', *Nanyang Siang Pau*, 4 February 1971; 'Clarifying our Political Atmosphere', *Nanyang Siang Pau*, 25 March 1971; and 'Changes in Singapore's Political Climate', *Nanyang Siang Pau*, 27 March 1971. All found in *Mirror of Opinion: Highlights of Malay, Chinese and Tamil Press*, a report of the vernacular press published weekly by the Singapore Ministry of Culture after independence.
44. 'Freedom of Speech in Singapore', *Nanyang Siang Pau*, 31 March 1971.
45. Cherian George, *Freedom from the Press: Journalism and State Power in Singapore*, Singapore: National University of Singapore Press, 2012, pp. 28, 29.
46. Barr, 'Marxists in Singapore?'; Lenore Lyons, 'Internalised Boundaries: AWARE's Place in Singapore's Emerging Civil Society', in Barr and Trocki (eds), *Paths Not Taken*, pp. 248–63; George, *Freedom from the Press*, pp. 42, 43, 103; and Lee Kuan Yew, *From Third World to First: The Singapore Story: 1965–2000. Memoirs of Lee Kuan Yew*, Singapore: Singapore Press Holdings and Times Editions, 2000, pp. 218–25.
47. Lily Zubaidah Rahim, *Singapore in the Malay World: Building and Breaching Regional Bridges*, London and New York: Routledge, 2009, p. 2.
48. Tim Huxley, *Defending the Lion City: The Armed Forces of Singapore*, St Leonards, NSW: Allen & Unwin, 2000, pp. 56, 57.
49. Michael D. Barr, 'No Island is a Man: The Enigma of Lee Kuan Yew', *Harvard Asia Quarterly*, 11(2/3), 2008, p. 51.
50. Daniel Wei Boon Chua, 'Reinventing Lee Kuan Yew's 1965–66 Anti-Americanism', *Asian Studies Review*, 38(3), 2014, pp. 442–60.
51. T.N. Harper, *The End of Empire and the Making of Malaya*, Cambridge, UK: Cambridge University Press, 2001 (1999), p. 87.
52. By the middle of the twentieth century, this cosmopolitanism was to make Singapore a hot spot of internationalist activism and fervour. See Sunil Amrith, 'Internationalism and Political Pluralism in Singapore, 1950–1963', in Barr and Trocki (eds), *Paths Not Taken*, pp. 37–56.
53. Timothy P. Barnard and Jan van der Putten, 'Malay Cosmopolitan Activism in Post-War Singapore', in Barr and Trocki (eds), *Paths Not Taken*, pp. 132–53.
54. William R. Roff, *Studies on Islam and Society in Southeast Asia*, Singapore: National University of Singapore Press, 2009, pp. 82, 83.
55. Harper, *The End of Empire*, pp. 91, 92.
56. See, for instance, Chua Ai Lin, 'Imperial Subjects, Straits Citizens: Anglophone Asians and the Struggle for Political Rights in Inter-War Singapore', in Barr and Trocki (eds), *Paths Not Taken*, pp. 16–36; Amrith, 'Internationalism and Political Pluralism in Singapore, 1950–1963'; Yeo Kim Wah, *Political Development in Singapore 1945–1955*, Singapore: University of Singapore Press, 1973, pp. 88–97 (on the Malayan Democratic Union); and Harper, *The End of Empire*, pp. 74, 286.
57. Hong Lysa, 'Politics of the Chinese-Speaking Communities in Singapore in the 1950s: The Shaping of Mass Politics', in Tan Jing Quee, Tan Kok Chiang and Hong Lysa (eds), *The May 13 Generation: The Chinese Middle Schools Student Movement and Singapore Politics in the 1950s*, Petaling Jaya: Strategic Information and Research Development Centre, 2011, pp. 57–102, especially pp. 88, 98, 99.

58. Turnbull, *A History of Singapore*, p. 18.
59. Ibid.; Victoria Glendinning, *Raffles and the Golden Opportunity*, London: Profile Books, 2012, Chapters 10–13, pp. 196–258; and C.M. Turnbull, *The Straits Settlements 1826–67: Indian Presidency to Crown Colony*, London: The Athlone Press of the University of London, 1972, Introduction, pp. 1–5.
60. Carl A. Trocki, *Prince of Pirates: The Temenggongs and the Development of Johor and Singapore 1784–1885*, Singapore: National University of Singapore Press, 2007 (1979), pp. 59, 75.
61. Ibid., p. 19.
62. Carl A. Trocki, *Opium and Empire: Chinese Society in Colonial Singapore, 1800–1910*, Ithaca and London: Cornell University Press, 1990.
63. Ibid., pp. 139–43. Also see Leon Comber, *The Triads: Chinese Secret Societies in 1950s Malaya and Singapore*, Singapore: Talisman Publishing and the Singapore Heritage Society, 2009 for the loose continuation of this pattern into the twentieth century.

CHAPTER 3 SINGAPORE CENTRAL: THE ROLE OF LOCATION IN SINGAPORE'S HISTORY

1. TeleGeography, 'Map of Submarine Cables' and 'Frequently Asked Questions', http://www.telegeography.com, accessed 25 April 2017.
2. Ibid.
3. Robert Martinage, 'Under the Sea: The Vulnerability of the Commons', *Foreign Affairs*, January/February 2015, pp. 117–19.
4. Ibid., p. 119.
5. Lee Kuan Yew, *From Third World to First: The Singapore Story: 1965–2000. Memoirs of Lee Kuan Yew*, Singapore: Singapore Press Holdings and Times Editions, 2000.
6. For an example where the role of place is totally ignored, see Mark T.S. Hong and Amy Lugg (eds), *The Rise of Singapore, Volume 1: The Reasons for Singapore's Success*, Singapore: World Scientific, 2016. For an exception to the rule, see John Curtis Perry, *Singapore: Unlikely Power*, New York: Oxford University Press, 2017.
7. BP, *BP Statistical Review 2018: China's Energy Market in 2017*, https://www.bp.com/content/dam/bp/en/corporate/pdf/energy-economics/statistical-review/bp-stats-review-2018-china-insights.pdf, accessed 9 August 2018; and BP, *BP Statistical Review of World Energy June 2018*, p. 9, https://www.bp.com/content/dam/bp/en/corporate/pdf/energy-economics/statistical-review/bp-stats-review-2018-full-report.pdf, accessed 9 July 2018.
8. Maritime and Port Authority of Singapore, *World's Busiest Port*, Singapore: Maritime and Port Authority of Singapore, c.2004.
9. Christopher M. Dent, *East Asian Regionalism*, London and New York: Routledge, 2008, Chapter 2, especially pp. 75–80.
10. W.G. Huff, *The Economic Growth of Singapore: Trade and Development in the Twentieth Century*, Cambridge, UK: Cambridge University Press, 1997 (1994), pp. 243–50, 278, 279.
11. Hon Sui Sen (ed. Linda Low and Lim Bee Lum), *Strategies of Singapore's Economic Success*, Singapore: Marshall Cavendish Academic, 2004, pp. 310–12.
12. BP, *BP Statistical Review of World Energy June 2018*.
13. C.M. Turnbull, *A History of Singapore 1819–1988*, 2nd edn, Singapore: Oxford University Press, 1989 (1977), p. 7; Christina Skott, 'Imagined Centrality: Sir Stamford Raffles and the Birth of Modern Singapore', in Karl Hack and Jean-Louis Margolin, with Karine Delaye (eds), *Singapore from Temasek to the 21st Century: Reinventing the Global City*, Singapore: National University of Singapore Press, 2010, p. 164.
14. John Bastin, *Raffles and Hastings: Private Exchanges Behind the Founding of Singapore*, Singapore: National Library Board and Marshall Cavendish, 2014, pp. 122, 123.
15. Malcolm H. Murfett, John N. Miksic, Brian P. Farrell and Chiang Ming Shun, *Between Two Oceans: A Military History of Singapore from 1275 to 1971*, 2nd edn, Singapore: Marshall Cavendish, 2011 (1999), p. 41.

16. Apart from being a bit small, Penang was too far north to protect west-bound Asian trade. Pirates based in the islands of the Riau Archipelago and on Singapore posed such a high risk to small native craft that Penang was unable to attract as much trade from the east as was hoped. See F.J. Moorhead, *A History of Malaya, Volume Two*, Kuala Lumpur: Longmans of Malaya, 1963, pp. 112, 113.
17. Victoria Glendinning, *Raffles and the Golden Opportunity*, London: Profile Books, 2012, p. 215; Carl A. Trocki, *Singapore: Wealth, Power and the Culture of Control*, London and New York: Routledge, 2006, p. 9.
18. John N. Miksic, *Singapore and the Silk Road of the Sea, 1300–1800*, Singapore: National University of Singapore Press and National Museum of Singapore, 2013, pp. 156–60.
19. Carl A. Trocki, *Prince of Pirates: The Temenggongs and the Development of Johor and Singapore 1784–1885*, Singapore: National University of Singapore Press, 2007 (1979), pp. 28, 29, 44, 45, 61.
20. Murfett *et al.*, *Between Two Oceans*, p. 37.
21. Glendinning, *Raffles and the Golden Opportunity*, p. 210.
22. See Skott, 'Imagined Centrality', p. 166. Also see Turnbull, *A History of Singapore*, p. 8.
23. See R.O. Winstedt, *A History of Johore (1365–1941)*, Kuala Lumpur: Malaysian Branch of the Royal Asiatic Society, 1992 (1932), p. 91, where he concludes that Raffles was focused on 'tackl[ing] the vital Johor problem'.
24. Bastin, *Raffles and Hastings*, p. 28.
25. Ibid., p. 32.
26. Turnbull, *A History of Singapore*, p. 7.
27. Bastin, *Raffles and Hastings*, p. 35. Bastin presents this passage as showing 'beyond all doubt' that Raffles had Singapore as his principal objective 'when he set out from Calcutta'. I read the same passage and came to the conclusion that Raffles' preference for Singapore firmed up only during his stay in Penang, after receiving the news that the Dutch had beaten him to 'Rhio'.
28. Ibid., p. 36.
29. Ibid., p. 37.
30. Ibid., p. 46.
31. Ibid.; Turnbull, *A History of Singapore*, pp. 6–8. Note that Turnbull reports a slightly different timeline in which Raffles sailed into Singapore River on the 29th, but Bastin has used Raffles' correspondence to establish that it was the 28th.
32. Note that there were also well-travelled land and riverine routes across the Malay Peninsula, mostly centred on Kedah. See Maziar Mozaffari Falarti, *Malay Kingship in Kedah: Religion, Trade and Society*, Lanham, MD: Lexington, 2013, Chapter 4, 'Bay to Gulf or Gulf to Bay'. The Sunda Straits also posed some attraction to Dutch sailors before the opening of the Suez Canal.
33. Note that most of the ancient and early modern references to Singapore and Singapore Strait refer to it as either a gateway between two oceans or as a stopping point between the oceans. See Peter Borschberg, 'Singapura in Early Modern Cartography: A Sea of Challenges', National Library Board, *Visualising Space: Maps of Singapore and the Region: Collections from the National Library and National Archives of Singapore*, Singapore: National Library Board, [2015], pp. 16, 17.
34. Miksic, *Silk Road of the Sea*, Chapters 1 and 2. Also see Anthony Reid, *Southeast Asia in the Age of Commerce, 1450–1680, Volume Two: Expansion and Crisis*, Chiang Mai, Thailand: Silkworm Books, 1993; and O.W. Wolters, *History, Culture, and Region in Southeast Asian Perspectives*, rev. edn, Ithaca, NY: Southeast Asia Program Publications, Southeast Asia Program, Cornell University, 1999 (1982).
35. Miksic, *Silk Road of the Sea*, pp. 72–7.
36. Falarti, *Malay Kingship in Kedah*, p. 12.
37. R.O. Winstedt, *Malaya and its History*, New York: Hutchinson's University Library, 1948, p. 31.
38. Miksic, *Silk Road of the Sea*, p. 94; Tansen Sen, 'The Military Campaigns of Rajendra Chola and the Chola–Srivajaya–China Triangle', in Hermann Kulke, K. Kesavapany and Vijay Sakhuja (eds), *Nagapattinam to Suvarnadwipa: Reflections of the Chola Naval Expeditions to Southeast Asia*, Singapore: Institute of Southeast Asian Studies, 2009, pp. 61–75.

39. Ibid., and Hermann Kulke, 'The Naval Expeditions of the Cholas in the Context of Asian History', in Kulke *et al.*, *Nagapattinam to Suvarnadwipa*, p. 9.
40. Miksic, *Silk Road of the Sea*, pp. 78, 79, 110.
41. O.W. Wolters, *The Fall of Srivajaya in Malay History*, Kuala Lumpur and Singapore: Oxford University Press, 1970, p. 78.
42. Miksic, *Silk Road of the Sea*, p. 172.
43. Wolters, *The Fall of Srivajaya*, p. 5.
44. See Barbara Watson Andaya and Leonard Y. Andaya, *A History of Malaysia*, 2nd edn, Honolulu: University of Hawai'i Press, 2001 (1982), pp. 7–9, 33–6. There are several versions of the Malay Annals in existence and there is considerable variation between them due to what Winstedt variously calls 'revisions' or 'tampering' (see R.O. Winstedt, *A History of Classical Literature*, Kuala Lumpur and Singapore: Oxford University Press, 1969, pp. 158, 159). I have used a translation of the oldest known version: C.C. Brown (ed. and transl.), *Sejarah Melayu or 'Malay Annals'*, Kuala Lumpur: Oxford University Press, 1970 (1953).
45. Peter Borschberg, 'Singapore in the Cycles of the Long Durée', *Journal of the Malaysian Branch of the Royal Asiatic Society*, 90 (Part 1, Number 312), 2017, pp. 36–8.
46. Ibid., pp. 38, 39.
47. Brown, *Malay Annals*, pp. 18, 19; Miksic, *Silk Road of the Sea*, p. 149; and Wolters, *The Fall of Srivajaya*, pp. 75–8.
48. Wolters, *The Fall of Srivajaya*, pp. 76, 77; and Miksic, *Silk Road of the Sea*, pp. 148–51.
49. Winstedt, *Malaya and its History*, p. 32.
50. Miksic, *Silk Road of the Sea*, p. 150.
51. Borschberg, 'Singapore in the Cycles of the Long Durée', p. 39.
52. Brown, *Malay Annals*, p. 21.
53. Wolters, *The Fall of Srivajaya*, pp. 79–81.
54. See Miksic, *Silk Road of the Sea*, Chapter 5. Also see references to Peter Borschberg's research, which is given proper attention later in this chapter.
55. Borschberg, 'Singapore in the Cycles of the Long Durée'.
56. Mark Ravinder Frost and Yu-Mei Balasingamchow, *Singapore: A Biography*, Singapore: Editions Didier Millet and National Museum of Singapore, 2009, pp. 35, 36.
57. See Leonard Y. Andaya, *Leaves of the Same Tree: Trade and Ethnicity in the Straits of Melaka*, Singapore: National University of Singapore Press, 2010, pp. 193–6.
58. Geoff Wade, 'Melaka in Ming Dynasty Texts', in Goeff Wade (ed.), *Southeast Asia-China Interactions, Reprint of Articles from the Journal of the Malaysian Branch, Royal Asiatic Society*, Singapore: National University of Singapore Press, in association with The Malaysian Branch of the Royal Asiatic Society, 2007, pp. 327–66. Also see Wang Gungwu, 'The First Three Rulers of Malacca', in Wade (ed.), *Southeast Asia-China Interactions*, p. 326.
59. Miksic, *Silk Road of the Sea*, pp. 192, 193.
60. Merle C. Ricklefs, *A History of Modern Indonesia Since c.1200*, 4th edn, London: Palgrave Macmillan, 2008, p. 25.
61. Leonard Y. Andaya, *The Kingdom of Johor 1641–1728*, Kuala Lumpur: Oxford University Press, 1975, p. 22.
62. Note that in the fifteenth to eighteenth centuries the Asian polities were sovereign powers, both in theory and in fact. Hence when we speak of alliances between Asian and European powers in these centuries, this is not a euphemism for a master–servant relationship but a reference to genuine strategic alliances borne out of mutual self-interest. See Peter Borschberg, *Hugo Grotius, the Portuguese and Free Trade in the East Indies*, Singapore: National University of Singapore Press, 2011.
63. Winstedt, *A History of Johore*, pp. 43–5.
64. Andaya, *The Kingdom of Johor*, p. 27.
65. Ibid., pp. 4, 38, 39, 174, 190, 191, 285, 312, 313.
66. Trocki, *Prince of Pirates*, p. 43.
67. Andaya and Andaya, *A History of Malaysia*, pp. 92–108.

68. Ibid., p. 112.
69. Peter Borschberg (ed.), *Jacques de Coutre's Singapore and Johor 1594–c.1625*, Singapore: National University of Singapore Press, 2015, pp. 10, 11.
70. Ibid., pp. 32–5; Borschberg, 'Singapura in Early Modern Cartography', p. 20.
71. Andaya, *The Kingdom of Johor*, p. 256; Borschberg, *Hugo Grotius*, pp. 78–81; and Peter Borschberg, *The Singapore and Melaka Straits: Violence, Security and Diplomacy in the 17th Century*, Singapore: National University of Singapore Press, 2010, pp. 71–5.
72. Paulo Jorge de Sousa Pinto, *The Portuguese and the Straits of Melaka 1575–1619: Power, Trade and Diplomacy*, Singapore: National University of Singapore Press, 2012, pp. 54, 55; and Borschberg, *The Singapore and Melaka Straits*, pp. 60–4.
73. Borschberg, *The Singapore and Melaka Straits*, pp. 118–24.
74. Ibid., pp. 173–5.
75. Ibid., p. 174.
76. Trocki suggests that the departure of the Bugis from Riau may have left the entire area around Johor vulnerable to pirates, and that this may have driven the population away. See Trocki, *Prince of Pirates*, p. 58.
77. Murfett *et al.*, *Between Two Oceans*, pp. 34, 35.
78. See Peter Borschberg (ed.) and Roopanjali Roy (transl.), *The Memoirs and Memorials of Jacques de Coutre: Security, Trade and Society in 16th and 17th-Century Southeast Asia*, Singapore: National University of Singapore Press, 2014, pp. 46, 76, 77, 231, 232, 236, 361.
79. Derek Heng Thiam Soon, 'Temasik as an International and Regional Trading Port in the Thirteenth and Fourteenth Centuries: A Reconstruction Based on Recent Archaeological Data', in Wade (ed.), *Southeast Asia-China Interactions*, p. 297.
80. Murfett *et al.*, *Between Two Oceans*, Chapters 3 and 4.
81. Karl Hack and Kevin Blackburn, *Did Singapore Have to Fall? Churchill and the Impregnable Fortress*, London and New York: Routledge, 2003, p. 30.
82. See Carl A. Trocki, *Opium and Empire: Chinese Society in Colonial Singapore, 1800–1910*, Ithaca and London: Cornell University Press, 1990, p. 4.
83. Carl A. Trocki, 'Chinese Capitalism and the British Empire', paper presented to the International Association of Historians of Asia Conference, Taiwan, Taipei, 6–10 December 2004.
84. Chan Heng Chee, *Singapore: The Politics of Survival 1965–1967*, Singapore and Kuala Lumpur: Oxford University Press, 1971.
85. Lee Kuan Yew, 'Speech to Pasir Panjang Residents on 5th December, 1965', National Archives of Singapore Online.
86. World Shipping Council, 'Top 50 World Container Ports', http://www.worldshipping.org/about-the-industry/global-trade/top-50-world-container-ports, accessed 8 July 2018; and *Port Strategy: Insight for Port Executives*, 'Port Klang Edges Closer to Top Ten Ranking', 18 January 2017, http://www.portstrategy.com/news101/world/asia/port-klang-nears-top-ten-container-ranking, accessed 10 July 2018.
87. Sree Kumar and Sharon Siddique, *Batam – Whose Hinterland? The Influence of Politics on Development*, Singapore: Select Publishing, 2013; and Rodolphe De Koninck, Julie Drolet and Marc Girard, *Singapore: An Atlas of Perpetual Territorial Transformation*, Singapore: National University of Singapore Press, 2008, pp. 48–51.
88. Dent, *East Asian Regionalism*, pp. 77, 78; and Lee Tsao Yuan (ed.), *Growth Triangle: The Johor–Singapore–Riau Experience*, Singapore: Institute of Southeast Asian Studies, 1991.

CHAPTER 4 GOVERNANCE IN PREMODERN SINGAPORE

1. Ministry of Information and the Arts, *The Singapore Story: Overcoming the Odds*, CD-ROM, 1999. There are several acceptable variations in the national narrative's periodisation. This particular version is taken from one of the earliest official versions; a CD-ROM produced for school children.

2. Curriculum Planning and Development Division, Ministry of Education, *History Syllabus, Lower Secondary, Express Course; Normal (Academic) Course*, Singapore: Ministry of Education, 2016.
3. Maziar Mozaffari Falarti, *Malay Kingship in Kedah: Religion, Trade and Society*, Lanham, MD: Lexington, 2013, pp. 111, 112.
4. R. Roolvink, 'The Variant Versions of the Malay Annals', p. xxxii in C.C. Brown (ed. and transl.), *Sejarah Melayu or 'Malay Annals'*, Kuala Lumpur: Oxford University Press, 1970 (1953).
5. A.C. Milner, *Kerajaan: Malay Political Culture on the Eve of Colonial Rule*, Tucson, AZ: University of Arizona Press for the Association for Asian Studies, 1982; Anthony Milner, *The Malays*, Chichester, UK: Wiley-Blackwell, 2008; Anthony Reid, *Southeast Asia in the Age of Commerce, 1450–1680, Volume One: The Lands Below the Wind*, New Haven and London: Yale University Press, 1988; Anthony Reid, *Southeast Asia in the Age of Commerce, 1450–1680, Volume Two: Expansion and Crisis*, Chiang Mai, Thailand: Silkworm Books, 1993; O.W. Wolters, *History, Culture, and Region in Southeast Asian Perspectives*, rev. edn, Ithaca, NY: Southeast Asia Program Publications, Southeast Asia Program, Cornell University, 1999 (1982); Falarti, *Malay Kingship in Kedah.*
6. Brown, *Malay Annals*, pp. 54–8.
7. Ibid., p. 60.
8. Ibid., p. 80.
9. John N. Miksic, *Singapore and the Silk Road of the Sea, 1300–1800*, Singapore: National University of Singapore Press and National Museum of Singapore, 2013, p. 156.
10. Brown, *Malay Annals*, p. 116.
11. Clifford Geertz, *Negara: The Theatre State in Nineteenth-Century Bali*, Princeton, NJ: Princeton University Press, 1980.
12. Milner, *The Malays*, p. 30.
13. Carl A. Trocki, *Prince of Pirates: The Temenggongs and the Development of Johor and Singapore 1784–1885*, Singapore: National University of Singapore Press, 2007 (1979), pp. 23–5.
14. Peter Borschberg (ed.), *Jacques de Coutre's Singapore and Johor 1594–c.1625*, Singapore: National University of Singapore Press, 2015, pp. 10, 11; Peter Borschberg (ed.), *Journals, Memorials and Letters of Cornelis Matelieff de Jonge: Security, Diplomacy and Commerce in 17th-Century Southeast Asia*, Singapore: National University of Singapore Press, 2015, pp. 64, 150, 194 n. 278, 516. Jacques de Coutre was an adventurer from Flanders who was seeking his fortune in the East Indies and Cornelis Matelieff de Jonge was an Admiral in the Dutch East Indies Navy.
15. Borschberg, *Jacques de Coutre's Singapore and Johor*, p. 11.
16. R.O. Winstedt, *A History of Johore (1365–1941)*, Kuala Lumpur: Malaysian Branch of the Royal Asiatic Society, 1992 (1932), pp. 59–66. According to the eighteenth-century account written by Ali al-Haji ibn Ahmad, Raja Kecil may have even been conceived posthumously immediately following the Sultan's murder, though even Ali does not take the story at face value. See Ali al-Haji ibn Ahmad, *The Precious Gift: Tuhfat Al-Nafis; an Annotated Translation by Virginia Matheson Hooker and Barbara Watson Andaya*, Kuala Lumpur: Oxford University Press, 1982, p. 22.
17. Barbara Watson Andaya and Leonard Y. Andaya, *A History of Malaysia*, 2nd edn, Honolulu: University of Hawai'i Press, 2001 (1982), pp. 108–9.
18. Falarti, *Malay Kingship in Kedah*, pp. 111, 112.
19. C.M. Turnbull, *A History of Singapore 1819–1988*, 2nd edn, Singapore: Oxford University Press, 1989 (1977), p. 10.
20. Trocki, *Prince of Pirates*, p. 59.
21. Ibid., p. 61.
22. Ibid.
23. John Bastin, *Raffles and Hastings: Private Exchanges Behind the Founding of Singapore*, Singapore: National Library Board and Marshall Cavendish, 2014, p. 46.
24. Ibid., Chapter 10, 'Proposal for the Amalgamation of Pinang, Singapore and Bengkulu'.
25. Turnbull, *A History of Singapore*, pp. 18, 19.
26. Trocki, *Prince of Pirates*, pp. 61, 62.
27. Bastin, *Raffles and Hastings*, pp. 122, 123; and Turnbull, *A History of Singapore*, pp. 12, 13.
28. Trocki, *Prince of Pirates*, p. 65.

29. Ibid., pp. 64–6.
30. F.J. Moorhead, *A History of Malaya, Volume Two*, Kuala Lumpur: Longmans of Malaya, 1963, pp. 86, 87.
31. See Carl A. Trocki, *Opium, Empire and the Global Political Economy: A Study of the Asian Opium Trade 1750–1950*, London and New York: Routledge, 1999.
32. Turnbull, *A History of Singapore*, pp. 25–31.
33. Loh Wei Leng, 'Penang's Trade and Shipping in the Imperial Age', in Yeoh Seng Guan, Loh Wei Leng, Khoo Salma Nasution and Neil Khor (eds), *Penang and Its Region: The Story of an Asian Entrepôt*, Singapore: National University of Singapore Press, 2009, pp. 83–102; and C.M. Turnbull, *The Straits Settlements 1826–67: Indian Presidency to Crown Colony*, London: The Athlone Press of the University of London, 1972, pp. 16, 17.
34. Turnbull, *The Straits Settlements*, p. 55.
35. Loh, 'Penang's Trade and Shipping', p. 96; and Turnbull, *A History of Singapore*, p. 36.
36. Turnbull, *The Straits Settlements*, pp. 16–21.
37. Goh Chor Boon, *Technology and Entrepôt Colonialism in Singapore, 1819–1940*, Singapore: Institute of Southeast Asian Studies, 2013, pp. 36, 52.
38. Turnbull, *The Straits Settlements*, p. 4.
39. Carl A. Trocki, *Opium and Empire: Chinese Society in Colonial Singapore, 1800–1910*, Ithaca and London: Cornell University Press, 1990, pp. 73, 74.
40. Ibid., p. 72, 96, 97.
41. Turnbull, *The Straits Settlements*, p. 55.
42. Ibid., pp. 54, 57, 58, 74.
43. Ibid., pp. 61–5, 75–81.
44. Brenda S.A. Yeoh, *Contesting Space in Colonial Singapore: Power Relations and the Urban Built Environment*, Singapore: Singapore University Press, 2003 (1996), 'Part 1. Sanitizing the Private Environment'.
45. Ibid., 'Part II: Ordering the Public Environment'.
46. Carl A. Trocki, *Singapore: Wealth, Power and the Culture of Control*, London and New York: Routledge, 2006, pp. 77, 78, 89–93. Also see Trocki, *Opium and Empire*, Chapter 1, 'The Kongsi and the History of the Singapore Chinese'. Colonial hostility towards the secret societies began to emerge as early as 1830, though it would be decades before they were treated fully as an enemy to be destroyed.
47. Trocki, *Prince of Pirates*, pp. 76, 79.
48. Ibid., pp. 78–83.
49. Turnbull, *The Straits Settlements*, pp. 275, 276.
50. Ibid., pp. 276, 277; and Trocki, *Prince of Pirates*, pp. 100–3.
51. Carl A. Trocki, 'Chinese Revenue Farms and Borders in Southeast Asia', *Modern Asian Studies*, 43(1), 2009, pp. 356, 357; Trocki, *Opium and Empire*, Chapter 4.
52. See J.S. Furnivall, *Colonial Policy and Practice: A Comparative Study of Burma and Netherlands India*, Cambridge, UK: Cambridge University Press, 1948; and J.S. Furnivall, *Netherlands India: A Study of Plural Economy*, Cambridge, UK: Cambridge University Press, 1944.
53. C.M. Turnbull, 'The European Mercantile Community in Singapore, 1819–1867', *Journal of Southeast Asian History*, 10(1), 1969, pp. 12–35.
54. Turnbull, *The Straits Settlements*, Chapter 9, 'Constitutional Reform: The Transfer Movement'.
55. John Curtis Perry, *Singapore: Unlikely Power*, New York: Oxford University Press, 2017, pp. 89–95, 106.
56. Goh, *Technology and Entrepôt Colonialism in Singapore*, p. 97.
57. Perry, *Singapore: Unlikely Power*, p. 106.
58. Goh, *Technology and Entrepôt Colonialism in Singapore*, pp. 100, 101.

CHAPTER 5 GOVERNANCE IN MODERN SINGAPORE, 1867–1965

1. C.M. Turnbull, *A History of Singapore 1819–1988*, 2nd edn, Singapore: Oxford University Press, 1989 (1977), p. 76.
2. Goh Chor Boon, *Technology and Entrepôt Colonialism in Singapore, 1819–1940*, Singapore: Institute of Southeast Asian Studies, 2013, pp. 126, 127.
3. Brenda S.A. Yeoh, *Contesting Space in Colonial Singapore: Power Relations and the Urban Built Environment*, Singapore: Singapore University Press, 2003 (1996), pp. 119–21, 153, 190–5, 251–3, 257–71.
4. Carl A. Trocki, *Opium and Empire: Chinese Society in Colonial Singapore, 1800–1910*, Ithaca and London: Cornell University Press, 1990, p. 236, Chapters 2 and 3.
5. Also see James Francis Warren, *Ah Ku and Karayuki-San: Prostitution in Singapore 1870–1940*, Singapore: Singapore University Press, 2003 (1993); and James Francis Warren, *Rickshaw Coolie: A People's History of Singapore 1880–1940*, Singapore: Singapore University Press, 2003 (1986). In the more isolated gambier farms and tin mines in Johor the *kangchu* held full monopolies over all consumables.
6. Trocki, *Opium and Empire*, Chapters 4 and 5.
7. Carl A. Trocki, 'Boundaries and Transgressions: Chinese Enterprise in Eighteenth- and Nineteenth-Century Southeast Asia', in Aiwah Ong and Donald M. Nonini (eds), *Underground Empires: The Cultural Politics of Modern Chinese Transnationalism*, London and New York: Routledge, 1997, pp. 63–78.
8. Warren, *Ah Ku and Karayuki-San*, pp. 94, 95.
9. For more fulsome accounts of community histories, see Phyllis Ghim-Lian Chew, *A Sociolinguistic History of Early Identities in Singapore: From Colonialism to Nationalism*, Basingstoke: Palgrave Macmillan, 2013.
10. Yeoh, *Contesting Space in Colonial Singapore*, pp. 76–85.
11. Turnbull, *A History of Singapore*, p. 76.
12. Trocki, *Opium and Empire*, p. 215.
13. Turnbull, *A History of Singapore*, pp. 151–3.
14. C.F. Yong and R.B. McKenna, *The Kuomintang Movement in British Malaya 1912–1949*, Singapore: Singapore University Press, 1990.
15. Lee Su Yin, *British Policy and the Chinese in Singapore, 1939 to 1955: The Public Service Career of Tan Chin Tuan*, Singapore: Talisman, 2011, pp. 31–47.
16. Ernest Koh, 'Remembrance, Nation, and the Second World War in Singapore: The Chinese Diaspora and their Wars', in Loh Kah Seng, Ernest Koh and Stephen Dobbs (eds), *Oral History in Southeast Asia: Memories and Fragments*, New York: Palgrave Macmillan, 2013, pp. 61–80.
17. Christopher Bayley and Tim Harper, *Forgotten Wars: The End of Britain's Empire*, London: Allen Lane, 2007, pp. 44, 45.
18. Chua Ai Lin, 'Imperial Subjects, Straits Citizens: Anglophone Asians and the Struggle for Political Rights in Inter-War Singapore', in Michael D. Barr and Carl A. Trocki (eds), *Paths Not Taken: Political Pluralism in Post-War Singapore*, Singapore: National University of Singapore Press, 2008, pp. 16–36.
19. Paul H. Kratoska, *The Japanese Occupation of Malaya: 1941–1945*, Honolulu: University of Hawai'i Press, 1997.
20. Mark Ravinder Frost and Yu-Mei Balasingamchow, *Singapore: A Biography*, Singapore: Editions Didier Millet and National Museum of Singapore, 2009, pp. 278, 280–2.
21. Bayley and Harper, *Forgotten Wars*, p. 328.
22. Ibid., pp. 87–8.
23. Ibid., p. 54.
24. Kratoska, *The Japanese Occupation of Malaya*, pp. 108, 109.
25. Frost and Balasingamchow, *Singapore: A Biography*, pp. 284, 285.
26. Kratoska, *The Japanese Occupation of Malaya*, pp. 182–4.

27. Bayley and Harper, *Forgotten Wars*, p. 46, 47.
28. Kratoska, *The Japanese Occupation of Malaya*, pp. 159–64, and Chapter 9, 'Rationing and Food Production'; and Frost and Balasingamchow, *Singapore: A Biography*, pp. 306–12.
29. Kratoska, *The Japanese Occupation of Malaya*, Chapter 5, 'Education and Propaganda'.
30. Cheah Boon Kheng, *Red Star Over Malaya: Resistance and Social Conflict During and After the Japanese Occupation, 1941–1946*, 3rd edn, Singapore: Singapore University Press, 2003 (1983), Chapters 5–7.
31. Karl Hack, *Defence and Decolonisation in Southeast Asia: Britain, Malaya and Singapore 1941–68*, London and New York: Routledge, 2014 (2001), p. 129.
32. T.N. Harper, *The End of Empire and the Making of Malaya*, Cambridge, UK: Cambridge University Press, 2001 (1999), pp. 111, 144.
33. Turnbull, *A History of Singapore*, p. 223.
34. Richard Clutterbuck, *Conflict and Violence in Singapore and Malaysia 1945–1983*, Singapore: Graham Brash, 1985, p. 81.
35. C.C. Chin, 'The United Front Strategy of the Malayan Communist Party in Singapore, 1950s–1960s', in Barr and Trocki (eds), *Paths Not Taken*, pp. 58–60.
36. Even the period of quiet included a two-day general strike of 173,000 workers in Singapore early in 1946. See Turnbull, *A History of Singapore*, p. 224.
37. Harper, *The End of Empire*, pp. 142–4.
38. Ibid., Chapter 3. Also see Chin Peng, *Alias Chin Peng, My Side of History*, Singapore: Media Masters, 2003, Chapter 13.
39. Department of Social Welfare, Singapore, *A Social Survey of Singapore: A Preliminary Study of Some Aspects of Social Conditions in the Municipal Area of Singapore, December 1947*, Singapore: Department of Social Welfare, 1947, p. 7.
40. Rodolphe De Koninck, Julie Drolet and Marc Girard, *Singapore: An Atlas of Perpetual Territorial Transformation*, Singapore: National University of Singapore Press, 2008, pp. 28, 29.
41. Loh Kah Seng, *Squatters Into Citizens: The 1961 Bukit Ho Swee Fire and the Making of Modern Singapore*, Singapore and Copenhagen: Asian Studies Association of Australia in association with National University of Singapore Press and the Nordic Institute of Asian Studies, 2013, pp. 26–40.
42. Department of Social Welfare, Singapore, *A Social Survey of Singapore*, pp. 85, 86.
43. Barrington Kaye, *Upper Nankin Street: A Sociological Study of Chinese Households Living in a Densely Populated Area*, Singapore: University of Malaya Press, 1960.
44. Singapore Legislative Council, *Proceedings of the Legislative Council of the Colony of Singapore*, Singapore: [Government Printing Office], 1953, B78.
45. Singapore Legislative Council, *Proceedings of the Legislative Council of the Colony of Singapore*, Singapore: [Government Printing Office], 1954/55, B41; *Straits Times*, 10 March 1954.
46. Singapore Legislative Council, *Proceedings of the Legislative Council*, 1953, B78.
47. Saw Swee-Hock, *The Population of Singapore*, 3rd edn, Singapore: Institute of Southeast Asian Studies, 2012, pp. 14, 15.
48. Ibid., p. 37.
49. Joan Sara Thomas, Ong Suan Ee, Chia Kee Seng and Lee Hin Ping, 'A Brief History of Public Health in Singapore', in Lee Chien Earn and K. Satku (eds), *Singapore's Health Care System: What 50 Years Have Achieved*, Singapore: World Scientific, 2016, pp. 36, 37.
50. Hack, *Defence and Decolonisation in Southeast Asia*, pp. 113–31; Clutterbuck, *Conflict and Violence in Singapore and Malaysia*, Chapters 11–14.
51. Loh, *Squatters Into Citizens*, pp. 33, 34.
52. Clutterbuck, *Conflict and Violence in Singapore and Malaysia*, p. 71. Chin, 'The United Front Strategy', pp. 59, 60.
53. Chin, 'The United Front Strategy', p. 62.
54. T.N. Harper, 'Lim Chin Siong and the "Singapore Story"', in Tan Jing Quee and Jomo K.S. (eds), *Comet in Our Sky: Lim Chin Siong in History*, Kuala Lumpur: Insan, 2001, p. 39.
55. Chin, 'The United Front Strategy', pp. 62–6; Clutterbuck, *Conflict and Violence in Singapore and Malaysia*, pp. 77–83.

56. Chin, 'The United Front Strategy', pp. 68–72. Also see Lee Kuan Yew, *The Singapore Story: Memoirs of Lee Kuan Yew*, Singapore: Prentice Hall, 1998, Chapters 16 and 17.
57. Chin, 'The United Front Strategy', p. 68.
58. Said Zahari, *Dark Clouds at Dawn: A Political Memoir*, Kuala Lumpur: Insan, 2001, p. 301.
59. Chin Peng, *My Side of History*, Chapters 22 and 23.
60. Cited in Geoff Wade, 'Operation Coldstore: A Key Event in the Creation of Modern Singapore', in Poh Soo Kai, Tan Kok Fang and Hong Lysa (eds), *The 1963 Operation Coldstore in Singapore: Commemorating 50 Years*, Petaling Jaya: Strategic Information and Research Development Centre; Kuala Lumpur: Pusat Sejarah Rakyat, 2013, p. 38.
61. Harper, 'Lim Chin Siong and the "Singapore Story"', p. 31.
62. Ibid., pp. 32–41.
63. Wade, 'Operation Coldstore', p. 38.
64. Harper, 'Lim Chin Siong and the "Singapore Story"', p. 32.
65. Wade, 'Operation Coldstore', especially around pp. 31–3 and 53.
66. Ibid., p. 38.
67. Ibid., p. 53.
68. Lee Ting Hui, *The Open United Front: The Communist Struggle in Singapore, 1954–1966*, Singapore: South Seas Society, 1996, p. 257.
69. Ibid.
70. Wade, 'Operation Coldstore', p. 57.
71. Ibid., pp. 55–60.
72. Ibid., p. 64.
73. See, for instance, Kumar Ramakrishna, *'Original Sin'? Revising the Revisionist Critique of the 1963 Operation Coldstore in Singapore*, Singapore: Institute of Southeast Asian Studies, 2015; Bilveer Singh, *Quest for Political Power: Communist Subversion and Militancy in Singapore*, Singapore: Marshall Cavendish, 2015.
74. *Straits Times*, 11 October 1949. Also see John Drysdale, *Singapore: Struggle for Success*, Singapore: Times Books International, 1984, p. 61.
75. Albert Lau, 'Decolonization and the Cold War in Singapore, 1955–9', in Albert Lau (ed.), *Southeast Asia and the Cold War*, London and New York: Routledge, 2012, p. 44.
76. Drysdale, *Singapore: Struggle for Success*, pp. 38, 39, 96, 97.
77. Turnbull was fulsome in her praise of Marshall on this point, as was John Drysdale, but Lee in his memoirs glossed over the significance of the achievement, and gave no credit to Marshall at all. He concluded his two-page account of the episode dismissively: 'I was having fun with Marshall, but there was more serious business at hand.' See Turnbull, *A History of Singapore*, p. 256; Drysdale, *Singapore: Struggle for Success*, Chapter 10 and pp. 128, 129; and Lee, *The Singapore Story*, pp. 211–13.
78. Kevin Y.L. Tan, *Marshall of Singapore: A Biography*, Singapore: Institute of Southeast Asian Studies, 2008, Chapter 11. Tan describes Marshall's failures in this field as 'a mortal blow' to his credibility (p. 275).
79. Turnbull, *A History of Singapore*, p. 256.
80. Drysdale, *Singapore: Struggle for Success*, pp. 139–44.
81. Tan, *Marshall of Singapore* and Carl A. Trocki, 'David Marshall and the Struggle for Civil Rights in Singapore', in Barr and Trocki (eds), *Paths Not Taken*, pp. 116–30.
82. Michael D. Barr and Jevon Low, 'Assimilation as Multiracialism: The Case of Singapore's Malays', *Asian Ethnicity*, 6(3), 2005, pp. 163, 164.
83. Drysdale, *Singapore: Struggle for Success*, pp. 206, 207. Presumably Marshall saw the irony of having protected Lee from politically motivated detention in 1959, only to see Lee committing the same offence against others in 1963 and on many other occasions thereafter.
84. Ibid., Chapter 18; and Francis Thomas, *Memoirs of a Migrant*, Singapore: Ethos Books, 2013, pp. 109–11. Thomas was Minister for Communications and Works in the Marshall Government and in the first two years of the Lim Yew Hock Government.

85. C.J. W-L. Wee, 'The Vanquished: Lim Chin Siong and a Progressivist National Narrative', in Lam Peng Er and Kevin Y.L. Tan (eds), *Lee's Lieutenants: Singapore's Old Guard*, St Leonard's, NSW: Allen & Unwin, 1999, pp. 177, 178; Lee, *The Singapore Story*, Chapter 16.
86. Drysdale, *Singapore: Struggle for Success*, Chapter 13, especially pp. 147–9.
87. A full list of Singapore's 1,190 political detainees (1950–2013) can be found at Poh *et al.* (eds), *The 1963 Operation Coldstore in Singapore*, pp. 432–88. The UPP members appear on p. 451.
88. Kevin Blackburn, 'Family Memories as Alternative Narratives to the State's Construction of Singapore's National History', in Loh *et al.* (eds), *Oral History in Southeast Asia*, pp. 32, 33.
89. Loh, *Squatters Into Citizens*, Chapter 6 onwards; Christopher Tremewan, *The Political Economy of Social Control in Singapore*, London: Macmillan Press; New York: St Martin's Press, 1994, p. 47.
90. Tremewan, *The Political Economy of Social Control*, Chapter 3.
91. 'Singapore seen as New York of the Nation', *Straits Times*, 30 July 1962; Turnbull, *A History of Singapore*, p. 270.
92. Interview in Melanie Chew (ed.), *Leaders of Singapore*, Singapore: Resources Press, 1996, p. 92.
93. Lee, *The Singapore Story*, p. 601.
94. This paragraph is drawn, substantially unchanged, from Michael D. Barr, *Lee Kuan Yew: The Beliefs Behind the Man*, Richmond, UK: Curzon Press, 2000, p. 31.
95. Goh Keng Swee's interview in Chew (ed.), *Leaders of Singapore*, p. 147.

CHAPTER 6 GOVERNANCE IN INDEPENDENT SINGAPORE

1. Melanie Kirkpatrick, 'Lee Kuan Yew vs. the News', *The Wall Street Journal*, 22 March 2015. Ms Kirkpatrick, a former deputy editor of the *Wall Street Journal*'s editorial page, twice faced criminal contempt charges in Singapore for editorials. She and other *Journal* editors were fined.
2. Terence Lee, *The Media, Cultural Control and Government in Singapore*, London and New York: Routledge, 2010.
3. Daniel Wei Boon Chua, 'Reinventing Lee Kuan Yew's 1965–66 Anti-Americanism', *Asian Studies Review*, 38(3), 2014, pp. 442–60.
4. Khong Yuen Foong, 'Singapore and the Great Powers', in Barry Desker and Ang Cheng Guan (eds), *Perspectives on the Security of Singapore: The First 50 Years*, Singapore: World Scientific, 2016, pp. 207–28; Mark Beeson, *Regionalism and Globalization in East Asia: Politics, Security and Economic Development*, Basingstoke: Palgrave Macmillan, 2007; Mark Beeson, 'Geopolitics and the Making of Regions: The Fall and Rise of East Asia', *Political Studies*, 57, 2009, pp. 498–516; and Richard Stubbs, *Rethinking Asia's Economic Miracle: The Political Economy of War, Prosperity and Crisis*, Basingstoke and New York: Palgrave Macmillan, 2005.
5. Kevin Blackburn, 'Family Memories as Alternative Narratives to the State's Construction of Singapore's National History', in Loh Kah Seng, Ernest Koh and Stephen Dobbs (eds), *Oral History in Southeast Asia: Memories and Fragments*, New York: Palgrave Macmillan, 2013, pp. 25–41; Ian Buchanan, *Singapore in Southeast Asia: An Economic and Political Appraisal*, London: G. Bell & Sons, 1972; Christopher Tremewan, *The Political Economy of Social Control in Singapore*, London: Macmillan Press; New York: St Martin's Press, 1994.
6. Chan Heng Chee, *Singapore: The Politics of Survival 1965–1967*, Singapore and Kuala Lumpur: Oxford University Press, 1971.
7. Chan Heng Chee, *Politics in an Administrative State: Where Has the Politics Gone?*, Singapore: Department of Political Science, University of Singapore, 1975.
8. Garry Rodan, 'Consultative Authoritarianism and Regime Change Analysis: Implications of the Singapore Case', in Richard Robison (ed.), *Routledge Handbook of Southeast Asian Politics*, London and New York: Routledge, 2012, pp. 120–34.
9. Daniel Wei Boon Chua, 'Reinventing Lee Kuan Yew's 1965–66 Anti-Americanism', *Asian Studies Review*, 38(3), 2014, pp. 442–60.
10. Lee Kuan Yew, *From Third World to First: The Singapore Story: 1965–2000. Memoirs of Lee Kuan Yew*, Singapore: Singapore Press Holdings and Times Editions, 2000, p. 73. Also see Chapters 3 and 28.

11. Ibid., pp. 74, 75.
12. Harvard University Institute of Politics, 'Kuan Yew Lee', http://www.iop.harvard.edu/kuan-yew-lee#comment-0, accessed 5 June 2018.
13. Prime Minister's Office, Singapore, 'Mr LEE Hsien Loong', http://www.pmo.gov.sg/cabinet/mr-lee-hsien-loong, accessed 5 June 2018.
14. *Harvard Kennedy School Magazine*, Summer 2012.
15. Tim Huxley, *Defending the Lion City: The Armed Forces of Singapore*, St Leonards, NSW: Allen & Unwin, 2000, p. 208.
16. Ibid., pp. 208–12.
17. Natasha Hamilton-Hart, *Hard Interests, Soft Illusions: Southeast Asia and American Power*, Ithaca and London: Cornell University Press, 2012.
18. David Harvey, *A Brief History of Neoliberalism*, Oxford: Oxford University Press, 2005, Chapter 1.
19. Jeff D. Colgan and Robert O. Keohane, 'The Liberal Order is Rigged: Fix It Now or Watch It Wither', *Foreign Affairs*, May–June 2017, pp. 38, 39.
20. Harvey, *A Brief History of Neoliberalism*, Chapter 1.
21. Michael D. Barr, 'Perpetual Revisionism in Singapore: The Limits of Change', *The Pacific Review*, 16(1), 2003, pp. 77–97.
22. Zheng Yongnian and Lim Wen Xin, 'Lee Kuan Yew: The Special Relationship with China', in Zheng Yongnian and Lye Liang Fook (eds), *Singapore–China Relations: 50 Years*, Singapore: World Scientific, 2016, pp. 31–48.
23. Lee, *From Third World to First*, Chapters 36–40; Lee Kuan Yew (interviews and selections by Graham Allison and Robert D. Blackwill, with Ali Wyne), *Lee Kuan Yew: The Grand Master's Insights on China, the United States and the World*, Cambridge, MA and London: The MIT Press, 2013, Chapters 1–3; Lee Kuan Yew, *One Man's View of the World*, Singapore: Straits Times Press, 2013, Chapters 1 and 2.
24. John Wong and Lye Liang Fook, 'China–Singapore Relations: Looking Back and Looking Forward', in Zheng and Lye (eds), *Singapore–China Relations*, p. 2. Also see Santander Trade Portal, 'China: Foreign Investment', https://en.portal.santandertrade.com/establish-overseas/china/foreign-investment, accessed 11 July 2018.
25. Michael D. Barr and Zlatko Skrbiš, *Constructing Singapore: Elitism, Ethnicity and the Nation-Building Project*, Copenhagen: Nordic Institute of Asian Studies, 2008, p. 224; Public Service Commission, *Public Service Commission Annual Report 2009*, Singapore: Public Service Commission, 2010.
26. Wong and Lye, 'China–Singapore Relations', p. 3.
27. 'China warns PM Lee over South China Sea', *The Independent Singapore*, 7 August 2016; 'Troubled waters: Beijing's "anger" lurks beneath surface of Singapore *Global Times* South China Sea row', *South China Morning Post*, 30 September 2016; 'Blow-by-blow account of the China–Singapore spat over *Global Times'* South China Sea report', *South China Morning Post*, 28 September 2016 (updated online 17 October 2016).
28. 'Merger still leaves Japanese shippers in middle of pack', *Nikkei Asian Review*, 1 November 2016.
29. Tang Hsiao Ling, 'Industrial Planning in Singapore', in Heng Chye Kiang (ed.), *50 Years of Urban Planning in Singapore*, Singapore: World Scientific, 2016, pp. 153–76.
30. Ibid., p. 154.
31. Michael D. Barr, *Lee Kuan Yew: The Beliefs Behind the Man*, Richmond, UK: Curzon Press, 2000, p. 81.
32. Chan, *Singapore: The Politics of Survival*, p. 49.
33. See Barr, *Lee Kuan Yew*, Chapter 3.
34. Chan, *Politics in an Administrative State*. Also see Jothie Rajah, *Authoritarian Rule of Law: Legislation, Discourse and Legitimacy in Singapore*, Cambridge, UK: Cambridge University Press, 2012, Chapter 3.
35. Thomas J. Bellows, *The People's Action Party of Singapore: Emergence of a Dominant Party System*, Monograph Series No. 14, New Haven, CT: Yale University Southeast Asia Studies, 1970.

36. Raj Vasil, *Governing Singapore: A History of National Development and Democracy*, St Leonards, NSW: Allen & Unwin, 2000, Chapter 1.
37. A fuller account can be found in Michael D. Barr, *The Ruling Elite of Singapore: Networks of Power and Influence*, London: I.B.Tauris, 2014, Chapter 3, among many other secondary sources.
38. Francis T. Seow, *The Media Enthralled: Singapore Revisited*, Boulder, CO and London: Lynne Rienner Publishers, 1998; Cherian George, *Freedom from the Press: Journalism and State Power in Singapore*, Singapore: National University of Singapore Press, 2012; Cherian George, 'History Spiked: Hegemony and the Denial of Media Diversity', in Michael D. Barr and Carl A. Trocki (eds), *Paths Not Taken: Political Pluralism in Post-War Singapore*, Singapore: National University of Singapore Press, 2008, pp. 264–80.
39. Michael Fernandez and Loh Kah Seng, 'The Left-Wing Trade Unions in Singapore, 1940–1970', in Barr and Trocki, *Paths Not Taken*, pp. 206–26; Diane K. Mauzy and R.S. Milne, *Singapore Politics Under the People's Action Party*, London and New York: Routledge, 2002, pp. 30–5; Barr, *The Ruling Elite of Singapore*, p. 40.
40. See Ross Worthington, *Governance in Singapore*, London and New York: Routlege-Curzon, 2003, Chapter 5, 'The Government in the Market: Government linked corporations and boards'.
41. Rajah, *Authoritarian Rule of Law*; Tsun Hang Tey, *Legal Consensus: Supreme Executive, Supine Jurisprudence, Suppliant Profession of Singapore*, Hong Kong: Centre for Comparative and Public Law, 2011; Kevin Y.L. Tan, 'State and Institution Building through the Singapore Constitution 1965–2005' and Arun K. Thiruvengadam, 'Comparative Law and Constitutional Interpretation in Singapore: Insights from Constitutional Theory', both in Li-ann Thio and Kevin Y.L. Tan (eds), *Evolution of a Revolution: Forty Years of the Singapore Constitution*, London and New York: Routledge-Cavendish, 2009, pp. 50–78 and 114–52 respectively.
42. Barr and Skrbiš, *Constructing Singapore*, pp. 238–40.
43. This paragraph is drawn substantially from ibid., pp. 63–70 and 239–43.
44. Cheong Koon Hean, 'The Evolution of HDB Towns', in Heng (ed.), *50 Years of Urban Planning*, pp. 101–25.
45. Cecelia Tortajada, Yugal Joshi and Asit K. Biswas, *The Singapore Water Story: Sustainable Development in an Urban City-State*, London and New York: Routledge, 2013, p. 139, 145.
46. Keng We Koh, 'The Deity Proposes, The State Disposes: The Vicissitudes of a Chinese Temple in Post-1965 Singapore', in Jason Lim and Terence Lee (eds), *Negotiating State and Society, 1965–2015*, London and New York: Routledge, 2016, pp. 126–42.
47. Peter van der Veer, 'Nation, Politics, Religion', *Journal of Religious and Political Practice*, 1(1), 2015, p. 17.
48. See, for instance, John Drysdale, *Singapore: Struggle for Success*, Singapore: Times Books International, 1984; and Kernial Singh Sandhu and Paul Wheatley, *Management of Success: The Moulding of Modern Singapore*, Singapore: Institute of Southeast Asian Studies, 1989.
49. Geraldine Heng and Janadas Devan, 'State Fatherhood: The Politics of Nationalism, Sexuality, and Race in Singapore', in Andrew Parker, Mary Russo, Doris Sommer and Patricia Yaeger (eds), *Nationalisms and Sexualities*, New York and London: Routledge, 1992, pp. 343–64; Barr, 'Perpetual Revisionism in Singapore'.
50. Michael D. Barr, 'Singapore: The Limits of a Technocratic Approach to Health Care', *Journal of Contemporary Asia*, 38(3), 2008, pp. 395–416.
51. Lily Zubaidah Rahim, *The Singapore Dilemma: The Political and Educational Marginality of the Malay Community*, Kuala Lumpur: Oxford University Press, 1998, pp. 75–7.
52. Garry Rodan, 'Goh's Consensus Politics of Authoritarian Rule', in Bridget Welsh, James Chin, Arun Mahizhnan and Tan Tarn How (eds), *Impressions of the Goh Chok Tong Years in Singapore*, Singapore: National University of Singapore Press, 2009, pp. 61–70; Michael D. Barr, 'The Bonsai Under the Banyan Tree: Democracy and Democratisation in Singapore', *Democratization*, 21(1), 2014, pp. 29–48.
53. Rodan, 'Consultative Authoritarianism and Regime Change Analysis'.
54. Ibid., p. 121.

55. Natasha Hamilton-Hart, 'The Singapore State Revisited', *The Pacific Review*, 13(2), 2000, pp. 195–216.
56. Li-ann Thio, 'Protecting Rights', and Michael Hor, 'Constitutionalism and Subversion – An Exploration', both in Thio and Tan (eds), *Evolution of a Revolution*, pp. 193–233 and 260–87 respectively.
57. This paragraph is derived directly from Michael D. Barr, 'Ordinary Singapore: The Decline of Singapore Exceptionalism', *Journal of Contemporary Asia*, 46(1), 2016, pp. 1–17.
58. Michael D. Barr, 'Marxists in Singapore? Lee Kuan Yew's Campaign Against Catholic Social Justice Activists in the 1980s', *Critical Asian Studies*, 42(3), 2010, p. 337.
59. Barr, *The Ruling Elite of Singapore*, pp. 54–6.
60. Ibid., pp. 100, 108.
61. Ibid., pp. 62–4.
62. See Welsh *et al.*, *Impressions of the Goh Chok Tong Years*, for a variety of mostly favourable accounts of the Goh years.
63. Barr, *The Ruling Elite of Singapore*, p. 64.
64. Ibid., pp. 99, 100.
65. Barr, 'Ordinary Singapore'.
66. This assessment is based on the author's interviews with nearly 20 opposition and civil society activists conducted a few months before the election was called.
67. Barr, 'Ordinary Singapore'.
68. Garry Rodan, 'Capitalism, Inequality and Ideology in Singapore: New Challenges for the Ruling Party', *Asian Studies Review*, 40(2), 2016, pp. 211–30.
69. Ibid., p. 225.

CHAPTER 7 THE ECONOMY: SINGAPORE, STILL AT THE CENTRE

1. Philippe Regnier, *Singapore: City-State in South-East Asia*, Honolulu: University of Hawai'i Press, 1987, p. 1.
2. W.G. Huff, *The Economic Growth of Singapore: Trade and Development in the Twentieth Century*, Cambridge, UK: Cambridge University Press, 1997 (1994), p. 31.
3. Peter Borschberg (ed.), *Admiral Matelieff's Singapore and Johor (1606–1616)*, Singapore: National University of Singapore Press, 2015, p. 166.
4. Ibid., p. 151.
5. I am indebted to Peter Borschberg for identifying this economic periodisation. See Peter Borschberg, 'Singapore in the Cycles of the Long Durée', *Journal of the Malaysian Branch of the Royal Asiatic Society*, 90 (Part 1, Number 312), 2017, pp. 29–60.
6. Ibid., p. 51.
7. Carl A. Trocki, *Prince of Pirates: The Temenggongs and the Development of Johor and Singapore 1784–1885*, Singapore: National University of Singapore Press, 2007 (1979), p. 61.
8. Conversation with the author early in the 2000s.
9. Carl A. Trocki, *Opium and Empire: Chinese Society in Colonial Singapore, 1800–1910*, Ithaca and London: Cornell University Press, 1990, pp. 44–9.
10. Borschberg, 'Singapore in the Cycles of the Long Durée', pp. 51, 52.
11. See especially Chapter 4.
12. Mark Ravinder Frost and Yu-Mei Balasingamchow, *Singapore: A Biography*, Singapore: Editions Didier Millet and National Museum of Singapore, 2009, p. 63.
13. Trocki, *Opium and Empire*, Chapters 6 and 7.
14. Ibid., p. 188.
15. Carl A. Trocki, *Singapore: Wealth, Power and the Culture of Control*, London and New York: Routledge, 2006, p. 18.
16. Ibid., p. 9.

17. Ratios are extrapolated from the figures for 1829/30, 1835/6, 1841/2 and 1847/8. See Anthony Reid, 'Chinese Trade and Southeast Asian Economic Expansion in the Later Eighteenth and Early Nineteenth Centuries: An Overview', in Nola Cooke and Tana Li (eds), *Water Frontier: Commerce and the Chinese in the Lower Mekong Region 1750–1880*, Singapore: National University of Singapore Press, 2004, Table 2.2, p. 30.
18. C.M. Turnbull, *A History of Singapore 1819–1988*, 2nd edn, Singapore: Oxford University Press, 1989, pp. 42, 43.
19. Goh Chor Boon, *Technology and Entrepôt Colonialism in Singapore, 1819–1940*, Singapore: Institute of Southeast Asian Studies, 2013, pp. 45–6.
20. Lee Soo Ann, 'Governance and Economic Change in Singapore', *The Singapore Economic Review*, 60(3), 2015, p. 1550028-3. Also see statistics provided in Wong Lin Ken, *The Malayan Tin Industry to 1914, with Special Reference to the States of Perak, Selangor, Negri Sembilan and Pahang*, Tucson: The Association for Asian Studies and The University of Arizona Press, 1965, p. 245. Note that these figures cover the whole of the Straits Settlements and not just Singapore.
21. Trocki, *Prince of Pirates*, pp. 90, 100, 101.
22. Trocki, *Opium and Empire*, p. 119.
23. Trocki, *Prince of Pirates*, pp. 87, 111, 117.
24. Huff, *The Economic Growth of Singapore*, pp. 8–12.
25. Huff, *The Economic Growth of Singapore*, p. 14; Lee, 'Governance and Economic Change in Singapore', pp. 1550028-4, 1550028-5.
26. Wong, *The Malayan Tin Industry to 1914*, especially Chapters 1 and 2.
27. F.J. Moorhead, *A History of Malaya, Volume Two*, Kuala Lumpur: Longmans of Malaya, 1963, pp. 191, 192.
28. Ibid.; and Lim Teck Ghee, *Peasants and their Agricultural Economy in Colonial Malaya 1874–1941*, Kuala Lumpur: Oxford University Press, 1977, p. 71.
29. Moorhead, *A History of Malaya*, p. 193; and Turnbull, *A History of Singapore*, p. 89.
30. T.H. Silcock, *The Economy of Malaya*, Singapore: Donald Moore, 1956, p. 17.
31. Turnbull, *A History of Singapore*, pp. 89, 90.
32. Richard Stubbs, *Rethinking Asia's Economic Miracle: The Political Economy of War, Prosperity and Crisis*, Basingstoke and New York: Palgrave Macmillan, 2005, pp. 78–82.
33. Hiroyoshi Kano, *Indonesian Exports, Peasant Agriculture and the World Economy 1850–2000: Economic Structures in a Southeast Asian State*, Singapore: National University of Singapore Press; Athens, OH: Ohio University Press, 2008, Chapter 4, Tables 4.1, 4.2 and 4.3.
34. Shakila Yacob, *The United States and the Malaysian Economy*, London and New York: Routledge, 2008, Chapter 3.
35. Commodity.com, 'Singapore's Top Commodity Imports & Exports', https://commodity.com/country-profiles/singapore/, accessed 12 July 2018.
36. Huff, *The Economic Growth of Singapore*, pp. 238, 239.
37. Ibid., pp. 236, 240–2.
38. Edgar H. Schein, *Strategic Pragmatism: The Culture of Singapore's Economic Development Board*, Singapore: Toppan with The MIT Press, 1996, p. 118.
39. See Ng Weng Hoong, *Singapore, the Energy Economy: From the First Refinery to the End of Cheap Oil, 1960–2010*, London and New York: Routledge, 2012; and Hon Sui Sen (ed. Linda Low and Lim Bee Lum), *Strategies of Singapore's Economic Success*, Singapore: Marshall Cavendish Academic, 2004, Part 2.
40. Goh, *Technology and Entrepôt Colonialism in Singapore*, pp. 49, 70, 71, 81.
41. John Curtis Perry, *Singapore: Unlikely Power*, New York: Oxford University Press, 2017, pp. 108, 109, 115.
42. Huff, *The Economic Growth of Singapore*, pp. 245–9.
43. Ibid., Chapter 1.
44. Ibid., p. 16.
45. Garry Rodan, *The Political Economy of Singapore's Industrialization: National State and International Capital*, Kuala Lumpur: Forum, 1991 (1989), Chapter 4.

46. Gavin Peebles and Peter Wilson, *Economic Growth and Development in Singapore: Past and Future*, Cheltenham, UK; Northampton, MA: Edward Elgar, 2002, p. 26.
47. Saw Swee-Hock, *The Population of Singapore*, 3rd edn, Singapore: Institute of Southeast Asian Studies, 2012, p. 37.
48. Peebles and Wilson, *Economic Growth and Development*, p. 27.
49. Chan Chin Bock *et al.*, *Heart Work*, Singapore: Economic Development Board and EDB Society, 2002; and Schein, *Strategic Pragmatism*.
50. Lee Kuan Yew, *From Third World to First: The Singapore Story: 1965–2000. Memoirs of Lee Kuan Yew*, Singapore: Singapore Press Holdings and Times Editions, 2000, Chapter 5; Peebles and Wilson, *Economic Growth and Development*, p. 35; and Christl Li, 'Connecting to the World: Singapore as a Hub Port', *Ethos*, 19, 8 July 2018, https://www.csc.gov.sg/articles/connecting-to-the-world-singapore-as-a-hub-port, accessed 31 July 2018.
51. Goh Keng Swee, interview with the author, Singapore, 1 September 1996.
52. Peebles and Wilson, *Economic Growth and Development*, p. 90.
53. Lee Kuan Yew, *From Third World to First*, Chapter 31.
54. Schein, *Strategic Pragmatism*.
55. This description is a simplification of Garry Rodan's analysis of Singapore as a node in the New International Division of Labour. See Rodan, *The Political Economy of Singapore's Industrialization*.
56. Lee Kuan Yew, *From Third World to First*, p. 73.
57. Linda Y.C. Lim, 'Singapore's Success: After the Miracle', in Robert E. Looney (ed.), *Routledge Handbook of Emerging Economies*, London and New York: Routledge, 2014, p. 205.
58. Marc Levinson, *The Box: How the Shipping Container Made the World Smaller and the World Economy Bigger*, Princeton and Oxford: Princeton University Press, 2006, pp. 209–11; Tatania Backes Vier, 'Hub Ports: A Case Study of Port of Singapore', Master's dissertation, Universidade Federal do Rio Grande do Sul, Porto Alegre, 2010, http://hdl.handle.net/10183/60515, accessed 5 June 2018.
59. See, for instance, 'The 13,466-island problem', *The Economist*, 27 February 2016.
60. Ngiam Tong Dow, *A Mandarin and the Making of Public Policy*, Singapore: National University of Singapore Press, 2006, p. 33.
61. Michael D. Barr, *The Ruling Elite of Singapore: Networks of Power and Influence*, London: I.B.Tauris, 2014, Chapters 3 and 5.
62. For readings on GLCs, Temasek Holdings, the GIC and Singapore Technologies see, for instance, Peebles and Wilson, *Economic Growth and Development*, Chapter 1; Tim Huxley, *Defending the Lion City: The Armed Forces of Singapore*, St Leonards, NSW: Allen & Unwin, 2000, Chapter 8; Ross Worthington, *Governance in Singapore*, London and New York: Routledge-Curzon, 2003, Chapter 5; Barr, *The Ruling Elite of Singapore*, Chapters 3–5, 7.
63. Joshua Kurlantzick, *State Capitalism: How the Return of Statism is Transforming the World*, New York: Oxford University Press, 2016, p. 29.
64. For more on the urbanisation programme, see Loh Kah Seng, *Squatters Into Citizens: The 1961 Bukit Ho Swee Fire and the Making of Modern Singapore*, Singapore and Copenhagen: Asian Studies Association of Australia in association with National University of Singapore Press and the Nordic Institute of Asian Studies, 2013.
65. Michael Fernandez and Loh Kah Seng, 'The Left-Wing Trade Unions in Singapore, 1945–1970', in Michael D. Barr and Carl A. Trocki (eds), *Paths Not Taken: Political Pluralism in Post-War Singapore*, Singapore: National University of Singapore Press, 2008, pp. 206–26; Rodan, *The Political Economy of Singapore's Industrialization*, pp. 68–72, 106–9.
66. Huff, *The Economic Growth of Singapore*, p. 348; Tilak Abeysinghe and Keen Meng Choy, *The Singapore Economy: An Econometric Perspective*, London and New York: Routledge, 2009, p. 70; Noorashikin Abdul Rahman, 'Managing Labour Flows: Foreign Talent, Foreign Workers and Domestic Help', in Terence Chong (ed.), *Management of Success: Singapore Revisited*, Singapore: Institute of Southeast Asian Studies, 2010, p. 200; Ministry of Manpower, 'Foreign workforce numbers', http://www.mom.gov.sg/documents-and-publications/foreign-workforce-numbers, accessed 12 July 2018. For a more comprehensive set of figures covering 1970–2014, with some gaps, see Yap Mui Teng and Christopher

Gee, 'Singapore's Demographic Transition, The Labour Force and Government Policies: The Last Fifty Years', *The Singapore Economic Review*, 60(3), 2015, p. 1550035-8.
67. Huff, *The Economic Growth of Singapore*, p. 348.
68. Abeysinghe and Choy, *The Singapore Economy*, pp. 81, 85, 136.
69. Stubbs, *Rethinking Asia's Economic Miracle*, pp. 136–8.
70. *Trading Economics*, 'Singapore GDP Annual Growth Rate 1976–2018', http://www.tradingeconomics.com/singapore/gdp-growth-annual, accessed 12 July 2018.
71. Ngiam Tong Dow (Zhang Zhibin, ed.), *Dynamics of the Singapore Success Story: Insights by Ngiam Tong Dow*, Singapore: Cengage Learning, 2011, p. 6.
72. Peter E. Robertson, 'Why the Tigers Roared: Capital Accumulation and the East Asian Miracle', *Pacific Economic Review*, 7(2), 2002, p. 269.
73. Goh Chor Boon, *From Traders to Innovators: Science and Technology in Singapore since 1965*, Singapore: ISEAS Publishing, 2016, pp. 71–9.
74. Perry, *Singapore: Unlikely Power*, p. 236.
75. Ngiam, *Dynamics of the Singapore Success Story*, p. 6. For a much more nuanced reading of the failure of the Second Industrial Revolution, see Rodan, *The Political Economy of Singapore's Industrialization*, Chapter 5.
76. Paul Krugman, 'The Myth of Asia's Miracle', *Foreign Affairs*, November/December 1994, pp. 70, 71.
77. For a restrained and balanced assessment of the state of this debate as it stood in 2002, see Peebles and Wilson, *Economic Growth and Development*, Chapter 3. Also see Pang Eng Fong and Linda Y.C. Lim, 'Labour Productivity and Singapore's Development Model', *The Singapore Economic Review*, 60(3), 2015, pp. 1550033-1–30.
78. Ngiam, *Dynamics of the Singapore Success Story*, p. 6.
79. Department of Statistics, Singapore, http://www.tablebuilder.singstat.gov.sg/publicfacing/createDataTable.action?refId=1408, accessed 12 July 2018.
80. Perry, *Singapore: Unlikely Power*, pp. 287, 288.
81. Rodolphe De Koninck, Julie Drolet and Marc Girard, *Singapore: An Atlas of Perpetual Territorial Transformation*, Singapore: National University of Singapore Press, 2008, especially pp. 14, 15, 24, 25, 42, 43, 60, 61; and Cheong Koon Hean, Tommy Koh and Lionel Yee, *Malaysia and Singapore: The Land Reclamation Case From Dispute to Settlement*, Singapore: Straits Times Press, 2013, especially p. 14.
82. Arun Mahizhnan, 'Developing Singapore's External Economy', *Southeast Asian Affairs*, 1994, pp. 285–301.
83. Andrea Goldstein and Pavida Pananond, 'Singapore Inc. Goes Shopping Abroad: Profits and Pitfalls', *Journal of Contemporary Asia*, 38(3), 2008, pp. 417–38.
84. Robyn Klingler-Vidra, 'The Pragmatic "Little Red Dot": Singapore's US Hedge Against China', in Nicholas Kitchen (ed.), *The New Geopolitics of Southeast Asia* (IDEAS Special Reports), London: London School of Economics and Political Science, Kindle edition, 2012, Figures 2 and 3.
85. Department of Statistics, Singapore, http://www.tablebuilder.singstat.gov.sg/publicfacing/createDataTable.action?refId=9132, accessed 13 July 2018.
86. Ibid.; Department of Statistics, *Singapore's Direct Investment Abroad*, Singapore: Department of Statistics, 2017; and World Integrated Trade Solution, 'Singapore exports, imports and trade balance by country 2016', https://wits.worldbank.org/CountryProfile/en/Country/SGP/Year/LTST/TradeFlow/EXPIMP/Partner/by-country, accessed 13 July 2018.
87. Department of Statistics, http://www.tablebuilder.singstat.gov.sg/publicfacing/createDataTable.action?refId=9132, accessed 13 July 2018. The comparison is accurate as of the latest statistics at the time of writing (i.e. 2016 figures), but even at that point mainland China was not far behind ASEAN as the biggest recipient of Singapore's OFDI. If Hong Kong is included as part of China, then China is already far ahead of ASEAN.
88. Peebles and Wilson, *Economic Growth and Development*, pp. 188, 189.
89. Koi Nyen Wong and Soo Khoon Goh, 'Outward FDI, Merchandise and Services Trade: Evidence from Singapore', Munich Personal RePEc Archive, 2011, https://mpra.ub.uni-muenchen.

de/35377/1/MPRA_paper_35377.pdf, p. 13, Table 3; Goldstein and Pananond, 'Singapore Inc. Goes Shopping Abroad', p. 420, Table 2.
90. Wong and Goh, 'Outward FDI, Merchandise and Services Trade', p. 13, Table 3.
91. 'Warwick votes against Singapore campus', *Financial Times*, 14 October 2005; 'Red faces, millions lost as uni closes campus', *Sydney Morning Herald*, 24 May 2007.
92. Joseph Wong, *Betting on Biotech: Innovation and the Limits of Asia's Developmental State*, Ithaca and London: Cornell University Press, 2011.
93. Goh, *From Traders to Innovators*, p. 71.
94. Ibid., pp. 94–100.
95. See Department of Statistics, Singapore, http://www.singstat.gov.sg/statistics/visualising-data/charts/share-of-gdp-by-industry, accessed 19 January 2016 (link no longer functioning). Also see Ministry of Trade and Industry, 'Economic Survey of Singapore 2017', https://www.mti.gov.sg/ResearchRoom/Pages/Economic-Survey-of-Singapore-2017.aspx, accessed 13 July 2018.
96. Kent E. Calder, *Singapore: Smart City, Smart State*, Washington, DC: Brookings Institution Press; Singapore: Talisman Press, 2017, p. 135.
97. Lim, 'Singapore's Success', pp. 204, 208.
98. Michael D. Barr, 'Ordinary Singapore: The Decline of Singapore Exceptionalism', *Journal of Contemporary Asia*, 46(1), 2016, pp. 1–17.
99. Saskia Sassen, *Cities in a World Economy*, 4th edn, Thousand Oaks, CA and London: Pine Forge Press, 2012, various tables in Chapter 4.

CHAPTER 8 MAKING MODERN SINGAPOREANS: PEOPLE, SOCIETY AND PLACE

1. Manuel Castells, *The City and the Grassroots: A Cross-Cultural Theory of Urban Social Movements*, Berkeley and Los Angeles: University of California Press, 1983, pp. 3, 4.
2. James Francis Warren, *Rickshaw Coolie: A People's History of Singapore 1880–1940*, Singapore: Singapore University Press, 2003 (1986), pp. 161, 162.
3. Stephen Dobbs, *The Singapore River: A Social History 1819–2012*, Singapore: Singapore University Press, 2003; Brenda S.A. Yeoh, *Contesting Space in Colonial Singapore: Power Relations and the Urban Built Environment*, Singapore: Singapore University Press, 2003; Loh Kah Seng, *Squatters Into Citizens: The 1961 Bukit Ho Swee Fire and the Making of Modern Singapore*, Singapore and Copenhagen: Asian Studies Association of Australia in association with National University of Singapore Press and the Nordic Institute of Asian Studies, 2013; Barrington Kaye, *Upper Nankin Street: A Sociological Study of Chinese Households Living in a Densely Populated Area*, Singapore: University of Malaya Press, 1960.
4. John Clammer, *Singapore: Ideology, Society and Culture*, Singapore: Chopmen Publishers, 1985, p. 27.
5. Peter Borschberg, 'Singapore in the Cycles of the Long Durée', *Journal of the Malaysian Branch of the Royal Asiatic Society*, 90 (Part 1, Number 312), 2017, pp. 36–8; and an email exchange with Carl Trocki, 13 July 2017.
6. Ibid. (both references).
7. Carl A. Trocki, *Prince of Pirates: The Temenggongs and the Development of Johor and Singapore 1784–1885*, Singapore: National University of Singapore Press, 2007 (1979), p. 59.
8. Dobbs, *The Singapore River*, pp. 3, 7.
9. Ibid., Chapter 3.
10. I put 'Malay' in inverted commas because they would not have self-identified thus. If they identified themselves as a group at all they would have used a much more specific, localised term, such as 'Bugis' or 'Siak'.
11. C.M. Turnbull, *A History of Singapore 1819–1988*, 2nd edn, Singapore: Oxford University Press, 1989 (1977), pp. 36, 37.
12. Saw Swee-Hock, *The Population of Singapore*, 3rd edn, Singapore: Institute of Southeast Asian Studies, 2012, pp. 9–11.

13. Warren, *Rickshaw Coolie*; and James Francis Warren, *Ah Ku and Karayuki-San: Prostitution in Singapore 1870–1940*, Singapore: Singapore University Press, 2003.
14. Ibid., especially Chapters 8 and 16; Goh Chor Boon, *Technology and Entrepôt Colonialism in Singapore, 1819–1940*, Singapore: Institute of Southeast Asian Studies, 2013, pp. 104–6.
15. See Carl A. Trocki, *Singapore: Wealth, Power and the Culture of Control*, London and New York: Routledge, 2006, pp. 54–7.
16. Cecelia Tortajada, Yugal Joshi and Asit K. Biswas, *The Singapore Water Story: Sustainable Development in an Urban City-State*, London and New York: Routledge, 2013, p. 145; S.R. Joey Long, 'Desecuritisation and after Desecuritisation: The Water Issue in Singapore', in Barry Desker and Ang Cheng Guan (eds), *Perspectives on the Security of Singapore: The First 50 Years*, Singapore: World Scientific, 2016, pp. 103–20.
17. Dobbs, *The Singapore River*, Chapters 3 and 5.
18. Jürgen Osterhammel (transl. Patrick Camiller), *The Transformation of the World: A Global History of the Nineteenth Century*, Princeton, NJ: Princeton University Press, 2014, pp. 275, 276.
19. Saw, *The Population of Singapore*, pp. 31–4.
20. Turnbull, *A History of Singapore*, p. 36.
21. Phyllis Ghim-Lian Chew, *A Sociolinguistic History of Early Identities in Singapore: From Colonialism to Nationalism*, Basingstoke: Palgrave Macmillan, 2013, p. 41.
22. Ibid., pp. 42, 43.
23. Felix Chia, *The Babas*, Singapore: Landmark Books, 2015 (1993, 1980).
24. Ibid.; Chew, *A Sociological History of Early Identities*, pp. 171–4; and Thienny Lee, 'Defining the Aesthetics of the *Nyonyas*' Batik Sarongs in the Straits Settlements, Late Nineteenth to Early Twentieth Century', *Asian Studies Review*, 40(2), 2016, pp. 173–91. Note that there were also *peranakan* Indians, but they were less prominent.
25. See Sikko Visscher, *The Business of Politics and Ethnicity: A History of the Singapore Chinese Chamber of Commerce and Industry*, Singapore: National University of Singapore Press, 2007, pp. 12–17. Also see Carl A. Trocki, *Opium and Empire: Chinese Society in Colonial Singapore, 1800–1910*, Ithaca and London: Cornell University Press, 1990, Chapters 1–5.
26. Trocki, *Opium and Empire*, p. 117.
27. J.S. Furnivall, *Colonial Policy and Practice: A Comparative Study of Burma and Netherlands India*, Cambridge, UK: Cambridge University Press, 1948.
28. Joel S. Kahn, *Other Malays: Nationalism and Cosmopolitanism in the Modern Malay World*, Singapore: National University of Singapore Press, 2006, p. 170.
29. William R. Roff, *Studies on Islam and Society in Southeast Asia*, Singapore: National University of Singapore Press, 2009, Chapter 4, 'The Malayo-Muslim World of Singapore at the Close of the Nineteenth Century'. Also see Timothy P. Barnard (ed.), *Contesting Malayness: Malay Identity Across Boundaries*, Singapore: Singapore University Press, 2004; and Anthony Milner, *The Malays*, Chichester: Wiley-Blackwell, 2008.
30. Trocki, *Singapore*, p. 39.
31. Ibid., pp. 66–8; and Benedict R.O.G. Anderson, *Imagined Communities: Reflections on the Origin and Spread of Nationalism*, London: Verso, 2006 (1983).
32. Trocki, *Singapore*, p. 68.
33. E. Kay Gillis, *Singapore Civil Society and British Power*, Singapore: Talisman Press, 2005.
34. Goh, *Technology and Entrepôt Colonialism in Singapore*, p. 41.
35. Mark Ravinder Frost and Yu-Mei Balasingamchow, *Singapore: A Biography*, Singapore: Editions Didier Millet and National Museum of Singapore, 2009, pp. 177, 179.
36. Goh, *Technology and Entrepôt Colonialism in Singapore*, pp. 170–82.
37. Turnbull, *A History of Singapore*, p. 45.
38. Frost and Balasingamchow, *Singapore: A Biography*, pp. 205–7.
39. Audrey Chin and Constance Singam, *Singapore Women Re-Presented*, Singapore: Landmark Books, 2004, pp. 99–101.
40. Iain Buchanan, *Singapore in Southeast Asia: An Economic and Political Appraisal*, London: G. Bell and Sons, 1972, pp. 170–2.

41. Edna Lim, 'Singapore Cinema: Connecting the Golden Age and the Revival', in Liew Kai Khiun and Stephen Teo, *Singapore Cinema: New Perspectives*, London and New York: Routledge, 2017, pp. 60–74.
42. E. Kay Gillis, 'Civil Society and the Malay Education Council', in Michael D. Barr and Carl A. Trocki (eds), *Paths Not Taken: Political Pluralism in Post-War Singapore*, Singapore: National University of Singapore Press, 2008, pp. 154–69.
43. Ernest Koh, *Singapore Stories: Language, Class and the Chinese of Singapore 1945–2000*, Amherst, NY: Cambria Press, 2010, pp. 48–50.
44. Eddie C.Y. Kuo, 'The Sociolinguistic Situation in Singapore: Unity in Diversity', in Evangelos A. Afendras and Eddie C.Y. Kuo (eds), *Language and Society in Singapore*, Singapore: Singapore University Press, 1980, p. 48.
45. Department of Social Welfare, Singapore, *A Social Survey of Singapore: A Preliminary Study of Some Aspects of Social Conditions in the Municipal Area of Singapore, December 1947*, Singapore: Department of Social Welfare, 1947, p. 61.
46. Yeoh, *Contesting Space in Colonial Singapore*, p. 67.
47. Frost and Balasingamchow, *Singapore: A Biography*, pp. 183–9; Turnbull, *A History of Singapore*, pp. 108–10.
48. Turnbull, *A History of Singapore*, pp. 126, 127.
49. Ibid., p. 145.
50. Barbara Watson Andaya and Leonard Y. Andaya, *A History of Malaysia*, 2nd edn, Honolulu: University of Hawai'i Press, 2001 (1982), pp. 256–300.
51. Yoshimura Mako, 'Japan's Economic Policy for Occupied Malaya', in Akashi Yoji and Yoshimura Mako (eds), *New Perspectives on the Japanese Occupation in Malaya and Singapore, 1941–1945*, Singapore: National University of Singapore Press, 2008, pp. 113–38.
52. Jim Baker, *Crossroads: A Popular History of Malaysia and Singapore*, 3rd edn, Singapore: Marshall Cavendish, 2014, p. 207. Also see Paul Kratoska, *The Japanese Occupation of Malaya: 1941–1945*, Honolulu: University of Hawai'i Press, 1997, pp. 202, 203.
53. Kratoska, *The Japanese Occupation of Malaya*, Chapter 5, 'Education and Propaganda'.
54. Turnbull, *A History of Singapore*, pp. 220, 221.
55. Kevin Blackburn and Karl Hack, *War Memory and the Making of Malaysia and Singapore*, Singapore: National University of Singapore Press, 2012.
56. Lee Su Yin, *British Policy and the Chinese in Singapore, 1939 to 1955: The Public Service Career of Tan Chin Tuan*, Singapore: Talisman, 2011, p. 71.
57. Diana Wong, 'Memory Suppression and Memory Production: The Japanese Occupation of Singapore', in T. Fujitani, Geoffrey M. White and Lisa Yoneyama (ed.), *Perilous Memories: The Asia-Pacific War(s)*, Durham, NC and London: Duke University Press, 2001, p. 232.
58. See Visscher, *The Business of Politics and Ethnicity*, Chapters 1, 2 and 3.
59. Ong Chu Meng, Lim Hoon Yong and Ng Lai Yang (eds), *Tan Lark Sye: Advocator and Founder of Nanyang University*, Singapore: World Scientific, 2015; Yao Souchou, 'All Quiet on Jurong Road: Nanyang University and Radical Vision in Singapore', in Barr and Trocki (eds), *Paths Not Taken*, pp. 170–87; and Lee Ting Hui, *The Open United Front: The Communist Struggle in Singapore, 1954–1966*, Singapore: South Seas Society, 1996, pp. 137, 303–15.
60. Hong Lysa, 'Politics of the Immigrant Chinese Communities in Singapore in the 1950s: Narratives of Belonging in the Time of Emergency', in Tan Jing Quee, Tan Kok Chiang and Hong Lysa (eds), *The May 13 Generation: The Chinese Middle Schools Student Movement and Singapore Politics in the 1950s*, Petaling Jaya: Strategic Information and Research Development Centre, 2011, p. 31.
61. Lim Huan Boon, 'My Recollections of Learning Malay' (transl. Edgar Liao Bolum), in Tan *et al.* (eds), *The May 13 Generation*, pp. 217–25.
62. Scholars who subscribe uncritically to the Special Branch view of history assume that Lim, Fong and many others were members and operatives of the MCP. Considering that most of the evidence for these claims was never tested outside a Special Branch interrogation cell, I regard such accusations with scepticism. Yet it would be naïve to deny that the MCP was actively trying to influence the students and that it must have had some personnel on the ground. Student activists such

as Tan Kok Chiang agree that there were communists in the mix, even as they argue that the communists were not central to the movement and that most of the students accused of being communists were innocent. See Lee, *The Open United Front*; Kumar Ramakrishna, *'Original Sin'? Revising the Revisionist Critique of the 1963 Operation Coldstore in Singapore*, Singapore: Institute of Southeast Asian Studies, 2015; Hong Lysa, 'Politics of the Chinese-speaking Communities in Singapore in the 1950s: The Shaping of Mass Politics', in Tan *et al.* (eds), *The May 13 Generation*, pp. 84–99; Tan Kok Chiang, 'My Story', in Tan *et al.* (eds), *The May 13 Generation*, pp. 123–86.

63. Hong, 'Politics of the Chinese-speaking Communities in Singapore', pp. 80–4.
64. Ibid., pp. 88, 89.
65. Lee, *The Open United Front*, pp. 36 n 52, 47–54, 70 n 37, 72 n 61, 134, 135; Ramakrishna, *'Original Sin'?*, pp. 33, 34, 45, 46.
66. *Utusan Melayu*, 25 August 1954, cited in Colony of Singapore, *Weekly Digest of Non-English Press*, Singapore: Singapore Public Relations 1954.
67. See, for instance, the editorials in the *Nanfang Evening Post*, 8 February 1956; *Nanyang Siang Pau*, 9 February 1956; *Chung Shing Jit Pao*, 9 February 1956; *Sin Chew Jit Poh*, 11 February 1956; *Tamil Murasa*, 5 February 1956; *Utusan Melayu*, 6 February 1956. All are cited in Colony of Singapore, *Weekly Digest of Non-English Press*, 1956. Also see Koh, *Singapore Stories*, pp. 93–9.
68. Rizwana Abdul Azeez, *Negotiating Malay Identities in Singapore: The Role of Modern Islam*, Brighton, UK, Chicago and Toronto: Sussex Academic Press, 2016, Chapters 2, 3 and 5; Michael D. Barr, *The Ruling Elite of Singapore: Networks of Power and Influence*, London: I.B.Tauris, 2014, pp. 30–41; Lily Zubaidah Rahim, *The Singapore Dilemma: The Political and Educational Marginality of the Malay Community*, Kuala Lumpur: Oxford University Press, 1998, Chapters 5 and 6; Visscher, *The Business of Politics and Ethnicity*, Chapters 4 and 5; Cherian George, *Freedom From the Press: Journalism and State Power in Singapore*, Singapore: National University of Singapore Press, 2012, Chapter 2.
69. *Sin Chew Jit Poh*, 8 July 1969, cited in Ministry of Culture, Singapore, *Mirror of Opinion: Highlights of Malay, Chinese and Tamil Press.*
70. The previous few paragraphs are drawn substantially from Michael D. Barr and Jevon Low, 'Assimilation as Multiracialism: The Case of Singapore's Malays', *Asian Ethnicity*, 6(3), 2005, pp. 162–5.
71. Michael D. Barr and Zlatko Skrbiš, *Constructing Singapore: Elitism, Ethnicity and the Nation-Building Project*, Copenhagen: Nordic Institute of Asian Studies, 2008, Chapters 7, 8 and 9.
72. For an overview of developments in education see Aaron Koh and Terence Chong (eds), *Education in the Global City: The Manufacturing of Education in Singapore*, London and New York: Routledge, 2016.
73. For a thoroughgoing exploration of the challenges facing the government in the 2010s, see Donald Low and Sudhir Vadaketh with contributions from Linda Lim and Thum Ping Tjin, *Hard Choices: Challenging the Singapore Consensus*, Singapore: National University of Singapore Press, 2014. Also see Lily Zubaidah Rahim, 'Reclaiming Singapore's "Growth with Equity" Social Compact', *Japanese Journal of Political Science*, 16(2), 2015, pp. 160–76; and Garry Rodan, 'Capitalism, Inequality and Ideology in Singapore: New Challenges for the Ruling Party', *Asian Studies Review*, 40(2), 2016, pp. 211–30.

AFTERWORD

1. 'Bicentennial of S'pore's founding offers teachable moment', *Straits Times*, 22 May 2017.
2. Michael D. Barr and Zlatko Skrbiš, *Constructing Singapore: Elitism, Ethnicity and the Nation-Building Project*, Copenhagen: Nordic Institute of Asian Studies, 2008.
3. 'Guidelines issued on use of name and image of Lee Kuan Yew', *Channel NewsAsia*, 16 March 2016.
4. Lee Kuan Yew in Han Fook Kwang, Zuraidah Ibrahim, Chua Mui Hoong, Lydia Lim, Ignatius Low, Rachel Lin, Robin Chan, *Lee Kuan Yew: Hard Truths to Keep Singapore Going*, Singapore: Straits Times Press, 2011, p. 399.

Bibliography

Abdul Azeez, Rizwana, *Negotiating Malay Identities in Singapore: The Role of Modern Islam*, Brighton, UK, Chicago and Toronto: Sussex Academic Press, 2016.

Abeysinghe, Tilak and Keen Meng Choy, *The Singapore Economy: An Econometric Perspective*, London and New York: Routledge, 2009.

Abshire, Jean E., *The History of Singapore*, Santa Barbara, CA: Greenwood, 2011.

Afendras, Evangelos A. and Eddie C.Y. Kuo (eds), *Language and Society in Singapore*, Singapore: Singapore University Press, 1980.

Ali al-Haji ibn Ahmad, *The Precious Gift: Tuhfat Al-Nafis; an Annotated Translation by Virginia Matheson Hooker and Barbara Watson Andaya*, Kuala Lumpur: Oxford University Press, 1982.

Amrith, Sunil, 'Internationalism and Political Pluralism in Singapore, 1950–1963', in Michael D. Barr and Carl A. Trocki (eds), *Paths Not Taken: Political Pluralism in Post-War Singapore*, Singapore: National University of Singapore Press, 2008, pp. 37–56.

Andaya, Barbara Watson and Leonard Y. Andaya, *A History of Malaysia*, 2nd edn, Honolulu: University of Hawai'i Press, 2001 (1982).

Andaya, Leonard Y., *The Kingdom of Johor 1641–1728*, Kuala Lumpur: Oxford University Press, 1975.

———, *Leaves of the Same Tree: Trade and Ethnicity in the Straits of Melaka*, Singapore: National University of Singapore Press, 2010.

Anderson, Benedict R.O.G., *Imagined Communities: Reflections on the Origin and Spread of Nationalism*, London: Verso, 2006 (1983).

Baker, Jim, *Crossroads: A Popular History of Malaysia and Singapore*, 3rd edn, Singapore: Marshall Cavendish, 2014.

Barnard, Timothy P. (ed.), *Contesting Malayness: Malay Identity Across Boundaries*, Singapore: Singapore University Press, 2004.

Barnard, Timothy P. and Jan van der Putten, 'Malay Cosmopolitan Activism in Post-War Singapore', in Michael D. Barr and Carl A. Trocki (eds), *Paths Not Taken: Political*

Pluralism in Post-War Singapore, Singapore: National University of Singapore Press, 2008, pp. 132–53.

Barr, Michael D., 'The Bonsai Under the Banyan Tree: Democracy and Democratisation in Singapore', *Democratization*, 21(1), 2014, pp. 29–48.

———, *Lee Kuan Yew: The Beliefs Behind the Man*, Richmond, UK: Curzon Press, 2000.

———, 'Marxists in Singapore? Lee Kuan Yew's Campaign Against Catholic Social Justice Activists in the 1980s', *Critical Asian Studies*, 42(3), 2010, pp. 335–62.

———, 'No Island is a Man: The Enigma of Lee Kuan Yew', *Harvard Asia Quarterly*, 11(2/3), 2008, pp. 45–56.

———, 'Ordinary Singapore: The Decline of Singapore Exceptionalism', *Journal of Contemporary Asia*, 46(1), 2016, pp. 1–17.

———, 'Perpetual Revisionism in Singapore: The Limits of Change', *The Pacific Review*, 16(1), 2003, pp. 77–97.

———, 'Review of Kumar Ramakrishna, *"Original Sin"? Revising the Revisionist Critique of the 1963 Operation Coldstore in Singapore*', *The Developing Economies*, 54(3), 2016, pp. 260–3.

———, *The Ruling Elite of Singapore: Networks of Power and Influence*, London: I.B.Tauris, 2014.

———, 'Singapore: The Limits of a Technocratic Approach to Health Care', *Journal of Contemporary Asia*, 38(3), 2008, pp. 395–416.

Barr, Michael D. and Jevon Low, 'Assimilation as Multiracialism: The Case of Singapore's Malays', *Asian Ethnicity*, 6(3), 2005, pp. 162–5.

Barr, Michael D. and Zlatko Skrbiš, *Constructing Singapore: Elitism, Ethnicity and the Nation-Building Project*, Copenhagen: Nordic Institute of Asian Studies, 2008.

Barr, Michael D. and Carl A. Trocki (eds), *Paths Not Taken: Political Pluralism in Post-War Singapore*, Singapore: National University of Singapore Press, 2008.

Bastin, John, *Raffles and Hastings: Private Exchanges Behind the Founding of Singapore*, Singapore: National Library Board and Marshall Cavendish, 2014.

Bayley, Christopher and Tim Harper, *Forgotten Wars: The End of Britain's Empire*, London: Allen Lane, 2007.

Beeson, Mark, 'Geopolitics and the Making of Regions: The Fall and Rise of East Asia', *Political Studies*, 57, 2009, pp. 498–516.

———, *Regionalism and Globalization in East Asia: Politics, Security and Economic Development*, Basingstoke: Palgrave Macmillan, 2007.

Bell, Daniel A. and Avner de-Shalit, *The Spirit of Cities: Why the Identity of a City Matters in a Global Age*, Princeton and Oxford: Princeton University Press, 2011.

Bellows, Thomas J., *The People's Action Party of Singapore: Emergence of a Dominant Party System*, Monograph Series No. 14, New Haven, CT: Yale University Southeast Asia Studies, 1970.

Blackburn, Kevin, 'Family Memories as Alternative Narratives to the State's Construction of Singapore's National History', in Loh Kah Seng, Ernest Koh and Stephen Dobbs (eds), *Oral History in Southeast Asia: Memories and Fragments*, New York: Palgrave Macmillan, 2013, pp. 25–41.

———, 'Mary Turnbull's History Textbook for the Singapore Nation', in Nicholas Tarling (ed.), *Studying Singapore's Past: C.M. Turnbull and the History of Modern Singapore*, Singapore: National University of Singapore Press, 2012, pp. 65–86.

Blackburn, Kevin and Karl Hack, *War Memory and the Making of Malaysia and Singapore*, Singapore: National University of Singapore Press, 2012.

Borschberg, Peter (ed.), *Admiral Matelieff's Singapore and Johor (1606–1616)*, Singapore: National University of Singapore Press, 2015.

———, *Hugo Grotius, the Portuguese and Free Trade in the East Indies*, Singapore: National University of Singapore Press, 2011.

——— (ed.), *Iberians in the Singapore-Melaka Area and Adjacent Regions (16th to 18th Century)*, Wiesbaden: Harrassowitz Verlag; Lisbon: Fundação Oriente, 2004.

——— (ed.), *Jacques de Coutre's Singapore and Johor 1594–c.1625*, Singapore: National University of Singapore Press, 2015.

——— (ed.), *Journals, Memorials and Letters of Cornelis Matelieff de Jonge: Security, Diplomacy and Commerce in 17th-Century Southeast Asia*, Singapore: National University of Singapore Press, 2015.

Borschberg, Peter, 'Malacca as a "Sea-Borne Empire" – Continuities and Discontinuities from Sultanate to Portuguese Colony (Fifteenth and Sixteenth Century)', in Peter Borschberg and Martin Krieger (eds), *Water and State in Europe and Asia*, New Delhi: Manohar, 2008, pp. 35–71.

———, 'Security, VOC Penetration and Luso-Spanish Co-operation: The Armada of Philippine Governor Juan de Silva in the Straits of Singapore, 1616', in Peter Borschberg (ed.), *Iberians in the Singapore-Melaka Area and Adjacent Regions (16th to 18th Century)*, Wiesbaden: Harrassowitz Verlag; Lisbon: Fundação Oriente, 2004, pp. 35–62.

———, *The Singapore and Melaka Straits: Violence, Security and Diplomacy in the 17th Century*, Singapore: National University of Singapore Press, 2010.

———, 'Singapore in the Cycles of the Long Durée', *Journal of the Malaysian Branch of the Royal Asiatic Society*, 90 (Part 1, Number 312), 2017, pp. 29–60.

———, 'Singapura in Early Modern Cartography: A Sea of Challenges', National Library Board, *Visualising Space: Maps of Singapore and the Region: Collections from the National Library and National Archives of Singapore*, Singapore: National Library Board, [2015].

Borschberg, Peter and Martin Krieger (eds), *Water and State in Europe and Asia*, New Delhi: Manohar, 2008.

Borschberg, Peter (ed.) and Roopanjali Roy (transl.), *The Memoirs and Memorials of Jacques de Coutre: Security, Trade and Society in 16th and 17th-Century Southeast Asia*, Singapore: National University of Singapore Press, 2014.

Brown, C.C. (ed. and transl.), *Sejarah Melayu or 'Malay Annals'*, Kuala Lumpur: Oxford University Press, 1970 (1953).

Buchanan, Iain, *Singapore in Southeast Asia: An Economic and Political Appraisal*, London: G. Bell & Sons, 1972.

Calder, Kent E., *Singapore: Smart City, Smart State*, Washington, DC: Brookings Institution Press; Singapore: Talisman Press, 2017.

Castells, Manuel, *The City and the Grassroots: A Cross-Cultural Theory of Urban Social Movements*, Berkeley and Los Angeles: University of California Press, 1983.

Chan Chin Bock *et al.*, *Heart Work*, Singapore: Economic Development Board and EDB Society, 2002.

Chan Heng Chee, *The Dynamics of One Party Dominance: The PAP at the Grassroots*, Singapore: Oxford University Press, 1976.

———, *Politics in an Administrative State: Where Has the Politics Gone?*, Singapore: Department of Political Science, University of Singapore, 1975.

———, *Singapore: The Politics of Survival 1965–1967*, Singapore and Kuala Lumpur: Oxford University Press, 1971.

Cheah Boon Kheng, *Red Star Over Malaya: Resistance and Social Conflict During and After the Japanese Occupation, 1941–1946*, 3rd edn, Singapore: Singapore University Press, 2003 (1983).

Cheong Koon Hean, 'The Evolution of HDB Towns', in Heng Chye Kiang (ed.), *50 Years of Urban Planning in Singapore*, Singapore: World Scientific, 2016, pp. 101–25.

Cheong Koon Hean, Tommy Koh and Lionel Yee, *Malaysia and Singapore: The Land Reclamation Case From Dispute to Settlement*, Singapore: Straits Times Press, 2013.

Chew, Melanie (ed.), *Leaders of Singapore*, Singapore: Resources Press, 1996.

Chew, Phyllis Ghim-Lian, *A Sociolinguistic History of Early Identities in Singapore: From Colonialism to Nationalism*, Basingstoke: Palgrave Macmillan, 2013.

Chia, Felix, *The Babas*, Singapore: Landmark Books, 2015 (1993, 1980).

Chin, Audrey and Constance Singam, *Singapore Women Re-Presented*, Singapore: Landmark Books, 2004.

Chin, C.C., 'The United Front Strategy of the Malayan Communist Party in Singapore, 1950s–1960s', in Michael D. Barr and Carl A. Trocki (eds), *Paths Not Taken: Political*

Pluralism in Post-War Singapore, Singapore: National University of Singapore Press, 2008, pp. 58–77.

Chin Peng, *Alias Chin Peng, My Side of History*, Singapore: Media Masters, 2003.

Chong, Terence (ed.), *Management of Success: Singapore Revisited*, Singapore: Institute of Southeast Asian Studies, 2010.

Chua Ai Lin, 'Imperial Subjects, Straits Citizens: Anglophone Asians and the Struggle for Political Rights in Inter-War Singapore', in Michael D. Barr and Carl A. Trocki (eds), *Paths Not Taken: Political Pluralism in Post-War Singapore*, Singapore: National University of Singapore Press, 2008, pp. 16–36.

Chua, Daniel Wei Boon, 'Reinventing Lee Kuan Yew's 1965–66 Anti-Americanism', *Asian Studies Review*, 38(3), 2014, pp. 442–60.

Clammer, John, *Singapore: Ideology, Society and Culture*, Singapore: Chopmen Publishers, 1985.

Clutterbuck, Richard, *Conflict and Violence in Singapore and Malaysia 1945–1983*, Singapore: Graham Brash, 1985.

Colgan, Jeff D. and Robert O. Keohane, 'The Liberal Order is Rigged: Fix It Now or Watch It Wither', *Foreign Affairs*, May–June 2017, pp. 36–44.

Comber, Leon, *The Triads: Chinese Secret Societies in 1950s Malaya and Singapore*, Singapore: Talisman Publishing and the Singapore Heritage Society, 2009.

Cooke, Nola and Tana Li (eds), *Water Frontier: Commerce and the Chinese in the Lower Mekong Region 1750–1880*, Singapore: National University of Singapore Press, 2004.

Curriculum Planning and Development Division, Ministry of Education, *Singapore: The Making of a Nation-State, 1300–1975*, Singapore: Star Publishing, 2014.

De Koninck, Rodolphe, Julie Drolet and Marc Girard, *Singapore: An Atlas of Perpetual Territorial Transformation*, Singapore: National University of Singapore Press, 2008.

de Sousa Pinto, Paulo Jorge, *The Portuguese and the Straits of Melaka 1575–1619: Power, Trade and Diplomacy*, Singapore: National University of Singapore Press, 2012.

Dent, Christopher M., *East Asian Regionalism*, London and New York: Routledge, 2008.

Desker, Barry and Ang Cheng Guan (eds), *Perspectives on the Security of Singapore: The First 50 Years*, Singapore: World Scientific, 2016.

Discovery Channel, *The History of Singapore: Lion City, Asian Tiger*, Hoboken, NJ: John Wiley & Sons, 2010.

Dobbs, Stephen, *The Singapore River: A Social History 1819–2012*, Singapore: Singapore University Press, 2003.

Drysdale, John, *Singapore: Struggle for Success*, Singapore: Times Books International, 1984.

Falarti, Maziar Mozaffari, *Malay Kingship in Kedah: Religion, Trade and Society*, Lanham, MD: Lexington, 2013.

Fernandez, Michael and Loh Kah Seng, 'The Left-Wing Trade Unions in Singapore, 1940–1970', in Michael D. Barr and Carl A. Trocki (eds), *Paths Not Taken: Political Pluralism in Post-War Singapore*, Singapore: National University of Singapore Press, 2008, pp. 206–26.

Frost, Mark Ravinder and Yu-Mei Balasingamchow, *Singapore: A Biography*, Singapore: Editions Didier Millet and National Museum of Singapore, 2009.

Fujitani, T., Geoffrey M. White and Lisa Yoneyama (ed.), *Perilous Memories: The Asia-Pacific War(s)*, Durham, NC and London: Duke University Press, 2001.

Furnivall, J.S., *Colonial Policy and Practice: A Comparative Study of Burma and Netherlands India*, Cambridge, UK: Cambridge University Press, 1948.

———, *Netherlands India: A Study of Plural Economy*, Cambridge, UK: Cambridge University Press, 1944.

Geertz, Clifford, *Negara: The Theatre State in Nineteenth-Century Bali*, Princeton, NJ: Princeton University Press, 1980.

George, Cherian, *Freedom from the Press: Journalism and State Power in Singapore*, Singapore: National University of Singapore Press, 2012.

———, 'History Spiked: Hegemony and the Denial of Media Diversity', in Michael D. Barr and Carl A. Trocki (eds), *Paths Not Taken: Political Pluralism in Post-War Singapore*, Singapore: National University of Singapore Press, 2008, pp. 264–80.

Gillis, E. Kay, 'Civil Society and the Malay Education Council', in Michael D. Barr and Carl A. Trocki (eds), *Paths Not Taken: Political Pluralism in Post-War Singapore*, Singapore: National University of Singapore Press, 2008, pp. 154–69.

———, *Singapore Civil Society and British Power*, Singapore: Talisman Press, 2005.

Glendinning, Victoria, *Raffles and the Golden Opportunity*, London: Profile Books, 2012.

Goh Chor Boon, *From Traders to Innovators: Science and Technology in Singapore since 1965*, Singapore: ISEAS Publishing, 2016.

———, *Technology and Entrepôt Colonialism in Singapore, 1819–1940*, Singapore: Institute of Southeast Asian Studies, 2013.

Goldstein, Andrea and Pavida Pananond, 'Singapore Inc. Goes Shopping Abroad: Profits and Pitfalls', *Journal of Contemporary Asia*, 38(3), 2008, pp. 417–38.

Hack, Karl, *Defence and Decolonisation in Southeast Asia: Britain, Malaya and Singapore 1941–68*, London and New York: Routledge, 2014 (2001).

———, 'Framing Singapore's History', in Nicholas Tarling (ed.), *Studying Singapore's Past: C.M. Turnbull and the History of Modern Singapore*, Singapore: National University of Singapore Press, 2012, pp. 17–64.

Hack, Karl and Kevin Blackburn, *Did Singapore Have to Fall? Churchill and the Impregnable Fortress*, London and New York: Routledge, 2003.

Hack, Karl and Jean-Louis Margolin, with Karine Delaye (eds), *Singapore from Temasek to the 21st Century: Reinventing the Global City*, Singapore: National University of Singapore Press, 2010.

Hamilton-Hart, Natasha, *Hard Interests, Soft Illusions: Southeast Asia and American Power*, Ithaca and London: Cornell University Press, 2012.

———, 'The Singapore State Revisited', *The Pacific Review*, 13(2), 2000, pp. 195–216.

Han Fook Kwang, Zuraidah Ibrahim, Chua Mui Hoong, Lydia Lim, Ignatius Low, Rachel Lin and Robin Chan, *Lee Kuan Yew: Hard Truths to Keep Singapore Going*, Singapore: Straits Times Press, 2011.

Harper, T.N., *The End of Empire and the Making of Malaya*, Cambridge, UK: Cambridge University Press, 2001 (1999).

———, 'Lim Chin Siong and the "Singapore Story"', in Tan Jing Quee and Jomo K.S. (eds), *Comet in Our Sky: Lim Chin Siong in History*, Kuala Lumpur: Insan, 2001, pp. 3–55.

Harvey, David, *A Brief History of Neoliberalism*, Oxford: Oxford University Press, 2005.

Heng Chye Kiang (ed.), *50 Years of Urban Planning in Singapore*, Singapore: World Scientific, 2016.

Heng, Geraldine and Janadas Devan, 'State Fatherhood: The Politics of Nationalism, Sexuality, and Race in Singapore', in Andrew Parker, Mary Russo, Doris Sommer and Patricia Yaeger (eds), *Nationalisms and Sexualities*, New York and London: Routledge, 1992, pp. 343–64.

Heng Thiam Soon, Derek, 'Temasik as an International and Regional Trading Port in the Thirteenth and Fourteenth Centuries: A Reconstruction Based on Recent Archaeological Data', in Geoff Wade (ed.), *Southeast Asia-China Interactions, Reprint of Articles from the Journal of the Malaysian Branch, Royal Asiatic Society*, Singapore: National University of Singapore Press, in association with The Malaysian Branch of the Royal Asiatic Society, 2007, pp. 296–308.

Hobsbawm, Eric and Terence Ranger (eds), *The Invention of Tradition*, Cambridge: Cambridge University Press, 1983.

Hon Sui Sen (ed. Linda Low and Lim Bee Lum), *Strategies of Singapore's Economic Success*, Singapore: Marshall Cavendish Academic, 2004.

Hong Lysa, 'Politics of the Chinese-Speaking Communities in Singapore in the 1950s: The Shaping of Mass Politics', in Tan Jing Quee, Tan Kok Chiang and Hong Lysa (eds), *The May 13 Generation: The Chinese Middle Schools Student Movement and Singapore Politics in the 1950s*, Petaling Jaya: Strategic Information and Research Development Centre, 2011, pp. 57–102.

———, 'Politics of the Immigrant Chinese Communities in Singapore in the 1950s: Narratives of Belonging in the Time of Emergency', in Tan Jing Quee, Tan Kok

Chiang and Hong Lysa (eds), *The May 13 Generation: The Chinese Middle School Student Movement and Singapore Politics in the 1950s*, Petaling Jaya: Strategic Information and Research Development Centre, 2011, pp. 27–55.

Hong Lysa and Huang Jianli, *The Scripting of a National History: Singapore and Its Pasts*, Singapore: National University of Singapore Press, 2008.

Hong, Mark T.S. and Amy Lugg (eds), *The Rise of Singapore, Volume 1: The Reasons for Singapore's Success*, Singapore: World Scientific, 2016.

Hor, Michael, 'Constitutionalism and Subversion – An Exploration', in Li-ann Thio and Kevin Y.L. Tan (eds), *Evolution of a Revolution: Forty Years of the Singapore Constitution*, London and New York: Routledge-Cavendish, 2009, pp. 260–87.

Huff, W.G., *The Economic Growth of Singapore: Trade and Development in the Twentieth Century*, Cambridge, UK: Cambridge University Press, 1997 (1994).

Huxley, Tim, *Defending the Lion City: The Armed Forces of Singapore*, St Leonards, NSW: Allen & Unwin, 2000.

Kahn, Joel S., *Other Malays: Nationalism and Cosmopolitanism in the Modern Malay World*, Singapore: National University of Singapore Press, 2006.

Kano, Hiroyoshi, *Indonesian Exports, Peasant Agriculture and the World Economy 1850–2000: Economic Structures in a Southeast Asian State*, Singapore: National University of Singapore Press; Athens, OH: Ohio University Press, 2008.

Kaye, Barrington, *Upper Nankin Street: A Sociological Study of Chinese Households Living in a Densely Populated Area*, Singapore: University of Malaya Press, 1960.

Keng We Koh, 'The Deity Proposes, The State Disposes: The Vicissitudes of a Chinese Temple in Post-1965 Singapore', in Jason Lim and Terence Lee (eds), *Negotiating State and Society, 1965–2015*, London and New York: Routledge, 2016, pp. 126–42.

Khong Yuen Foong, 'Singapore and the Great Powers', in Barry Desker and Ang Cheng Guan (eds), *Perspectives on the Security of Singapore: The First 50 Years*, Singapore: World Scientific, 2016, pp. 207–28.

King, Ross, *Kuala Lumpur and Putrajaya: Negotiating Urban Space in Malaysia*, Singapore: National University of Singapore Press; Copenhagen: Nordic Institute of Asian Studies, 2008.

Kitchen, Nicholas (ed.), *The New Geopolitics of Southeast Asia* (IDEAS Special Reports), London: London School of Economics and Political Science, Kindle edition, 2012.

Klingler-Vidra, Robyn, 'The Pragmatic "Little Red Dot": Singapore's US Hedge Against China', in Nicholas Kitchen (ed.), *The New Geopolitics of Southeast Asia* (IDEAS Special Reports), London: London School of Economics and Political Science, Kindle edition, 2012, Chapter 11 (no page numbers provided).

Koh, Aaron and Terence Chong (eds), *Education in the Global City: The Manufacturing of Education in Singapore*, London and New York: Routledge, 2016.

Koh, Ernest, 'Remembrance, Nation, and the Second World War in Singapore: The Chinese Diaspora and their Wars', in Loh Kah Seng, Ernest Koh and Stephen Dobbs (eds), *Oral History in Southeast Asia: Memories and Fragments*, New York: Palgrave Macmillan, 2013, pp. 61–80.

———, *Singapore Stories: Language, Class and the Chinese of Singapore 1945–2000*, Amherst, NY: Cambria Press, 2010.

Kratoska, Paul H., *The Japanese Occupation of Malaya: 1941–1945*, Honolulu: University of Hawai'i Press, 1997.

Krugman, Paul, 'The Myth of Asia's Miracle', *Foreign Affairs*, November/December 1994, pp. 62–78.

Kulke, Hermann, 'The Naval Expeditions of the Cholas in the Context of Asian History', in Hermann Kulke, K. Kesavapany and Vijay Sakhuja (eds), *Nagapattinam to Suvarnadwipa: Reflections of the Chola Naval Expeditions to Southeast Asia*, Singapore: Institute of Southeast Asian Studies, 2009, pp. 1–19.

Kulke, Hermann, K. Kesavapany and Vijay Sakhuja (eds), *Nagapattinam to Suvarnadwipa: Reflections of the Chola Naval Expeditions to Southeast Asia*, Singapore: Institute of Southeast Asian Studies, 2009.

Kumar, Sree and Sharon Siddique, *Batam – Whose Hinterland? The Influence of Politics on Development*, Singapore: Select Publishing, 2013.

Kuo, Eddie C.Y., 'The Sociolinguistic Situation in Singapore: Unity in Diversity', in Evangelos A. Afendras and Eddie C.Y. Kuo (eds), *Language and Society in Singapore*, Singapore: Singapore University Press, 1980, pp. 39–62.

Kurlantzick, Joshua, *State Capitalism: How the Return of Statism is Transforming the World*, New York: Oxford University Press, 2016.

Kwa Chong Guan (ed.), *S. Rajaratnam on Singapore: From Ideas to Reality*, Singapore: World Scientific and Institute of Defence and Strategic Studies, 2006.

Kwa Chong Guan, Derek Heng and Tan Tai Yong, *Singapore: A 700-Year History from Early Emporium to World City*, Singapore: National Archives of Singapore, 2009.

Lam Peng Er and Kevin Y.L. Tan (eds), *Lee's Lieutenants: Singapore's Old Guard*, St Leonard's, NSW: Allen & Unwin, 1999.

Lau, Albert, 'Decolonization and the Cold War in Singapore, 1955–9', in Albert Lau (ed.), *Southeast Asia and the Cold War*, London and New York: Routledge, 2012, pp. 43–66.

——— (ed.), *Southeast Asia and the Cold War*, London and New York: Routledge, 2012.

Lee Chien Earn and K. Satku (eds), *Singapore's Health Care System: What 50 Years Have Achieved*, Singapore: World Scientific, 2016.

Lee Kuan Yew, *From Third World to First: The Singapore Story: 1965–2000. Memoirs of Lee Kuan Yew*, Singapore: Singapore Press Holdings and Times Editions, 2000.

——— (interviews and selections by Graham Allison and Robert D. Blackwill, with Ali Wyne), *Lee Kuan Yew: The Grand Master's Insights on China, the United States and the World*, Cambridge, MA and London: The MIT Press, 2013.

———, *One Man's View of the World*, Singapore: Straits Times Press, 2013.

———, *The Singapore Story: Memoirs of Lee Kuan Yew*, Singapore: Prentice Hall, 1998.

Lee Soo Ann, 'Governance and Economic Change in Singapore', *The Singapore Economic Review*, 60(3), 2015, pp. 1550028-1–15.

Lee Su Yin, *British Policy and the Chinese in Singapore, 1939 to 1955: The Public Service Career of Tan Chin Tuan*, Singapore: Talisman, 2011.

Lee, Terence, *The Media, Cultural Control and Government in Singapore*, London and New York: Routledge, 2010.

Lee, Thienny, 'Defining the Aesthetics of the *Nyonyas*' Batik Sarongs in the Straits Settlements, Late Nineteenth to Early Twentieth Century', *Asian Studies Review*, 40(2), 2016, pp. 173–91.

Lee Ting Hui, *The Open United Front: The Communist Struggle in Singapore, 1954–1966*, Singapore: South Seas Society, 1996.

Lee Tsao Yuan (ed.), *Growth Triangle: The Johor–Singapore–Riau Experience*, Singapore: Institute of Southeast Asian Studies, 1991.

Leifer, Michael, *Singapore's Foreign Policy: Coping with Vulnerability*, London and New York: Routledge, 2000.

Levinson, Marc, *The Box: How the Shipping Container Made the World Smaller and the World Economy Bigger*, Princeton and Oxford: Princeton University Press, 2006.

Liew Kai Khiun and Stephen Teo, *Singapore Cinema: New Perspectives*, London and New York: Routledge, 2017.

Lim, Edna, 'Singapore Cinema: Connecting the Golden Age and the Revival', in Liew Kai Khiun and Stephen Teo, *Singapore Cinema: New Perspectives*, London and New York: Routledge, 2017, pp. 60–74.

Lim Hock Siew, '"I would never lift one finger to justify my own detention"', in Poh Soo Kai, Tan Kok Fang and Hong Lysa (eds), *The 1963 Operation Coldstore in Singapore: Commemorating 50 Years*, Petaling Jaya: Strategic Information and Research Development Centre; Kuala Lumpur: Pusat Sejarah Rakyat, 2013, pp. 203–237.

Lim Huan Boon, 'My Recollections of Learning Malay' (transl. Edgar Liao Bolum), in Tan Jing Quee, Tan Kok Chiang and Hong Lysa (eds), *The May 13 Generation: The Chinese Middle Schools Student Movement and Singapore Politics in the 1950s*, Petaling Jaya: Strategic Information and Research Development Centre, 2011, pp. 217–25.

Lim, Jason and Terence Lee (eds), *Negotiating State and Society, 1965–2015*, London and New York: Routledge, 2016.

Lim, Linda Y.C., 'Singapore's Success: After the Miracle', in Robert E. Looney (ed.), *Routledge Handbook of Emerging Economies*, London and New York: Routledge, 2014, pp. 203–26.

Lim Teck Ghee, *Peasants and their Agricultural Economy in Colonial Malaya 1874–1941*, Kuala Lumpur: Oxford University Press, 1977.

Loh Kah Seng, *Squatters Into Citizens: The 1961 Bukit Ho Swee Fire and the Making of Modern Singapore*, Singapore and Copenhagen: Asian Studies Association of Australia in association with National University of Singapore Press and the Nordic Institute of Asian Studies, 2013.

Loh Kah Seng, Ernest Koh and Stephen Dobbs (eds), *Oral History in Southeast Asia: Memories and Fragments*, New York: Palgrave Macmillan, 2013.

Loh Wei Leng, 'Penang's Trade and Shipping in the Imperial Age', in Yeoh Seng Guan, Loh Wei Leng, Khoo Salma Nasution and Neil Khor (eds), *Penang and Its Region: The Story of an Asian Entrepôt*, Singapore: National University of Singapore Press, 2009, pp. 83–102.

Long, S.R. Joey, 'Desecuritisation and after Desecuritisation: The Water Issue in Singapore', in Barry Desker and Ang Cheng Guan (eds), *Perspectives on the Security of Singapore: The First 50 Years*, Singapore: World Scientific, 2016, pp. 103–20.

Looney, Robert E. (ed.), *Routledge Handbook of Emerging Economies*, London and New York: Routledge, 2014.

Low, Donald and Sudhir Vadaketh with contributions from Linda Lim and Thum Ping Tjin, *Hard Choices: Challenging the Singapore Consensus*, Singapore: National University of Singapore Press, 2014.

Lyons, Lenore, 'Internalised Boundaries: AWARE's Place in Singapore's Emerging Civil Society', in Michael D. Barr and Carl A. Trocki (eds), *Paths Not Taken: Political Pluralism in Post-War Singapore*, Singapore: National University of Singapore Press, 2008, pp. 248–63.

Mahizhnan, Arun, 'Developing Singapore's External Economy', *Southeast Asian Affairs*, 1994, pp. 285–301.

Mako, Yoshimura, 'Japan's Economic Policy for Occupied Malaya', in Akashi Yoji and Yoshimura Mako (eds), *New Perspectives on the Japanese Occupation in Malaya and Singapore, 1941–1945*, Singapore: National University of Singapore Press, 2008, pp. 113–38.

Maritime and Port Authority of Singapore, *World's Busiest Port*, Singapore: Maritime and Port Authority of Singapore, c.2004.

Martinage, Robert, 'Under the Sea: The Vulnerability of the Commons', *Foreign Affairs*, January/February 2015, pp. 117–26.

Mauzy, Diane K. and R.S. Milne, *Singapore Politics Under the People's Action Party*, London and New York: Routledge, 2002.

Miksic, John N., *Archaeological Research on 'Forbidden Hill' of Singapore: Excavations at Fort Canning, 1984*, Singapore: National Museum of Singapore, 1985.

———, *Singapore and the Silk Road of the Sea, 1300–1800*, Singapore: National University of Singapore Press and National Museum of Singapore, 2013.

Milner, A.C., *Kerajaan: Malay Political Culture on the Eve of Colonial Rule*, Tucson, AZ: University of Arizona Press for the Association for Asian Studies, 1982.

Milner, Anthony, *The Malays*, Chichester: Wiley-Blackwell, 2008.

Moorhead, F.J., *A History of Malaya, Volume Two*, Kuala Lumpur: Longmans of Malaya, 1963.

Murfett, Malcolm H., John N. Miksic, Brian P. Farrell and Chiang Ming Shun, *Between Two Oceans: A Military History of Singapore from 1275 to 1971*, 2nd edn, Singapore: Marshall Cavendish, 2011 (1999).

Ng Weng Hoong, *Singapore, the Energy Economy: From the First Refinery to the End of Cheap Oil, 1960–2010*, London and New York: Routledge, 2012.

Ngiam Tong Dow (Zhang Zhibin, ed.), *Dynamics of the Singapore Success Story: Insights by Ngiam Tong Dow*, Singapore: Cengage Learning, 2011.

———, *A Mandarin and the Making of Public Policy*, Singapore: National University of Singapore Press, 2006.

Ong, Aiwah and Donald M. Nonini (eds), *Underground Empires: The Cultural Politics of Modern Chinese Transnationalism*, London and New York: Routledge, 1997.

Ong Chu Meng, Lim Hoon Yong and Ng Lai Yang (eds), *Tan Lark Sye: Advocator and Founder of Nanyang University*, Singapore: World Scientific, 2015.

Osterhammel, Jürgen (transl. Patrick Camiller), *The Transformation of the World: A Global History of the Nineteenth Century*, Princeton, NJ: Princeton University Press, 2014.

Pang Eng Fong and Linda Y.C. Lim, 'Labour Productivity and Singapore's Development Model', *The Singapore Economic Review*, 60(3), 2015, pp. 1550033-1–30.

Parker, Andrew, Mary Russo, Doris Sommer and Patricia Yaeger (eds), *Nationalisms and Sexualities*, New York and London: Routledge, 1992.

Pearson, H.F., *Singapore: A Popular History*, Singapore: Times Books International, 1985 (1961).

Peebles, Gavin and Peter Wilson, *Economic Growth and Development in Singapore: Past and Future*, Cheltenham, UK; Northampton, MA: Edward Elgar, 2002.

Perry, John Curtis, *Singapore: Unlikely Power*, New York: Oxford University Press, 2017.

Poh Soo Kai, Tan Kok Fang and Hong Lysa (eds), *The 1963 Operation Coldstore in Singapore: Commemorating 50 Years*, Petaling Jaya: Strategic Information and Research Development Centre; Kuala Lumpur: Pusat Sejarah Rakyat, 2013.

Quah, Jon S.T., *Public Administration Singapore Style*, Talisman: Singapore, 2010.

Rahim, Lily Zubaidah, 'Reclaiming Singapore's "Growth with Equity" Social Compact', *Japanese Journal of Political Science*, 16(2), 2015, pp. 160–76.

———, *The Singapore Dilemma: The Political and Educational Marginality of the Malay Community*, Kuala Lumpur: Oxford University Press, 1998.

———, *Singapore in the Malay World: Building and Breaching Regional Bridges*, London and New York: Routledge, 2009.

Rahman, Noorashikin Abdul, 'Managing Labour Flows: Foreign Talent, Foreign Workers and Domestic Help', in Terence Chong (ed.), *Management of Success: Singapore Revisited*, Singapore: Institute of Southeast Asian Studies, 2010, pp. 199–216.

Rajah, Jothie, *Authoritarian Rule of Law: Legislation, Discourse and Legitimacy in Singapore*, Cambridge, UK: Cambridge University Press, 2012.

Rajaratnam, S., 'Singapore: Global City', in Kwa Chong Guan (ed.), *S. Rajaratnam on Singapore: From Ideas to Reality*, Singapore: World Scientific and Institute of Defence and Strategic Studies, 2006, pp. 227–237.

Ramakrishna, Kumar, *'Original Sin'? Revising the Revisionist Critique of the 1963 Operation Coldstore in Singapore*, Singapore: Institute of Southeast Asian Studies, 2015.

Regnier, Philippe, *Singapore: City-State in South-East Asia*, Honolulu: University of Hawai'i Press, 1987.

Reid, Anthony, 'Chinese Trade and Southeast Asian Economic Expansion in the Later Eighteenth and Early Nineteenth Centuries: An Overview', in Nola Cooke and Tana Li (eds), *Water Frontier: Commerce and the Chinese in the Lower Mekong Region 1750–1880*, Singapore: National University of Singapore Press, 2004, pp. 21–34.

———, *Southeast Asia in the Age of Commerce, 1450–1680, Volume One: The Lands Below the Wind*, New Haven and London: Yale University Press, 1988.

———, *Southeast Asia in the Age of Commerce, 1450–1680, Volume Two: Expansion and Crisis*, Chiang Mai, Thailand: Silkworm Books, 1993.

Ricklefs, Merle C., *A History of Modern Indonesia Since c.1200*, 4th edn, London: Palgrave Macmillan, 2008.

Robertson, Peter E., 'Why the Tigers Roared: Capital Accumulation and the East Asian Miracle', *Pacific Economic Review*, 7(2), 2002, pp. 259–74.

Robison, Richard (ed.), *Routledge Handbook of Southeast Asian Politics*, London and New York: Routledge, 2012.

Rodan, Garry, 'Capitalism, Inequality and Ideology in Singapore: New Challenges for the Ruling Party', *Asian Studies Review*, 40(2), 2016, pp. 211–30.

———, 'Consultative Authoritarianism and Regime Change Analysis: Implications of the Singapore Case', in Richard Robison (ed.), *Routledge Handbook of Southeast Asian Politics*, London and New York: Routledge, 2012, pp. 120–34.

———, 'Goh's Consensus Politics of Authoritarian Rule', in Bridget Welsh, James Chin, Arun Mahizhnan and Tan Tarn How (eds), *Impressions of the Goh Chok Tong Years in Singapore*, Singapore: National University of Singapore Press, 2009, pp. 61–70.

———, *The Political Economy of Singapore's Industrialization: National State and International Capital*, Kuala Lumpur: Forum, 1991 (1989).

Roff, William R., *Studies on Islam and Society in Southeast Asia*, Singapore: National University of Singapore Press, 2009.

Roolvink, R., 'The Variant Versions of the Malay Annals', in C.C. Brown (ed. and transl.), *Sejarah Melayu or 'Malay Annals'*, Kuala Lumpur: Oxford University Press, 1970 (1953), pp. xv–xxxv.

Sandhu, Kernial Singh and Paul Wheatley, *Management of Success: The Moulding of Modern Singapore*, Singapore: Institute of Southeast Asian Studies, 1989.

Sassen, Saskia, *Cities in a World Economy*, 4th edn, Thousand Oaks, CA and London: Pine Forge Press, 2012.

Saw Swee-Hock, *The Population of Singapore*, 3rd edn, Singapore: Institute of Southeast Asian Studies, 2012.

Schein, Edgar H., *Strategic Pragmatism: The Culture of Singapore's Economic Development Board*, Singapore: Toppan with The MIT Press, 1996.

Sen, Tansen, 'The Military Campaigns of Rajendra Chola and the Chola–Srivajaya–China Triangle', in Hermann Kulke, K. Kesavapany and Vijay Sakhuja (eds), *Nagapattinam to Suvarnadwipa: Reflections of the Chola Naval Expeditions to Southeast Asia*, Singapore: Institute of Southeast Asian Studies, 2009, pp. 61–75.

Seow, Francis T., *The Media Enthralled: Singapore Revisited*, Boulder, CO and London: Lynne Rienner Publishers, 1998.

Silcock, T.H., *The Economy of Malaya*, Singapore: Donald Moore, 1956.

Singapore History Project Team, *History of Modern Singapore (Secondary 1)*, Singapore: Addison Wesley Longman for the Curriculum Development Institute of Singapore, 1984–94.

Singapore Legislative Council, *Proceedings of the Legislative Council of the Colony of Singapore*, Singapore: [Government Printing Office], 1953.

———, *Proceedings of the Legislative Council of the Colony of Singapore*, Singapore: [Government Printing Office], 1954/55

Singh, Bilveer, *Quest for Political Power: Communist Subversion and Militancy in Singapore*, Singapore: Marshall Cavendish, 2015.

Skott, Christina, 'Imagined Centrality: Sir Stamford Raffles and the Birth of Modern Singapore', in Karl Hack and Jean-Louis Margolin, with Karine Delaye (eds), *Singapore from Temasek to the 21st Century: Reinventing the Global City*, Singapore: National University of Singapore Press, 2010, pp. 155–84.

Stubbs, Richard, *Rethinking Asia's Economic Miracle: The Political Economy of War, Prosperity and Crisis*, Basingstoke and New York: Palgrave Macmillan, 2005.

Taleb, Nassim Nicholas and Gregory F. Treverton, 'The Calm Before the Storm', *Foreign Affairs*, January–February 2015, pp. 86–95.

Tan Jing Quee and Jomo K.S. (eds), *Comet in Our Sky: Lim Chin Siong in History*, Kuala Lumpur: Insan, 2001.

Tan Jing Quee, Tan Kok Chiang and Hong Lysa (eds), *The May 13 Generation: The Chinese Middle Schools Student Movement and Singapore Politics in the 1950s*, Petaling Jaya: Strategic Information and Research Development Centre, 2011.

Tan, Kenneth Paul (ed.), *Renaissance Singapore? Economy, Culture, and Politics*, Singapore: National University of Singapore Press, 2007.

Tan, Kevin Y.L., *Marshall of Singapore: A Biography*, Singapore: Institute of Southeast Asian Studies, 2008.

———, 'State and Institution Building through the Singapore Constitution 1965–2005', in Li-ann Thio and Kevin Y.L. Tan (eds), *Evolution of a Revolution: Forty Years of the Singapore Constitution*, London and New York: Routledge-Cavendish, 2009, pp. 50–78.

Tan Kok Chiang, 'My Story', in Tan Jing Quee, Tan Kok Chiang and Hong Lysa (eds), *The May 13 Generation: The Chinese Middle Schools Student Movement and Singapore Politics in the 1950s*, Petaling Jaya: Strategic Information and Research Development Centre, 2011, pp. 123–86.

Tang Hsiao Ling, 'Industrial Planning in Singapore', in Heng Chye Kiang (ed.), *50 Years of Urban Planning in Singapore*, Singapore: World Scientific, 2016, pp. 153–76.

Tarling, Nicholas (ed.), *Studying Singapore's Past: C.M. Turnbull and the History of Modern Singapore*, Singapore: National University of Singapore Press, 2012.

Tey, Tsun Hang, *Legal Consensus: Supreme Executive, Supine Jurisprudence, Suppliant Profession of Singapore*, Hong Kong: Centre for Comparative and Public Law, 2011.

Thio, Li-ann, 'Protecting Rights', in Li-ann Thio and Kevin Y.L. Tan (eds), *Evolution of a Revolution: Forty Years of the Singapore Constitution*, London and New York: Routledge-Cavendish, 2009, pp. 193–233.

Thio, Li-ann and Kevin Y.L. Tan (eds), *Evolution of a Revolution: Forty Years of the Singapore Constitution*, London and New York: Routledge-Cavendish, 2009.

Thiruvengadam, Arun K., 'Comparative Law and Constitutional Interpretation in Singapore: Insights from Constitutional Theory', in Li-ann Thio and Kevin Y.L. Tan (eds), *Evolution of a Revolution: Forty Years of the Singapore Constitution*, London and New York: Routledge-Cavendish, 2009, pp. 238–40.

Thomas, Francis, *Memoirs of a Migrant*, Singapore: Ethos Books, 2013.

Thomas, Joan Sara, Ong Suan Ee, Chia Kee Seng and Lee Hin Ping, 'A Brief History of Public Health in Singapore', in Lee Chien Earn and K. Satku (eds), *Singapore's Health Care System: What 50 Years Have Achieved*, Singapore: World Scientific, 2016, pp. 33–55.

Thum Ping Tjin, '"Flesh and Bone Reunite as One Body": Singapore's Chinese-Speaking and Their Perspectives on Merger', in Poh Soo Kai, Tan Kok Fang and Hong Lysa (eds), *The 1963 Operation Coldstore in Singapore: Commemorating 50 Years*, Petaling Jaya: Strategic Information and Research Development Centre; Kuala Lumpur: Pusat Sejarah Rakyat, 2013, pp. 73–119.

Tortajada, Cecelia, Yugal Joshi and Asit K. Biswas, *The Singapore Water Story: Sustainable Development in an Urban City-State*, London and New York: Routledge, 2013.

Tremewan, Christopher, *The Political Economy of Social Control in Singapore*, London: Macmillan Press; New York: St Martin's Press, 1994.

Trocki, Carl A., 'Boundaries and Transgressions: Chinese Enterprise in Eighteenth- and Nineteenth-Century Southeast Asia', in Aiwah Ong and Donald M. Nonini (eds), *Underground Empires: The Cultural Politics of Modern Chinese Transnationalism*, London and New York: Routledge, 1997, pp. 63–78.

———, 'Chinese Capitalism and the British Empire', paper presented to the International Association of Historians of Asia Conference, Taiwan, Taipei, 6–10 December 2004.

———, 'Chinese Revenue Farms and Borders in Southeast Asia', *Modern Asian Studies*, 43(1), 2009, pp. 335–62.

———, 'David Marshall and the Struggle for Civil Rights in Singapore', in Michael D. Barr and Carl A. Trocki (eds), *Paths Not Taken: Political Pluralism in Post-War Singapore*, Singapore: National University of Singapore Press, 2008, pp. 116–30.

———, *Opium and Empire: Chinese Society in Colonial Singapore, 1800–1910*, Ithaca and London: Cornell University Press, 1990.

———, *Opium, Empire and the Global Political Economy: A Study of the Asian Opium Trade 1750–1950*, London and New York: Routledge, 1999.

———, *Prince of Pirates: The Temenggongs and the Development of Johor and Singapore 1784–1885*, Singapore: National University of Singapore Press, 2007 (1979).

———, *Singapore: Wealth, Power and the Culture of Control*, London and New York: Routledge, 2006.

Turnbull, C.M., 'The European Mercantile Community in Singapore, 1819–1867', *Journal of Southeast Asian History*, 10(1), 1969, pp. 12–35.

———, *A History of Singapore 1819–1988*, 2nd edn, Singapore: Oxford University Press, 1989 (1977).

———, *The Straits Settlements 1826–67: Indian Presidency to Crown Colony*, London: The Athlone Press of the University of London, 1972.

van der Veer, Peter, 'Nation, Politics, Religion', *Journal of Religious and Political Practice*, 1(1), 2015, pp. 7–21.

Vasil, Raj, *Governing Singapore: A History of National Development and Democracy*, St Leonards, NSW: Allen & Unwin, 2000.

Velayutham, Selvaraj, *Responding to Globalization: Nation, Culture and Identity in Singapore*, Singapore: Institute of Southeast Asian Studies, 2007.

Vier, Tatania Backes, 'Hub Ports: A Case Study of Port of Singapore', Master's dissertation, Universidade Federal do Rio Grande do Sul, Porto Alegre, 2010, http://hdl.handle.net/10183/60515, accessed 5 June 2018.

Visscher, Sikko, *The Business of Politics and Ethnicity: A History of the Singapore Chinese Chamber of Commerce and Industry*, Singapore: National University of Singapore Press, 2007.

Wade, Geoff, 'Melaka in Ming Dynasty Texts', in Geoff Wade (ed.), *Southeast Asia-China Interactions, Reprint of Articles from the Journal of the Malaysian Branch, Royal Asiatic Society*, Singapore: National University of Singapore Press, in association with The Malaysian Branch of the Royal Asiatic Society, 2007, pp. 327–66.

———, 'Operation Coldstore: A Key Event in the Creation of Modern Singapore', in Poh Soo Kai, Tan Kok Fang and Hong Lysa (eds), *The 1963 Operation Coldstore in Singapore: Commemorating 50 Years*, Petaling Jaya: Strategic Information and Research Development Centre; Kuala Lumpur: Pusat Sejarah Rakyat, 2013, pp. 15–72.

——— (ed.), *Southeast Asia-China Interactions, Reprint of Articles from the Journal of the Malaysian Branch, Royal Asiatic Society*, Singapore: National University of Singapore Press, in association with The Malaysian Branch of the Royal Asiatic Society, 2007.

Wang Gungwu, 'The First Three Rulers of Malacca', in Geoff Wade (ed.), *Southeast Asia-China Interactions, Reprint of Articles from the Journal of the Malaysian Branch, Royal Asiatic Society*, Singapore: National University of Singapore Press, in association with The Malaysian Branch of the Royal Asiatic Society, 2007, pp. 317–26.

Warren, James Francis, *Ah Ku and Karayuki-San: Prostitution in Singapore 1870–1940*, Singapore: Singapore University Press, 2003 (1993).

———, *Rickshaw Coolie: A People's History of Singapore 1880–1940*, Singapore: Singapore University Press, 2003 (1986).

Wee, C.J. W-L., 'The Vanquished: Lim Chin Siong and a Progressivist National Narrative', in Lam Peng Er and Kevin Y.L. Tan (eds), *Lee's Lieutenants: Singapore's Old Guard*, St Leonard's, NSW: Allen & Unwin, 1999, pp. 169–90.

Welsh, Bridget, James Chin, Arun Mahizhnan and Tan Tarn How (eds), *Impressions of the Goh Chok Tong Years in Singapore*, Singapore: National University of Singapore Press, 2009.

Winstedt, R.O., *A History of Classical Literature*, Kuala Lumpur and Singapore: Oxford University Press, 1969.

———, *A History of Johore (1365–1941)*, Kuala Lumpur: Malaysian Branch of the Royal Asiatic Society, 1992 (1932).

———, *Malaya and its History*, New York: Hutchinson's University Library, 1948.

Wolters, O.W., *The Fall of Srivajaya in Malay History*, Kuala Lumpur and Singapore: Oxford University Press, 1970.

———, *History, Culture, and Region in Southeast Asian Perspectives*, rev. edn, Ithaca, NY: Southeast Asia Program Publications, Southeast Asia Program, Cornell University, 1999 (1982).

Wong, Diana, 'Memory Suppression and Memory Production: The Japanese Occupation of Singapore', in T. Fujitani, Geoffrey M. White and Lisa Yoneyama (ed.), *Perilous Memories: The Asia-Pacific War(s)*, Durham, NC and London: Duke University Press, 2001, pp. 218–38.

Wong, John and Lye Liang Fook, 'China–Singapore Relations: Looking Back and Looking Forward', in Zheng Yongnian and Lye Liang Fook (eds), *Singapore–China Relations: 50 Years*, Singapore: World Scientific, 2016, pp. 1–29.

Wong, Joseph, *Betting on Biotech: Innovation and the Limits of Asia's Developmental State*, Ithaca and London: Cornell University Press, 2011.

Wong Lin Ken, *The Malayan Tin Industry to 1914, with Special Reference to the States of Perak, Selangor, Negri Sembilan and Pahang*, Tucson: The Association for Asian Studies and The University of Arizona Press, 1965.

Worthington, Ross, *Governance in Singapore*, London and New York: Routlege-Curzon, 2003.

Yacob, Shakila, *The United States and the Malaysian Economy*, London and New York: Routledge, 2008.

Yao Souchou, 'All Quiet on Jurong Road: Nanyang University and Radical Vision in Singapore', in Michael D. Barr and Carl A. Trocki (eds), *Paths Not Taken: Political Pluralism in Post-War Singapore*, Singapore: National University of Singapore Press, 2008, pp. 170–87.

Yap Mui Teng and Christopher Gee, 'Singapore's Demographic Transition, The Labour Force and Government Policies: The Last Fifty Years', *The Singapore Economic Review*, 60(3), 2015, pp. 1550035-1–22.

Yeo Kim Wah, *Political Development in Singapore 1945–1955*, Singapore: University of Singapore Press, 1973.

Yeoh, Brenda S.A., *Contesting Space in Colonial Singapore: Power Relations and the Urban Built Environment*, Singapore: Singapore University Press, 2003 (1996).

Yeoh Seng Guan, Loh Wei Leng, Khoo Salma Nasution and Neil Khor (eds), *Penang and Its Region: The Story of an Asian Entrepôt*, Singapore: National University of Singapore Press, 2009.

Yoji, Akashi and Yoshimura Mako (eds), *New Perspectives on the Japanese Occupation in Malaya and Singapore, 1941–1945*, Singapore: National University of Singapore Press, 2008.

Yong, C.F. and R.B. McKenna, *The Kuomintang Movement in British Malaya 1912–1949*, Singapore: Singapore University Press, 1990.

Zahari, Said, *Dark Clouds at Dawn: A Political Memoir*, Kuala Lumpur: Insan, 2001.

Zheng Yongnian and Lim Wen Xin, 'Lee Kuan Yew: The Special Relationship with China', in Zheng Yongnian and Lye Liang Fook (eds), *Singapore–China Relations: 50 Years*, Singapore: World Scientific, 2016, pp. 31–48.

Zheng Yongnian and Lye Liang Fook (eds), *Singapore–China Relations: 50 Years*, Singapore: World Scientific, 2016.

RESEARCH INTERVIEW

Goh Keng Swee, interview with the author, Singapore, 1 September 1996.

ARCHIVAL, MEDIA AND INTERNET SOURCES

BP, *BP Statistical Review 2018: China's Energy Market in 2017*, https://www.bp.com/content/dam/bp/en/corporate/pdf/energy-economics/statistical-review/bp-stats-review-2018-china-insights.pdf.

———, *BP Statistical Review of World Energy June 2018*, https://www.bp.com/content/dam/bp/en/corporate/pdf/energy-economics/statistical-review/bp-stats-review-2018-full-report.pdf.

Changi Airport Media Centre, 'Top 10 Country Markets', http://www.changiairport.com/corporate/media-centre/newsroom.html#/images/changi2015-top-10-country-markets-516931.

Channel NewsAsia, 2015, 2016.

Colony of Singapore, *Weekly Digest of Non-English Press*, 1954, 1956.

Commodity.com, 'Singapore's Top Commodity Imports & Exports', https://commodity.com/country-profiles/singapore/.

Curriculum Planning and Development Division, Ministry of Education, *History Syllabus, Lower Secondary, Express Course; Normal (Academic) Course*, Singapore: Ministry of Education, 2016.

Department of Social Welfare, Singapore, *A Social Survey of Singapore: A Preliminary Study of Some Aspects of Social Conditions in the Municipal Area of Singapore, December 1947*, Singapore: Department of Social Welfare, 1947.

Department of Statistics, Singapore, http://www.singstat.gov.sg.

———, *Singapore's Direct Investment Abroad*, Singapore: Department of Statistics, 2017.

The Economist, 2015, 2016.

Financial Times, 2005.

Goh Chok Tong, 'Speech by Mr Goh Chok Tong, Minister for Health and Second Minister of Defence, at the Singapore General Hospital (SGH) Nite 1982', 6 March 1982, National Archives of Singapore Online.

Government of Singapore, *White Paper: Salaries for a Capable and Committed Government*, Singapore: Government of Singapore, 10 January 2012.

Harvard Kennedy School Magazine, 2012.

Harvard University Institute of Politics, 'Kuan Yew Lee', http://www.iop.harvard.edu/kuan-yew-lee#comment-0.

The Independent Singapore, 2016.

Lee Hsien Loong, 'Prime Minister Lee Hsien Loong's 2004 National Day Rally Speech, Sunday 22 August 2004', National Archives of Singapore Online.

———, 'Transcript of Prime Minister Lee Hsien Loong's May Day Rally Speech on 1 May 2015', http://www.pmo.gov.sg/newsroom/transcript-prime-minister-lee-hsien-loong-may-day-rally-speech-1-may-2015.

Lee Kuan Yew, 'Speech to Pasir Panjang Residents on 5th December, 1965', National Archives of Singapore Online.

Li, Christl, 'Connecting to the World: Singapore as a Hub Port', *Ethos*, 19, 8 July 2018, https://www.csc.gov.sg/articles/connecting-to-the-world-singapore-as-a-hub-port.

Maritime Executive, 'World Oil Transit Chokepoints', https://www.maritime-executive.com/article/world-oil-transit-chokepoints-2014-11-15#gs.j2fa2_w.

Ministry of Culture, Singapore, *Mirror of Opinion: Highlights of Malay, Chinese and Tamil Press*, 1966, 1969, 1971.

Ministry of Information and the Arts, *The Singapore Story: Overcoming the Odds*, CD-ROM, 1999.

Ministry of Manpower, 'Foreign workforce numbers', http://www.mom.gov.sg/documents-and-publications/foreign-workforce-numbers.

Ministry of Trade and Industry, 'Economic Survey of Singapore 2017', https://www.mti.gov.sg/ResearchRoom/Pages/Economic-Survey-of-Singapore-2017.aspx.

National Archives of Singapore Online, http://www.nas.gov.sg/archivesonline/.

Nikkei Asian Review, 2016.

Port Strategy: Insight for Port Executives, 'Port Klang Edges Closer to Top Ten Ranking', 18 January 2017, http://www.portstrategy.com/news101/world/asia/port-klang-nears-top-ten-container-ranking.

Prime Minister's Office, Singapore, 'Mr LEE Hsien Loong', http://www.pmo.gov.sg/cabinet/mr-lee-hsien-loong.

Public Service Commission, *Public Service Commission Annual Report 2009*, Singapore: Public Service Commission, 2010.

Santander Trade Portal, 'China: Foreign Investment', https://en.portal.santandertrade.com/establish-overseas/china/foreign-investment.

South China Morning Post, 2016.

The Straits Times, 1949, 1954, 1962, 1963, 1966, 1985, 2017.

Sydney Morning Herald, 2007.

TeleGeography, 'Map of Submarine Cables' and 'Frequently Asked Questions', http://www.telegeography.com.

Today, 2014.

Trading Economics, 'Singapore GDP Annual Growth Rate 1976–2018', http://www.tradingeconomics.com/singapore/gdp-growth-annual.

The Wall Street Journal, 2015.

Wong, Koi Nyen and Soo Khoon Goh, 'Outward FDI, Merchandise and Services Trade: Evidence from Singapore', Munich Personal RePEc Archive, 2011, https://mpra.ub.uni-muenchen.de/35377/1/MPRA_paper_35377.pdf.

World History, 'John O'Sullivan and Manifest Destiny', https://worldhistory.us/american-history/john-osullivan-and-manifest-destiny.php.

World Integrated Trade Solution, 'Singapore exports, imports and trade balance by country 2016', https://wits.worldbank.org/CountryProfile/en/Country/SGP/Year/LTST/TradeFlow/EXPIMP/Partner/by-country.

World Shipping Council, 'Top 50 World Container Ports', http://www.worldshipping.org/about-the-industry/global-trade/top-50-world-container-ports.

Yap Mui Teng and Christopher Gee, 'Renewing the Sap: Civil Society Rejuvenates the Singapore's Public Sector Banyan Tree', interview with Dr Albert Bressand and Catherine Distler, 17 May 2001, National Archives of Singapore Online.

Yeo, George, 'Between North and South, Between East and West', speech at The SGH Lecture, 29 April 2001, National Archives of Singapore Online.

Index

www.ingramcontent.com/pod-product-compliance
Ingram Content Group UK Ltd.
Pitfield, Milton Keynes, MK11 3LW, UK
UKHW020655280225
455688UK00004B/129